# BEST-SELLING
# CHILDREN'S BOOKS

by

Jean Spealman Kujoth

The Scarecrow Press, Inc.
Metuchen, N.J.        1973

**Library of Congress Cataloging in Publication Data**

Kujoth, Jean Spealman.
  Best-selling children's books.

   1.  Children's literature--Bibliography.  2.  Best
sellers--Bibliography.  I.  Title.
Z1037.K83       028.52       72-11692
ISBN 0-8108-0571-5

To my Father and Mother

# TABLE OF CONTENTS

# ACKNOWLEDGMENTS

I wish to express appreciation to all of the publishers who kindly provided the information on their best sellers that made this survey possible, and to all those who replied to my information request.  The sixty-eight publishers whose best-selling children's books are listed in this book are:

Abingdon Press
Addison-Wesley Publishing Company, Inc.
Apollo Editions
William L. Bauhan, Inc.
Behrman House, Inc.
Benefic Press
Bethany Press
Bobbs-Merrill Company, Inc.
Boy Scouts of America
Caxton Printers, Ltd.
Children's Press, Inc.
Colonial Williamsburg Foundation
Columbia Children's Book & Record Library
Concordia Publishing House
Cornell University Press
Creative Educational Society, Inc.
Dell Publishing Company, Inc.
T. S. Denison & Company, Inc.
Doubleday & Company, Inc.
E. P. Dutton & Company, Inc.
Wm. B. Eerdmans Publishing Company
Farrar, Straus & Giroux, Inc.
Follett Publishing Company
Garrard Publishing Company
Grosset & Dunlap, Inc.
E. M. Hale & Company
Hammond Incorporated
Harper & Row Publishers, Inc.
Highlights for Children, Inc.
Holt, Rinehart & Winston, Inc.
Houghton Mifflin Company

Hubbard Press
John Day Company, Inc.
Johnson Publishing Company (Chicago)
Alfred A. Knopf, Inc.
Lawrence Publishing Company
Lerner Publications Company
J. B. Lippincott Company
Little, Brown & Company
Lothrop, Lee & Shepard Company (Division of William
    Morrow & Company)
Macrae Smith Company
Meredith Press, Consumer Division (Better Homes &
    Gardens Press)
G. & C. Merriam Company
Julian Messner, Inc.   (Division of Simon & Schuster,
    Inc. )
Metropolitan Museum of Art
William Morrow & Company, Inc.
Naturegraph Publishers
Thomas Nelson, Inc.
Oddo Publishing, Inc.
Pantheon Books
Pelican Publishing House
S. G. Phillips, Inc.
Platt & Munk Company
Price/Stern/Sloan, Publishers, Inc.
G. P. Putnam's Sons
Rand McNally & Company
Rutgers University Press
Charles Scribner's Sons
Seabury Press, Inc.
Simon & Schuster, Inc.
Steck-Vaughn Company
United States Committee for UNICEF
Vanguard Press, Inc.
Van Nostrand Reinhold Company
Viking Press, Inc.
Warner Press
Albert Whitman & Company
Zondervan Publishing House

--Jean Spealman Kujoth

Chapter One

A SURVEY OF BEST-SELLING CHILDREN'S BOOKS

Publishers, authors, librarians, parents, teachers, students of children's literature, and others have long had a personal or professional interest in children's books and children's reading interests. Best-selling children's books are of particular interest from a psychological and socio-logical standpoint also, for, since they get into the hands of more children than other books do, they are an especially important vehicle for the transmission of culture from generation to generation.

This book, the first survey of its kind, is an attempt to answer as objectively as possible the question: What children's books have been bought for, and read by, the most children, and can therefore roughly be assumed to have influenced the most people during the impressionable years of childhood? I say "roughly" because it is unjustifiable to assume that all books that are bought are read--especially children's books, which are usually bought by an adult and read (or not read) by the child(ren) for whom they are bought--and also unjustifiable to assume that all books read do influence the readers. However, if we can assume that a book not read influences fewer people than a book read, and that word-of-mouth "advertising" is a large factor in making any book a best seller, then it would seem to follow that best sellers are likely to influence more people than non-best sellers.

Some people, upon hearing the title of this book project, said skeptically, "But best sellers aren't necessarily the best books for children," or, doubtfully, "Is that the most valid basis for determining what are good books?" I explained that this book would not recommend what I thought were "good" books for children to read, for enough other books have done that and the term "good" meant different

things to different people; that rather, the main purpose of
this project would be to find out what children's books have
been of interest to the most people.

This is a survey of best-selling children's trade books
presently in print, for most publishers informed me that
their records on out-of-print books were too inaccessible to
unearth and that they preferred to name their in-print best
sellers. I thought that, especially in view of this, readers
of this book would not mind the complete omission of "ex-
tinct" (out-of-print) best sellers, since "living" best sellers
would be of far more practical interest anyway. Textbooks
and subscription books are not included in this survey.

The term "best seller" is a relative one that can be
defined in many ways. For the purposes of this book I define a "best seller" as a trade book that has sold 100,000
copies or more since its original publication. This defini-
tion is arbitrary, objective, consistent, and yielded a total
of 928 books reported by publishers, plus 30 more books
listed in Alice Payne Hackett's Seventy Years of Best Sellers,
making a grand total of 958 best sellers included in this
survey.

The information in this book was obtained by sending
the following information request to over 300 American publishers listed in Literary Market Place and in Children's
Books in Print--i. e., to all publishers in the U.S. that I
thought might have published at least one best-selling
children's book. (If any publisher who should have received
this questionnaire didn't, I hope he will let me know so that
the error won't be repeated.)

Dear [Publisher of children's books]:

I am compiling a book to be entitled Best-Selling
Children's Books, for publication by The Scarecrow
Press, a division of Grolier Inc. This book will
attempt to list and annotate all in-print juvenile
trade books published in the U.S. that have sold
100,000 or more copies. It is intended for use by
teachers, children's librarians, parents, and others
who buy books for children, and by writers and
others with a professional interest in juvenile books.
It will also benefit publishers by helping to publicize
their juvenile best sellers. Since this book can be

only as useful as it is comprehensive, I hope that you
will find this information request feasible to answer.

Can you send me a copy of your current annotated
catalog of juvenile trade books, with check marks made
by all titles in the catalog that have sold 100,000 or
more copies in trade, hardcover, paperback, library,
mass market, foreign, reprint, and/or combined editions since their publication by your firm? (Please
include all types of books, all age levels, both works
originally published by your firm and works originally
published by another firm but reprinted by your firm
or published in a new version by your firm.)

If you can state the number of copies sold for each
of these best sellers (even approximately), this information will be useful in the book. If sales figures
cannot be provided, just omit them from the marked
catalog that you send me. The most important information needed is the titles of all in-print children's books of which your firm has sold 100,000 or
more copies. If your catalog is copyrighted, can you
please give me written permission to include its descriptions of best sellers in Best-Selling Children's
Books, if there is no objection?

Thank you very much for participating in this
survey.

Sincerely,

(Mrs.) Jean S. Kujoth

Happily for this project, sixty-eight publishers replied identifying their best-selling children's books. Other
publishers who did not report any best sellers were kind
enough to reply explaining that they did not publish juvenile
books, that they did not publish trade books, that none of
their books had yet sold 100,000 copies, or that their policy
forbade them to provide the requested information.

The question "What makes a best seller?" has been
tossed around a good deal and has never been completely
answered to everyone's satisfaction. It can hardly be
answered at all in an informed way without first answering
another question--the one this book attempts to answer--

namely: "What books are we talking about?" It is hoped
that the information herein--particularly the descriptions
in Chapter Two, the chronological listing in Chapter Five,
and the categorical listing in Chapter Seven--will give the
reader a basis from which to observe and speculate on best-
seller trends.

The number of best-selling children's books has, of
course, increased with the general rise in book sales over
the past few decades, due in part to the population increase,
the paperback revolution, book clubs, the increase in and
specialization of knowledge, and eclecticism in education.

Mrs. Ann Heidbreder of Grosset & Dunlap remarked
upon the fact that some publishers had made best sellers
of high-quality books by publishing them in mass market
editions (e.g., the Grosset & Dunlap Wonder-Treasure
Books) sold through drugstores, supermarkets, etc., and
that even some schools are buying mass-market books.

Mr. William Sloane of Rutgers University Press ob-
served, "Many children's books have gone on to have sub-
stantial adult sales. For example, we published as an adult
book Frank R. Stockton's History of New Jersey, originally
published by the American Book Company and distributed to
the tune of several hundred thousand copies of which a large
number must surely have gone to the junior market. For
many years, one of the great American classics, Moby
Dick, which was obviously written as an adult book, was
kept alive in the publishing marketplace by sales to juvenile
readers."

Chapter Two

## BEST SELLERS LISTED BY AUTHOR, WITH DESCRIPTIONS

This chapter arranges all 958 best sellers alphabetically by author. For each book it tells the illustrator, publisher, date of publication, and grade level of the edition of the book reported for this survey, and the original date of publication. This chapter also tells something about the contents and noteworthy features of each book. Descriptions and annotations not otherwise credited are by the publisher who reported the book as a best seller--usually from the publisher's current annotated catalog of juvenile books. In some cases reviews are quoted in lieu of descriptions or annotations; and a few factual and descriptive statements are written by the compiler. No attempt is made here to name all the publishers of a given book, or to give prices, publishers' addresses, and other ordering information that can be found in Children's Books in Print and other available sources.

ADAMS, Don. Would You Believe? Price/Stern/Sloan, Publishers, Inc., 1966.
    The star of TV's "Get Smart" finds some highly improbable answers to his famous question.
Sister ADELE Marie, C.S.J. The Magic Wishbone. Illustrated by Sister Charlotte Anne, C.S.J. Lawrence Publishing Company. Grades 3-7.
    A delightful story for children from eight to twelve.
AESOP. Aesop's Fables, edited by John Warrington; illustrated by Joan Kiddell-Monroe. E.P. Dutton & Company, Inc. Grades 3-7.
    Moralized beast tales based directly or indirectly on Greek tradition. Their exact origin is unknown; Aesop was allegedly born about 620 B.C. and the first written collection of the fables made about 320 B.C. by Demetrius Phalerus, founder of the Alexandrian Library.

John Warrington has edited a handsome volume containing over 200 of the popular Aesop fables, translated
into clear, straightforward English from the early Greek
and Latin texts.  Stunning line drawings point up the
morals of the wise and charming stories in this collection which includes both familiar and unfamiliar selections.
_____.  Aesop's Stories, by Edward W. and M. P. Dolch.
Illustrated.  Garrard Publishing Company, 1951.  Grades
3 up.
Aesop's Fables rewritten almost entirely with the First
Thousand Words for Children's Reading, a list scien-
tifically derived by Dr. Dolch from the first words
children learn to read.  Reading level:  grade 4.  Excellent for supplemental classroom reading, and written
simply enough so that slower readers can derive pleasure not only from the stories themselves but from their
success in reading them.
_____.  Three Fox Fables, written and illustrated by
Paul Galdone.  The Seabury Press, 1971.  Grades ps-1.
Illustrated in four colors.  "This picture-book version
of three of Aesop's better-known fables includes the
fox's pursuit and rejection of the 'sour-grapes,' his
comeuppance at the hands of the stork over the shape of
their soup dishes, and his flattery of the crow....
Galdone's selection and his humorous, animated pictures
make Aesop accessible to younger children."--The
Kirkus Reviews.
ALCOTT, Louisa May.  Jo's Boys.  Illustrated.  Little,
Brown and Company.  Originally published 1886.
Grades 5 up.
A sequel to Little Men, telling what happens to the
characters in that novel some years later when they
prepare to leave home and go out on their own. --J. K.
_____.  Little Men.  Illustrated by Harry Toothill.
E. P. Dutton & Company, Inc., 1957.  Another illus-
trated edition published by Little, Brown and Company.
Originally published 1871.  Grades 5-9.
A sequel to Little Women.  Jo and Fritz Bhaer raise
their own children and run a lively boys' school. --J. K.
_____.  Little Women.  Illustrated by Jessie Willcox
Smith.  Little, Brown and Company, 1968.  Illustrated
by S. Van Abbe.  E. P. Dutton & Company, Inc., 1948.
Originally published 1868.  Grades 5-9.
The story, told with warmth and humor, of events in
the lives of the four March girls:  tomboyish Jo, who
wants to be an author; Meg, who longs for a gracious,
ladylike future; delicate homeloving Beth; and beautiful,
egotistical Amy. --J. K.

ALDEN, Raymond MacDonald. Why the Chimes Rang. Illustrated by R. Busoni. The Bobbs-Merrill Company, Inc.,
1954. Grades 2-6.
The story of the wonderful church with a chime of bells
that had not rung for many years. Why they did ring
at last is told in this Christmas classic.--H.W. Wilson
Company.

AMES, Gerald, and Wyler, Rose. The Earth's Story. Illustrated with photos. Creative Educational Society,
Inc., in cooperation with the American Museum of Natural History. 1967. Grades 5-9.
"Here is an open invitation by two of the best known
science writers in the country to enjoy the study of the
earth. The authors have chosen outstanding photographic
examples of geological processes and have accompanied
these pictures with brief, easy-to-understand popular
literature on geology.... This book is an outstanding
contribution to popular literature on geology."--Geotimes
(American Geological Institute).

_____. Food and Life. Illustrated with photos. Crea-
tive Educational Society, Inc. in cooperation with the
American Museum of Natural History. 1966. Grades
5-9.
"Here is a wealth of information on food, nutrition,
enzymes, digestion, world food problems, plus excellent historical sections on domestication and agricultural
advances.... The format is open and inviting, and the
writing clear, simple, well paced, and interesting. The
section on malnutrition in the world is excellent. Writing, format, coverage, approach, index, depth, and
photographs all contribute to making this the finest book
I have ever read on nutrition."--Library Journal.

ANDERSEN, Hans Christian. Hans Andersen's Fairy Tales.
Translated by Reginald Spink. Illustrated by Hans
Baumhauer. E.P. Dutton & Company, Inc., 1953.
Originally published 1835. Grades 3-6.
Included among these stories are "The Emperor's New
Clothes," "The Fir Tree," "Little Claus and Big Claus,"
"Little Mermaid," "The Princess and the Pea," "The
Steadfast Tin Soldier," "Snow Queen," "Thumbelina."
--J.K.

_____. The Steadfast Tin Soldier. Translated by M.R.
James. Illustrated by Marcia Brown. Charles Scribner's Sons, 1953. Originally published 1835. Grades
3-4.
This favorite story is illustrated with feeling and vital-
ity.

ANDERSON, Edna A.  The Extra Egg.  Illustrated by Lucile
Bruce.  T. S. Denison & Company, Inc.  Grades K-3.
An amusing story of the little duckling who is hatched by
a mother hen and soon discovers that he is different.
The little duck which hatched last in the setting of chicks
thought of himself as a queer little chicken with webbed
feet and a wide, flat bill.  He was separated from his
"family" when chasing bugs in a weed patch.  Sherry
found him and raised him in the sun porch.  She called
him "Queer Chick" because of his habit of watching the
chickens and wanting to be near them.  Reading level,
grade 3.  Four-color illustrations.

ANGLUND, Joan Walsh.  A Friend Is Someone Who Likes
You.  Illustrated by the author.  Harcourt Brace Jovanovich, Inc., 1958.  Grades K-3.
"... shows how a friend can be not only a boy or a
girl but a dog, a white mouse, a tree, a brook, or even
the wind.  It also talks about how to recognize or find a
friend and ends on the comforting note that everyone in
the whole world has at least one friend."--Booklist.

_____.  Love Is a Special Way of Feeling.  Illustrated by
the author.  Harcourt Brace Jovanovich, 1960.  Grade
1 up.
A picture book that identifies some typical pleasant experiences that give rise to this emotion.--J. K.

ATWATER, Richard and Florence.  Mr. Popper's Penguins.
Illustrated by Robert Lawson.  Little, Brown and Company, 1938.  Grades 4-6.
The modern classic about the penguins who came to live
with a house painter.

AUSTIN, Margot.  Barney's Adventure.  Illustrated by the
author.  E. P. Dutton & Company, Inc., 1941.  Grades
ps-2.
A brave small boy and his dog follow some big footprints
leading away from the circus grounds, hoping to find and
return a lost circus animal and be rewarded by free
tickets to see the circus.  Instead of an animal Barney
finds a clown, and returns him to the circus.--J. K.

_____.  Peter Churchmouse.  Illustrated by the author.
E. P. Dutton & Company, Inc., 1941.  Grades ps-2.
Picture-story book about a small, hungry churchmouse,
and the kitten who was supposed to clear the church of
rats--but not Peter Churchmouse.  Their adventures in
attempting to get cheese for Peter provide "spontaneous
fun, the kind that is truly funny to little children...."
--M. L. Becker, Books.

_____.  See also:  Mother Goose.

AVERILL, Esther.   The Fire Cat.   Illustrated by the author.
Harper & Row, Publishers, Inc., 1960.   Grades ps-3.
An "I Can Read" Book.   One day Pickles, a young cat,
chased a little cat up a tree.   But Pickles couldn't
climb down so his only friend, Mrs. Goodkind, called
the Fire Department.   Joe the fireman took Pickles back
to the firehouse where he learned to be a good fire cat
and to make friends with the other cats.   Then Pickles
got a chance to be a hero.


BAGNOLD, Enid.   "National Velvet."   Illustrated by Paul
Brown.   William Morrow and Company, Inc., 1949.
Grades 7 up.
New edition of the famous novel about a girl who raced
her beloved horse in the Grand National.   Ten illustra-
tions.
BAILEY, Carolyn Sherwin.   The Little Rabbit Who Wanted
Red Wings.   Illustrated by Dorothy Grider.   Platt &
Munk Company, 1945.   Grades ps-3.
The delightful story of a rabbit whose wish comes true.
Full-color illustrations on every page.
_____.   Miss Hickory.   Illustrated by Ruth Gannett.   The
Viking Press, Inc., 1946; paperback, 1968.   Grades 4-6.
Winner of the Newbery Award.   "Fascinating and harmo-
nious lithographs adorn this imaginative, delightful story
of a tiny country woman made out of apple twigs with a
hickory-nut head."--Horn Book.
BAKER, Rachel.   The First Woman Doctor:   The Story of
Elizabeth Blackwell, M. D.   Illustrated by Corinne Mal-
vern.   Julian Messner Division of Simon & Schuster,
Inc., 1944.   Grades 6 up.
Biography of Dr. Blackwell, 1821-1910, who came to the
United States from England in 1832, began medical prac-
tice in New York in 1851, and organized the New York
Infirmary for Women and Children. --J. K.
_____.   Sigmund Freud.   Julian Messner Division of Si-
mon & Schuster, Inc., 1952.   Grades 10 up.
Biography of Freud, 1856-1939, Austrian physician and
psychiatrist who was the founder of psychoanalysis. --J. K.
BAMMAN, Henry A. and Whitehead, Robert J.   City Be-
neath the Sea.   Illustrated.   Benefic Press, 1964.
Grades 4-9.
A book in The World of Adventure series.   Reading
level, grade 4.   This daring-packed adventure story skil-
fully combines fact, fiction, and fun to stimulate the
enthusiasm and fire the imagination of every young read-

er.   A purposeful expedition, undertaken by two young
adventurous men and supporting adult characters, form
the content and background.   Story development,  plot,
and suspense surrounding the expedition provide abundant
student interest--and an easy-to-read vocabulary provides
clear understanding.
In addition to the story, the book contains a vocabulary
listing, and a story map, news article, and a tall tale.
These features, directly related to the story action, are
utilized in conjunction with exercises provided in the
Teacher's Guide.
_____.   Fire on the Mountain.   Illustrated.   Benefic
Press, 1963.   Grades 4-9.
World of Adventure series.   Reading level, grade 3.
(See description of the authors' City Beneath the Sea.)
_____.   Flight to the South Pole.   Illustrated.   Benefic
Press, 1965.   Grades 4-9.
World of Adventure series.   Reading level, grade 2.
(See description of the authors' City Beneath the Sea.)
_____.   Hunting Grizzly Bears.   Illustrated.   Benefic
Press, 1963.   Grades 4-9.
World of Adventure series.   Reading level, grade 3.
(See description of the authors' City Beneath the Sea.)
_____.   Lost Uranium Mine.   Illustrated.   Benefic Press,
1964.   Grades 4-9.
World of Adventure series.   Reading level, grade 2.
(See description of the authors' City Beneath the Sea.)
_____.   Sacred Well of Sacrifice.   Illustrated.   Benefic
Press, 1964.   Grades 4-9.
World of Adventure series.   Reading level, grade 5.
(See description of the authors' City Beneath the Sea.)
_____.   The Search for Piranha.   Illustrated.   Benefic
Press, 1964.   Grades 4-9.
World of Adventure series.   Reading level, grade 4.
(See description of the authors' City Beneath the Sea.)
_____.   Viking Treasure.   Illustrated.   Benefic Press,
1965.   Grades 4-9.
World of Adventure series.   Reading level, grade 6.
(See description of the authors' City Beneath the Sea.)
BANNERMAN, Helen.   Little Black Sambo.   Illustrated.
Platt & Munk Company.   Originally published 1900 by
Stokes.   Grades ps-3.
Sambo's adventures with the tiger, told in Helen Banner-
man's classic version.   Illustrated in 4 colors and black
and white.
_____.   The Story of Little Black Sambo.   Illustrated by
the author.   J.B. Lippincott Company, 1923.

The jolly and exciting tale of the little boy who lost his
red coat and his blue trousers and his purple shoes but
who was saved from the tigers to eat 169 pancakes for
his supper, has been universally loved by generations of
children.  First written in 1899, the story has become a
childhood classic and the authorized American edition
with the original drawings by the author has sold hundreds of thousands of copies.
This is a book that speaks the common language of all
nations, and has added more to the joy of little children
than perhaps any other story.  They love to hear it
again and again; to read it to themselves; to act it out
in their play.
"I cannot imagine a childhood without it.  For it has fun
--hilarious, rollicking fun, and that is rare enough in
books of any size for any-sized children.  The gift of
being funny for little children is one of the rarest to be
bestowed upon authors or artists:  Helen Bannerman is
both at once...."--May L. Becker in First Adventures
in Reading.

BARBE, Walter B., compiler.  Creative Writing Activities;
A Highlights Handbook.  Illustrated.  Highlights For
Children, Inc., 1965.  Grades K-6.
This book "is a collection of imaginative devices to
stimulate original efforts by children in creating prose
and poetry.  The book stresses a variety of approaches
to creative writing, with something for every child on
every page, regardless of his age or ability.  It may be
used as a source book for small groups or by a child
working alone....
"Among the techniques employed are story starters, story
endings, story titles, and word descriptions of cartoons
and pictures.  In the area of poetry, children discover
the fun of expressing feelings and ideas in rhyming,
blank verse, and Haiku....
"This volume is based on materials which have appeared
in Highlights For Children...."--Foreword.

BARRIE, James M.  Peter Pan.  Illustrated by Nora S.
Unwin.  Charles Scribner's Sons, 1949.  Grades 4-6.
Adventurous fairy tale of the boy who did not want to
grow up.

BARTLETT, Janet LaSpisa.  See:  Helmrath, Marilyn Olear.

BAUM, L. Frank.  The Wizard of Oz.  Illustrated by Evelyn Copelman.  The Bobbs-Merrill Company, Inc.  Originally published 1900 by George M. Hill Company with
title:  The Wonderful Wizard of Oz.  Grades 3 up.
The adventures of Dorothy who, in her dreams, escaped

from her bed in Kansas to visit the Emerald City and
to meet the wonderful Wizard of Oz, the Scarecrow, the
Tin Woodman, and the Cowardly Lion.

_____. The Wonderful Wizard of Oz.   Illustrated by B. S.
Biro.   E. P. Dutton & Company, Inc.
The beloved story of Dorothy's adventures in the Land
of Oz here appears in a most attractive new edition
which is illustrated with more than forty line drawings
and four color plates.

BEARD, Charles A.   The Presidents in American History.
Updated by William Beard.   Julian Messner Division of
Simon & Schuster, Inc., 1969; originally 1948.   Grades
6 up.
Biographies, from Washington through Nixon.

BEARD, Isobel R.   Dot to Dot.   Follett Publishing Company,
1969.   Grades ps-3.
A Follett Activity Fun Book.

_____. Draw with Dots.   Follett Publishing Company.
Grades ps-3.
A Follett Activity Fun Book.

_____. Join the Dots.   Follett Publishing Company.
Grades ps-3.
A Follett Activity Fun Book.

_____. Link the Dots.   Follett Publishing Company, 1969.
Grades ps-3.
A Follett Activity Fun Book.

_____. Puzzles and Riddles.   Follett Publishing Compa-
ny.   Grades ps-3.
A Follett Activity Fun Book.

_____. Puzzles for Pleasure.   Follett Publishing Compa-
ny.   Grades ps-3.
A Follett Activity Fun Book.

BEARD, William.   See: Beard, Charles A.

BECKER, John.   See: Faulkner, Georgene.

BEDFORD, Annie N.   See: Chase, Alice.

BEIM, Jerrold.   The Smallest Boy in the Class.   Illustrated
by Meg Wohlberg.   William Morrow and Company, Inc.,
1949.   Grades ps-3.
"An appealing picture storybook illustrated with lifelike
pictures in color and black and white."--Booklist.

BEMELMANS, Ludwig.   Madeline.   Illustrated by the author.
The Viking Press, Inc., 1939; paperback, 1969.   Grades
K-3.
Runner-up, Caldecott Medal Award.   "Gaiety is the key-
note of the book in text and pictures; nevertheless, Mr.
Bemelmans' drawings of the Opera, of Notre Dame in
the rain, of the sun shining on birds and children in the

Luxembourg and Tuileries gardens have put an authentic Paris within the covers of this book. The rhymes in which the tale is told make it one that children will enjoy repeating."--New York Times.

_____. Madeline and the Bad Hat. Illustrated by the author. The Viking Press, Inc., 1957; paperback, 1968. Grades K-3.
Prizewinner, New York Herald Tribune's Children's Spring Book Festival. "This story about Madeline deals more with the little son of the Spanish Ambassador. With twelve little girls as neighbors, it was inevitable that he would turn out to be a show-off and a 'bad hat.' The pictures of Paris are enchanting."--Library Journal.

_____. Madeline and the Gypsies. Illustrated by the author. The Viking Press, Inc., 1959. Grades K-3.
"The irresistible Madeline and Pepito, stranded on a Ferris wheel in a storm, are rescued by gypsies with whom they lead an enchanting life for a while."--Library Journal.

_____. Madeline in London. Illustrated by the author. The Viking Press, Inc., 1961. Grades K-3.
"Miss Clavel's whole class of twelve leaves France for England and even the Queen's guard is involved when Madeline and Pepito, the Bad Hat, take a wild ride around the city. Ludwig Bemelmans again proves his skill with glowing pictures and a lively story."--Grade Teacher.

_____. Madeline's Rescue. Illustrated by the author. The Viking Press, Inc., 1953. Grades K-3.
"Madeline tumbles into the Seine and is rescued by a dog who comes back to school with the famous two-line walk of little girls. The story goes on to search all over Paris for the poor dog Genevieve who returns of her own accord and solves the problem of 'whose bed tonight' by having the right number of puppies."--New York Times.

BENÉT, William Rose, compiler. Poems for Youth: An American Anthology. E. P. Dutton & Company, Inc., 1923. Grades 7 up.
"A generous selection of the most striking poems of American poets old and new, compiled especially for young Americans...."--Literary Review.

BENSON, Sally. Junior Miss. Doubleday & Company, Inc. Originally published 1941 by Random House, Inc. Grades 7-12.
A novel for girls.

BERGEY, Alyce.  Beggar's Greatest Wish.  Illustrated.
  Concordia Publishing House, 1969.  Grades 4-6.
  An Arch Book.  Children, parents, and teachers are
  still discovering these colorful and easy-to-read little
  treasures.  They're long enough to tell a whole Bible
  story in bouncy verse or prose, and short enough to be
  interesting.
_____.  Boy Who Saved His Family.  Illustrated by Betty
  Wind.  Concordia Publishing House, 1966.
  An Arch Book, presenting a Bible story in colorful,
  easy-to-read form.
_____.  Fishermen's Surprise.  Illustrated.  Concordia
  Publishing House, 1967.
  An Arch Book, presenting a Bible story in colorful,
  easy-to-read form.
_____.  Great Promise.  Illustrated by B. Behm.  Con-
  cordia Publishing House, 1968.  Grade 5.
  An Arch Book, presenting a Bible story in colorful,
  easy-to-read form.
_____.  Rocky, the Rocket Mouse.  Illustrated by Law-
  rence Spiegel.  T. S. Denison & Company, Inc.  Grades
  1-3.
  A fantasy story of Rocky, a laboratory mouse, used on
  a rocket trip to the moon.  Rocky was a very ordinary,
  unimportant, and somewhat bored little mouse--until he
  was chosen to be sent to the moon in a rocket!  This is
  the story of his flight into space and his adventures on
  the moon.  After a trip to the moon, which all little
  girls and boys today dream about, Rocky is eager to get
  back to his simple little laboratory home.  Four-color
  illustrations.
_____.  World God Made.  Illustrated by Obata.  Con-
  cordia Publishing House, 1965.
  An Arch Book, presenting a Bible story in colorful,
  easy-to-read form.
BESKOW, Elsa Maartman.  Pelle's New Suit.  Illustrated
  by the author.  Harper & Row Publishers, Inc., 1929.
  Grades ps-1.
  A Swedish picture book, translated by Marion Letcher
  Woodburn, which tells "the story of how Pelle earned
  his new suit.  He is shown raking hay, bringing in wood,
  feeding pigs, going on errands and at the same time,
  each process in the making of the suit is followed beginning with the shearing of the lamb.  The coloring of the
  pictures (which show both Swedish peasant house interi-
  ors and out-of-doors scenes) is quite lovely."--New York
  Public Library.

BETTER HOMES AND GARDENS EDITORS.   Better Homes
and Gardens Junior Cook Book.   Illustrated.   Better
Homes and Gardens Press (Consumer Book Division,
Meredith Corporation), 1955.   Grades 5-8.
Excellent first cooking guide for the homemaker of to-
morrow.   Step-by-step instructions and illustrations
make learning easy and fun.   Recipes presented are
perfect for family meals or party planning.   Safety tips,
a glossary of standard cooking terms, an easy-to-follow
measuring chart, food trims, table settings and meal
plans are tailor-made for the beginner.   Washable, easy-
care cover.
_____.   Better Homes and Gardens Story Book.   Illus-
trated.   Better Homes and Gardens Press (Consumer
Book Division, Meredith Corporation), 1950.   Grades
K-3.
A collection of 47 classic stories and poems from the
rich heritage of children's literature.   Each selection
enhanced by reproductions of original illustrations.
Songs to sing.   Games to play.   Verses and stories to
learn by heart.   Perfect for "read-to-me," and begin-
ning readers.   Over 600 original illustrations.   A wash-
able cover.
BISHOP, Claire Huchet.   The Five Chinese Brothers.   Illus-
trated by Kurt Wiese.   Coward-McCann & Geoghegan,
Inc., 1938; E.M. Hale & Company.   Grades K-5.
"Each of the five identical Chinese brothers has a spe-
cial talent which he uses to save the lives of all."--
Hodges.
BLACK, Charles L.   Big Book of Airplanes.   Illustrated by
George J. Zaffo.   Grosset & Dunlap, Inc., 1951.
For parents to read aloud and for young readers to read
for themselves.   Illustrated in 4 colors.
BLACKMORE, Richard Doddridge.   Lorna Doone.   Illustrated
by Lionel Edwards.   E.P. Dutton & Company, Inc.
Originally published 1869.   Grades 7 up.
The story of John Ridd and the gentle, exquisite girl he
finds incongruously among his father's murderers, the
outlaw robber Doones.
BLANTON, Catherine.   Hold Fast to Your Dreams.   Julian
Messner Division of Simon & Schuster, Inc., 1955.
Grades 7 up.
"Determined to become a ballet dancer but aware that
the color of her skin is against her, Emmy Lou leaves
Alabama for a non-segregated school in Arizona with
high hopes, only to find that there, too, she must fight
prejudice before she can achieve her dream...."--Book-
list.

BOND, Michael. A Bear Called Paddington. Illustrated by
    Peggy Fortnum. Houghton Mifflin Company, 1960; Dell
    Publishing Company, Inc., 1968. Originally published
    in 1958 in England. Grades 2-6.
    A most endearing bear from Darkest Peru finds himself
    on a railway platform in London with a "Please look
    after this bear" sign hanging from his furry neck. The
    Brown family do just that, and discover that life is
    filled with adventure when there is a bear in the house.
BONHAM, Frank. Durango Street. E. P. Dutton & Company,
    Inc., 1965. Grades 7 up.
    "Rufus Henry had no choice. The only way he could
    escape the Gassers was to join another gang--even though
    it was a violation of his new parole.... In this unusual-
    ly moving and powerful novel, Frank Bonham, a leading
    writer for young people, sympathetically and accurately
    depicts the sad, boisterous, and violent world of teen-
    age gangs and the people who try to help them."--book
    jacket.
_____. The Nitty Gritty. Illustrated by Alvin Smith.
    E. P. Dutton & Company, Inc., 1968; Dell Publishing
    Company, Inc., 1971. Grades 7 up.
    Charlie lives in Dogtown, the black ghetto area of a
    large city. His father sees no future in education for
    a young black man and wants Charlie to work at shining
    shoes. But Charlie has other ideas. When he decides
    to escape from Dogtown with his freewheeling Uncle Bar-
    on, he meets the reality of his environment headon with
    drama and humor.
BONSALL, Crosby Newell. The Case of the Cat's Meow.
    Illustrated by the author. Harper & Row Publishers,
    Inc., 1965. Grades ps-3.
    An "I Can Read" Mystery. Snitch, Wizard, Skinny, and
    Tubby, "the same four young 'private eyes' who appeared
    in The Case of the Hungry Stranger, now solve the mys-
    tery of the puzzling disappearance of Snitch's cat Mil-
    dred."--Booklist.
_____. The Case of the Hungry Stranger. Illustrated by
    the author. Harper & Row Publishers, Inc., 1963.
    Grades ps-3.
    An "I Can Read" Mystery, about the hilarious hijinks of
    four young Private Eyes: Wizard, Tubby, Skinny and
    Snitch. Keeps beginning readers guessing--and laughing.
_____. Tell Me Some More. Illustrated by Fritz Siebel.
    Harper & Row Publishers, Inc., 1961. Grades ps-3.
    An "I Can Read" Book. Andrew tells Tim he knows a
    place where he can hold an elephant under his arm and

three camels in his two hands and pat a lion on the nose,
and do a few other miraculous things.  Finally he shows
Tim the place, and their imaginations go on a hilarious
spree.--J. K.
_____.  Who's a Pest?  Illustrated by the author.  Harper
& Row Publishers, Inc., 1962.  Grades ps-3.
An "I Can Read" Book.
BOWMAN, James Cloyd.  Pecos Bill.  Illustrated by Laura
Bannon.  Albert Whitman & Company, 1937.  Grades 5
up.
"Marvelous doings of 'the greatest cowboy of all times'."
--New York Times.
BOWMAN, James Cloyd and Bianco, Margery.  Tales from
a Finnish Tupa.  Illustrated by Laura Bannon.  Albert
Whitman & Company, 1936.  Grades 5 up.
Hero tales, folklore, fairy tales, and fables of Finland,
translated from original sources, are in this anthology.
BOY SCOUTS OF AMERICA.  Animal Industry.  Illustrated.
Boy Scouts of America, 1944.  Grades 6-12.
Explains the handling of farm animals for profit.
_____.  Archery.  Illustrated.  Boy Scouts of America,
1964.  Grades 6-12.
About bows, arrows, techniques of learning, and ways
to employ the knowledge for fun and skill.
_____.  Art.  Illustrated.  Boy Scouts of America, 1968.
Grades 6-12.
Tells background and emphasizes appreciation.
_____.  Astronomy.  Illustrated.  Boy Scouts of America,
1971.  Grades 6-12.
This book plots stars, planets, and their galaxies, ex-
plaining relationships to environmental factors.
_____.  Athletics.  Illustrated.  Boy Scouts of America,
1964.  Grades 6-12.
Gives management tips on training, staging, and super-
vising sports events.
_____.  Automotive Safety.  Illustrated.  Boy Scouts of
America, 1962.  Grades 6-12.
Contains checklist data for maintaining, operating, and
understanding vehicles.
_____.  Aviation.  Illustrated.  Boy Scouts of America,
1968.  Grades 6-12.
Gives descriptions of airports, jobs in aviation, and air-
craft power.
_____.  Basketry.  Illustrated.  Boy Scouts of America,
1968.  Grades 6-12.
Tells how to weave wicker, cane, reed, and willow ob-
jects.

_____. Bear Cub Scout Book. Illustrated. Boy Scouts
of America, 1967. Grade 4.
This book for nine-year-olds is a part of the Cub literature. It includes a parents' supplement.

_____. Bird Study. Illustrated. Boy Scouts of America,
1967. Grades 6-12.
Classifies species, concentrating on habits and protection
efforts.

_____. Boy Scout Handbook. Illustrated. Boy Scouts of
America, 1966. Originally published 1910. Grades 6-
12.
The basic book for Boy Scouts. This 7th edition is in
full color with facts on hiking, camping, nature study,
first aid, and skills.

_____. Boy Scout Songbook. Illustrated. Boy Scouts of
America, 1971. Grades 6-12.
A group-singing manual.

_____. Camping. Illustrated. Boy Scouts of America,
1966. Grades 6-12.
Extends the experiences of 60 years of camping by millions of American boys.

_____. Canoeing. Illustrated. Boy Scouts of America,
1968. Grades 6-12.
Explains repair, maintenance, and use of canoes with
paddles, as sailing rigs, and in other situations.

_____. Chemistry. Illustrated. Boy Scouts of America,
1962. Grades 6-12.
Describes both inorganic and organic fundamentals.

_____. Citizenship. Illustrated. Boy Scouts of America,
1966. Grades 6-12.
Shows how home, community, nation, and world depend
on integrity and responsibility.

_____. Coin Collecting. Illustrated. Boy Scouts of
America, 1966. Grades 6-12.
Carries examples of rare coins for the ever-growing
numbers of numismatists.

_____. Conservation of Natural Resources. Illustrated.
Boy Scouts of America, 1967. Grades 6-12.
Stresses the very real modern problems of water and
air pollution, interrelations of resources, laws for and
careers in conservation.

_____. Cooking. Illustrated. Boy Scouts of America,
1967. Grades 6-12.
Stresses outdoor preparations of food, but it also gives
menus, utensils, serving, and cleanup.

_____. Cub Scout Fun Book. Illustrated. Boy Scouts
of America, 1967. Grades 3-5.

This book contains 45 Cub-age projects.   Each project
has "how to" information with patterns.
_____.  Cub Scout Magic.   Illustrated.   Boy Scouts of
America, 1960.   Grades 3-5.
This book suggests stunts for dens and packs.
_____.  Cub Scout Songbook.   Illustrated.   Boy Scouts of
America, 1969.   Grades 3-5.
This book for boys and leaders contains 144 fun songs,
action songs, and rounds.
_____.  Cycling.   Illustrated.   Boy Scouts of America,
1971.   Grades 6-12.
Teaches vehicular safety with fun.
_____.  Den Chief's Denbook.   Illustrated.   Boy Scouts
of America, 1968.   Grades 6-12.
A handbook for the Boy Scout leader of a Cub Scout den.
It gives many suggestions for activities.
_____.  Dog Care.   Illustrated.   Boy Scouts of America,
1969.   Grades 6-12.
Discusses feeding, training, and first aid of several
breeds.
_____.  Electricity.   Illustrated.   Boy Scouts of America,
1964.   Grades 6-12.
Describes the nature of the power with equipment re-
pairs, things to make, and problems in use.
_____.  Explorer Member's Guide.   Illustrated.   Boy
Scouts of America, 1969.   Grades 6-12.
Replaces the Exploring manual; describes the program
of Exploring for young adults.
_____.  Fieldbook.   Illustrated.   Boy Scouts of America,
1967.   Grades 6-12.
Combines a half-century of outdoor experience in many
fields with five years of testing and compiling of facts
for a multisubject guide with 2,500 illustrations.
_____.  Fingerprinting.   Illustrated.   Boy Scouts of Amer-
ica, 1964.   Grades 6-12.
Methods and uses of the identification technique.
_____.  Firemanship.   Illustrated.   Boy Scouts of Amer-
ica, 1968.   Grades 6-12.
Contains information on causes of fires, prevention techniques, and fire-escape plans.
_____.  First Aid.   Illustrated.   Boy Scouts of America,
1960.   Grades 6-12.
Extends emergency care training to Boy Scouts and Explorers.
_____.  First Aid to Animals.   Illustrated.   Boy Scouts
of America, 1963.   Grades 6-12.
Warns of hit-and-miss methods as it tells how to treat
animal ailments and accidents.

_____. Fishing. Illustrated. Boy Scouts of America,
1954. Grades 6-12.
Supplies data on methods and gear.

_____. Forestry. Illustrated. Boy Scouts of America,
1971. Grades 6-12.
Suggests improvements in watersheds, soils, wildlife,
reforestation, and tools.

_____. Gardening. Illustrated. Boy Scouts of America,
1971. Grades 6-12.
Centers on growth of food plants, including most vege-
tables.

_____. Geology. Illustrated. Boy Scouts of America,
1953. Grades 6-12.
Traces the millenium changes in rocks, minerals, and
earth.

_____. Hiking. Illustrated. Boy Scouts of America,
1962. Grades 6-12.
Advances earlier Scout training for use by older boys.

_____. Home Repairs. Illustrated. Boy Scouts of Amer-
ica, 1961. Grades 6-12.
A do-it-yourself guide for household basic tools.

_____. Horsemanship. Illustrated. Boy Scouts of Amer-
ica, 1969. Grades 6-12.
About knowing horses and how to ride them.

_____. Indian Lore. Illustrated. Boy Scouts of Amer-
ica, 1959. Grades 6-12.
Tells characteristics and history of American Indians.

_____. Insect Life. Illustrated. Boy Scouts of Amer-
ica, 1963. Grades 6-12.
Classifies habits and tells how to turn insects into hob-
bies.

_____. Leatherwork. Illustrated. Boy Scouts of Amer-
ica, 1970. Grades 6-12.
Gives ways of turning hides into useful apparel and handicraft projects.

_____. Lifesaving. Illustrated. Boy Scouts of America,
1965. Grades 6-12.
Gives instructions about water rescues.

_____. Motorboating. Illustrated. Boy Scouts of Amer-
ica, 1962. Grades 6-12.
Examines boats, their care and operation, listing the
safety rules every owner must know.

_____. Music. Illustrated. Boy Scouts of America,
1968. Grades 6-12.
About instrumental and vocal music, and Boy Scout bugle
calls.

_____ . Nature. Illustrated. Boy Scouts of America,
1952. Grades 6-12.
Includes everything from birds to soils and rocks.
_____ . Patrol Leader's Handbook. Illustrated. Boy
Scouts of America, 1967. Grades 6-12.
Clips out short, fast-reading bursts of information for
many techniques a boy can use to exert leadership with
his peers.
_____ . Personal Fitness. Illustrated. Boy Scouts of
America, 1968. Grades 6-12.
Gives the answers to better body conditioning.
_____ . Pets. Illustrated. Boy Scouts of America,
1969. Grades 6-12.
Stresses care, attention, and love for all household
creatures and tells why.
_____ . Photography. Illustrated. Boy Scouts of Amer-
ica, 1960. Grades 6-12.
Shoots wide angle view of the camera, lighting, focus,
and subject matter with common errors in developing
and taking pictures.
_____ . Pioneering. Illustrated. Boy Scouts of America,
1967. Grades 6-12.
Emphasizes skills of ropework, wilderness engineering,
and primitive existence.
_____ . Public Health. Illustrated. Boy Scouts of Amer-
ica, 1969. Grades 6-12.
Lists dread diseases, insect carriers, contamination,
and benefits of community cleanliness.
_____ . Public Speaking. Illustrated. Boy Scouts of
America, 1969. Grades 6-12.
Describes voice; effectiveness of pitch, rhythm, pauses,
staging, appearance; helps on speech preparation.
_____ . Radio. Illustrated. Boy Scouts of America,
1965. Grades 6-12.
This book is more a "what is" than a "how to" of sending and receiving signals with proper equipment and
training.
_____ . Reading. Illustrated. Boy Scouts of America,
1965. Grades 6-12.
Encourages balance in the book fare of older boys in
news, technical fields, travel, fiction, poetry, and other
forms. It lists material by ages, too.
_____ . Reptile Study. Illustrated. Boy Scouts of America, 1971. Grades 6-12.
Classifies cold-blooded creatures for pet and study pos-
sibilities.

_____.  Rifle and Shotgun Shooting.  Illustrated.  Boy
Scouts of America, 1967.  Grades 6-12.
Teaches safe operation, hunting do's and don'ts.
_____.  Rowing.  Illustrated.  Boy Scouts of America,
1964.  Grades 6-12.
Gives the interdependence of boats, water, operation,
and maintenance.
_____.  Safety.  Illustrated.  Boy Scouts of America,
1971.  Grades 6-12.
Emphasizes accident prevention at home, on the highway,
in the woods, in water, in sports, and in the workaday
world.
_____.  Scholarship.  Illustrated.  Boy Scouts of Amer-
ica, 1970.  Grades 6-12.
Shows benefits of maximum effort in the classroom, re-
search, and reading.  Scholarship is exciting and re-
warding.
_____.  Scout How Book.  Illustrated.  Boy Scouts of
America, 1969.  Grades 6-12.
In comic-book style for the first two ranks in the Boy
Scout program, this book is designed for poor readers
who are eleven years old and older.
_____.  Signaling.  Illustrated.  Boy Scouts of America,
1940.  Grades 6-12.
Sends the message about semaphore, Morse, and other
codes.
_____.  Small-Boat Sailing.  Illustrated.  Boy Scouts of
America, 1965.  Grades 6-12.
Guides the learner on lakes and rivers in a growing
sport.
_____.  Soil and Water Conservation.  Illustrated.  Boy
Scouts of America, 1968.  Grades 6-12.
Recognizes in its analysis that proper management of
soil requires a close control of interrelated wildlife,
water, woods, grasslands, and drainage.
_____.  Stamp Collecting.  Illustrated.  Boy Scouts of
America, 1966.  Grades 6-12.
Evaluates categories of stamps for beginner hobbyists.
_____.  Swimming.  Illustrated.  Boy Scouts of America,
1960.  Grades 6-12.
Upgrades the fun aspects to valuable skills with dia-
grams and photographs.
_____.  Weather.  Illustrated.  Boy Scouts of America,
1963.  Grades 6-12.
Does something about it by explaining climate, wind
pressures, and other means of getting up a forecast.

_____. Webelos Scout Book. Illustrated. Boy Scouts
of America, 1967. Grade 5.
This book is a program for ten-year-old boys. The
Webelos Scout is between Cub Scouting and Boy Scouting.
_____. Wildlife Management. Illustrated. Boy Scouts
of America, 1952. Grades 6-12.
Helps understand protection from terrain, cover, water-
ways, and trees.
_____. Wolf Cub Scout Book. Illustrated. Boy Scouts
of America, 1967. Grade 3.
This book for eight-year-olds is a part of the Cub liter-
ature. It includes a parents' supplement.
_____. Wood Carving. Illustrated. Boy Scouts of Amer-
ica, 1966. Grades 6-12.
Lists objects to carve, kinds of wood, tools.
_____. Woodwork. Illustrated. Boy Scouts of America,
1970. Grades 6-12.
Has information about the wood industry and its projects.
BREM, M. M. Man Caught by a Fish. Concordia Publish-
ing House, 1967.
An Arch Book. Children, parents, and teachers are
still discovering these colorful and easy-to-read little
treasures. They're long enough to tell a whole Bible
story in bouncy verse or prose, and short enough to be
interesting.
_____. Mary's Story. Concordia Publishing House,
1967.
An Arch Book. A colorful, easy-to-read Bible story.
BROCK, Emma L. et al. Spooks and Spirits and Shadowy
Shapes. Illustrated by Robert L. Doremus. E. P. Dut-
ton & Company, Inc., 1949. Grades 2-5.
A book of stories about ghosts and witches. The sto-
ries are: "It Was So Spooky!" by E. L. Brock; "The
Friendly Ghost," by Elizabeth Yates; "The Witch in the
Wintry Wood," by Aileen Fisher; "Thirteen Witches,"
by Elizabeth Coatsworth; "The Ghost of Mad Maurice,"
by R. D. McCrea; "The Floogles Are Detectives," by
Gertrude Crampton; "A Strange Surprise," by Adele De
Leeuw; "Shamus and the Black Cat," by M. R. Walsh.
There is one poem: "Ghost in the Orchard," by Aileen
Fisher.
BROOKS, Charlotte, editor. The Outnumbered. Dell Pub-
lishing Company, Inc., 1967; Delacorte Press, 1969.
Grades 7 up.
Subtitle: Stories, essays and poems about minority
groups by America's leading writers. These writings
are about the minorities of past years, many of whom

have now assimilated into the mainstream of America,
and about the minorities of today, for whom the promise
of America has not been fulfilled.
Contents: "The Shimerdas," by Willa Cather; "O'Hal-
loran's Luck," by Stephen Vincent Benét; "Panic," by
Donn Byrne; "Angel Levine," by Bernard Malamud;
"The Jewish Cemetery at Newport," by Henry Wads-
worth Longfellow; "The Land of Room Enough," by E. P.
Maxwell; "Seventy Thousand Assyrians," by William
Saroyan; "The Indian Burying Ground," by Philip Fre-
neau; "Scars of Honor," by Dorothy Johnson; "Shock,"
by Marian Anderson; "The Cheerleaders," by John
Steinbeck; "My Dungeon Shook," by James Baldwin;
"Fate," by Richard Wright; "Let America Be America
Again," by Langston Hughes.

BROWN, Doris V. and McDonald, Pauline.  Creative Art
Activities for Home and School.  Illustrated.  Lawrence
Publishing Company, 1966.
Illustrated with photographs.  Endorsed by private, pub-
lic and parochial school authorities, praised by Health
Education and Welfare officials, libraries, the PTA and
NAEYC.  Aid to creative imagination at home and
school.

_____.  Learning Begins at Home--A Stimulus for a
Child's I. Q.  Illustrated.  Lawrence Publishing Company.
Illustrated with photographs.  The authors of Creative
Art Activities wrote this widely endorsed book, an excellent companion to their earlier work.  Praised by school
officials, solidly founded on the authors' knowledge of
child psychology and their wide experience as teachers,
administrators and parents, the book contains a wealth
of practical ideas.

BROWN, Lisette G.  Tales of the Sea Foam.  Illustrated
by Virginia Townsend.  Naturegraph Books, 1969.
Grades 6 up.
True adventures of an eleven-year-old white girl with
an Indian group of the northwestern California coast.
A wise and wonderful old Indian woman lends strong
interest to the story.  Aids relations and understanding
between white and Indian children.  5 photos, 12 drawings.

BROWN, Marcia.  Once a Mouse... A Fable Cut in Wood.
Illustrated by the author.  Charles Scribner's Sons,
1961.  Grades K-3.
A fable from India in which a hermit saves a mouse.
Awarded the Caldecott Medal, 1962.

_____. Stone Soup; An Old Tale. Illustrated by the
author. Charles Scribner's Sons, 1947. Grades K-3.
The villagers hid all the food when they saw the soldiers. But the soldiers showed them how to make stone
soup.

BROWN, Margaret Wise. The Golden Egg Book. Illustrated
by Leonard Weisgard. Simon & Schuster, Inc., 1947;
Western Publishing Company, Inc., 1963. Grades K-2.
"A lonely little bunny finds an egg and, hoping to find a
friend inside, he tries all sorts of ways to break it.
Not until he fell asleep did it crack open and out came
a little duck who was as pleased as the bunny to find a
friend."--Huntting.
"It is the pictures that distinguish the work.... Leonard Weisgard surrounds life-like little animals with
flowers of a loveliness one would call unearthly were it
not that flowers just like these do grow from our American earth."--New York Herald Tribune Books.

_____. Goodnight Moon. Illustrated by Clement Hurd.
Harper & Row Publishers, Inc., 1947. Grades ps-1.
"In a picture book with warm colors, progressing from
bright to soft dark tones, and rhythmic, lulling text, a
little rabbit says goodnight to all the familiar objects
in the room."--Booklist.

_____. The Runaway Bunny. Illustrated by Clement
Hurd. Harper & Row Publishers, Inc., 1942. Grades
ps-1.
Two generations of small children have been profoundly
comforted by the gentle magic of this classic picture
book.... Now, Clement Hurd has redrawn some of his
pictures--in the softly poetic spirit of the original draw-
ings--for this story about a little bunny's imaginary
game of hide-and-seek and the lovingly steadfast mother
who finds her child every time. 16 pictures in full col-
or, 18 pictures in black and white.

BROWNELL, Clifford, and Moore, Roy. Recreational
Sports. Illustrated. Creative Educational Society, Inc.,
1962. Grades 4 up.
This volume is for the young person who wants to learn
and study more about the recreational sports, their his-
tories, skills and rules. Teachers will find it to be a
valuable supplement to teaching the recreational sports
in school. Each chapter is prepared by a specialist
and is devoted to a separate sport: Archery, Badmin-
ton, Bowling, Canoeing, Figure Skating, Handball, Skiing, Table Tennis, Volleyball, Water Skiing.

BRUCE, Dana, editor. My Brimful Book. Illustrated by
Tasha Tudor; Margot Austin (pseud.); and Wesley Den-
nis. Platt & Munk Company, 1960. Grades ps-3.
An elegant, colorful volume with full-color illustrations,
containing favorite poems, animal stories, and Mother
Goose rhymes.
_____. The Tasha Tudor Book of Fairy Tales. Illus-
trated by Tasha Tudor. Platt & Munk Company, 1961.
Grades ps-2.
Thirteen favorite tales, illustrated in glowing full color
by America's foremost children's artist, Tasha Tudor.
"Luscious"--Life Magazine; "There couldn't be a warm-
er, lovelier introduction to fairy tales."--Chicago Trib-
une.
_____. Tell Me a Joke. Illustrated by Bill Sokol. Platt
& Munk Company, 1966. Grades 3-7.
Merry jokes children will enjoy telling their friends.
Bright illustrations add to the fun.
_____. Tell Me a Riddle. Illustrated by Frank Elkin.
Platt & Munk Company, 1966. Grades 3-7.
Brain-teasing riddles that will delight children. Amus-
ingly and colorfully illustrated.
BRYANT, Chester. The Lost Kingdom. Illustrated by
Margaret Ayer. Julian Messner Division of Simon &
Schuster, Inc., 1951. Grades 3-6.
"A wonderfully fascinating story of a Hindu boy, Rod-
mika, who discovers the mystery of the tattooed cobra
mark on his chest, in a vibrant jungle background of
authenticity and charm ... one of the best of all jungle
stories...."--Elementary English.
BUCHAN, John. The Thirty-Nine Steps. Illustrated by Edward Ardizzone. E.P. Dutton & Company, Inc., 1964.
Originally published 1915. Grades 7 up.
Richard Hannay, an Englishman, is told by an American
of a plot to destroy England; then the American is murdered and Hannay is suspected of the murder. Hunted
by the police and by the gang whose plot and murder he
knows of, he struggles to elude both groups and get the
truth to Scotland Yard.--J.K.
BUCK, Pearl Sydenstricker. The Big Wave. Illustrated by
Hiroshige and Hokusai. The John Day Company, Inc.,
1948. Grades 4-6.
Illustrated with Japanese prints in black and white. "To
live in the presence of danger makes us brave and
makes us know how good life is. This is the lesson
which Kino and his playmate Jiya learned when a big
tidal wave swept away the fishing village where Jiya
lived."--Huntting

"A gem of a story telling something about the eternal truths of life and death--and helping us to understand the Japanese heart."--Asia.

. The Water-Buffalo Children and The Dragon Fish. Illustrated by William A. Smith and Esther Bird. Dell Publishing Company, Inc., 1966. Originally published by John Day Company, Inc., 1943 and 1944 respectively. Grades 2-6.

In the first story, a little American girl thinks a magic stone has brought two Chinese children on the back of a water-buffalo. In the second, two girls, one American and one Chinese, run away with the help of a magic dragon fish.

BUFF, Mary and Conrad. Dash and Dart: Two Fawns. Illustrated by Conrad Buff. The Viking Press, Inc., 1942. K-3.

Runner-up, Caldecott Medal Award. "The first year of twin fawns ... perfect for reading aloud, so simple and direct is the style. It is difficult to convey the perfection and quality of this book."--Christian Science Monitor.

BULLOCK, Henry M., and Peterson, Edward C., editors. Young Readers Bible. Illustrated. Abingdon Press, 1968. Grades 4 up.

Revised Standard Version. Study helps by the Reverend Henry M. Bullock, Ph.D., and the Reverend Edward C. Peterson, Ed.D. Three different sizes of clear, easy-to-read type; bold-face subject headings inserted into text outlining each book of the Bible; chapter and verse headings in dictionary-like format; marginal color tabs for locating books of the Bible; more than 600 two-color illustrations; 8 pages of full-color general reference maps; and much, much more.

BUNYAN, John. Pilgrim's Progress. Illustrated by Frank G. Pape. E.P. Dutton & Company, Inc. Originally published 1678 (Part I) and 1684 (Part II). Grades 6-9. This volume contains the first and second parts of Pilgrim's famous "progress from this world to that which is to come delivered under the similitude of a dream, his dangerous journey and safe arrival at the desired country."

BURCH, Robert. Queenie Peavy. Illustrated by Jerry Lazare. The Viking Press, Inc., 1966. Grades 4-6. Winner of the 1966 Children's Book Award of the Child Study Association; the Seventeenth Annual Literary Achievement Award of the Georgia Writers Association; the Jane Addams Children's Book Award for 1967.

"Poignant realistic story set in rural Georgia during the
Great Depression, about a defiant girl--a tobacco chewer
and fighter--who learns to face responsibility."--New
York Times.

BURGESS, Thornton W.  Adventures of Peter Cottontail.
One version illustrated by Harrison Cady and George
Kerr; another illustrated by Phoebe Erickson.  Grosset
& Dunlap, Inc.  Grades K-3.
For parents to read aloud and for young readers to read
for themselves here are easy-to-read specially edited
versions of a great classic that boast all the charm of
the original.  Illustrated in 4 colors.

BURNETT, Frances Hodgson.  Little Lord Fauntleroy.  Illustrated by Harry Toothill.  E. P. Dutton & Company,
Inc.  Originally published 1886.  Grades 3-6.
A little boy, living on the edge of poverty in New York,
suddenly becomes an English lord with vast lands and
wealth, yet remains unspoiled by his change of fortune.
_____.  The Secret Garden.  Illustrated by Tasha Tudor.
J. B. Lippincott Company, 1962; Dell Publishing Company, Inc., 1971.  Originally published 1912.  Grades 5-9.
A favorite with generations of children since its original
publication, this is the story of Mary, a cross, self-
centered little girl, and Colin, a pampered invalid boy,
who learn compassion and generosity with the help of a
robin, a boy who loves and is loved by all living things,
and the quiet miracles of nature that they discover in
an abandoned garden.

BURNFORD, Sheila.  The Incredible Journey.  Illustrated
by Carl Burger.  Little, Brown and Company, 1961.
Grades 6 up.
An Atlantic Monthly Press book.
The adventures of "two dogs and a cat who set out to
cross three hundred rugged miles of northern Ontario.
The English bull terrier is old and not in condition for
a trip.  The cat is a Siamese, a breed noted for being
unable to stand cold weather.  Only the large Labrador
retriever is suited to strenuous fall conditions, but not
even he is used to dealing with lynxes, bears, porcu-
pines, rushing rivers, or angry human beings."--Li-
brary Journal.

BURTON, Virginia Lee.  Katy and the Big Snow.  Illustrated
by the author.  Houghton Mifflin Company, 1943.  Grades
K-3.
"Bright, vigorous pictures with plenty of action and endless detail portray Katy at work for the Highway Department of the city of Geoppolis.  Katy is a striking red
crawler tractor ... an absorbing tale."--Horn Book.

_____ . The Little House. Illustrated by the author.
Houghton Mifflin Company, 1942. Grades K-3.
A Caldecott Medal Winner and ALA Notable Book.
". . . This engaging picture book cleverly presents a
wealth of information--the changing seasons in the coun-
try, the advancement in architecture and transportation,
growth in population, and the accelerating tempo of city
life. "--Booklist.
_____ . Mike Mulligan and His Steam Shovel. Illustrated
by the author. Houghton Mifflin Company, 1939. Grades
K-3.
"This is fun both in its text and gay crayon drawings.
Mike Mulligan remains faithful to his steam shovel,
Mary Anne, against the threat of the new gas and Diesel-
engine contraptions and digs his way to a surprising and
happy ending. "--New Yorker.
BUTTERWORTH, Oliver. The Enormous Egg. Illustrated
by Louis Darling. Little, Brown and Company, 1956.
Grades 4-6.
Young Nate Twichell's hen laid a huge egg, and with
Nate's help hatched out--a Triceratops!
BYARS, Betsy. The Summer of the Swans. Illustrated by
Ted McConis. The Viking Press, Inc., 1970. Grades
7 up.
"Story of the longest day in the life of a 14-year-old
girl--the summer day her loved, mentally retarded
brother is lost, the day she discovers compassion in a
friend. A compelling story. "--Publishers Weekly.


CADBURY, B. Bartram. Fresh and Salt Water. Illustrated.
Creative Educational Society, Inc. in cooperation with
the National Audubon Society, 1967. Grades 4-8.
Young readers make a wondrous discovery when they
learn how living things relate to water in rivers, lakes,
swamps, the sea and on land. The book shows the importance of water in man's life, the role of plants, and
animals in or near aquatic environments, the sea as a
source of important chemicals and minerals as well as
food, and the need for control of floods, erosion, and
pollution. Text is by an authority in the subject, and
the photographs by top-notch specialists.
CAMERON, Elizabeth. Big Book of Real Trucks. Illustrated by George J. Zaffo. Grosset & Dunlap, Inc.,
1958. Originally written by George J. Zaffo, published
1950. Grades 1-5.
For parents to read aloud and for young readers to read
for themselves. Illustrated in 4 colors.

CANNON, Marian. Colonial Williamsburg Coloring Book.
Illustrated by the author. The Colonial Williamsburg
Foundation, 1948.
Imaginative line drawings and informative text form this
attractive coloring book.

CARLETON, Barbee. Benny and the Bear. Illustrated by
Dagmar Wilson. Follett Publishing Company, 1960.
Grades 2-4.
"How Benny became big and brave by taming the bear
the men thought they had to shoot. Illustrations in color
harmonize with the text."--School Library Journal.

CARLSON, Bernice Wells. Make It Yourself! Illustrated
by Aline Hansens. Abingdon Press, 1950. Grades 3-7.
Here are more than 150 handicraft projects that are
easy--and fun for boys and girls.

CARLSON, George. Jokes and Riddles. Illustrated. Platt
& Munk Company. Grades 3-7.
A selection of riddles and jokes children love.

CARLSON, Natalie Savage. The Empty Schoolhouse. Illustrated by John Kaufmann. Harper & Row Publishers,
Inc., 1965; Dell Publishing Company, Inc., 1968.
Grades 2-6.
Ten-year-old Lullah Royall was thrilled at the news that
the parochial schools in her state were to be desegre-
gated: she could be with her friends at last. But unexpected hostilities and the threat of violence make her
happiness short-lived.
Notable Children's Book of 1965, ALA; 1965 Children's
Book Award, CSA.

CARROLL, Lewis (pseud.). Alice's Adventures in Wonderland and Through the Looking Glass. Illustrated by
John Tenniel and Diana Stanley. E. P. Dutton & Company, Inc., 1954. Originally published 1865 and 1872
respectively. Grades 3-7.
In the first story Alice, in a dream, has strange adventures in a wonderful underground country with fantastic
talking animals and other creatures that have become
immortal characters in English literature, including the
Cheshire Cat, the March Hare, the Mad Hatter, the
Mock Turtle, etc.
In the second story Alice wonders about the world back
of the looking glass, then dreams that she enters the
looking-glass house, where everything is turned back-
ward. The story follows a game of chess with Alice as
the White Pawn. She encounters such fascinating characters as the White King and Queen, the Red King and
Queen, Tweedledum and Tweedledee, Humpty Dumpty,
and the Lion and the Unicorn.--J.K.

CHAMBERLAIN, Joseph M. and Nicholson, Thomas D.
   Planets, Stars and Space. Illustrated. Creative Educational Society, Inc. in cooperation with the American
   Museum of Natural History, 1962. Grades 5-9.
   This fascinating book begins with the earth and travels
   outward to define the structures and population of the
   universe. The reader is constantly exposed to one of
   the wonderful features of modern astronomy--the photo-
   graph. Through the photographs, original art, and text,
   the reader shares the finest hours of the leading astron-
   omers and the superlative vision of the best telescopes.
   His curiosity about our environment of planets, stars,
   and space will be satisfied--and extended.

CHANDLER, Edna Walker. Cowboy Sam. Illustrated by
   Jack Merryweather. Benefic Press, 1960. Grades K-3.
   Reading level for this book: K.
   The Cowboy Sam series of books tells exciting adventures
   of western life. Three levels of difficulty for each reading level offer unusual flexibility to meet a wide range
   of teaching situations and individual differences. Upon
   completion of basic and after-basic readers, assign high
   interest, controlled difficulty Cowboy Sam readers to
   youngsters. A section in each book lists the reading
   skills that are covered. The adult characters and high
   interest stories told in an easy vocabulary permit even
   slow readers to share the humorous and exciting adventures. The author knows the western way of life and
   writes about it in an intimate style that brings cowboys
   close to the reader's heart. Her Cowboy Sam adventures show that there's plenty of excitement in the West
   that doesn't involve blood and thunder.
   _____. Cowboy Sam and Big Bill. Illustrated by Jack
   Merryweather. Benefic Press, 1970. Grades ps-2.
   Reading level: ps. See description of Cowboy Sam.
   _____. Cowboy Sam and Dandy. Illustrated by Jack
   Merryweather. Benefic Press, 1962. Grades ps-2.
   Reading level: ps. See description of Cowboy Sam.
   _____. Cowboy Sam and Flop. Illustrated by Jack Mer-
   ryweather. Benefic Press, 1971. Grades 1-4.
   Reading level: grade 1. See description of Cowboy
   Sam.
   _____. Cowboy Sam and Freckles. Illustrated by Jack
   Merryweather. Benefic Press, 1971. Grades ps-2.
   Reading level: ps. See description of Cowboy Sam.
   _____. Cowboy Sam and Freddy. Illustrated by Jack
   Merryweather. Benefic Press, 1970. Grades 1-4.
   Reading level: grade 1. See description of Cowboy Sam.

_____. Cowboy Sam and Miss Lily. Illustrated by Jack
Merryweather. Benefic Press, 1971. Grades K-3.
Reading level: K. See description of Cowboy Sam.
_____. Cowboy Sam and Porky. Illustrated by Jack Mer-
ryweather. Benefic Press, 1971. Grades K-3.
Reading level: K. See description of Cowboy Sam.
_____. Cowboy Sam and Sally. Illustrated by Jack Mer-
ryweather. Benefic Press, 1959. Grades 2-5.
Reading level: grade 2. See description of Cowboy Sam.
_____. Cowboy Sam and Shorty. Illustrated by Jack
Merryweather. Benefic Press, 1962. Grades 1-4.
Reading level: grade 1. See description of Cowboy Sam.
_____. Cowboy Sam and the Airplane. Illustrated by
Jack Merryweather. Benefic Press, 1959. Grades 3-6.
Reading level: grade 3. See description of Cowboy Sam.
_____. Cowboy Sam and the Fair. Illustrated by Jack
Merryweather. Benefic Press, 1970. Grades 2-5.
Reading level: grade 2. See description of Cowboy Sam.
_____. Cowboy Sam and the Indians. Illustrated by Jack
Merryweather. Benefic Press, 1971. Grades 3-6.
Reading level: grade 3. See description of Cowboy Sam.
_____. Cowboy Sam and the Rodeo. Illustrated by Jack
Merryweather. Benefic Press, 1959. Grades 2-5.
Reading level: grade 2. See description of Cowboy Sam.
_____. Cowboy Sam and the Rustlers. Illustrated by Jack
Merryweather. Benefic Press, 1970. Grades 3-6.
Reading level: grade 3. See description of Cowboy Sam.
CHAPBOOK 2. The Bethany Press, 1966. Grades 4-9.
Compact song and source book for all informal occasions.
Contains hymns, ballads, and fun songs plus worship re-
sources including calls to worship, prayers, and litanies
on such topics as stewardship, seasonal celebrations and
God.
CHAPPEL, Bernice M. Harvey Hopper. Illustrated by Ruth
Brophy. T.S. Denison & Company, Inc. Grades K-3.
A nature study that encourages children to become in-
terested in the world of living things. This is a story
written in rhyme about a happy grasshopper and his
friend, a cricket, as they meet the dangers and pleas-
ures of life. Children will enjoy Harvey's and Jumper's
experiences as they escape from a huge fish, an owl,
and a mother killdeer. Four-color illustrations.
CHARLIP, Remy. Where Is Everybody? Illustrated by the
author. Addison-Wesley Publishing Company, 1957.
Grades ps-1.
First, there is only empty sky. A bird appears. Then
the sun comes out. Gradually a hill, a river, a boat,

trees, deer, a house, and people appear on the scene.
Then, as night comes, each of these things disappears.
An excellent book for beginning, remedial, and pre-
readers because the word for each object in the story is
printed right on the object. Illustrations in 2 colors.
CHASE, Alice. Walt Disney's Mary Poppins. Edited by
Annie N. Bedford. Illustrated by Grace Clark. Western
Publishing Company, Inc., 1964. Grades K-2.
A version for the very young, of the story by Pamela
Travers of the nonsensical adventures of the amazing
nursemaid with the British Banks children. --J. K.
CHASE, Alice Elizabeth. Famous Paintings: An Introduc-
tion to Art. Illustrated. Platt & Munk Company, 1962.
Originally published 1951. Grades 5 up.
This book has been acclaimed by art experts, educators
and readers of all ages as the book that makes art "un-
derstandable" even to a beginning student. More than
184 reproductions, 54 of them in full color. Cited by
the ALA as a Notable Children's Book. "Perhaps the
best introduction to art that has been done."--Virginia
Kirkus.
CHILDREN'S TELEVISION WORKSHOP. See: Moss, Jeffrey.
CHUTE, Marchette. Around and About. Illustrated by the
author. E.P. Dutton & Company, Inc., 1957. Grades
ps-2.
A book of rhymes.
CLARK, Ann Nolan. In My Mother's House. Illustrated by
Velino Herrera. The Viking Press, Inc., 1941. Grades
K-3.
Prizewinner, New York Herald Tribune's Children's
Spring Book Festival. Runner-up, Caldecott Medal
Award. "Rhythm and dignity of speech mark this simple
text, based on the notebooks of Indian children in schools
near Santa Fe. Describes the things they know best,
their homes, crops, work horses, and their festivals."
--Horn Book.
_____. Secret of the Andes. Illustrated by Jean Charlot.
The Viking Press, Inc., 1952; paperback, 1970. Grades
4-6.
Winner of the Newbery Award. "The story of Cusi, an In-
can boy who lives in a hidden valley high in the mountains
of Peru with old Chuto the llama herder. Unknown to
Cusi, he is of royal blood and is the 'chosen one.' A
compelling story."--Booklist.
CLARK, Margery (pseud.). The Poppy Seed Cakes. Illus-
trated by Maud and Miska Petersham. Doubleday &
Company, Inc., 1924. Grades ps-3.

Adventures in the nursery. "About four-year-old Andrewshek, four-and-a-half-year-old Erminka, and good Aunt Katushka, who came from the old country with a bag full of presents. The gay pictures resemble those of Czecho-Slovakian and Russian picture books."--Toronto.

CLARK, Mary L. The True Book of Dinosaurs. Illustrated by C. Maltman. Children's Press, 1955. Grades 1-5. Science and social studies ... these factual books explain so many of the things that puzzle inquisitive young minds. Students use the True Books for supplementary work in their classes. They use them to find out about special things that interest them. They read them to learn on their own. Each fascinating True Book encourages a child to further his search for the answers he wants. Easy to read, packed with information, the True Books are excellent for primary and intermediate grades. Color illustrations.

CLEARY, Beverly. Ellen Tebbits. Illustrated by Louis Darling. William Morrow and Company, Inc., 1951. Grades 3-7.
"Hilarious adventures of a little girl who is every inch the equal of Henry Huggins."--New York State Library Bookmark.

_____. Fifteen. Illustrated by Joe and Beth Krush. William Morrow and Company, Inc., 1956. Grades 6-9. Winner of the 1958 Dorothy Canfield Fisher Award.
"The boy-girl relationships are portrayed with perceptiveness, warmth, and kindly humor in this thoroughly enjoyable story, perfect for junior high readers."--Booklist.

_____. Henry and Beezus. Illustrated by Louis Darling. William Morrow and Company, Inc., 1952. Grades 3-7.
"A worthy sequel to Henry Huggins and just as hilarious."--Horn Book.

_____. Henry and Ribsy. Illustrated by Louis Darling. William Morrow and Company, Inc., 1954. Grades 3-7. Winner of the 1957 Young Readers' Choice Award from the Pacific Northwest Library Association. "Only a person who knows the minds and ways of children could continue to create such natural characters and such unhackneyed, genuinely funny situations."--Booklist.

_____. Henry and the Clubhouse. Illustrated by Louis Darling. William Morrow and Company, Inc., 1962. Grades 4-6.
"Henry Huggins' latest adventures are as lifelike and funny as ever, and Ramona, intrepid kindergartner, is still his chief source of discomfort."--Horn Book.

_____ . Henry and the Paper Route. Illustrated by Louis
Darling. William Morrow and Company, Inc., 1957.
Grades 3-7.
Winner of the 1960 Young Readers' Choice Award from
the Pacific Northwest Library Association. "More hu-
morous episodes with Henry Huggins are told with as
much zest as the previous stories of Henry and his
friends Ramona and Beezus. A good family story."--
Library Journal.
_____ . Henry Huggins. Illustrated by Louis Darling.
William Morrow and Company, Inc., 1950. Grades 3-7.
"We defy anyone under 70 not to chuckle over it."--
Saturday Review.
CLEMENS, Samuel Langhorne. See: Twain, Mark.
COLLINS, Stephen. Forest and Woodland. Illustrated.
Creative Educational Society, Inc. in cooperation with
the National Audubon Society, 1967. Grades 4-8.
"In this book the author's well-chosen pictures and text
make the woodland come to life. He reveals how young
people can come to recognize the importance of our
country's forest land for our enjoyment, our health, and
our economic future. Whatever else this book accom-
plishes, it seems safe to predict that no one who learns
what it has to tell need ever walk unseeing through the
woods."--Charles E. Mohr. Text is by an authority on
the subject, and the photographs by top-notch specialists.
COLLODI, Carlo. Pinocchio: The Story of a Puppet. Illustrated by Charles Folkard. E. P. Dutton & Company,
Inc., 1952. Originally published 1881. Grades 2-6.
Geppetto makes a wonderful wooden puppet, Pinocchio,
who can dance, fence, and perform like an acrobat.
Pinocchio, a rebellious "boy," has many wild adventures
and gets into and out of many difficulties. Finally he
becomes a real boy.--J. K.
COLVER, Anne. Abraham Lincoln: For the People. Illustrated by William Moyers. Garrard Publishing Company,
1960; Dell Publishing Company, Inc., 1966. Grades 1-7.
This warm, intimate portrait of Lincoln (1809-1865)
captures the fine mixture of seriousness and humor
which marked Lincoln's life. A Discovery Book, with
more than 18 full-page, 3-color illustrations.
_____ . Florence Nightingale: War Nurse. Illustrated
by Gerald McCann. Garrard Publishing Company, 1961;
Dell Publishing Company, Inc., 1966. Grades 1-7.
The inspiring story of Florence Nightingale (1820-1910),
heroic nurse in the Crimean War, illustrates that courage and perseverance can bring many rewarding divi-
dends. A Discovery Book, with 3-color illustrations.

COMFORT, Mildred H. Winter on the Johnny Smoker. Illustrated by Henry C. Pitz. T.S. Denison & Company, Inc. Grades 5-12.
An authentic Mississippi River tale of the 1875 period. Mississippi River packets, side-wheelers and stern-wheelers puffing up to the levee--the Dustin family knew and loved them all. Riverboats were in their blood but until the Johnny Smoker came along they had only dreamed of owning one. The family was to spend a winter on board and it was the happiest winter the Dustins ever had.

COMSTOCK, Anna Botsford. Handbook of Nature Study. Illustrated. Cornell University Press (including Comstock Publishing Associates), 1939. Grades 7 up.
This classic work on nature study, now in its 24th edition, has been used as a text, reference book, and general source of information by hundreds of thousands of students, teachers, and parents. The living subjects treated thoroughly and enthusiastically by Mrs. Comstock include birds, fish, reptiles, amphibians, mammals, insects, flowers, weeds, flowerless plants, cultivated crop plants, and trees. Her treatment of inanimate nature covers streams, water and water formations, soil and soil conservation, crystals, minerals, magnetism, the stars, and the weather. All in all, about 700 separate subjects in nature are discussed and bibliographies are provided....
This book has received the widest praise in journals and periodicals both abroad and in the U.S. "We cannot imagine a better guide to sensible and scientific nature study."--Independent. The late Anna Botsford Comstock was the founder and first head of the Department of Nature Study at Cornell University.

CONCORDIA PUBLISHING HOUSE. One Hundred Bible Stories (Illustrated King James Edition). Concordia Publishing House, 1966. Grades 4-7.
A revised edition of an old favorite--the same wonderful stories but all new illustrations. Homes with children 9 to 12 will find this book an invaluable aid in religious training. The stories are told in the words of Scripture. Explanatory notes help children understand the King James text. Each story includes a short memory verse and a prayer or hymn verse.

COOKE, Donald E. Atlas of the Presidents. Illustrated. Hammond Incorporated, 1964. Grades 6 up.
Biographies of all American presidents, including the 36th, President Nixon, with descriptions of the periods

in which they lived and the situations they faced. The
Presidents' pictures are based on photographs of por-
traits supplied by the Library of Congress. Biographical and election maps by Hammond cartographers, and
an index. "A good reference work for the young scholar ... a great deal of useful information in small com-
pass."--Saturday Review.
"An article on 'How to Prepare for the Presidency,'
which Kennedy wrote especially for young people, is the
foreword to this unusual new reference book."--New
York Times.

COSSI, Olga. Robin Deer. Illustrated by Rosinda Holmes
and Ned Westover. Naturegraph Books, 1968. Grades
4 up.
This true adventure of four California ranch children,
who raised a wild deer, will be entrancing to all the
young at heart. A crisis occurs when Robin Deer leaves
the ranch and instinctively returns to the wilderness.

COURTIS, Stuart A. and Watters, Garnette. Courtis-Watters
Illustrated Golden Dictionary for Young Readers. Illus-
trated by Beth and Joe Krush. Western Publishing
Company, Inc., 1965. Originally published 1952.
Grades 2-4.

CRAIG, Hazel. Becky Lou in Grandmother's Days. Illustrated by Sam Craig. T. S. Denison & Company, Inc.
Grades 1-5.
A splendid book to instruct children in the customs and
living habits during the first part of our century. After
a long Rip Van Winkle sleep, Becky Lou, a doll in the
attic, awakens amid her early 20th century furnishings.
Told delightfully by photographs of Becky Lou and what
she was doing and how she decided to get the place in
the house ready for her mistress' return.

CRANE, Stephen. The Red Badge of Courage. Illustrated
by Charles Mozley. E. P. Dutton & Company, Inc.
Originally published 1895. Grades 5-9.
Henry Fleming, a farm boy who volunteered with the
Union forces in the Civil War, loses his head and flees
when the firing begins. After undergoing some harrowing
and nightmarish experiences, he rejoins his regiment and
finds the courage to carry forward their colors in a heroic advance.--J. K.

CREDLE, Ellis. Down, Down the Mountain. Illustrated by
the author. Thomas Nelson, Inc., 1934. Grades ps-3.
The classic story of Hetty and Hank who go down the
mountain to sell their turnips and buy creaky, squeaky
shoes.

_____ . Tall Tales from the High Hills. Illustrated by
Richard Bennett. Thomas Nelson Inc., 1957. Grades
5-8.
Twenty lively stories that are part of our literary her-
itage--old tales that have been passed down from generation to generation by the mountain folk of the South. Included are two of the author's own; all reflect a way of
life that has almost disappeared, but they are as rele-
vant as today's headlines.
CROUTHERS, David D.   Flags of American History.   Illustrated.   Hammond Inc., 1964.   Grades 6 up.
A comprehensive collection of 89 flags which have played
a part in American history.   All state flags are reproduced, plus those of obscure background or unusual history:   the Viking Banner, the personal flag of Christopher Columbus, St. Andrew's Cross, confederate flags.
Additional sections:   U.S. Flag Code, glossary, flag information.   David D. Crouthers was formerly librarian
at Hammond.   "Brilliantly colored pictures of 89 flags
with a description of their significance in our history
from colonial times to the present...."--Horn Book.


DAHL, Roald.   Charlie and the Chocolate Factory.   Illustrated by Joseph Schindelman.   Alfred A. Knopf, Inc.,
1964.   Grades 5-6.
Mr. Willy Wonka has a factory where the world's most
wonderful candy is made.   Only five children were going
to be allowed to see the mysterious machinery there.
What happens when they meet Mr. Willy Wonka and dis-
obey his orders is the substance of this uproarious mo-
rality tale by a world-renowned storyteller.
_____ . James and the Giant Peach.   Illustrated by Nancy
Ekholm Burkert.   Alfred A. Knopf, Inc., 1961.   Grades
3 up.
A fairy tale about James Henry Trotter, an unhappy little
orphan who lives with his Aunt Sponge and Aunt Spiker.
"His peach, like Jack's beanstalk, grows to such an
enormous size that he, and a number of giant insects
who live in the peach, can cross the ocean in it.   There
are various adventures ... before James settles down
to live happily ever after."--Publishers Weekly.
DALGLIESH, Alice.   The Bears on Hemlock Mountain.   Illustrated by Helen Sewell.   Charles Scribner's Sons, 1952.
Grades 3-4.
Jonathan's mother did not believe there were bears on
Hemlock Mountain, but Jonathan did.

_____ . compiler.  Christmas: A Book of Stories Old
and New.  Illustrated by Hildegard Woodward.  Charles
Scribner's Sons, 1950; originally published 1934.  Grades
4-6.
Stories and poems, including those about Christmas in
American history and in other lands.
_____ . The Courage of Sarah Noble.  Illustrated by
Leonard Weisgard.  Charles Scribner's Sons, 1954.
Grades 3-4.
Story of Sarah, an eight-year-old, who went with her
father into the wilderness in 1707.
DAUGHERTY, James.  Andy and the Lion.  Illustrated by
the author.  The Viking Press, Inc., 1938; paperback,
1970.  Grades K-3.
Runner-up, Caldecott Medal Award.  "Masterly drawings
build up the story of a small boy and a lion into a pre-
posterous adventure.  It is a tonic book for all ages."
_____ . Daniel Boone.  Illustrated by the author.  The
Viking Press, Inc., 1939.  Grades 7 up.
"Superb drawings and text.  Only a pioneer at heart
could have reached back with so warm a handclasp for
the Pioneer of the Wilderness."--Horn Book.
D'AULAIRE, Ingri and Edgar Parin.  Abraham Lincoln.
Illustrated by the authors.  Doubleday & Company, Inc.,
1940.  Grades 3-5.
The 1939 winner of the Caldecott Medal.  An "introduc-
tory biography and picture book for younger children.
All the essential facts of Lincoln's life are included
from early childhood to the end of the Civil War."--
Huntting.
_____ . Animals Everywhere.  Illustrated by the authors.
Doubleday & Company, Inc., 1954.  Grades ps-3.
Introduces to very small children the animals from the
tropics to the arctic regions.  The animals are pictured
in their settings.--H.W. Wilson Company.
_____ . Benjamin Franklin.  Illustrated by the authors.
Doubleday & Company, Inc., 1950.  Grades 3-6.
The story of a famous runaway, of his arrival, almost
penniless, in Philadelphia, and of his steady rise to
wealth and fame.--H.W. Wilson Company.
_____ . Columbus.  Illustrated by the authors.  Doubleday & Company, Inc., 1955.  Grades 3-5.
An "account of Columbus's adventure-filled life, from
his boyhood in Genoa through the excitement, achievements of his celebrated voyages."--Junior Literary
Guild.

_____ . D'Aulaires' Book of Greek Myths. Illustrated by
the authors. Doubleday & Company, Inc., 1962.
Grades 3-5.
These myths of the gods and goddesses of ancient
Greece are divided into the following sections: In Olden
Times: Gaea, Mother Earth; The Titans; Zeus and his
family; Minor gods, nymphs, satyrs, and centaurs;
Mortal descendants of Zeus.
_____ . George Washington. Illustrated by the authors.
Doubleday & Company, Inc., 1936. Grades 3-5.
"Large size picture-story book depicting scenes in the
life of George Washington. For the pictures, which are
in 5 colors, the author-artists have used their technique
of lithographing on stone."--Book Review Digest.
DAY, Veronique. Landslide! Illustrated by Margot Tomes.
Translated from the French by Margaret Morgan.
Coward-McCann & Geoghegan, Inc., 1963; Dell Publish-
ing Company, Inc., 1966. Grades 3-7.
Five children, on vacation in the mountains, are trapped
in a lonely cabin by a landslide until finally the oldest
boy invents a way of signaling for help. An ALA Notable Book 1964.
De ANGELI, Marguerite. Book of Nursery & Mother Goose
Rhymes. Illustrated by the author. Doubleday & Com-
pany, Inc., 1954. Grades ps-3.
_____ . Bright April. Illustrated by the author. Dou-
bleday & Company, Inc., 1946. Grades 3-5.
A story, with a Philadelphia background, of April, a
little Negro girl, her happy family, her friends, her
Brownie scout troop, and the remarkable surprise which
her tenth birthday brought.--H.W. Wilson Company.
_____ . The Door in the Wall. Illustrated by the author.
Doubleday & Company, Inc., 1949. Grades 3-6.
Awarded the Newbery Medal 1950. "Set in 13th century
England, it tells the dramatic story of Robin, crippled
son of a great lord, who overcomes his disabilities by
craftsmanship and eventually wins his knighthood by a
courageous act."--Retail Bookseller.
_____ . Thee, Hannah! Illustrated by the author. Dou-
bleday & Company, Inc., 1940. Grades 4-6.
"Story of a large Quaker family of old Philadelphia,
more particularly of a very real little nine-year-old
who found it difficult to fit her tastes and behavior into
a conservative pattern."--Booklist.
DeCLEMENTE, Frank F. Baseball. Illustrated. Creative
Educational Society, Inc., 1962. Grades 4 up.
All of the varied techniques and plays of baseball are

presented in a simple, informative style. Batting,
pitching, fielding, catching, first, second and third
base play, shortstop play, outfielding, team defense,
base running and sliding are discussed and illustrated
with action photographs of school age players and major
leaguers.

DeFOE, Daniel. Robinson Crusoe. Illustrated by J. Ayton-
Symington. E.P. Dutton & Company, Inc., 1954; Dell
Publishing Company, Inc. Originally published 1719.
Grades 5-9.
The story of a young sailor shipwrecked and cast ashore
on a deserted island, Robinson Crusoe recounts the
twenty-four years of loneliness endured by its hero and
his final triumph of hope and belief.

DeJONG, Meindert. The Wheel on the School. Illustrated
by Maurice Sendak. Harper & Row Publishers, Inc.,
1954. Grades 5 up.
Newbery Award Winner. "The efforts of six school
children to bring the stork back to their little Dutch
village, written with dramatic power and a deep insight
into the minds and hearts of children."--Booklist.

DENNIS, Wesley. Flip. Illustrated by the author. The
Viking Press, Inc., 1941. Grades K-3.
"Flip is as engaging a colt as ever grazed on Kentucky
bluegrass. He grows, in spirited pictures, from grace
to glory, kicking and bucking with gusto."--New York
Times.

_____. Flip and the Morning. Illustrated by the author.
The Viking Press, Inc., 1951. Grades K-3.
"An engaging tale of Flip, the colt, introducing other
occupants of the barn. All ages will chuckle over the
drawings of Flip capering through the pages in early
morning play and of Willie the goat, whose proud plan
for getting more sleep had a different outcome than he'd
expected."--Horn Book.

DICKENS, Charles. A Christmas Carol and The Cricket
on the Hearth. Illustrated by C.E. Brock. E.P. Dutton & Company, Inc., 1963. Originally published 1843
and 1845 respectively. Grades 3-7.
Bound in one volume, the famous Christmas story of
the transformation of the avaricious Scrooge into a generous benefactor, and the less well-known, but equally
appealing, tale of a cricket's benevolent role in the
lives of John Peerybingle and his young wife, Dot.

DR. SEUSS. See: Seuss, Dr.

DODGE, Mary Mapes. Hans Brinker: Or The Silver
Skates. Illustrated by Hans Baumhauer. E.P. Dutton

& Company, Inc., 1956.   Originally published 1865.
Grades 4-7.
All the fascination of life in Holland is unfolded in this
story of Hans and Gretel and the winning of the silver
skates.
DODGSON, Charles Lutwidge.   See:  Carroll, Lewis.
DOLCH, Edward W. and M. P.   Animal Stories.  Illustrated.
Garrard Publishing Company, 1952.   Grades 1-6.
A Basic Vocabulary Book written almost entirely with
the Dolch 220 Basic Sight Words and 95 Commonest
Nouns.   Reading level:  grade 2.   Provides easy-to-
read practice material for an enrichment program.
Children will seek out Dolch books because they know
they can read the stories by themselves.   Full-page
illustrations.
In this book many countries are represented in stories
in which animals talk, think, and act like real people.
            .  Circus Stories.  Illustrated.  Garrard Publish-
ing Company, 1956.   Grades 1-6.
A Basic Vocabulary Book written almost entirely with
the Dolch 220 Basic Sight Words and 95 Commonest
Nouns.  (See description of the authors' Animal Stories.)
This book contains selected real stories about clowns,
acrobats, and animals, that "bring the circus to town"
for every young reader.   Children learn about life under
the Big Top.
            .  Dog Stories.  Illustrated.  Garrard Publishing
Company, 1954.   Grades 1-6.
A Basic Vocabulary Book written almost entirely with
the Dolch 220 Basic Sight Words and 95 Commonest
Nouns.   (See description of the authors' Animal Stories.)
This book contains 18 delightful, true stories about the
intelligence and devotion displayed by dogs of many dif-
ferent breeds.
            .  Folk Stories.  Illustrated.  Garrard Publishing
Company, 1952.   Grades 1-6.
A Basic Vocabulary Book written almost entirely with
the Dolch 220 Basic Sight Words and 95 Commonest
Nouns.   (See description of the authors' Animal Stories.)
This book contains beloved folk tales handed down for
generations, including "The Three Bears," "Little Red
Riding Hood," "The Gingerbread Boy," and others.
            .  Horse Stories.  Illustrated.  Garrard Publishing
Company, 1958.   Grades 1-6.
A Basic Vocabulary Book written almost entirely with
the Dolch 220 Basic Sight Words and 95 Commonest
Nouns.   (See description of the authors' Animal Stories.)

In this book children will find real reading pleasure
with these action-packed stories about all kinds of
horses ... race horses, work horses, and circus horses.
_____. "Why" Stories. Illustrated. Garrard Publishing
Company, 1958. Grades 1-6.
A Basic Vocabulary Book written almost entirely with
the Dolch 220 Basic Sight Words and 95 Commonest
Nouns. (See description of the authors' Animal Stories.)
The fascinating tales in this book answer many frequent-
ly-asked questions of children, as "Why do dogs wag
their tails?"
_____. See also: Aesop.
DU BOIS, William Pene. See: Pene du Bois, William.
DUENEWALD, Doris, editor. Big Book of Real Trains.
Illustrated. Grosset & Dunlap, Inc., 1970. Grades
2-7.
For parents to read aloud and for young readers to
read for themselves. Illustrated in 4 colors.
_____. Fairy Tales and Fables. Illustrated by Gyo
Fujikawa. Grosset & Dunlap, Inc., 1970. Grades K-3.
DUPRE, Ramona. Too Many Dogs. Illustrated by Howard
Baer. Follett Publishing Company, 1960. Grades 1-3.
"Amusing book about two dachshunds who bring home
another dog and her nine pups. Recommended for beginning readers."--School Library Journal.
DUVALL, Evelyn Millis and Sylvanus. Facts of Life and
Love for Teenagers. Association Press, 1956; original-
ly 1950. Grades 7 up.
The authors put into this book the pertinent facts and
insights that are available from social counselors, phys-
iology, psychology, sociology, ethics, human development and other fields. The 1956 edition adds new material on dating, entertaining, appearance, manners and
courtesy, loving and being loved, and courtship.--H.W.
Wilson Company.
DYPWICK, Otis J. and Jacobs, Helen Hull. Golf, Swimming
and Tennis. Illustrated. Creative Educational Society,
Inc., 1962. Grades 4 up.
This basic guidebook on golf, swimming, and tennis is
used extensively by clubs, teams, camps, athletic centers, schools and libraries. The text is exceptionally
clear and comprehensive. The three sections are written by an authority who is also an experienced teacher.
The numerous photographs and drawings are instructive
and demonstrate the poise and body efficiency that are
developed through these sports.

EASTMAN, Phillip D.   The Cat in the Hat Beginner Book
     Dictionary.   Illustrated.   Random House, Inc., 1964.
     Grades 1-4.
EGERMEIER, Elsie E.   Egermeier's Bible Story Books.
     Illustrated by Clive Uptton.   Warner Press Publishers,
     1969; originally 1923.   Grades K-6.
     Here are 312 stories with pictures that cover the Bible
     from Genesis to Revelation.   Beauty and simplicity of
     style invite the meaning of the Bible into the child's
     heart and mind to become an active part of his life,
     never to be forgotten.   Features:  the complete Bible in
     story form; chronological order of stories; consistent
     art style; 121 full-color pictures; true to the Bible; ap-
     proved by all Faiths; written to be understood by chil-
     dren.
EINSEL, Walter.   Did You Ever See?   Illustrated by the
     author.   Addison-Wesley Publishing Company, 1962.
     Grades ps-1.
     Did you ever see a giraffe laugh?   Or a pig dig?   Or
     a sheep sleep?   In this very young picture book of non-
     sense rhymes, even pre-schoolers will soon be able to
     "read" the simple words which accompany the author's
     colorful and witty illustrations, and then make up new
     rhymes of their own.
ELLIS, Mary Jackson.   Gobble, Gobble, Gobble.   Illustrated
     by Jewel Sears.   T. S. Denison & Company, Inc.   Grades
     K-2.
     A story about a small, underfed turkey all alone on a
     big turkey farm.   It will win the adoration of everyone.
     Little boys and girls have such boundless imaginations
     that they will discover the surprise in store for them
     in this exciting book.   Excellent information about actual
     life on an Upper Midwest turkey farm.   Four-color il-
     lustrations.
_____.   Spaghetti Eddie.   Illustrated by Sylvia Myers.
     T. S. Denison & Company, Inc.   Grades K-4.
     An entertaining story which emphasizes safety and
     health rules, and teaches the importance of sharing
     with others.   Eddie, with his uncontrollable red hair,
     sparkling eyes and sprinkling of freckles, had always
     yearned to have a spaghetti party for all his friends.
     It seemed as if his wish would never come true until
     one day Eddie had an idea that grew quite out of hand!
     Four-color illustrations.
_____.   Swimmer Is a Hopper.   Illustrated by Earl W.
     Moline, Jr.   T. S. Denison & Company, Inc.   Grades
     K-4.

A science story showing the evolution of a frog. Billy
was sad because it was the last day of his vacation at
the lake and he had wanted to do something very special.
He was sad no longer because his brother thought of a
way for them to spend the day. Four-color illustrations.
ELMER, Irene. Boy Who Ran Away. Illustrated by S.
Mathews. Concordia Publishing House, 1964.
An Arch Book. Children, parents, and teachers are
still discovering these colorful and easy-to-read little
treasures. They're long enough to tell a whole Bible
story in bouncy verse or prose, and short enough to be
interesting.
ELTING, Mary. The Answer Book. Illustrated by Tram
Mawicke. Grosset & Dunlap, Inc., 1959. Grades 4-6.
A beautiful large-size book resplendent with color illus-
trations throughout.
_____. Answers and More Answers. Illustrated by J.
Mawicke. Grosset & Dunlap, Inc., 1961. Grades 4-6.
A beautiful large-size book resplendent with color illus-
trations throughout.
_____ and Folsom, Franklin. Still More Answers.
Illustrated by Glen Fleischmann. Grosset & Dunlap,
Inc., 1970. Grades 4-6.
A beautiful large-size book resplendent with color illus-
trations throughout.
ENRIGHT, Elizabeth. The Four-Story Mistake. Illustrated
by the author. Holt, Rinehart & Winston, Inc., 1942;
Dell Publishing Company, Inc., 1967. Grades 3-7.
The four Melendy children settle down to busy and excit-
ing country living in an intriguing old house appropriately
called the Four-Story Mistake.
_____. The Saturdays. Illustrated by the author. Holt,
Rinehart & Winston, Inc., 1941; Dell Publishing Company, Inc., 1966. Grades 3-7.
The four Melendy children organize a Saturday outing
club, pooling allowances so that each in turn can go on
a glorious adventure.
EPSTEIN, Sam and Beryl. George Washington Carver, Negro Scientist. Illustrated. Garrard Publishing Company,
1960. Grades 2-5.
A memorable picture of a great American is simply presented in this informative story of a world-famous scientist. A Discovery Book. More than 18 full-page, 3-
color illustrations.
_____. Stories of Champions: Baseball Hall of Fame.
Illustrated. Garrard Publishing Company, 1965. Grades
3-6.

Profile biographies of the first five men to be named to
the Baseball Hall of Fame--Walter Johnson, Christy
Mathewson, Honus Wagner, Ty Cobb, and Babe Ruth are
vividly described.  The facts are accurate in these well-
documented accounts which emphasize that the key to
greatness in athletics is a combination of ability, determination, hard work, and constant practice.

EPSTEIN, Samuel, and Williams, Beryl.  The Great Houdini,
Magician Extraordinary.  Julian Messner Division of
Simon & Schuster, Inc., 1950.  Grades 7 up.
Biography of Harry Houdini, 1874-1926, U.S. magician
and author, whose real name was Erich Weiss.

ERICKSON, Phoebe.  Just Follow Me.  Illustrated by the
author.  Follett Publishing Company, 1960.  Grades 1-3.
"Little Dog follows six animals to their homes.  Fortu-
nately, the last one lives in Little Dog's barnyard.  The
simple vocabulary is repetitive without being monotonous."
--School Library Journal.

ETS, Marie Hall.  Gilberto and the Wind.  Illustrated by the
author.  The Viking Press, Inc., 1963; paperback, 1969.
Grades K-3.
An ALA Notable Book.  "The story of a small Mexican
boy and his discovery of the wind.  The pictures are
very effective and the short text is exactly perfect to
underscore the action of the pictures."--Grade Teacher.

_____.  In the Forest.  Illustrated by the author.  The
Viking Press, Inc., 1944; paperback, 1970.  Grades K-3.
Runner-up, Caldecott Medal Award.  "As effortless and
unself-conscious as a child's own make-believe, it takes
the reader of any age along with the little boy, as with
his new horn and a paper hat, he goes for a walk in the
forest."--New York Times.

_____.  Just Me.  Illustrated by the author.  The Viking
Press, Inc., 1965; paperback, 1970.  Grades K-3.
Runner-up, Caldecott Medal Award.  "Here is a perfect
companion to Play With Me.  A little boy discovered for
himself that he could imitate some of the movements and
habits of both wild and domestic animals, but others he
could not.  When he ran to meet his dad, he found out
that 'I ran like nobody else at all.  Just Me.' "--Instruc-
tor.

_____.  Play With Me.  Illustrated by the author.  The
Viking Press, Inc., 1955.  Grades K-3.
Runner-up, Caldecott Medal Award.  "A little girl wanted
to play with the animals in a meadow.  In her eagerness
she frightened them away, and it was not until she sat
still that they came back to her.  A rare and lovely picture book."--Saturday Review.

_____ and Labastida, Aurora.  Nine Days to Christmas.
Illustrated by Marie Hall Ets.  The Viking Press, Inc.,
1959.  Grades K-3.
Winner of the Caldecott Award.  "Small Ceci has her
first 'posada' and searches the Christmas market for
exactly the right 'piñata.'  The pictures and text convey
the mirth and glory of the season."--Library Journal.

FAULKNER, Georgene, and Becker, John.  Melindy's Medal.
Illustrated by Elton C. Fax.  Julian Messner Division
of Simon & Schuster, Inc., 1945.  Grades 3-6.
"Two wonderful things happened to Melindy, a little Negro girl.  First, the family moved from shabby quarters
to a fine new housing project, and next, she was a her-
oine when there was a fire at the school."--Adventuring
with Books.

FEAGLES, Anita.  Casey, the Utterly Impossible Horse.
Illustrated by Dagmar Wilson.  Addison-Wesley Publishing Company, 1960.  Grades 2-4.
Casey is a talking horse.  This would seem to make
him an ideal pet.  But the endless demands he makes
of the children in the story, and the lengths to which
they have to go in order to please him, make them wonder.  A very funny story, illustrated with drawings.

_____ .  Twenty-Seven Cats Next Door.  Illustrated by
Robert Shipman.  Addison-Wesley Publishing Company,
1965.  Grades 2-4.
Mrs. Ames has twenty-seven cats.  When the neighbors
sign a petition to compel her to get rid of them, her
young friend Jim tries to help.  He soon finds that there
are moral problems which have no easy or happy solution.  A story which explores the relationship between
the rights of an individual and his obligations to a larger
community.  Illustrated with drawings.

FELSEN, Henry Gregor.  Hot Rod.  Illustrated.  E. P. Dutton & Company, Inc., 1950.  Grades 7 up.
Bud Crayne's genius for hot rodding brought not only
idolizing from his contemporaries, but death to two
small boys.  "Shocking and tragic yet true to fact, this
story about teen-age drivers is certain to rouse wide
interest....  The story is packed with action and suspense...."--New York Times.

FERRIS, Helen Josephine, editor.  Favorite Poems Old and
New.  Illustrated by Leonard Weisgard.  Doubleday &
Company, Inc., 1957.  Grades 3-7.
A book of about 700 poems selected for boys and girls

by the editor of the Junior Literary Guild, who states
in the Preface, "This book had its beginning years ago
when two parents, loving poetry, made it as much a
part of their children's every day as getting up in the
morning, eating breakfast, going to school, playing outdoors until suppertime." A.A. Milne, Robert Louis
Stevenson, William Shakespeare, Robert Frost, and Carl
Sandburg are among the poets represented.--J. K.

FIELD, Eugene. The Gingham Dog and the Calico Cat. Illustrated by Helen Page. Follett Publishing Company,
1956. Grades ps-3.
The classic poems with colorful illustrations.

FISHER, Dorothy Canfield. Understood Betsy. Illustrated
by Martha Alexander. Holt, Rinehart and Winston,
Inc., 1972. Originally published 1916. Grades 4-6.
All of the sheltered nine years of her life, Elizabeth
Ann has heard her Aunt Frances refer in whispers to
"those horrid Putney, Vermont, cousins." But now
Aunt Frances can no longer take care of her niece and
Elizabeth Ann is shipped off, rigid with fear, to the
wilds of Vermont. There are lots of new experiences
in store--making butter from cream, herding cows,
learning not to be afraid of arithmetic. However, it
takes a long time for Elizabeth Ann to realize that she's
become someone else: a healthier, prouder girl with a
new name and a new pleasure in being alive.... The
illustrations for this new edition perfectly capture all
the charm and fascination of an earlier era.

FISHER, Lois. You and the United Nations. Illustrated by
the author. Children's Press, 1958; originally 1951.
Grades 5-10.
A brief, lively description, with humorous black-and-
white line drawings, of the kinds of problems the United
Nations deals with, and its divisions and functions, including the General Assembly, the Security Council, the
International Court of Justice, the Secretariat, the
Trusteeship Council, the Economic and Social Council,
the Military Staff Committee, the World Health Organiza-
tion, and the United Nations Children's Fund. The Universal Declaration of Human Rights is included in the
third edition. --J. K.

FITCH, Florence Mary. One God: The Ways We Worship
Him. Illustrated. Lothrop, Lee & Shepard Company,
1944. Grades 4-6.
Illustrated with photos; contains an index. "Explains the
fundamentals of the major forms of religions in Amer-
ica--Jewish, Catholic and Protestant. It stresses the

common belief in one God.   An excellent book for building up understanding and tolerance among groups of different faiths."--Association for Childhood Education International.

FITZHUGH, Louise.   Harriet the Spy.   Illustrated by the
author.   Harper & Row Publishers, Inc., 1964; Dell
Publishing Company, Inc., 1967.   Grades 4-7.
Harriet the Spy has a secret notebook which she fills
with utterly honest jottings about her parents, her class-
mates, and her neighbors.   But one day Harriet's notebook is found by her schoolmates--to their anger, and to
Harriet's rue.   A New York Times Best Children's Book
1964.

FLACK, Marjorie.   Angus and the Cat.   Illustrated by the
author.   Doubleday & Company, Inc., 1931.   Grades
ps-2.
Tale of a Scottie dog and his friend.   This "simple little
story ... has an element of surprise and humor that 7
and 8 year olds thoroughly enjoy."--New York Times.

_____.   Angus and the Ducks.   Illustrated by the author.
Doubleday & Company, Inc., 1930.   Grades ps-2.
The other side of the hedge.

_____.   Angus Lost.   Illustrated by the author.   Double-
day & Company, Inc., 1932.   Grades ps-2.
The Scottie explores other places.

_____.   The Boats on the River.   Illustrated by Jay Hyde
Barnum.   The Viking Press, Inc., 1946.   Grades ps-3.
Runner-up, Caldecott Medal Award.   "Brief, rhythmical
text and fresh-looking colored illustrations picture the
different boats--from rowboat to ocean liner--that go up
and down a busy river that flows through a big city."--
Booklist.

_____.   The Story about Ping.   Illustrated by Kurt Wiese.
The Viking Press, Inc., 1933.   Grades K-3.
"An irresistible picture book.   Kurt Wiese has created
in Ping a duckling of great individuality against a background [the Yangtze River] that has both accuracy and
charm."--New York Times.

_____.   Tim Tadpole and the Great Bullfrog.   Illustrated
by the author.   Doubleday & Company, Inc., 1934.
Grades ps-3.
Tale of an ambitious tadpole.
"Following the advice of the big bullfrog, Tim the little
tadpole began to swim and one day found he had legs and
arms, was no longer a tadpole but Tim Frog."--Ontario.

FOLSOM, Franklin.   See: Elting, Mary.

FORBES, Esther. Johnny Tremain. Illustrated by Lynd
    Ward. Houghton Mifflin Company, 1943; Dell Publishing
    Company, Inc. Grades 7-12.
    Winner of the Newbery Medal, this novel is set in the
    Boston of 1775 and follows the young apprentice from a
    tragic accident in the silversmith's shop to his dramatic
    involvement as a patriot in the exciting days just before
    the American Revolution.
    "This is Esther Forbes at her brilliant best. She has
    drawn the character of Johnny with such sympathy and
    insight that he may take his place with Jim Hawkins,
    Huck Finn and other young immortals...."--Book Week.
FORD, F. M. Pony Engine. Illustrated by George Presto-
    pino. Grosset & Dunlap, Inc. Grade ps.
    A giant-size favorite for the youngest reader, with glow-
    ing full-color illustrations on every page. Edited by
    Doris Garn.
FORD, Lauren. Little Book about God (Protestant). Illus-
    trated by the author. Doubleday & Company, Inc., 1934.
    Grades ps-2.
    God's care of His people.
FORELL, Betty. Little Benjamin and the First Christmas.
    Illustrated by Betty Wind. Concordia Publishing House,
    1964.
    An Arch Book, presenting a Bible story in colorful,
    easy-to-read form.
FOSTER, Celeste K. Casper, the Caterpillar. Illustrated
    by the author. T. S. Denison & Company, Inc. Grades
    K-3.
    A science story showing the discontented and humdrum
    life of Casper as a caterpillar, and his yearning to be-
    come a pretty butterfly. Children will enjoy the story
    of Casper's struggle to identify himself with bees, crick-
    ets, birds, ants, and flies. When it all seems futile,
    a change begins and he evolves from his covering into a
    beautiful Monarch butterfly. Four-color illustrations.
_____. Jonathan and the Octopus. Illustrated by the
    author. T. S. Denison & Company, Inc. Grades K-3.
    A story of fantasy woven about the dream of a typical
    little boy who is always making messes for his already
    overworked mother to clean up. One morning, in des-
    peration, Jonathan's mother says she wishes she were
    an octopus so she'd have eight arms to work with in-
    stead of only two. This sets Jonathan thinking about
    how he can obtain an octopus for his mother. With this
    idea on his mind, he goes fishing to a neighborhood
    stream, but he soon falls asleep and begins to dream.
    Four-color illustrations.

FOSTER, Laura Louise. Keer-Loo. Illustrated by the author. Naturegraph Books, 1965. Grades 4 up.
Keer-Loo started life as a wild wood duck, but, soon
after he tumbled out of his tree hollow nest, he became
an extraordinary and exceedingly lively and humorous
member of a human family. Has 27 attractive illustrations of the life of Keer-Loo.

FRANCO, John M. Afro-American Contributors to American
Life. Benefic Press, 1971. Grades 4-8.
Introduces great Afro-American contributors to our heritage, each at three different reading levels; maximum
flexibility attained for within grade usage as well as
multi-grade application. Three-reading-levels approach
permits teacher to individualize presentation according
to student ability. Contains subject area correlation
charts; life lines that highlight major contributions; and
Afro-American landmarks and milestones.

FRANÇOISE. Jeanne-Marie Counts Her Sheep. Illustrated
by the author. Charles Scribner's Sons, 1951. Grades
K-3.
A little French girl counts the number of lambs her
sheep may have.

_____. Springtime for Jeanne-Marie. Illustrated by the
author. Charles Scribner's Sons, 1955. Grades K-3.
Jeanne-Marie searches for her lost duck and finds a
new friend.

FREEMAN, Don. Corduroy. Illustrated by the author.
The Viking Press, Inc., 1968; paperback, 1970. Grades
K-3.
A department store teddy bear longs for a real home.
"Endearing, brightly colored pictures together with the
text affectionately recount Corduroy's adventures in the
big store one night as he hunts for a button missing
from his overalls and his happiness at being taken home
to live with Lisa."--Booklist.

_____. Dandelion. Illustrated by the author. The Viking
Press, Inc., 1964. Grades K-3.
"Invited to a come-as-you-are tea party, a foolish lion
turns himself into such a dapper dandy that his hostess
does not recognize him and shuts the door in his face.
The vain but lovable lion and the consequences of his
folly are wonderfully amusing."--Booklist.

_____. Mop Top. Illustrated by the author. The Viking
Press, Inc., 1955. Grades K-3.
"An amusing book about a boy who never wanted to have
his hair cut. Moppy didn't mind what people called him,
but Mother said that something had to be done. The

pictures are as funny as the story."--Saturday Review.
_____.  Norman the Doorman.  Illustrated by the author.
The Viking Press, Inc., 1959; paperback, 1969.  Grades
K-3.
An ALA Notable Book.  "Whimsical text and colorful
illustrations tell the story of an ingenious mouse who
won an art contest with his creation made from mouse-
traps.  Norman is allowed to choose his own award, a
tour unmolested by guards through the art museum."--
Saturday Review.
FRIIS-BAASTAD, Babbis.  Don't Take Teddy.  Translated
by Lise Somme McKinnon.  Charles Scribner's Sons,
1967.  Grades 4-6.
A story about Mikkel and his older brother Teddy who
is mentally retarded.
FRISKEY, Margaret.  Chicken Little Count-to-Ten.  Illustrated by Katherine Evans.  Children's Press, 1946.
Grades K-3.
"Outstanding book in color and design for one-to-ten
stage of counting."--Childhood Education.
Primary grade children respond to this captivating Easy
Reading Picture Story Book as they reinforce their newly acquired reading skills.  Illustrated in full color.
_____.  The True Book of Air Around Us.  Illustrated
by Katherine Evans.  Children's Press, 1953.  Grades
K-4.
Science and social studies ... these factual books explain so many of the things that puzzle inquisitive young
minds.  Students use the True Books for supplementary
work in their classes.  They use them to find out about
special things that interest them.  They read them to
learn on their own.  Each fascinating True Book encourages a child to further his search for the answers he
wants.  Easy to read, packed with information, the
True Books are excellent for primary and intermediate
grades.  Color illustrations.
_____.  The True Book of Birds We Know.  Illustrated
by A. Pistorius.  Children's Press, 1954.  Grades K-4.
See description of the author's True Book of Air Around
Us.
FROST, Robert.  You Come Too.  Illustrated by Thomas W.
Nason.  Holt, Rinehart and Winston, Inc., 1959.  All
ages.
Robert Frost's simplicity, wisdom, and humanity come
through in this collection of his poems for young people.
Illustrated in black and white.  Foreword by Hyde Cox.
An ALA Notable Book.

FUJIKAWA, Gyo, compiler. A Child's Book of Poems.
Illustrated by the compiler. Grosset & Dunlap, Inc.,
1969. Grades 3-7.
About 200 short famous poems and excerpts that express
universal childhood experiences and philosophical thoughts.
Among the poets represented are William Blake, Christ-
ina Rossetti, William Wordsworth, Eugene Field, Ralph
Waldo Emerson, Emily Dickinson, Edward Lear, James
Whitcomb Riley, Lewis Carroll, and William Shakespeare.
Illustrations in color and in black and white. --J. K.


GALDONE, Paul. Henny Penny. Illustrated by the author.
The Seabury Press, 1968. Originally published about
1860. Grades ps-1.
An English fairy tale. "How nice of Paul Galdone to
bring back 'Henny Penny'! And to bring back that famous Cassandra in the most ebullient Galdone fashion!
Now there's a man who knows gusto when he sees it.
And his happy readers will know it, too, when they see
his jolly pictures."--Publishers Weekly.
_____. The Monkey and the Crocodile: A Jataka Tale
from India. Illustrated by the author. The Seabury
Press, 1969. Originally written about 300 A. D. Grades
ps-1.
The Jatakas, or birth stories of Buddha, related adventures of Buddha in his former existence and each contained a moral.
"Galdone astounds the reader with the variety of colorful pictures in which just the two animals appear. The
monkey uses his wits to escape the jaws of the hungry
predator. For him it is a matter of life and death.
For Galdone--a tour de force."--Book Week.
_____. See also: Aesop; Grimm, Jakob and Wilhelm.
GARELICK, May. What's Inside the Egg? Illustrated by
Rena Jakobsen. Addison-Wesley Publishing Company,
1955. Grades 2-4.
The hatching and development of a baby goose, shown
in a series of close-up photographs that document each
step from the first tiny crack in the egg to the eventual
emergence of the tiny gosling and his subsequent gosling-
hood. The reader's interest is held because, until the
egg hatches, he doesn't know what's inside. Dramatic
photographs by Rena Jakobsen.
_____. Where Does the Butterfly Go When It Rains?
Illustrated by Leonard Weisgard. Addison-Wesley Publishing Company, 1961. Grades ps-1.

A young child wonders where the animals and insects
go when it rains. What he knows from personal experience he can answer for himself; what he doesn't know,
he questions. Playfully and poetically, this book explores aspects of the rich realm of speculation. Beautiful three-color illustrations of a rainy-day world.
GARRETT, Helen. Angelo the Naughty One. Illustrated by
Leo Politi. The Viking Press, Inc., 1944; paperback,
1970. Grades K-3.
"Amusing text and charming pictures tell what happened
to a little Mexican boy the day of his sister's wedding
when, refusing to take a bath, he ran off to the soldiers
at the fort. A colorful book with a Mexican village
background."--Booklist.
GARST, Shannon. Sitting Bull, Champion of His People.
Illustrated by Elton C. Fax. Julian Messner Division
of Simon & Schuster, Inc., 1946. Grades 6 up.
Biography of Sitting Bull, 1734-1890, Indian chief of the
Sioux tribe; fought against General Custer (1876).--J.K.
GATES, Doris. Blue Willow. Illustrated by Paul Lantz.
The Viking Press, Inc., 1940; paperback, 1969. Grades
4-6.
Runner-up, Newbery Medal Award. "Janey, whose father was an itinerant farm worker, wanted desperately
a settled home and friends and a well-ordered life. This
story, based on realism, is neither sordid nor sentimen-
tal. Told with sensitive beauty, its emphasis placed on
courage, stamina, and family devotion, it should widen
the horizons of the little girls who read it."--Horn Book.
_____. Little Vic. Illustrated by Kate Seredy. The
Viking Press, Inc., 1951. Grades 4-6.
"An effortlessly told and entirely credible story of a boy
and a race horse. Pony Rivers, stable boy and orphaned
son of a jockey, fell in love with Little Vic the day the
colt was foaled."--Booklist.
_____. Sensible Kate. Illustrated by Marjorie Torrey.
The Viking Press, Inc., 1943; paperback, 1970. Grades
4-6.
"Being neither cute nor pretty, ten-year-old Kate, orphan
and family helper, felt she'd better stick to being just
sensible--and she was sensible. How Kate learns the
meaning of nonsense and joy and that even a red-headed
freckled little girl is needed by someone, makes a heart-
warming story."--Booklist.
GAULT, William Campbell. Drag Strip. E.P. Dutton &
Company, Inc., 1959. Grades 5-10.
Terry and Bud are drawn to a racially mixed group of

boys by their common interest in hot rods, and learn to
overcome their resentments, resolve their personal differences, and gain a new insight of themselves. "Ex-
citingly written.... A must for the young driver...."
--Virginia Kirkus.

      . Thunder Road. E.P. Dutton & Company, Inc.,
1952. Grades 5 up.
Peter Elliot progresses from an enthusiastic adolescent
interested mainly in speed, to racing mechanic and finally drives to victory in the Indianapolis 500. "An exciting
story written in the first person with the vernacular of
the auto race track, a sense of fair play, and good par-
ent and child relationships."--Library Journal.

GEHM, Katherine. Happiness Is Smiling. Illustrated by
Ruth Brophy. T.S. Denison & Company, Inc. Grades
K-4.
A story to encourage children in cultivating a happy dis-
position. Smiley Sam, always happy and smiling, and
Freddy Frown, always glum and frowning, are good
friends but different as can be. Sam tells Freddy the
way to be happy is to feel happy. If he will but wear
a smile then everything will look differently to him.
Four-color illustrations.

GEIS, Darlene. Dinosaurs and Other Prehistoric Animals.
Illustrated by Russell F. Peterson. Grosset & Dunlap,
Inc., 1959. Grades 4-6.
A beautiful large-size book resplendent with color illus-
trations throughout.

GEISEL, Theodor Seuss. See: Seuss, Dr.

GEORGE, Jean Craighead. The Hole in the Tree. Illustrated by the author. E.P. Dutton & Company, Inc.,
1957. Grades K-3.
Nature facts are skillfully woven into this story of the
hole in the tree, the small insects, birds, and mammals
that inhabit it, and two observant children. "This authentic nature book for younger children ... has special
appeal in its friendly 'human' approach and in the beautiful black-and-white drawings on every page."--New
York Times.

      . My Side of the Mountain. Illustrated by the au-
thor. E.P. Dutton & Company, Inc., 1959. Grades
5-9.
Runner-up for Newbery Medal; International Hans Christian Andersen Award. "An extraordinary book ... young
Sam Gribley's story of his year of complete self-suffi-
ciency spent in the Catskill Mountains is as credible as
a factual record ... unforgettable experiences in the

heart of nature [which] I believe will be read year after
year."--Horn Book.
GEORGE, John and Jean.   Dipper of Copper Creek.   Illus-
trated by Jean George.   E. P. Dutton & Company, Inc.,
1956.   Grades 5-9.
"Young Doug and his prospector grandfather summer in
the Rockies and find fascinating the life of the dipper or
water ouzel."--McClurg, Book News.
GEORGIADY, Nicholas, and Romano, Louis.   Gertie the
Duck.   Illustrated by Dagmar Wilson.   Follett Publishing
Company, 1959.   Grades 1-3.
Old bridge pilings in the middle of a busy city become
a new home for Gertie and her family.
GERSH, Harry, and Levinger, Elma E. and Lee J.   The
Story of the Jew.   Illustrated.   Behrman House, Inc.
Grades 8-11.
This classic one-volume history of the Jewish people,
which in the past thirty years has sold over 100,000
copies, is now revised and brought up to date.   This is
social history at its finest and most discerning.   Forces
and figures, failures and successes are woven into a
brightly colored textured fabric that stresses the concept
of God as the foundation of Jewish life and highlights the
Covenant between God and Israel in Jewish history.
Charged with feeling for Jewish tradition and emotionally
bound to the men and majesty of Jewish life, this greatly revised and improved edition is a book to make its
readers feel their own Jewish roots more keenly, their
own identification with Jewish life, past and present,
more sharply, and their own history with greater pride
and insight.
Profusely illustrated with photographs, maps and charts,
all of which serve to give added dimension to the text,
this is the ideal summary and survey of Jewish history
for the confirmation years and beyond.
GIBSON, Katherine, editor.   The Tall Book of Bible Stories.
Illustrated by Ted Chaiko.   Harper & Row Publishers,
Inc., 1957.   Grades ps-3.
GILES, Lucille.   Color Me Brown.   Illustrated by Louis F.
Holmes.   Johnson Publishing Company, Inc. (Chicago).
Grades K-3.
A story-coloring book about black men and women who
have made contributions to world history.
GOCKEL, Herman W., and Saleska, Edward J., compilers.
A Child's Garden of Prayer.   Illustrated.   Concordia
Publishing House, 1948.   Grades K-3.
Easy-to-learn prayers that fit into every activity of the

child's busy day. Prayers for attending school, Sunday school, meal blessings, bedtime, etc. Colorful illustrations.

GODDEN, Rumer. Mouse House. Illustrated by Adrienne Adams. The Viking Press, Inc., 1957. Grades K-3. An ALA Notable Book. "The enchanting story tells how, through the adventures of Bonnie, the little mouse that was crowded out of the nest and found her way upstairs, Mouse House became the new home of a family of real mice."--Booklist.

GOLD, Robert S., editor. Point of Departure. Dell Publishing Company, Inc.; Delacorte Press, 1971. Grades 7 up. Nineteen stories of youth and discovery.

GOLDILOCKS AND THE THREE BEARS. Illustrated. Grosset & Dunlap, Inc. Originally published about 1831. Grade ps. A giant-size favorite for the youngest reader, with glowing full-color illustrations on every page.

GOUDEY, Alice E. The Day We Saw the Sun Come Up. Illustrated by Adrienne Adams. Charles Scribner's Sons, 1961. Grades K-3. Sue and her brother talk with Mother about day and night and the movement of the earth.

———. Houses from the Sea. Illustrated by Adrienne Adams. Charles Scribner's Sons, 1959. Grades K-3. An introduction to shells in rhythmic prose. Describes a variety of shells and how they serve as houses for sea creatures.

GRAFF, Stewart. George Washington: Father of Freedom. Illustrated by Robert Doremus. Garrard Publishing Company, 1964; Dell Publishing Company, Inc., 1966. Grades 2-6. The warm humanity as well as the nobility of the father of our country is revealed in this refreshing story. A Discovery Book, with more than 18 full-page, 3-color illustrations.

GRAFF, Stewart and Polly Anne. Helen Keller: Toward the Light. Illustrated by Paul Frame. Garrard Publishing Company, 1965; Dell Publishing Company, Inc., 1966. Grades 2-7. Although blind and deaf at an early age, this remarkable woman went to college and devoted her life to the handicapped. A Discovery Book, with 3-color illustrations.

GRAHAM, Al. Timothy Turtle. Illustrated by Tony Palazzo. The Viking Press, Inc., 1949; paperback, 1970. Grades K-3.

"Children delight in following Timothy as, in quest of
adventure, he climbs Took-a-Look Hill and comes safely
home."--Christian Science Monitor.
GRAHAM, Lillian S.  See:  Wackerbarth, Marjorie.
GRAHAM, Shirley, and Lipscomb, George D.  Dr. George
  Washington Carver, Scientist.  Illustrated by Elton C.
  Fax.  Julian Messner Division of Simon & Schuster,
  Inc., 1944.  Grades 6 up.
  Biography of Dr. Carver, 1864, 1943, U.S. Negro edu-
  cator, botanist, and agricultural chemist.
GRAHAME, Kenneth.  The Wind in the Willows.  Illustrated
  by Ernest H. Shepard.  Charles Scribner's Sons, 1961.
  Originally published 1908.  Grades 4-6.
  Mole went adventuring and met delightful companions in
  Rat, Badger, Toad, and others.
GRAMATKY, Hardie.  Little Toot.  Illustrated by the author.
  G. P. Putnam's Sons, 1939.  Grades K-3.
  Story and pictures describe the early career of a saucy
  little tugboat too pleased with himself to do any real
  work until one day when he found himself out on the
  ocean in a storm.  Then Little Toot earned the right
  to be called a hero.--H. W. Wilson Company.
GRANT, Bruce.  The Boy Scout Encyclopedia.  Illustrated
  by F. and J. Mastri and William Timmins.  Rand Mc-
  Nally and Company, 1965; originally 1952.  Grades 3-11.
  Authorized by the Boy Scouts of America.  An A to Z
  encyclopedia illustrated with 200 color drawings.  It is
  the perfect gift book for every Scout, as well as the
  non-Scout who enjoys outdoor life.  "... a real adventure for the boys of America ... the color, the drama
  and the zest that make Scouting the greatest game on
  earth for boys."--From Introduction by Joseph A.
  Brunton, Jr., Chief Scout Executive.
GRAVES, Charles P.  Benjamin Franklin:  Man of Ideas.
  Illustrated.  Garrard Publishing Company, 1960.  Grades
  2-5.
  Here is a lively account of a man beloved by his contemporaries and remembered by the world--a man of
  many varied talents.  A Discovery Book, with more than
  18 full-page, 3-color illustrations.
  _____.  John F. Kennedy:  New Frontiersman.  Illustrated
  by Paul Frame.  Garrard Publishing Company, 1965;
  Dell Publishing Company, Inc., 1966.  Grades 1-7.
  This is the dramatic story of the courage and leadership
  of our late President, from his days as a Boy Scout to
  his tragic death.  A Discovery Book, with more than
  18 full-page, 3-color illustrations.

_____. A World Explorer: Marco Polo. Illustrated.
Garrard Publishing Company, 1963. Grades 3-6.
Marco Polo was only seventeen when he left Venice for
China. At forty he returned home with a fortune in
jewels, and other precious cargo. He settled down and
wrote a guidebook for later explorers. Illustrated in
color.
Conquest of continents, struggles for power and wealth,
exotic cultures, intrigue, and physical danger--all the
agonies and triumphs of the age of World Exploration
come to life in this easy-to-read book. It is filled with
action and vigor so important to the success of reading
programs at this age level. Carefully checked by experts for historical accuracy, it will introduce or underscore important social studies concepts. Endsheet maps
tracing the explorer's route further clarify the patterns
of world exploration.

GRAVES, Robert. Greek Gods and Heroes. Illustrated by
Dimitris Davis. Doubleday & Company, Inc., 1960;
Dell Publishing Company, Inc. Grades 7-11.
The pantheon of Olympian gods, the Underworld of Tar-
tarus, Midas and his golden touch, the labors of Hera-
cles--these and many other myths and legends of ancient
Greece are retold in a clear, fast-moving style. With
an introduction by the author.

GRAY, Elizabeth Janet. Adam of the Road. Illustrated by
Robert Lawson. The Viking Press, Inc., 1942. Grades
7 up.
A Newbery Award winner. "Elizabeth Gray has re-cre-
ated, with superb effect, a period of English history
glowing with life and color.... With the sympathetic
pictures by Robert Lawson this absorbing story will take
its place among the finest historical stories for children."
--Horn Book.

GREENE, Carla. I Want to Be a Nurse. Illustrated by
B. and E. Krehbiel. Children's Press, 1957. Grades
K-3.
Primary children can learn two things at once with the
"I Want To Be" books. Each easy-to-read story rein-
forces budding reading skills while it introduces children
to the working world. Children gain social studies concepts about community helpers, transportation, commu-
nication and other areas basic to our social and economic structure as they eagerly read each new title. Two-
color illustrations.

GRIMM, Jakob and Wilhelm. Grimm's Fairy Tales. Illustrated by Charles Folkard. E.P. Dutton & Company,

Inc., 1949. Originally published 1812 and 1815. Grades K-6.
Forty-seven favorite stories by the Brothers Grimm, based on the selection of Marion Edwardes. The Grimm stories, originally published in German as Kinder-und Hausmärchen, include "Hansel and Gretel," "The Golden Goose," "The House in the Wood," "The Hedgehog and the Hare," "Little Red Riding Hood," "King Thrush-beard," "Rapunzel," "Rumpelstiltskin," "The Seven Ravens," "Sleeping Beauty," "Snow White and the Seven Dwarfs."

_____. Little Red Riding Hood. Illustrated. Grosset & Dunlap, Inc. Grade ps.
A retelling of the traditional tale of a little girl who meets a wolf in the forest on the way to her grandmother's house. A giant-size favorite for the youngest reader, with glowing full-color illustrations on every page.

_____. The Three Little Pigs. Retold and illustrated by Paul Galdone. The Seabury Press, 1970. Grades ps-1.
"Paul Galdone gives new life to the childhood classic with his colorful and realistic pictures. In each one, he manages to capture the mood of the moment, and through subtle touches, adds much to the story."-- School Library Journal.

_____. The Three Little Pigs. Retold by Margaret Hillert. Illustrated by Irma Wilde. Follett Publishing Company, 1963. Grades 1-3.
Adapted from the classic tale, this book can be read independently as a preprimer.

GROSS, Arthur W. A Child's Garden of Bible Stories. Illustrated. Concordia Publishing House, 1948. Grades 1-4.
A unified, progressive account of God's action among men. Sixty stories in all--28 from the Old Testament and 32 from the New Testament. 156 illustrations in color and black and white.

GROSSMAN, Shelly and Mary Louise. The How and Why Wonder Book of Ecology. Illustrated by Shelly Grossman. Wonder-Treasure Books, Inc., 1971. Grades 2-7.
A well-known ecologist and photographer explain the plight which has befallen the animal world for the young reader. Lavishly illustrated with color and black-and-white photography, this is a book to capture the imagination of young people and explain to them the endangered wonders of their world. Edited under the supervision of Dr. Paul Blackwood, U.S. Office of Education; all text and art are checked for accuracy by Oakes White of the Brooklyn Children's Museum.

GROVER, Eulalie O.  See:  Mother Goose.

GUILFOILE, Elizabeth.  Have You Seen My Brother?  Illus-
    trated by Mary Stevens Andrew.  Follett Publishing Com-
    pany, 1962.  Grades 1-3.
    Andrew is searching for his big brother who, in turn,
    is searching for Andrew.  Andrew describes his brother
    to various people--but no one has seen him.  Finally,
    at the police station, they find each other.
    _____.  Nobody Listens to Andrew.  Illustrated by Mary
    Stevens.  Follett Publishing Company, 1957.  Grades
    1-3.
    "A highly successful attempt to provide a good story in
    a form that first graders can read independently...."
    --Booklist.


HACKER, Rich.  See:  Meyers, Earl "Bud."

HACKLER, David.  How Maps and Globes Help Us.  Illus-
    trated by William Tanis.  Benefic Press, 1970; original-
    ly 1962.  Grades 4-7.
    A book in the Basic Concepts Series systematically ar-
    ranged to develop in students a complete understanding
    of today's world and to develop vital skills.  Concepts
    and terms are underlined and defined as introduced.
    Summary at end of book presents overview of each basic
    concept and refers to pages where discussed.  Glossary
    lists new words, pronunciation and page where used.
    Photographs, drawings, charts and graphs expand and
    reinforce learning.  Contains a thought-provoking ques-
    tion section at end of each chapter.  A full-color film-
    strip and a transparency set is available for use with
    the book.

HADFIELD, A. M.  King Arthur and the Round Table.  Illus-
    trated by Donald S. Cammell.  E. P. Dutton & Company,
    Inc., 1953.  Grades 5-9.
    Courage, romance, humor, and honour belong to the
    real people of a real world in this version of the King
    Arthur story which focuses on the quest for the Holy
    Grail.

HAGGARD, H. Rider.  King Solomon's Mines.  Illustrated
    by A. R. Whitear.  E. P. Dutton & Company, Inc.  Orig-
    inally published 1886.  Grades 6 up.
    Allan Quartermain's breath-taking search for great treas-
    ure through the deserts and mountains of Africa.

HALLIBURTON, Richard.  The Book of Marvels.  Illustrated.
    The Bobbs-Merrill Company, Inc., 1937, 1938.
    First issued in two separate volumes:  Richard Halli-

burton's Book of Marvels: The Occident, published in
1937, and Second Book of Marvels: The Orient, pub-
lished in 1938. Contains maps and illustrations.
HAMILTON, Edith. Mythology. Illustrated by Steele Savage.
Little, Brown and Company, 1942. Grades 7-11.
A source book for Greek, Roman and Norse myths.
HAMMOND Incorporated. Illustrated Atlas for Young
America. Illustrated. Hammond Incorporated, 1967.
The story of maps: how they originated, what they do
and how to read them, with text and diagrams. Con-
tents: Facts about Our Earth; Different Kinds of Maps;
What a Map Does; How to Use a Map; What Scale Means;
Projections; Contours; Hemisphere Views; Reading a Re-
lief Map; Reading a Political Map; Man's Story in Maps.
Contains 30 full-color political, physical and pictorial
maps, many of them double spreads. Contains an Index.
An excellent atlas for children beginning map study; an
appropriate first atlas for the librarian to recommend
for personal ownership.
HANDFORTH, Thomas. Mei Li. Illustrated. Doubleday &
Company, Inc., 1938. Grades K-3.
Tale of a Chinese girl at the New Year Fair. Winner
of the Caldecott Medal Award. "It tells of Mei Li, a
little girl of North China, and her day at the Fair in
the town and of her part in all the doings along with
her brother, San Yu, his kitten Igo and her thrush, until at the end of a long day she goes riding home on a
camel just in time to greet the Kitchen God at midnight
on New Year's Eve."--Horn Book.
HARRINGTON, Mark Raymond. The Indians of New Jersey:
Dickon Among the Lenapes. Illustrated. Rutgers University Press, 1963. Grades 4-6.
Originally published by Winston with title: Dickon Among
the Lenape Indians.
HARRIS, Joel Chandler. Walt Disney's Uncle Remus Stories. Edited by Marion Palmer. Illustrated by Al
Dempster and Bill Justice. Western Publishing Company, Inc., 1964. This version originally published by
Golden Press, 1946. Grades 3-5.
In the Uncle Remus stories, the first collection of which
was published in 1880, Old Uncle Remus, a family servant and former slave, tells in authentic dialect Negro
folk tales about Brer Rabbit, Brer Fox, Brer Wolf, and
other beloved characters.--J.K.
HASTINGS, Evelyn. Big New School. Illustrated by Polly
Jackson. Follett Publishing Company, 1959. Grades
1-3.

The story of a "big new school," built for the children
from nearby farms, that becomes the "little old school"
with the passing of time.

HAWES, Charles Boardman. The Dark Frigate. Illustrated
by Warren Chappell. Little Brown and Company, 1934;
revised 1971. Originally published 1924. Grades 7 up.
Since its publication in 1924, this book has become a
classic. At that time, The New York Tribune said, "No
one, we think, has written so perfect a pirate tale since
Treasure Island," and it was honored with the Newbery
Medal. Forty-six years later young people are still
finding adventure and suspense in the story of Philip
Marsham, who boards the English frigate, Rose of Devon,
to train as a seaman. In mid-ocean, the frigate rescues twelve men from a sinking ship. Within three days
they have murdered the captain, seized the ship, and
changed its course for the Caribbean in hopes of plunder
and bounty. Philip is forced to become an involuntary
member of the band of pirates. Excitement, action, and
suspense--pirate style--plague him until he escapes, only
to be rescued by a British man-of-war and accused of
piracy. This new edition has been completely redesigned
by Warren Chappell and has an introduction by Lloyd
Alexander.

HAWTHORNE, Nathaniel. Tanglewood Tales. Illustrated by
S. Van Abbe. E. P. Dutton & Company, Inc., 1952.
Originally published 1853. Grades 4-9.
A famous author brings his imaginative genius to the re-
telling of six Greek myths for the children who enjoyed
the tales in A Wonder Book.

_____. A Wonder Book. Illustrated by S. Van Abbe.
E. P. Dutton & Company, Inc. Originally published 1851.
Grades 4-9.
Six classical legends fancifully retold and connected by
diverting incidents drawn from the life of the young peo-
ple gathered around the author's old country home.

HAYDEN, Gwendolen L. Skip, the Pioneer Boy. Illustrated.
T. S. Denison & Company, Inc. Grades 5-9.
An authentic story of early pioneer days of the West.
Skip was happy when Pa and Ma decided to move from
busy Nevada City to lonely Rocky Point. He was sure
that nothing could be as thrilling as the 500-mile trip
in their big covered wagon drawn by six horses. But
Skip little dreamed of all the exciting events that lay
ahead: living in a hillside dugout, helping Pa build a
log cabin, trapping a huge gray wolf, killing a cougar,
and escaping from Indians on the warpath. Reading level, fifth grade.

HAYNES, Doris, and Hurley, Jane. Afro-Americans Then and Now. Benefic Press, 1969. Grades 2-4.
Presents an interdisciplinary biographical approach to Afro-American heritage for use at the primary level. Emphasis on Afro-American culture, unit openings to biographies, commentary for teacher, challenging unit end activities, bibliography.

HAYWOOD, Carolyn. Little Eddie. Illustrated by the author. William Morrow and Company, Inc., 1947. Grades 1-5.
Forty illustrations. "Eddie's exploits are hilarious. Highly recommended."--Library Journal.

HEILBRONER, Joan. The Happy Birthday Present. Illustrated by Mary Chalmers. Harper & Row Publishers, Inc., 1961. Grades ps-3.
An "I Can Read" Book. Peter and his younger brother Davy go on a humorous search to many stores to find the perfect birthday gift for their mother.--J. K.

HEINLEIN, Robert A. Between Planets. Illustrated by Clifford Geary. Charles Scribner's Sons, 1951. Grades 5-11.
Topnotch science fiction with some very interesting characters.

_____ . Citizen of the Galaxy. Illustrated. Charles Scribner's Sons, 1957. Grades 5-11.
Thorby's adventures take him from one planet to another as he tries to solve the mystery of his own past.

_____ . Farmer in the Sky. Illustrated by Clifford Geary. Charles Scribner's Sons, 1950. Grades 5-11.
Exciting story of the colonization of the planet Ganymede.

_____ . Have Space Suit--Will Travel. Illustrated. Charles Scribner's Sons, 1958. Grades 5-11.
A boy repairs a space suit, and becomes involved in an interspatial cold war.

_____ . Red Planet: A Colonial Boy on Mars. Illustrated by Clifford Geary. Charles Scribner's Sons, 1949. Grades 5-11.
Mars is colonized by a group of earthlings who must fight for their liberties and independence.

_____ . Rocket Ship Galileo. Illustrated by Thomas W. Voter. Charles Scribner's Sons, 1947. Grades 5-11.
Three boys accompany a scientist on a rocket ship flight to the moon.

_____ . The Rolling Stones. Illustrated by Clifford Geary. Charles Scribner's Sons, 1952. Grades 5-11.
Humorous story of a family vacation trip to Mars and the asteroids.

_____ . Space Cadet. Illustrated by Clifford Geary.
Charles Scribner's Sons, 1948. Grades 5-11.
In 2075 two cadets from the rocket training school make
a flight to Venus.
_____ . The Star Beast. Illustrated. Charles Scribner's
Sons, 1954. Grades 5-11.
A fascinating story of a very unusual creature named
Lummox.
_____ . Starman Jones. Illustrated by Clifford Geary.
Charles Scribner's Sons, 1953. Grades 5-11.
Story of interplanetary voyaging and a special pet with
unusual qualities.
_____ . Starship Troopers. G. P. Putnam's Sons, 1959.
Grades 7 up.
A trooper's first-person account of his military training
experiences. --J. K.
_____ . Time for the Stars. Charles Scribner's Sons,
1956. Grades 5-11.
Humorous adventure story of twins and the telepathy
between them.
_____ . Tunnel in the Sky. Illustrated. Charles Scrib-
ner's Sons, 1955. Grades 5-11.
Exciting story of an advanced survival test on an unknown planet.
HELMRATH, Marilyn Olear, and Bartlett, Janet LaSpisa.
Bobby Bear and the Bees. Illustrated by Marilue. Oddo
Publishing, Inc., 1968. Grades ps-1.
A happy trip to the woods turns out to be not so happy
for Bobby Bear when he is stung by a bee. His mother
removes the stinger from Bobby's paw and explains to
the tearful Bobby and Little Hare why Bobby was stung
and the nature of bees and their work. While reading
for pleasure, children learn about bees, their hives,
why bees sting. The full-color illustrations add humor
to this story.
_____ . Bobby Bear Finds Maple Sugar. Illustrated by
Marilue. Oddo Publishing, Inc., 1968. Grades ps-1.
A wonderful aroma in the air takes Bobby and Little
Hare to a sugar bush. Fascinated, they watch the maple
sugar process from the tapping of the trees to the deli-
cious finished product. But Bobby's main interest is to
eat the maple sugar. He makes many attempts but none
of them work. He finally does get some maple sugar
when he decides to tap his own maple tree. This is an
easily-read, accurate story of maple sugar. Full-color
illustrations.
_____ . Bobby Bear Goes Fishing. Illustrated by Marilue.

Oddo Publishing, Inc., 1968. Grades ps-1.
After several unsuccessful fishing trips, Bobby finally
does get a bite on his fishing hook. With great excitement, he enlists the help of Father Bear and a robin.
But he is disappointed again when he sees a pail on his
hook and not a fish. To his surprise, he discovers a
fish in the pail and is very happy. His fish is so pretty
that Bobby decides to keep it as a pet and not eat it.
Full-color illustrations.
_____. Bobby Bear in the Spring. Illustrated by Marilue.
Oddo Publishing, Inc., 1968. Grades ps-1.
One spring day Bobby awakes to find a bright new green
world. Everything is warm and pretty, and Bobby and
his friends are off to the woods to make the best of this
lovely day. Through the reading of this book, children
become acquainted with the seasons of the year and what
nature does during each one. Full-color illustrations.
_____. Bobby Bear's Halloween. Illustrated by Marilue.
Oddo Publishing, Inc., 1968. Grades ps-1.
A delightful story depicting appreciation of nature in the
fun of this special day. When all Bobby's friends are
too busy to play, he amuses himself by romping in the
colorful autumn leaves. Upon his return home through
the dark woods, he meets with some elements of Halloween surprises. Full-color illustrations.
_____. Bobby Bear's Rocket Ride. Illustrated by Mari-
lue. Oddo Publishing, Inc., 1968. Grades ps-1.
It is an adventurous story of Bobby and his friend, the
robin. Bobby's great desire to fly takes the two friends
to a rocket ship. This ship blasts off, rockets on a
pleasurable and informative ride through space, and returns to Bobby's home in the woods. This easily-read
story is aimed to inform the young reader of the planets,
the moon and the sun. Full-color illustrations.
HENRY, Marguerite. Album of Horses. Illustrated by
Wesley Dennis. Rand McNally & Company, 1951.
Grades 4 up.
Interesting accounts of 22 important breeds of horses,
plus the mule and burro. Each is accompanied by a
full-page portrait in full color by Wesley Dennis. "A
happy collaboration of author and artist, both of whom
know and love horses, has produced an enticing treasury
of horse lore. All kinds of information, anecdotes, and
stories about 24 important breeds of horses."--Booklist.
_____. Black Gold. Illustrated by Wesley Dennis. Rand
McNally & Company, 1957. Grades 4-9.
Black-and-white drawings. The story of the famous Ken-

tucky Derby winner, and of a boy and a man who fixed
their sights upon the same hard goal.   Winner of the
1960 Sequoyah Children's Book Award.   "The true story
of a small but great-hearted stallion that won the Kentucky Derby in 1924 and three years later, with a broken
leg, gallantly insisted on finishing his race ... a thoroughly satisfying horse story."--Booklist.
          .   Born to Trot.   Illustrated by Wesley Dennis.
Rand McNally & Company, 1950.   Grades 3-11.
An ALA Notable Children's Book of 1950.   Filled with
dramatic action--the true story of an American boy and the
great trotting mare, Rosalind.   Tells how the boy becomes
her owner and shares in the triumph at the Hambletonian.
"Against an exciting background of horses and harness
racing the author writes of real people and real events....
Beautifully illustrated."--Booklist.
          .   Brighty of the Grand Canyon.   Illustrated by
Wesley Dennis.   Rand McNally & Company, 1956.
Grades 2-9.
Illustrated with full-color and black-and-white drawings.
The true and captivating story of a little burro who
blazed trails for men in the Grand Canyon.   How Brighty
helps solve a mystery is an enchanting story.   Breath-
taking illustrations.   Winner, William Allen White Award.
"... not only an entertaining animal story, but also an
interesting history of the development of Grand Canyon
as a national park."--Bulletin of the Center for Children's Books.
          .   Justin Morgan Had a Horse.   Illustrated by Wes-
ley Dennis.   Rand McNally & Company, 1954.   Grades
2-9.
Black-and-white drawings; Source Bibliography.   Friends
of Literature Award winner; Newbery Medal Runner-up.
A superb story of the pint-sized stallion who sired an
illustrious breed of horses.   "... a remarkably fine
piece of work and Wesley Dennis has added superb new
illustrations."--Elementary English.
          .   King of the Wind.   Illustrated by Wesley Dennis.
Rand McNally & Company, 1948.   Grades 2-9.
Illustrated with black-and-white and full-color drawings;
contains Source Bibliography.   An ALA Notable Children's Book of 1948; winner of the Newbery Medal.   The
story of the ancestor of Man O'War and a founder of the
entire thoroughbred strain.   An exciting tale that begins
in Morocco, sweeps across France and into England.
"A sympathetic story of the famous Godolphin Arabian,
a spirited stallion, and the mute Arabian stable boy who

accompanies him on his journey across the seas to
France and England.... The moving quality of the writ-
ing is reflected in the handsome illustrations."--ALA
Notable Children's Books, 1940-1959.
_____ . Misty of Chincoteague. Illustrated by Wesley
Dennis. Rand McNally & Company, 1947. Grades 2-9.
Illustrated with black-and-white drawings. Lewis Carroll
Shelf Award. Newbery Medal Runner-up. A magnificent
story of a brother and sister who capture and tame two
wild ponies. Setting and many characters and events are
real in this exceptionally appealing tale. "... Two children have their hearts set on owning a wild pony and
her colt ... a story that is vividly real. The many illustrations are in the spirit of the text."--Booklist.
_____ . Mustang, Wild Spirit of the West. Illustrated
by Robert Lougheed. Rand McNally & Company, 1966.
Grades 4 up.
The true story of America's wild horses--the mustangs--
and of one girl's brave battle to save them from exter-
mination. How "Wild Horse Annie" carried her fight to
the White House makes a grand book. 1970 Winner,
Sequoyah Children's Book Award. Western Heritage
Award (Outstanding Western Juvenile of 1966). Illustrated with black-and-white and 4-color drawings.
"... the story of 'Wild Horse Annie,' a real person....
The book is the best this author has written for many
years, engrossing as a story of the preservation of wild
animals and truly moving as a story of a dauntless woman."--Bulletin of the Center for Children's Books.
_____ . Sea Star, Orphan of Chincoteague. Illustrated
by Wesley Dennis. Rand McNally & Company, 1949.
Grades 2-9.
Illustrated with black-and-white and full-color drawings.
A heart-warming story about the wild ponies of Chinco-
teague. Misty's new adventures and the struggle to save
Little Sea Star make enthralling reading. "Most horse
stories are so harrowingly sad that it is a relief to come
upon this delightful story of a little wild horse orphan
rescued by two children and eventually saved from starva-
tion by a bereft mare."--Childhood Education.
_____ . Stormy, Misty's Foal. Illustrated by Wesley
Dennis. Rand McNally & Company, 1963. Grades 2-9.
Illustrated with black-and-white and full-color drawings.
The true and thrill-packed story of how Misty's foal
was born in the aftermath of a great storm that devas-
tated Chincoteague Island, and how the islanders rebuilt
their land. "The story is, for the most part, a true

one and Marguerite Henry fills it with human understanding. Here, side by side, are humor and pathos, elation and suffering, and victory rising from defeat."--Elementary English.

_____. White Stallion of Lipizza. Illustrated by Wesley Dennis. Rand McNally & Company, 1964. Grades 3-8. Illustrated with black-and-white and full-color drawings. The world-famous horses of the Spanish Riding School are featured in the story of a baker's boy who becomes a riding master. Delightful glimpses of Vienna are the background. "Miss Henry's descriptions ... are real and vivid. But it is the almost mystical rapport between horse and boy, which she portrays so well, that grips the reader."--Young Readers' Review.

HENTOFF, Nat. I'm Really Dragged But Nothing Gets Me Down. Simon & Schuster, Inc., 1968; Dell Publishing Company, Inc. Grades 7 up.
Jeremy Wolf is beset by deeply conflicting responsibilities--to himself, to his family, to his country. Jeremy is in the process of finding out who he is. With wit and understanding, this novel examines both sides of the generation gap. "A taut, highly articulate exposition of today's hangups...."--The Kirkus Service; "... the book has provocative timeliness."--Horn Book.

_____. Jazz Country. Harper & Row Publishers, Inc., 1965; Dell Publishing Company, Inc., 1967. Grades 7 up.
High school senior Tom Curtis has lived for little but his trumpet, but when he tries to make it as a professional jazz-man, he learns he has yet to find himself as an artist and as a person. A Herald Tribune Honor Book 1965.
This novel "portrays the jazz world as seen by a boy who longs to be a jazz musician and who discovers, from the Negro professionals who become his friends, that being a true jazz artist does not depend on the color of one's skin."--McClurg. Book News.

HERBERT, Don. Mr. Wizard's Experiments for Young Scientists. Illustrated by Dan Noonan. Doubleday & Company, Inc., 1959. Grades 5-9.
Thirteen experiments using household equipment are enriched by information on the work of adult scientists--astronomers, botanists, chemists, geologists, and others. The author demonstrates how each tackles his research and the important discoveries each has made.

HEYERDAHL, Thor. Kon-Tiki for Young People. Illustrated. Rand McNally & Company, 1960. Grades 4 up.

A handsome, profusely illustrated edition for young people which preserves the exciting first-hand appeal of the
famous Kon-Tiki expedition.  With 130 photographs and
drawings in color.  "Extremely entertaining reading and
has scientific worth in its insights into anthropology,
oceanography, and zoology."--AAAS Science Book List
for Children.

HEYWARD, Dubose.  The Country Bunny and the Little Gold
Shoes.  Illustrated by Marjorie Flack.  Houghton Mifflin
Company, 1939.  Grades K-3.
"It was Easter of 1939 when this happy, inspiring story
won its first group of devoted readers.  Many have read
it every year since, always finding new pleasure in the
story...."--Chicago Sun-Times.

The Editors of HIGHLIGHTS.  Holiday (Craft) Handbook No.
4.  Illustrated.  Highlights For Children, Inc., 1965.
Grades K-6.
Contains 181 creative suggestions for Halloween, Thanksgiving, Christmas, Valentine Day, Easter, Mother's Day,
and Year 'Round Ideas.  "Most of the features are suited
for use in several different grades, recognizing the wide
individual differences, interests, art skills, and creative
talents among children of any grade....  The aim has
been to keep material costs down and teacher-effort at
a minimum."--From Foreword.

_____ .  Tricks and Teasers; A Highlights Handbook.  Illustrated.  Highlights For Children, Inc., 1965.  Grades
K-6.
Puzzles and brain teasers which have appeared in Highlights For Children are collected and reprinted here.
They range in difficulty from very easy ones the child
from 5 to 7 can do, to harder ones challenging the
brightest older child or the adult....  "Tricks and teasers
afford a strong appeal to the child to read for meaning
[and] ... provide an opportunity for good fun for the
whole family."--From Foreword.

HILL, Dave.  Boy Who Gave His Lunch Away.  Illustrated.
Concordia Publishing House, 1967.
An Arch Book, presenting a Bible story in colorful,
easy-to-read form.

_____ .  Most Wonderful King.  Illustrated by B. Wind.
Concordia Publishing House, 1968.
An Arch Book, presenting a Bible story in colorful,
easy-to-read form.

_____ .  Secret of the Star.  Illustrated by Roberts.  Concordia Publishing House, 1966.
An Arch Book, presenting a Bible story in colorful,
easy-to-read form.

_____. Walls Came Tumbling Down. Illustrated. Concordia Publishing House, 1967.
An Arch Book, presenting a Bible story in colorful, easy-to-read form.

HILLERT, Margaret. See: Grimm, Jakob and Wilhelm.

HINTON, S.E. The Outsiders. The Viking Press, Inc., 1967; Dell Publishing Company, Inc. Grades 7 up.
Honor Book, Book World's Children's Spring Book Festival. A revealing novel about teenagers--written by a teenager. It's the story of a gang of toughs from the wrong side of the tracks whose mode of expression is violence--directed toward the group of privileged kids who are the object of their envy and their hatred. "No social scientist can fault this talented teen-age author's sympathetic observations of the members of a city gang, their relationships to each other, and their detachment from prevailing standards. The killing pride of the disadvantaged is captured and conveyed in the novel's action and suspense."--Library Journal.

HOFF, Carol. The Four Friends. Illustrated by Jim Porter. Follett Publishing Company, 1955. Grades 1-3.
"Recommended wherever beginning reading books are needed."--School Library Journal.

HOFF, Syd. Danny and the Dinosaur. Illustrated by the author. Harper & Row Publishers, Inc., 1958. Grades ps-3.
An "I Can Read" Book. When Danny decided to visit the museum he never expected to make friends with the largest object there. But the dinosaur was as eager to play with Danny as Danny was to play with the dinosaur, so what could have been more natural than for the two of them to leave the museum together?

_____. Julius. Illustrated by the author. Harper & Row Publishers, Inc., 1959. Grades ps-3.
An "I Can Read" Book. Julius, a friendly African gorilla, is brought to America and employed in the circus, and gets lost one day.--J.K.

_____. Little Chief. Illustrated by the author. Harper & Row Publishers, Inc., 1961. Grades ps-3.
An "I Can Read" Book.

_____. Oliver. Illustrated by the author. Harper & Row Publishers, Inc., 1960. Grades ps-3.
An "I Can Read" Book. This is "the story of Oliver, an elephant who longed to be a circus star and who achieved his ambition."--McClurg. Book News.

_____. Sammy the Seal. Illustrated by the author. Harper & Row, Publishers, Inc., 1959. Grades ps-3.
An "I Can Read" Book.

_____. Who Will Be My Friends? Illustrated by the au-
thor. Harper & Row Publishers, Inc., 1960. Grades
ps-3.

An Early "I Can Read" Book. How young Freddy tries,
fails, and finally succeeds in making friends in his new
neighborhood.--J. K.

HOFFMAN, Vern B. See: Hutton, Joe.

HOLLAND, Joyce. Bessie, the Messy Penguin. Illustrated
by Carvel Lee. T.S. Denison & Company, Inc., 1960.
Grades K-4.

A story to encourage children to be satisfied with their
home, friends, and family. Bessie is a very messy
little penguin who can't manage to keep her formal black
and white feathers clean. All the penguins laugh at her
and call her "Messy Bessie." Bessie decides to run
away and find some different feathers to wear. However,
in her travels, Bessie learns that her own feathers are
the best for her, and that it is best to stay at home.
Four-color illustrations.

HOLLING, Holling C. Minn of the Mississippi. Illustrated
by the author. Houghton Mifflin Company, 1951. Grades
4-6.

"The Mississippi River is the subject of the fourth book
in Mr. Holling's series about America.... Outstanding
book with beautiful colored illustrations and marginal
drawings similar to those in his previous books. Wide
interest level, including adults."--Library Journal.

_____. Paddle-to-the-Sea. Illustrated by the author.
Houghton Mifflin Company, 1941. Grades 4-6.

ALA Notable Book. "Paddle-to-the-Sea is a little person in a canoe, carved by an Indian boy ... to follow
his course through the different waterways to the
ocean.... Geography of the best kind, made vivid by
the power of imagination...."--Horn Book.

_____. Tree in the Trail. Illustrated by the author.
Houghton Mifflin Company, 1942. Grades 4-6.

"The story of a cottonwood tree that watched the pageant
of history on the Santa Fe trail where it stood, a land-
mark to travelers and a peace-medicine tree to Indians,
for over 200 years...."--Booklist.

HOOFNAGLE, Keith Lundy. The Story of Linda Lookout.
Illustrated. Naturegraph Books. Grades 4 up.

A charming little cartoon story of how a very human
fire look-out lady does her job on a lonely mountain top.

HOOPES, Ned, editor. Wonderful World of Horses. Dell
Publishing Company, Inc., 1966. Grades 7-11.

Excitement, humor, pathos and magic are ingredients

in this collection of horse stories by some of our most distinguished writers. Contents: "The Sorrel Colt," by Benito Lynch; "Throw Your Heart Over," by Stuart Cloete; "Pool of Sand," by Charlotte Edwards; "I Ride a Bucking Horse," by Mark Twain; "The Magic Winged Horse," from The Arabian Nights; "The Chimaera," by Nathaniel Hawthorne; "A Horseman and His Horse," from Aesop's Fables; "The Summer of the Beautiful White Horse," by William Saroyan; "Coaly-Bay, the Outlaw Horse," by Ernest Thompson Seton; "The Perverse Horse," by Edward Noyes Westcott; "The Horse Looked at Him," by MacKinlay Kantor; "Horses--One Dash," by Stephen Crane; "Midnight," by Will James; "The Gift," by John Steinbeck; "Chu Chu," by Bret Harte.

       and Peck, Richard, editors. Edge of Awareness. Dell Publishing Company, Inc., 1966; Delacorte Press, 1970. Grades 7 up.
A stimulating collection of 25 essays by outstanding contemporary writers. Statesmen, poets, anthropologists, critics and scientists here express their personal views on many subjects, from the problem of young people to the exploration of outer space. Many provocative ideas are set forth which will sharpen the reader's own points of view about man in a complex world.

HOWARD, Matthew V. Blink, the Patchwork Bunny. Illustrated by Earl W. Moline, Jr. T.S. Denison & Company, Inc., 1959. Grades K-3.
A rollicking fun-filled verse-fantasy about Easter and a multicolored bunny with a secret. Enjoyment through understanding. Careful coordination of big, bright, full-color illustrations with a studied and tested selection of words and phrases insures enjoyment from listening as well as learning to read.

HUDNUT. A Horse of Her Own. Van Nostrand Reinhold Company.

HUGHES, Thomas. Tom Brown's Schooldays. Illustrated by S. Van Abbe. E.P. Dutton & Company, Inc. Originally published 1857. Grades 6-9.
The life of a typical middle class English boy, from his timid entrance to his triumphant graduation, in the Rugby of Dr. Arnold.

HUNT, Irene. Across Five Aprils. Follett Publishing Company, 1964. Grades 7 up.
Runner-up for the Newbery Award, 1965. "An impressive book both as a historically authenticated Civil War novel and as a beautifully written family story."--Center for Children's Books, University of Chicago Bulletin.

_____. Up a Road Slowly. Follett Publishing Company,
    1966. Grades 7 up.
    Awarded the John Newbery Medal for 1967. "The per-
    ceptive though nostalgic portrayal of a girl growing to
    maturity is well written...."--Booklist.
HUNTER, Kristin. The Soul Brothers and Sister Lou.
    Charles Scribner's Sons, 1968. Grades 7 up.
    Louretta is a lonely Negro teenager in an urban ghetto.
HUNTINGTON, Harriet E. Let's Go Outdoors. Illustrated.
    Doubleday & Company, Inc., 1939. Grades ps-4.
    Answers to youngsters' questions about nature's crea-
    tures.
HURD, Edith Thacher. Come and Have Fun. Illustrated by
    Clement Hurd. Harper & Row Publishers, Inc., 1962.
    Grades ps-2.
    An Early "I Can Read" Book. A cat invites a mouse to
    come out of his mouse house and play.--J.K.
_____. Last One Home Is a Green Pig. Illustrated by
    Clement Hurd. Harper & Row Publishers, Inc., 1959.
    Grades ps-3.
    An "I Can Read" Book. An easy-to-read book about the
    day a Duck and a Monkey decided to race each other
    home. 'Last one home is a green pig,' said the Monkey,
    and they started off. It was a close race all the way,
    and neither contestant was ever sure who would win.
    They used their legs, their wits, and every available
    conveyance, from a horse to a submarine.
HURLBUT, Jesse Lyman. Hurlbut's Story of the Bible. Il-
    lustrated. Zondervan Publishing House. Originally pub-
    lished 1966 by Revell. Grades K-4.
    A continuous narrative of the Scriptures that brings the
    great heroes and events of Bible days to life. Features
    168 stories covering the whole Bible; 192 illustrations;
    69 pages of suggestions for teaching; 62 pages on the
    history of the Books of the Bible; presentation page; pro-
    nunciation key.
HURLEY, Jane. See: Haynes, Doris.
HURLEY, William J. Dan Frontier. Illustrated by Jack
    Boyd. Benefic Press, 1959. Grades ps-2.
    Reading level of this book: ps.
    The Dan Frontier series of books and companion record-
    ings is about early frontier life--settling the Midwest.
    Vigorous and adventurous, this likable young frontiers-
    man--not unlike Daniel Boone--becomes a lifelike inspira-
    tional hero to children of many ages. Many exciting ad-
    ventures--hunting, fishing, exploring, fighting Indians--
    hold reader's interest. Mature characters and adult ac-

tion assure high interest via advanced social studies concepts such as neighborhood and community development, and home and family relationships.  Each book contains a unique teacher's guide for use in promoting growth in interpretive skills, word perception skills and language. All factors affecting readability are carefully controlled. Vocabulary chart in each book shows words at above and below grade level.

_____. Dan Frontier and the Big Cat.  Illustrated by Jack Boyd.  Benefic Press, 1961.  Grades K-3. Reading level of this book:  K.  See description of the author's Dan Frontier.

_____. Dan Frontier and the New House.  Illustrated by Don Simmons.  Benefic Press, 1961.  Grades ps-2. Reading level:  ps.  See description of the author's Dan Frontier.

_____. Dan Frontier and the Wagon Train.  Illustrated by Jack Boyd.  Benefic Press, 1959.  Grades 2-5. Reading level:  grade 2.  See description of the author's Dan Frontier.

_____. Dan Frontier Goes Exploring.  Illustrated by Jack Boyd.  Benefic Press, 1963.  Grades 3-6. Reading level:  grade 3.  See description of the author's Dan Frontier.

_____. Dan Frontier Goes Hunting.  Illustrated by Jack Boyd.  Benefic Press, 1959.  Grades K-3. Reading level:  K.  See description of the author's Dan Frontier.

_____. Dan Frontier Goes to Congress.  Illustrated by George Rohrer.  Benefic Press, 1964.  Grades 4-7. Reading level:  grade 4.  See description of the author's Dan Frontier.

_____. Dan Frontier Scouts with the Army.  Illustrated by Jack Boyd.  Benefic Press, 1962.  Grades 2-5. Reading level:  grade 2.  See description of the author's Dan Frontier.

_____. Dan Frontier, Sheriff.  Illustrated by Jack Boyd. Benefic Press, 1960.  Grades 3-6. Reading level:  grade 3.  See description of the author's Dan Frontier.

_____. Dan Frontier, Trapper.  Illustrated by Jack Boyd. Benefic Press, 1962.  Grades 1-4. Reading level:  grade 1.  See description of the author's Dan Frontier.

_____. Dan Frontier with the Indians.  Illustrated by Jack Boyd.  Benefic Press, 1959.  Grades 1-4. Reading level:  grade 1.  See description of the author's Dan Frontier.

HUTTON, Joe, and Hoffman, Vern B. Basketball. Illustrated. Creative Educational Society, Inc., 1962.
Grades 4 up.
This book has become very popular among those who
play, watch, and coach one of the most widely played
games in the country. Beginners and advanced players
use it to learn coordination, precision, and team plays.
Spectators enjoy its many explanations. Coaches adopt
it to teach their players fundamental skills--the excellent photographs and text serve to fully explain each
fundamental in detail.


JACOBS, Helen Hull. See: Dypwick, Otis J.
JACOBS, Joseph, editor. English Folk and Fairy Tales.
Illustrated by John D. Batten. G. P. Putman's Sons,
1904. Grades 3-6.
A popular collection of folktales drawn from many
sources, retold by the editor.
JAHSMANN, Allan H., reviser. Little Folded Hands. Illustrated by F. Hook. Concordia Publishing House, 1959.
Grades 1-5.
A wonderful help in teaching simple prayers of thanks
to children. Beautiful full-color illustrations and large,
easy-to-read type make learning a joy to the youngsters.
Many prayers included are appropriate for family blessings also.
JAHSMANN, Allan H. and Simon, Martin P. Little Visits
with God. Illustrated. Concordia Publishing House,
1957. Grades ps-5.
This devotional book has become an established favorite
with Christian families everywhere. With 200 devotions,
it shows children that being a Christian is an everyday
experience. Familiar incidents in a child's world, Bible
readings, discussion questions and prayers provide devotions that children can read, understand and apply to
their own lives with the rest of the family. Beautifully
illustrated.
_____. More Little Visits with God. Illustrated. Con-
cordia Publishing House, 1961. Grades ps-5.
Contains 197 devotions. See description of the authors'
Little Visits with God.
JAMES, M. R., translator. See: Andersen, Hans Christian.
JAMES, Will. Smoky, the Cow Horse. Illustrated by the
author. Charles Scribner's Sons, 1954; originally 1926.
Grades 7-11.
A cowpony's life on the range. Awarded the Newbery
Medal, 1927.

JATAKA Tales.  See: Galdone, Paul.
JAYNES, Ruth.  Yo-Ho and Kim.  Illustrated.  Lawrence
   Publishing Company.  Grades 1-6.
   A high motivation reader for encouraging interest and a
   positive attitude in the slower reader, and for extending
   the basic vocabulary of children in all grades.  Edited
   by Ida Mulock.
   _____.  Yo-Ho and Kim at Sea.  Illustrated.  Lawrence
   Publishing Company.  Grades 1-6.
   See description of the author's Yo-Ho and Kim.
JOHNSON, Crockett (pseud.).  Harold and the Purple Crayon.
   Illustrated by the author.  Harper & Row Publishers,
   Inc., 1958; originally 1955.  Grades ps-3.
   "Fantasy of a small boy who decides to go for a walk
   one night.  He uses his purple crayon to draw all the
   things necessary for a successful walk--a moon, a path,
   houses, the ocean, a boat, a mountain, a balloon, and
   finally his own room again...."--Chicago.  Children's
   Book Center.
JONES, Jessie Orton, editor.  Small Rain:  Verses from
   the Bible.  Illustrated by Elizabeth Orton Jones.  The
   Viking Press, Inc., 1943.  Grades K-3.
   Runner-up, Caldecott Medal Award.  "Joyous sensitive
   drawings bring some beautiful verses of the Bible into
   close and intimate association with a child's daily life."
   --Horn Book.
JONES, Mary Alice.  Bible Stories.  Rand McNally & Company, 1952.  Grades ps-K.
   _____.  Tell Me About Christmas.  Illustrated by Mar-
   jorie Cooper.  Rand McNally & Company, 1958.  Grades
   ps-4.
   Teaches small children the true and lovely meaning, the
   greatness and beauty of Christmas, not merely as a day
   for giving and receiving, but as the celebration of a
   beautiful way of life.  Illustrated with beautiful drawings,
   many in full color.
   _____.  Tell Me About God.  Illustrated by Dorothy
   Grider.  Rand McNally & Company, 1967; originally
   1943.  Grades ps-4.
   Completely rewritten and newly illustrated for today's
   children.  Answers such questions as:  "Is God real?"
   "Does God care about us?" and "Can we know God?"
   A best-seller for over two decades.  Illustrated with
   beautiful drawings, many in full color.
   _____.  Tell Me About Heaven.  Illustrated by Marjorie
   Cooper.  Rand McNally & Company, 1956.  Grades ps-
   4.

The child's questions about heaven--where it is, what it
is like, etc.--are answered in an honest, sincere and
convincing manner that will impress and satisfy the very
young.  Lovely, meaningful drawings, many in full color.
_____.  Tell Me About Jesus.  Illustrated by Dorothy
Grider.  Rand McNally & Company, 1967; originally
1944.  Grades ps-4.
A completely new edition, with new text and new full-
color pictures.  Helps children understand the meaning
of the life of Jesus and to feel closer to Him.  Nonde-
nominational and in accord with today's religious teaching.
_____.  Tell Me About Prayer.  Illustrated by Dorothy
Grider.  Rand McNally & Company, 1948.  Grades 3-5.
Through simple, natural conversation, Miss Jones explains why we pray, how we pray, and the different
types of prayers for children.  Non-denominational and
planned for family use.  Illustrated with beautiful drawings, many in full color.
_____.  Tell Me About the Bible.  Illustrated by Pelagie
Doane.  Rand McNally & Company, 1945.  Grades 1-5.
In simple, conversational style, Miss Jones answers
the child's natural questions about the Bible.  The book
makes the Bible live for children and does it with rare
attractiveness.  Illustrated with beautiful drawings, many
in full color.
JONK, Clarence.  Jimmy, a Little Pup.  Illustrated by Hugh
Berta.  T.S. Denison & Company, Inc.  Grades K-3.
A story about a puppy who gets lost when he plays tag
with a squirrel.  Jimmy was the smallest puppy in the
family.  He just never could catch his brothers and sis-
ters.  Playing tag with a small squirrel one day is fun
all right, but suddenly night falls.  Now Jimmy is lost.
He howls and cries.  The owls answer.  Four-color illustrations.
JORDAN, Emil L.  Nature Atlas of America.  Illustrated.
Hammond Incorporated, 1952.  Grades 6 up.
An introduction to day-by-day nature: rocks, trees and
wildflowers, birds and animals, amphibians, reptiles,
fishes and insects.  Includes distribution and physical
maps, tables of wildlife refuges, glossary.  Original
paintings and Hammond maps in color.  Index.
JOSEPH, James.  Careers Outdoors.  Thomas Nelson Inc.,
1969; originally 1962.  Grades 7-12.
A carefully researched guide to the whole spectrum of
outdoor occupations, suggesting government jobs as well
as those connected with sports and vacationing.

JOSLIN, Sesyle.  What Do You Say, Dear?  Illustrated by
    Maurice Sendak.  Addison-Wesley Publishing Company,
    1958.  Grades 2-4.
    What does a young gentleman say when he is introduced
    to a baby elephant?  What does a young lady say when
    she bumps into a crocodile?  However ridiculous the
    situation, there is still an appropriate social response.
    This lively book of manners is amusingly illustrated in
    two colors.
JUDSON, Clara Ingram.  Abraham Lincoln.  Illustrated by
    Polly Jackson.  Follett Publishing Company, 1961.
    Grades 2-4.
    An easy-to-read biography of the sixteenth President of
    the United States.
_____.  Christopher Columbus.  Illustrated by Polly Jack-
    son.  Follett Publishing Company, 1964.  Grades 2-4.
    A child's biography of Columbus:  his boyhood desire to
    be a sailor, and his eventual discovery of the Americas.
_____.  George Washington.  Illustrated by Bob Patterson.
    Follett Publishing Company, 1961.  Grades 2-4.
    Beginning with his boyhood in Virginia, this book de-
    scribes Washington's career as the first President of the
    United States.


KAMM, Herbert.  Junior Illustrated Encyclopedia of Sports.
    Illustrated by Willard Mullin.  The Bobbs-Merrill Com-
    pany, Inc., 1970; originally 1960, edited by Willard Mul-
    lin.  Grades 8 up.
    "The history, players, outstanding events, and statistics
    of all the popular sports, including baseball, football,
    basketball, tennis, track and field, ice hockey, boxing,
    and golf.  Illustrated with drawings, photographs, and
    cartoons by Willard Mullin."--Book Buyer's Guide.
KAUNE, Merriman.  My Own Little House.  Illustrated by
    the author.  Follett Publishing Company, 1957.  Grades
    1-3.
    A child tells how he paints a house, and what interesting
    variations he can make.
KEATS, Ezra Jack.  The Snowy Day.  Illustrated by the au-
    thor.  The Viking Press, Inc., 1962.  Grades K-3.
    "In this book sparkling with atmosphere, a small boy
    experiences the joys of a snowy day.  The brief, vividly
    expressed text points out his new awareness."--Horn
    Book.
_____.  Whistle for Willie.  Illustrated by the author.
    The Viking Press, Inc., 1964; paperback, 1969.  Grades
    K-3.

An ALA Notable Book.  "We are delighted to see Peter
again.  Now he wants to whistle so that he can call his
dog, Willie....  A companion to The Snowy Day, this
has a different but equal charm."--Saturday Review.

KEEN, Martin L.  The How and Why Wonder Book of the
Human Body.  Illustrated by Darrell Sweet.  Wonder-
Treasure Books, Inc.  Grades 2-7.
Questions most commonly asked by boys and girls are
answered in this authoritative and handsome volume of
easy-to-understand information.  Illustrated in full color
and black and white.  Edited under the supervision of
Dr. Paul Blackwood, U.S. Office of Education.  All text
and art are checked for accuracy by Oakes White of the
Brooklyn Children's Museum.

KENNEDY, John F.  The Kennedy Years and the Negro.
Edited by Doris E. Saunders.  Illustrated.  Johnson Publishing Company, Inc.  (Chicago), 1964.
Introduction by Andrew T. Hatcher.  The impact of
President Kennedy on the nation's black people and their
impact on him is captured in photos and text.  "Makes
its point by illustrating as words could not, the unprec-
edented entry of Negroes into the White House."--Hart-
ford Times.

KERR, James S.  Dandy, the Dime.  Illustrated by S.
Schofer Mathews.  T.S. Denison & Company, Inc.
Grades K-3.
A story of a dime written in verse to encourage young
children in thrift and saving money.  Dandy, the dime,
is discouraged because no one places much value on him
and he is bounced around from pocket to pocket careless-
ly.  He'd like to be a quarter or a half dollar because
no one heard his jingling.  He finally lands in a real
bank and enjoys the company of other coins and is pleased
because he has taught Jimmy to save.  Four-color illustrations.

KESSLER, Leonard.  Here Comes the Strikeout.  Illustrated
by the author.  Harper & Row Publishers, Inc., 1965.
Grades ps-3.
A Sports "I Can Read" Book.  Every time young Bobby
comes up to bat he strikes out, until he learns, with
his friend Willie's help, that good hitting is the result
of hard work. --H.W. Wilson Company.

KEYES, Nelson Beecher.  Story of the Bible World.  Illustrated.  Hammond Incorporated, 1962.  Grades 6 up.
Account of the main events of Bible history, from ancient civilizations of Egypt and Babylonia to modern ar-
chaeological work in Israel and Jordan today.  Maps of

Jerusalem in Old and New Testament times, time chart
of Bible history.  100 photographs, 30 full-color Hammond maps.  Map and text indexes.

KIDDER, Barbara.  Mr. Wonderful.  Illustrated by the author.  T. S. Denison & Company, Inc.  Grades K-3.
A health treatment of the five senses of the human body.
"Mr. Wonderful" is a factual account about the five
senses of sight, hearing, taste, touch and smell written
in first and second grade vocabulary.  A delightful little
pixie guides the young reader to an appreciation of his
own physical capabilities.  Three-color illustrations.

KIDDER, M. Worden and Barbara.  Mr. Mighty.  Illustrated
by Barbara Kidder.  T. S. Denison & Company, Inc.
Grades 1-4.
Structure of the muscles of the human body and how they
function.  Mr. Mighty has the strength and physique that
most growing children admire.  He tells about the three
kinds of muscles found in our bodies, what they are,
what they do, how they work and how they grow.  Four-
color illustrations.

KING, Martin Luther, Jr.  Martin Luther King Jr., 1929-
1968: An Ebony Picture Biography.  Illustrated.  Johnson Publishing Company, Inc. (Chicago), 1969.
Eighty-two pages of photographs, some of them never
before published, accompanied by an eloquent text taken
from the speeches of Dr. King himself, tells the story
from beginning to end of the national black leader who
"tried to love and serve humanity."

KING, Patricia.  Mable the Whale.  Illustrated by Katherine
Evans.  Follett Publishing Company, 1958.  Grades 1-3.
This clever tale of a whale with a sunburned fin is based
on a true incident.

KINGMAN, Lee.  The Peter Pan Bag.  Houghton Mifflin
Company, 1970; Dell Publishing Company, Inc., 1971.
Grades 8 up.
Seventeen-year-old Wendy leaves home to join the hippie
scene on Beacon Hill in Boston.  She finds a world of
communal living, crash pads and pot, and meets other
young people who have come to look for intangible mean-
ings they can't find at school or at home.

KIPLING, Rudyard.  The Jungle Books.  Illustrated.  Double-
day & Company, Inc., 1964; Dell Publishing Company,
Inc.  Originally published 1894.  Grades 5-9.
In this classic collection of animal tales, the Indian boy
Mowgli, lost in the jungle, finds refuge with a family of
wolves and learns the lore of the jungle from various
animals.  Among the tales are "Rikki-Tikki-Tavi" and
"How Fear Came."

_____. Kim. Doubleday & Company, Inc.; Dell Publishing Company, Inc. Originally published 1901. Grades 5-9.
An orphan boy, son of an Irish soldier, grows up in India free to explore the alleys and bazaars of Lahore. But when he meets his father's regiment he trades his Indian life for schooling and yet other adventures.

_____. New Illustrated Just So Stories. Illustrated by Nicholas. Doubleday & Company, Inc., 1952; originally 1912. Grades 1-6.
Fables of men and beasts. Contents: How the whale got his throat; How the camel got his hump; How the rhinoceros got his skin; How the leopard got his spots; Elephant's child; Sing-song of Old Man Kangaroo; Beginning of the armadillos; How the first letter was written; How the alphabet was made; The crab that played with the sea; Cat that walked by himself; Butterfly that stamped.

KLOTS, Alexander and Elsie. The Desert. Illustrated. Creative Educational Society, Inc. in cooperation with the National Audubon Society, 1967. Grades 4-8.
"The authors have written out of a background of personal experience and study. And the photographic illustrations reproduced in large size, represent some of the finest desert camera studies in existence. Together, the text, carefully prepared, and the album of photographs, detailed and artistic, form a valuable addition to the excellent series."--Edwin Way Teale.

KNIGHT, Eric. Lassie Come-Home. Illustrated by Don Bolognese. Holt, Rinehart and Winston, Inc., 1941. Grades 4-9.
This beautiful epic is told with profound understanding not only of a relationship between a young boy and his loyal dog, but of the vibrant lives of the Yorkshire people whom Eric Knight knew and loved so well. Originally published in 1939 as a short story in The Saturday Evening Post, it became the basis for the successful film and television series. The full-length book, published in 24 languages, has sold millions of copies. Illustrated in black and white by Don Bolognese. 30th Anniversary Edition, 1971.

KNIGHT, Hilary. Christmas Nutshell Library. Illustrated by the author. Harper & Row Publishers, Inc., 1963. Consists of four books: Angels and Berries and Candy Canes; Christmas Stocking Story; A Firefly in a Fir Tree; and The Night Before Christmas.

KOHLER, J. See: Witty, Paul.

KOMROFF, Manuel. Marco Polo. Illustrated by Edgard
Cirlin. Julian Messner Division of Simon & Schuster,
Inc., 1952. Grades 7 up.
Biography of Marco Polo, 1254?-1324?, Venetian trav-
eler in Asia.

KORFKER, Dena. My Picture Story Bible. Illustrated.
Zondervan Publishing House. Grades 1-4.
Picture and story skillfully blended to increase the child's
interest in the Bible. 270 stories.

KRAMER, A.H. Baby Born in a Stable. Illustrated by
Lampher. Concordia Publishing House.
An Arch Book. Children, parents, and teachers are
still discovering these colorful and easy-to-read little
treasures. They're long enough to tell a whole Bible
story in bouncy verse or prose, and short enough to be
interesting.

KRAMER, Janice. Donkey Daniel in Bethlehem. Illustrated.
Concordia Publishing House, 1970. Grades ps-4.
An Arch Book, presenting a Bible story in colorful,
easy-to-read form.

_____. Eight Bags of Gold. Illustrated by S. Mathews.
Concordia Publishing House, 1964. Grades ps-4.
An Arch Book, presenting a Bible story in colorful,
easy-to-read form.

_____. Good Samaritan. Illustrated by S. Mathews.
Concordia Publishing House, 1964. Grades ps-4.
An Arch Book, presenting a Bible story in colorful,
easy-to-read form.

_____. Princess and the Baby. Illustrated. Concordia
Publishing House, 1969. Grades ps-4.
An Arch Book, presenting a Bible story in colorful,
easy-to-read form.

_____. The Rich Fool. Illustrated by S. Mathews. Con-
cordia Publishing House, 1964. Grades ps-4.
An Arch Book, presenting a Bible story in colorful,
easy-to-read form.

_____. Simeon's Secret. Illustrated. Concordia Publish-
ing House, 1969. Grades ps-4.
An Arch Book, presenting a Bible story in colorful,
easy-to-read form.

_____. Unforgiving Servant. Illustrated by S. Mathews.
Concordia Publishing House, 1968. Grades ps-4.
An Arch Book, presenting a Bible story in colorful,
easy-to-read form.

KRAUSS, Ruth. A Hole Is To Dig: A First Book of First
Definitions. Illustrated by Maurice Sendak. Harper &
Row Publishers, Inc., 1952. Grades ps-2.

A small book which gives "children-size definitions of everyday things, such as 'A book is to look at,' etc." --Retail Bookseller.

KRUMGOLD, Joseph. And Now Miguel. Illustrated by Jean Charlot. Thomas Y. Crowell Company, 1953; Apollo Editions, 1970. Grades 6 up.
Newbery Award winner. This is Miguel--Miguel Chavez who held in his heart a secret wish and yearned to go with the men of his family to the Sangre de Cristo mountains. He lives near Taos, New Mexico, where the members of the Chavez family have lived on a sheep-raising farm for many generations. --H. W. Wilson Company.

_____. Onion John. Illustrated by Symeon Shimin. Thomas Y. Crowell Company, 1959; Apollo Editions, 1970. Grades 5 up.
Newbery Award Book, 1960. Tells a warm story of a young boy and his friendship with an old and quite unusual man, Onion John.


LABASTIDA, Aurora. See: Ets, Marie Hall.

LAMB, Charles and Mary. Tales from Shakespeare. Illustrated by Arthur Rackham. E. P. Dutton & Company, Inc. Originally published 1807. Grades 6-9.
Twenty plays, both comedies and tragedies, recreated in a vocabulary mirroring Shakespeare's in range and choice, yet presented with a simplicity and economy suitable for young readers.

LAMOURISSE, Albert. The Red Balloon. Illustrated. Doubleday & Company, Inc., 1956. Grades 3-5.
Moods of childhood in Paris.
The "adventures of a little Parisian boy who finds a magic balloon that follows him everywhere. The photographs were taken during the filming of the movie The Red Balloon, which won an Academy Award."--Publishers Weekly.

LANG, Andrew. The Adventures of Odysseus. Illustrated by Joan Kiddell-Monroe. E. P. Dutton & Company, Inc. Originally published 1879. Grades 5-9.
Following closely the Iliad and Odyssey, an expert classical scholar retells the ancient, thrilling epic of the Trojan War and the adventures of Odysseus homeward-bound across the "wine-dark sea" to Ithaca.

LARRICK, Nancy. Junior Science Book of Rain, Hail, Sleet, and Snow. Illustrated. Garrard Publishing Company, 1961. Grades 2-5.

This story of weather was written by the editor of the
Junior Science series. She explains how to identify various cloud formations and what they foretell. Two-color
illustrations or photos.

LATHAM, Jean Lee. Carry On, Mr. Bowditch. Illustrated
by John O'Hara Cosgrave II. Houghton Mifflin Company,
1955. Grades 7-12.
Winner of the Newbery Medal; ALA Notable Book. "Delightful, interesting, and inspiring biography of a rather
obscure yet important figure in the maritime history of
our country.... Illustrations, rich in detail ... add
authenticity and value. Excellent format...."--Library
Journal.

_____. Sam Houston: Hero of Texas. Illustrated. Gar-
rard Publishing Company, 1965. Grades 2-5.
The stirring story of Sam Houston, a great American
soldier and statesman, was written by a Newbery Award
winner. A Discovery Book, with more than 18 full-page,
3-color illustrations.

LATOURETTE, Jane. Daniel in the Lion's Den. Illustrated
by S. Mathews. Concordia Publishing House, 1966.
Grades ps-4.
An Arch Book, presenting a Bible story in colorful,
easy-to-read form.

_____. House on the Rock. Illustrated by S. Mathews.
Concordia Publishing House, 1966. Grades ps-4.
An Arch Book, presenting a Bible story in colorful,
easy-to-read form.

_____. Jon and the Little Lost Lamb. Illustrated by
Betty Wind. Concordia Publishing House, 1965. Grades
ps-4.
An Arch Book, presenting a Bible story in colorful,
easy-to-read form.

_____. Story of Noah's Ark. Illustrated by S. Mathews.
Concordia Publishing House, 1965. Grades ps-4.
An Arch Book, presenting a Bible story in colorful,
easy-to-read form.

LATTIN, Anne. Peter's Policeman. Illustrated by Gertrude
Espenschied. Follett Publishing Company, 1958. Grades
2-4.
Peter gets a chance to ride in the sidecar of Officer
Green's motorcycle and see some of the things that keep
a policeman busy.

LAUBER, Patricia. Junior Science Book of Icebergs and
Glaciers. Illustrated. Garrard Publishing Company,
1961. Grades 2-5.
This is a vivid, scientific report on the Big Ice that has

baffled the world for centuries.  It tells about the Ice
Age and the prospects of a second Ice Age to come, as
well as how glaciers and icebergs are formed.  Two-
color illustrations or photos.
_____.  Junior Science Book of Penguins.  Illustrated.
Garrard Publishing Company, 1963.  Grades 2-5.
Among the world's most remarkable birds, penguins have
fascinated men for centuries.  This account of their cu-
rious habits is illustrated with stunning photographs from
three nations.
_____.  Junior Science Book of Volcanoes.  Illustrated.
Garrard Publishing Company, 1965.  Grades 2-5.
The awesome forces in the earth that create volcanoes
are described in this informative and exciting book.
Readers learn how this strange kind of mountain grows,
how it becomes active or quiet, and how they have existed
for centuries.  Two-color illustrations or photos.
LAWSON, Robert.  Ben and Me.  Illustrated by the author.
Little, Brown and Company, 1939.  Grades 4-6.
Benjamin Franklin as seen by his friend, a mouse.
_____.  Mr. Revere and I.  Illustrated by the author.
Little, Brown and Company, 1953.  Grades 4-6.
His horse tells about Paul Revere.
_____.  Rabbit Hill.  Illustrated by the author.  The Vik-
ing Press, Inc., 1944; Dell Publishing Company, Inc.,
1968.  Grades 2-6.
Awarded the Newbery Medal.  "The story of the animals
on Rabbit Hill and their excitement when they learn that
'New Folks' are coming to live in the 'Big House.'"--
Kirkus.
"Robert Lawson has made immortal the animals on Rab-
bit Hill by the rich texture and lively humor which en-
dow both the story and illustrations.  His own delight
and appreciation of the flavor of the Connecticut countryside and the animals is conveyed in harmonious pages.
The individuality of each animal is fully realized."--
Saturday Review.
_____.  They Were Strong and Good.  Illustrated by the
author.  The Viking Press, Inc., 1940.  Grades 4-6.
Winner of the Caldecott Award.  "This is not ancestor
worship; it is feeling the sap ascend in one's veins.
None of Mr. Lawson's folks reached the headlines, but
this is their memorial ... an expression of that ideal
of individual value on which the destiny of the world de-
pends."--New York Herald Tribune.
_____.  The Tough Winter.  Illustrated by the author.
The Viking Press, Inc., 1954.  Grades 4-6.

Father and Uncle Analdas, Little Georgie and Willie
Fieldmouse, with help from the other Rabbit Hill animals, deal with the dire emergencies brought by ice
storms and food shortages and, worst of all, a caretaker
and his stupid dog. A perfect combination of text and
drawings.

LEAF, Munro. The Story of Ferdinand. Illustrated by Robert Lawson. The Viking Press, Inc., 1936. Grades
K-3.
The story of the little bull who would rather just sit and
smell the flowers than fight. A childhood classic.

_____. Wee Gillis. Illustrated by Robert Lawson. The
Viking Press, Inc., 1938. Grades K-3.
Runner-up, Caldecott Medal Award. "Prepare for a
winter of bonnets and plaids, for here comes Wee Gillis
with the biggest bagpipe in all Scotland. Robert Lawson
brings us the Highlands and the Lowlands just as vividly
as he did pre-war Spain. His Scotchmen's faces are
superb. Welcome Wee Gillis!"--Saturday Review.

LEIPOLD, Edmond L. Famous American Indians. T.S.
Denison & Company, Inc. Grades 5-7.
Contents: Will Rogers, Jim Thorpe, Sitting Bull, Geron-
imo, Pocahontas, Charles Curtis, Maria Martinez,
Osceola, Pontiac, Oscar Howe. Each biography details
vibrantly the character and personality of the person
being considered. Not only are the lives of these people
written about, but the reader is given a taste of the
times, and feels as if he is living history itself. America
is great because its people have made it so. These
books will be a most valuable addition to any classroom's
reference library.

_____. Famous American Negroes. T.S. Denison &
Company, Inc. Grades 5-7.
Contents: Matt Hensen, Jean Du Sable, James Beck-
wourth, Paul Laurence Dunbar, Crispus Attucks, Esteban,
George Washington Carver, Edward W. Brooke, Marian
Anderson, Dr. Ralph Bunche. Each biography details
vibrantly the character and personality of the person being considered, and the reader is given a taste of the
times in which the biographee lived.

LEMMON, Robert S. Parks and Gardens. Illustrated.
Creative Educational Society, Inc. in cooperation with
the National Audubon Society, 1967. Grades 4-8.
Text is by an authority in the subject, and the photographs by top-notch specialists. In this book young readers are invited to discover the rich world of living activity just beyond their doors--the communities of birds,

insects, plants, and other forms of life that exist in ur-
ban and suburban areas.  This book "guides the city
child to nature study in his own backyard and introduces
him to the more familiar plants and animals found
there."--Booklist.
LENARD, Alexander, translator.  See: Milne, A.A.
L'ENGLE, Madeleine.  A Wrinkle in Time.   Farrar, Straus
& Giroux, Inc., 1962.  Grades 6 up.
Won the Newbery Medal, 1963; an ALA Notable Book,
1962.  "Two children, accompanied by an older boy, go
on a search for their missing scientist-father--a dangerous search that takes them through space by means of
a 'tesseract,' or wrinkle in time, to the dark planet
Camazotz, whose puppetlike inhabitants are controlled by
IT, a disembodied brain.  The spellbinding, thought-
provoking story is written with the same perceptive char-
acterization and warm family relationships which marked
the author's Meet the Austins."--ALA Booklist.
LENSKI, Lois.  Cotton in My Sack.  Illustrated by the author.  J.B. Lippincott Company, 1949; Dell Publishing
Company, Inc., 1966.  Grades 3-7.
Written at the request of Arkansas children, this story
is a revealing account of life among the sharecroppers,
tenant farmers, and farm owners of the Cotton Belt.
_____ .  The Little Family.  Illustrated by the author.
Doubleday & Company, Inc., 1932.  Grades ps-1.
Things a family does.
_____ .  Strawberry Girl.  Illustrated by the author.  J.B.
Lippincott Company, 1945; Dell Publishing Company, Inc.,
1967.  Grades 3-7.
Winner of the Newbery Medal in 1946.  Birdie Boyer
was a Florida Cracker.  She belonged to a large "strawberry family," who lived on a flatwoods farm in the lake
section of the state.  They raised strawberries for a
living.
Through all the hazards of the uncertain crop--battling
against dry weather and grass fires, the roving hogs and
cattle of their neighbors--Birdie dreamed of an education that would include playing the organ.  In the end
she won not only the title of "strawberry girl," but book
learning as well.
This is a regional story full of enterprise and fun and
the excitement of real life in this interesting part of
America.  The author's illustrations are distinguished
for their action and fascinating detail.  They add greatly
to this true picture of Florida life at a time when old
Florida ways were changing to new.

LEOKUM, Arkady.  Lots More Tell Me Why.  Illustrated by
     Cynthia and Alvin Koehler.  Grosset & Dunlap, Inc.,
     1971.
     In the same format as the first three volumes in this
     series, with material arranged in convenient sections,
     covering such subjects as the Human Body, Animals,
     Plants, The World We Live In, the Universe, and other
     topics.  Here are more than 400 questions and answers,
     with illustrations in one and two colors.  A complete
     list of Questions and Answers at the back of the book
     makes it simple to find specific questions on any subject
     covered.
          .  More Tell Me Why.  Illustrated by Cynthia and
     Alvin Koehler.  Grosset & Dunlap, Inc., 1967.  Grades
     ps-2.
          .  Still More Tell Me Why.  Illustrated by Cynthia
     and Alvin Koehler.  Grosset & Dunlap, Inc., 1968.
     Grades 4-9.
          .  Tell Me Why.  Illustrated by Cynthia and Alvin
     Koehler.  Grosset & Dunlap, Inc., 1969.  Grades 4-9.
     Three volumes of the series.
LEVINE, I.E.  Electronics Pioneer, Lee De Forest.  Julian
     Messner Division of Simon & Schuster, Inc., 1964.
     Grades 7 up.
     Biography of "the father of radio" (1873-1961), a U.S.
     inventor.
LEVINGER, Elma Ehrlich.  Albert Einstein.  Julian Mes-
     sner Division of Simon & Schuster, Inc., 1949.  Grades
     7-10.
     Biography of the German-born physicist (1879-1955) who
     introduced the theory of relativity, received the Nobel
     Prize in Physics, 1921, and became an American citizen
     in 1940.
          and Lee J.  See:  Gersh, Harry.
LEWELLEN, John.  The True Book of Farm Animals.  Illus-
     trated by D. Mutchler.  Children's Press, 1954.  Grades
     K-4.
     Science and social studies ... these factual books ex-
     plain so many of the things that puzzle inquisitive young
     minds.  Students use the True Books for supplementary
     work in their classes; to find out about special things
     that interest them; and to learn on their own.  Each fas-
     cinating True Book encourages a child to further his
     search for the answers he wants.  Easy to read, packed
     with information, the True Books are excellent for pri-
     mary and intermediate grades.  Color illustrations.

LEWIS, Richard, editor.   Miracles: Poems by Children of
the English-Speaking World.  Illustrated.  Simon &
Schuster, Inc., 1966.   Grades 2-6.
An ALA Notable Children's Book.   Black-and-white and
halftone illustrations by children.   "... If there were
Caldecott and Newbery awards for poetry this year,
surely at the top of everybody's list would be Miracles."
--Lavinia Russ.
LINDGREN, Astrid.   Pippi Goes on Board.   Illustrated by
Louis S. Glanzman.   The Viking Press, Inc., 1957.
Grades 4-6.
Translated by Florence Lamborn.   "Nothing ever happens
in an ordinary way around Pippi, not even departure for
the cannibal isles.   Superior nonsense."--New York Her-
ald Tribune.
_____.   Pippi in the South Seas.   Illustrated by Louis S.
Glanzman.   The Viking Press, Inc., 1959; paperback,
1970.   Grades 4-6.
Translated by Gerry Bothmer.   "Any reappearance of
the irrepressible Pippi Longstocking is cause for celebra-
tion.   This installment is no exception."--New York
Times.
_____.   Pippi Longstocking.   Illustrated by Louis S.
Glanzman.   The Viking Press, Inc., 1950.   Grades 4-6.
Translated by Florence Lamborn.   "A rollicking story
of Pippi who lives without any grownups in a little house
at the edge of the village.   The matter-of-fact way in
which her absurd adventures are related is one of the
chief charms of this story."--Horn Book.
LINDMAN, Maj.   Flicka, Ricka, Dicka and the New Dotted
Dresses.  Illustrated by the author.  Albert Whitman
& Company, 1939.   Grades ps-2.
"Mrs. Lindman writes and paints pictures for the pre-
school children and those in the first grade--simple little
stories of Swedish children like those in any family whose
children are loving and want to be good....   They are
just what their readers want; they are loved and they
last."--New York Herald Tribune.
_____.   Flicka, Ricka, Dicka and the Three Kittens.  Il-
lustrated by the author.   Albert Whitman & Company,
1941.   Grades ps-2.
See description of the author's Flicka, Ricka, Dicka and
the New Dotted Dresses.
_____.   Snipp, Snapp, Snurr and the Big Surprise.  Illus-
trated by the author.   Albert Whitman & Company, 1937.
Grades ps-2.
See description of the author's Flicka, Ricka, Dicka and
the New Dotted Dresses.

_____. Snipp, Snapp, Snurr and the Buttered Bread. Il-
lustrated by the author. Albert Whitman & Company,
1934. Grades ps-2.
See description of the author's Flicka, Ricka, Dicka and
the New Dotted Dresses.
_____. Snipp, Snapp, Snurr and the Gingerbread. Illus-
trated by the author. Albert Whitman & Company, 1936.
Grades ps-2.
See description of the author's Flicka, Ricka, Dicka and
the New Dotted Dresses.
_____. Snipp, Snapp, Snurr and the Magic Horse. Illus-
trated by the author. Albert Whitman & Company, 1933.
Grades ps-2.
See description of the author's Flicka, Ricka, Dicka and
the New Dotted Dresses.
_____. Snipp, Snapp, Snurr and the Red Shoes. Illus-
trated by the author. Albert Whitman & Company, 1932.
Grades ps-2.
See description of the author's Flicka, Ricka, Dicka and
the New Dotted Dresses.
_____. Snipp, Snapp, Snurr and the Yellow Sled. Illus-
trated by the author. Albert Whitman & Company, 1936.
Grades ps-2.
See description of the author's Flicka, Ricka, Dicka and
the New Dotted Dresses.
LIONNI, Leo. Swimmy. Illustrated by the author. Pantheon
Books, 1963. Grades ps-1.
Illustrated in full color. "An exquisite picture book
which truly reflects the ethereal quality of underwater
life.... A little fish, the lone survivor of a school of
fish swallowed by a tuna, devises a plan to camouflage
himself and his new companions.... The pictures will
evoke continuing awe from artistic, perceptive children."
--Library Journal.
LIPSCOMB, George D. See: Graham, Shirley.
LLOYD, Mary Edna. Jesus, the Little New Baby. Illustrated by Grace Paull. Abingdon Press, 1951. Grades
ps-2.
A simple retelling of the Nativity. Gray Donkey, Brown
Cow, and White Dove join all creatures in loving worship
of the Christ Child.
LOFTING, Hugh. The Story of Doctor Dolittle. Illustrated
by the author. J.B. Lippincott Company, 1920; Dell
Publishing Company, Inc. Grades 3 up.
Doctor Dolittle--a little old doctor who has so many
animal pets all over his house that his patients won't
visit him--becomes the animals' own doctor, able to

speak their languages and cure their sufferings.  When
he learns of an epidemic among the monkeys in Africa,
the good old doctor sets sail at once.
Hugh Lofting was an officer in the Irish Guards when he
found that writing illustrated letters to his children eased
the terrific strain of war which he felt so keenly.  These
letters became The Story of Doctor Dolittle, published in
1920.  Since then children all over the world have read
it with the other books that followed.  They have been
translated into almost every language.
"The most delightful nonsense story of the year....  Any
father with a sense of nonsense and love of animal and
human-kind will enjoy reading it aloud.  I fancy it will
be found as often in the hands of big boys as little ones,
since it is the real thing in the way of a 'funny book.' "
--Anne Carroll Moore, New York Public Library.
_____ .  The Voyages of Doctor Dolittle.  Illustrated by
the author.  J.B. Lippincott Company, 1922; Dell Publishing Company, Inc.  Grades 3 up.
Winner of the Newbery Medal in 1923.  It is Tommy
Stubbins, the cobbler's son, who tells this story of Doctor Dolittle's wonderful voyage to Spidermonkey Island.
Tommy Stubbins was a little boy who wanted to be a
naturalist when he grew up.
One day he got acquainted with Doctor Dolittle, and after
that his dreams began to come true; for that kindly little
man promised to teach him all he knew about animals
and their languages, and to take him along on his next
voyage of discovery.  They decided where to go by open-
ing the atlas with their eyes shut and touching the page
with a pencil.
All in all it was perhaps the most amazing voyage that
has ever been heard of.  The excitement began with four
stowaways (one of them the cat's-meat-man!); then came
the Doctor's discovery of the key to the language of the
shellfish, through his meeting with a Fidgit.  After that,
events crowd thick and fast:  the stop at a Spanish island where the Doctor creates a sensation as matador
at a bullfight; the shipwreck; the landing on a Floating
Island; and all the adventures there till the Doctor is
crowned king by the devoted natives and has to be got
away home to Puddleby by stealth.
LONDON, Jack.  The Call of the Wild.  Illustrated by
Charles Pickard.  E.P. Dutton & Company, Inc., 1968.
Originally published 1903.  Grades 7 up.
From a life of ease as a puppy, Buck was thrust into
a fiercely embattled existence, where both men and dogs

behaved like savages.  The only law was the law of the
club and the fang.
LONGFELLOW, Henry Wadsworth.  The Song of Hiawatha.
Illustrated by Joan Kiddell-Monroe.  E. P. Dutton & Company, Inc., 1959.  Originally published 1855.  Grades 4-
8.
Romantic Indian epic of the legendary Hiawatha and his
bride, Minnehaha, in the unrhymed verse of one of
America's favorite poets.
LOW, Donald F.  The How and Why Wonder Book of Sea
Shells.  Illustrated by Cynthia and Alvin Koehler.  Wonder-Treasure Books, Inc.  Grades 2-7.
Questions most commonly asked by boys and girls are
answered in this authoritative and handsome volume of
easy-to-understand information.  Illustrated in full color
and black and white.  Edited under the supervision of
Dr. Paul Blackwood, U. S. Office of Education.  All text
and art are checked for accuracy by Oakes White of the
Brooklyn Children's Museum.


McCALL, Yvonne.  Braggy King of Babylon.  Illustrated.
Concordia Publishing House, 1969.
An Arch Book, presenting a Bible story in colorful,
easy-to-read form.
McCLOSKEY, Robert.  Blueberries for Sal.  Illustrated by
the author.  The Viking Press, Inc., 1948; paperback,
1968.  Grades K-3.
Runner-up, Caldecott Medal Award.  "The adventures of
a little girl and a baby bear while hunting for blueberries
with their mothers one bright summer day.  All the col-
or and flavor of the sea and the pine-covered Maine
countryside."--Library Journal.
_____ .  Centerburg Tales.  Illustrated by the author.
The Viking Press, Inc., 1951.  Grades 4-6.
"The inimitable Homer Price will be assured of a warm
welcome by scores of admirers in these fresh escapades....  The illustrations evoke a spontaneous sense
of recognition and mirth."--Grade Teacher.
_____ .  Homer Price.  Illustrated by the author.  The
Viking Press, Inc., 1943.  Grades 4-6.
"Rollicking fun breaks through every page and picture
in this new book.  In six hilarious episodes it introduces
a genuine small boy in the best Tom Sawyer tradition,
living in a truly American town."--Horn Book.
_____ .  Lentil.  Illustrated by the author.  The Viking
Press, Inc., 1940.  Grades K-3.
"Puts before the reader a complete small Middle-West-

ern town. Boys and girls from nine on are entertained
by Lentil's problems and his final triumph as a musician.... Older boys and adults are particularly appre-
ciative of the humor and human nature of the drawings.
Lentil adds to the gaiety of life."--New York Times.
_____. Make Way for Ducklings. Illustrated by the au-
thor. The Viking Press, Inc., 1941; paperback, 1969.
Grades K-3.
Winner of the Caldecott Medal Award. "One of the mer-
riest picture-books ... told in very few words with a
gravity that underscores the delightful comedy of the pic-
tures--fine large pictures, strongly drawn, with a wealth
of detail."--New York Times.
_____. One Morning in Maine. Illustrated by the author.
The Viking Press, Inc., 1952. Grades K-3.
Runner-up, Caldecott Medal Award. "In crisp blue ink
see a happy young family on an island off the Maine
coast. The story will delight those of four to eight who
know about losing that first wobbly tooth. The pictures
will alternately amuse those small ones the age of Sal,
and charm the grownups who share this artist's love of
shores where pines meet big red rocks, where a seal
might poke up his nose to see a little girl with a hole
in her mouth."--New York Herald Tribune.
_____. Time of Wonder. Illustrated by the author. The
Viking Press, Inc., 1957. Grades K-3.
Winner of the Caldecott Award. "In prose that has the
quality of poetry, and in beautiful pictures, [here is] a
Maine island from a foggy morning in spring through the
approach of fall. A book of great beauty."--Horn Book.
McCORMICK, Dell J. Paul Bunyan Swings His Axe. Illustrated by the author. The Caxton Printers, Ltd., 1936.
Grades 4-6.
Stories of the fabulous deeds of Paul Bunyan, mythical
giant lumberjack of the north woods, are here arranged
for children, together with amazing details about his
camp and Babe, the Blue Ox. Colored frontispiece and
black-and-white drawings by the author.
McCORMICK, Jack. Atoms, Energy, and Machines. Illustrated. Creative Educational Society, Inc. in cooperation
with the American Museum of Natural History, 1967.
Grades 5-9.
In this book the reader learns principles of chemistry
and physics through clear explanations based on simple,
everyday examples. Then he sees how these principles
are applied in modern technology. Numerous diagrams
and photographs are coordinated closely with the text to

develop understanding. Strategically placed questions
encourage the reader to think and respond on his own.
MacDONALD, George. At the Back of the North Wind. Illustrated by Ernest H. Shepard. E.P. Dutton & Company, Inc. Originally published 1871. Grades 4-7.
The haunting beauty of MacDonald's fairy tales illumines
this story of the friendship between the little son of a
coachman and the lovely lady with the flowing hair who
whisked him off to the back of the north wind.
     . The Lost Princess: A Double Story. Illustrated
by D.J. Watkins-Pitchford. E.P. Dutton & Company,
Inc., 1965. Grades 3-7.
Rosamund, the selfish princess, and Agnes, the arrogant
shepherdess, come mysteriously to the dwelling place of
the Wise Woman and experience the wonders and terrors
of her strange teachings. "Only George MacDonald, the
master of the allegorical fairy tale, could have given
such a story the power to live: it is as important today
as it was in the nineteenth century. Children of every
period should have available books that can give such
imaginative and philosophical experiences as this one
can."--Horn Book.
MacDONALD, Golden. The Little Island. Illustrated by
Leonard Weisgard. Doubleday & Company, Inc., 1946.
Grades 1-3.
All about the seasons.
     . Red Light Green Light. Illustrated by Leonard
Weisgard. Doubleday & Company, Inc., 1944. Grades
ps-2.
Children's traffic lesson.
McDONALD, Pauline. See: Brown, Doris V.
McINTIRE, Alta. Follett Beginning-To-Read Picture Diction-
ary. Illustrated by Janet LaSalle. Follett Publishing
Company, 1959. Grades 1-3.
Each of the 174 attractive pictures illustrates a basic
word in the primary vocabulary.
McKAY, Don, editor. On Two Wheels: An Anthology about
Men and Motorcycles. Dell Publishing Company, Inc.,
1971. Grades 7 up.
Stories, essays, poems and songs about motorcycling
chosen for their literary merit as well as for their
readability and appeal, these pieces by Arlo Guthrie,
Hunter S. Thompson, Horace McCoy and others make
exciting and gripping reading.
     . Wild Wheels. Dell Publishing Company, Inc.,
1969. Grades 7 up.
The excitement of the race, the terror of the accident,
and the humor of the road are captured in this collection

of great stories about men and their cars.

McKINNON, Lise Somme, translator. See: Friis-Baastad, Babbis.

McSWIGAN, Marie. Snow Treasure. Illustrated by Mary Reardon. E. P. Dutton & Company, Inc., 1942. Grades 3-7.
The story, based on fact, of how Norwegian children smuggled gold out of Norway during the German occupation. "Well written and superior to previous books about the war in that the actions of the children are planned and controlled by their elders. Striking black-and-white illustrations."--Booklist.

MARTIGNONI, Margaret E., editor. Illustrated Treasury of Children's Literature. Illustrated. Grosset & Dunlap, Inc., 1969; originally 1955. Grades 5-8.
Compiled with the original illustrations under the direction of P. Edward Ernest; Staff editors; Doris Duenewald; Evelyn Andreas and Alice Thorne. "More than 250 of the world's best-loved stories--some complete, some brief excerpts--fairy tales, fables, poems, nursery rhymes and legends--plus a picture alphabet. A few of the 163 well-known authors and illustrators whose works appear in this book are: Robert Louis Stevenson, Rudyard Kipling, William Shakespeare, Aesop, Beatrix Potter, Leonard Weisgard, Willy Pogany."--McClurg. Book News.

MARTIN, Patricia Miles. Show and Tell. Illustrated by Tom Hamil. G. P. Putnam's Sons, 1962. Grades K-3.
Jeffry and his mother take his dog Bongo to school to present at Show and Tell, but Bongo chases a cat out the window, so Jeffry presents his mother to the class instead.--J. K.

MARTINI, Teri. The True Book of Indians. Illustrated by C. Heston. Children's Press, 1954. Grades K-4.
These factual books explain so many of the things that puzzle inquisitive young minds. Students use the True Books for supplementary work in their classes, to find out about special things that interest them, and to learn on their own. Each fascinating True Book encourages a child to further his search for the answers he wants. Easy to read, packed with information, the True Books are excellent for primary and intermediate grades. Color illustrations.

MATHEWSON, Robert. The How and Why Wonder Book of Birds. Illustrated by Walter Ferguson. Wonder-Treasure Books, Inc., 1960. Grades 2-7.
Questions most commonly asked by boys and girls are answered in this authoritative and handsome volume of

easy-to-understand information.  Illustrated in full color
and black and white.  Edited under the supervision of
Dr. Paul Blackwood, U.S. Office of Education.  All text
and art are checked for accuracy by Oakes White of the
Brooklyn Children's Museum.

    .  The How and Why Wonder Book of Reptiles and
Amphibians.  Illustrated by Allen D. Sweet.  Wonder-
Treasure Books, Inc., 1960.  Grades 2-7.
See description of the author's How and Why Wonder
Book of Birds.

MAXWELL, Gavin.  Ring of Bright Water.  Illustrated.
E. P. Dutton & Company, Inc., 1961.  Grades 7 up.
"It was a good idea to bring out this shortened edition
of Ring of Bright Water prepared by the author himself.
Added episodes describe fun with a third otter, Tako,
and new photographs are included.  The more than eighty
pictures, five in color, are completely captivating."--
Horn Book.  The latest edition is entitled The Otters'
Tale.

MAY, Madeline.  Fun with Dots.  Illustrated.  Follett Publishing Company, 1969 (3d ed.).  Grades ps-3.
A Follett Activity Fun Book.

MAZER, Bill.  The Answer Book of Sports.  Illustrated.
Grosset & Dunlap, Inc., 1969.  Grades 9 up.
A beautiful large-size book resplendent with color illus-
trations throughout.  Edited by Lud Durosks.

MEEKS, Esther.  The Curious Cow.  Illustrated by Mel
Pekarsky.  Follett Publishing Company, 1960.  Grades
1-3.
A humorous account of the misadventures of a cow with
one fault--curiosity.  "... gay spoof that children like
to relax with...."--Scholastic Teacher.

    .  In John's Back Yard.  Illustrated by Jessica
Zemsky.  Follett Publishing Company, 1957.  Grades
1-3.
While looking for a lost ball, John discovers that his
back yard is full of interesting things.  An introduction
to nature study.

    .  Something New at the Zoo.  Illustrated by Hazel
Hoecke.  Follett Publishing Company, 1957.  Grades 1-3.
Alice and her mother visit the zoo and are surprised to
find a children's zoo for baby animals.

MEIGS, Cornelia.  Invincible Louisa.  Illustrated.  Little,
Brown and Company, 1968; originally 1933.  Grades 7 up.

A new edition of the Newbery Award biography of Louisa
May Alcott with a new introduction by the author.   Published to honor the Centennial of Little Women.   Illustrated with 19 photographs.

MELVILLE, Herman.   Moby Dick.   Illustrated.   Grosset &
Dunlap, Inc.   Originally published 1851.   Grades 4 up.
For parents to read aloud and for young readers to read
for themselves here is an easy-to-read specially edited
version of a great classic that boasts all the charm of
the original.   Illustrated in 4 colors.

G. & C. MERRIAM Company.   Webster's Elementary Dictionary.   Illustrated.   G. & C. Merriam Company, 1966.
Grades 4-7.
The only dictionary specifically written for boys and girls
in the fourth, fifth, sixth, and in some instances the
seventh grades.   All materials carefully compiled to help
in actual schoolwork.   18,000 vocabulary entries selected
for school needs in the elementary grades.   1,600 pictures to increase understanding and interest.   Three special sections to teach each boy and girl how to use the
dictionary.   Large, clear, easily readable type with sim-
plified pronunciation.   Important tables of special information conveniently listed.

MERRILL, Jean.   The Pushcart War.   Illustrated by Ronni
Solbert.   Addison-Wesley Publishing Company, 1964.
Grades 4-6.
Twenty-ton trucks versus defenseless pushcarts is the
theme of this miniature epic about the pushcart peddlers'
guerilla war against the truckers who had conspired to
run them off the streets of New York.   Warm characters
and dramatic situations enhance this funny book about a
famous episode in American history that has not happened
--yet.   Illustrated with drawings.

_____.   Shan's Lucky Knife.   Illustrated by Ronni Solbert.
Addison-Wesley Publishing Company, 1960.   Grades 2-4.
Everyone appreciates a good trick, especially if the trick
is played on a greedy trickster.   This spirited Burmese
folktale tells how Shan, a boy from the hills, is tricked
by Ko Tin, a sly boatmaster from the city of Rangoon,
and how Shan eventually evens the score by using his
head.   Illustrated in three colors.

_____.   The Superlative Horse.   Illustrated by Ronni Sol-
bert.   Addison-Wesley Publishing Company, 1961.
Grades 4-6.
A tale of ancient China about a young boy's selection of
a superlative horse for the Duke, his master.   The members of the court are not convinced, because the horse

does not appear to be anything out of the ordinary. But, when put to the test in a chariot race, the stallion wins easily and proves the boy's acuteness of judgment. Illustrated in 2 colors.

MEYERS, Earl "Bud" and Hacker, Rich. Track and Field. Illustrated. Creative Educational Society, Inc., 1962. Grades 4 up.
In many elementary and secondary schools, track and field are not taught by professionally trained sports instructors but by teachers with a background in academic subjects. This book is particularly helpful in this learning-and-teaching situation. The text and hundreds of pictures provide the reader with step-by-step explanations. All popular track and field sports are included: sprints, running, steeple-chase, low hurdles, high hurdles, relays, high jump, pole vault, shot put, discus throw, javelin, hammer throw, and cross country.

MIERS, Earl S. America and Its Presidents. Illustrated by Stanley Dersh. Grosset & Dunlap, Inc., 1970; originally 1959. Grades 6 up.
A beautiful large-size book resplendent with color illustrations throughout.

MILHOUS, Katherine. The Egg Tree. Illustrated by the author. Charles Scribner's Sons, 1950. Grades 3-4.
How to decorate an Easter egg tree is shown in this Pennsylvania Dutch story. Awarded the Caldecott Medal, 1951.

MILLER, Natalie M. The Story of Mount Vernon. Illustrated by C. Burger. Children's Press, 1965. Grades 3-5.
The bravery and daring of America's colonial and revolutionary heroes injects vibrant excitement into every page, every story of our heritage. Each book in the collection focuses on a major event, symbol or place and delves into the details that are not found in textbooks. Students react to the Cornerstones of Freedom books because they make history real and meaningful. From the personal trials of young William Bradford through the boldness of John Paul Jones and the inspiration of the Statue of Liberty, these books re-kindle an appreciation of what the United States of America means. Illustrated in color.

_____. The Story of the Liberty Bell. Illustrated by Betsy Warren. Children's Press, 1965. Grades 3-5. See description of author's The Story of Mount Vernon.

_____. The Story of the Lincoln Memorial. Illustrated by Tom Dunnington. Children's Press, 1966. Grades 3-5.

See description of author's The Story of Mount Vernon.
_____. The Story of the Star-Spangled Banner.  Illus-
trated by G. Wilde.  Children's Press, 1965.  Grades
3-5.
See description of author's The Story of Mount Vernon.
_____. The Story of the Statue of Liberty.  Illustrated
by John and Lucy Hawkinson.  Children's Press, 1965.
Grades 3-5.
See description of author's The Story of Mount Vernon.
MILLS, Dorothy.  The Book of the Ancient Greeks.  Illus-
trated.  G. P. Putnam's Sons, 1925.  Grades 8 up.
Contains black-and-white illustrations and maps.  "An
introduction to the history and civilization of Greece
from the coming of the Greeks to the conquest of Corinth
by Rome in 146 B. C."--subtitle.
_____. The Book of the Ancient Romans.  Illustrated.
G. P. Putnam's Sons, 1927.  Grades 9 up.
Contains illustrations, bibliography, and maps.  "An
introduction to the history and civilization of Rome from
the traditional date of the founding of the city to its fall
in 476 A. D."--subtitle.
_____. The Book of the Ancient World for Younger Read-
ers.  Illustrated.  G. P. Putnam's Sons, 1923.  Grades
5-9.
Contains illustrations and maps.  "An account of our
common heritage from the dawn of civilization to the
coming of the Greeks."--subtitle.
_____. The Middle Ages.  Illustrated.  G. P. Putnam's
Sons, 1935.  Grades 9 up.
Illustrated with photographs.  Tells "the story of the
Middle Ages in such a way as to bring out the most
characteristic features of the period and to emphasize
those things in medieval life which have most significance
for us today, [beginning with] the fall of Rome.... Reference is made to the invention of gunpowder and to that
of printing, to the fall of Constantinople and to the discovery of America, to the passing of feudalism and to the
work of Wycliffe...."--From Preface.
_____. Renaissance and Reformation Times.  Illustrated.
G. P. Putnam's Sons, 1939.  Grades 7-9.
"The period of the Renaissance and Reformation is in-
creasingly important for the student of today.  Miss Mills
re-creates this exciting period in history, and once more
proves her unique ability to write history which is interesting and at the same time based on sound scholarship.
She shows the essential meaning of the Renaissance period, what brought about this great change in thought and

how it affected the outward experience of the peoples of
Italy, Germany, Spain, France and England.  Included
are interesting illustrations from contemporary sources,
maps, and a time chart."--From book jacket.
MILNE, A.A.   The House at Pooh Corner.   Illustrated by
Ernest H. Shepard.   E.P. Dutton & Company, Inc.,
1961; originally 1928.   Dell Publishing Company, Inc.,
1970.   Grades K-7.
"Silly old bear," "the best bear in the world"--here
comes Pooh walking through the forest, humming proudly
to himself.   This time he and his friends, Christopher
Robin, Eeyore, Owl, Piglet, and Kanga and Little Roo
are joined by the hilarious Tigger.   Their escapades are
the funniest reading anywhere.
"This is an example of a sequel in which there seems
to be no let-down, and from all sides I catch echoes of
most joyous reactions to it."--New York Herald Tribune.
_____. Now We Are Six.   Illustrated by Ernest H. Shep-
ard.   E.P. Dutton & Company, Inc., 1961; originally
1927.   Dell Publishing Company, Inc., 1970.   Grades
K-5.
More entertaining verses and delightful pictures in the
style of When We Were Very Young.   "Gay verses about
all manner of things, which with their original rhythm
dance their way into memory."--Four to Fourteen.
This is verse for people who now are six and for people
who were that age a long time ago.   It's especially verse
for Winnie-the-Pooh fans.   Even though he has two books
of his own, he has a way of working his way into these
pages.
_____. When We Were Very Young.   Illustrated by Er-
nest H. Shepard.   E.P. Dutton & Company, Inc., 1924;
Dell Publishing Company, Inc., 1970.   Grades K-5.
Verses full of bubbling nonsense and rhythm, written for
the author's son, Christopher Robin.   It is for "very
small children (and for their elders who get a surrepti-
tious joy from what is meant for their little ones)....
Mr. Milne's gay jingles have found a worthy accompaniment in the charming illustrations...."--Saturday Review.
_____. Winnie-the-Pooh.   Illustrated by Ernest H. Shep-
ard.   E.P. Dutton & Company, Inc., 1926; Dell Publishing Company, Inc., 1970.   Grades K-7.
In the beginning, his name was Edward Bear.   His
friend, Christopher Robin, thought he should be called
Winnie-the-Pooh.   Since then Pooh has become the most
famous and loved bear in literature.   With his friends,

Piglet, Rabbit, Owl, Kanga and Little Roo, and Eeyore,
he joins Christopher Robin in adventurous exploits which
delight readers of all ages.

"Winnie-the-Pooh is a joy; full of solemn idiocies and
the sort of jokes one weeps over helplessly, not even
knowing why they are so funny, and with it all the real
wit and tenderness which alone could create a priceless
little masterpiece.   Kanga and baby Roo, Piglet, and
above all Pooh and Christopher Robin himself, are characters no one can afford to miss....   The drawings by
E.H. Shepard which accompany the story are thoroughly
delightful."--Saturday Review.

_____.   Winnie-the-Pooh's Calendar Book.   Illustrated
by Ernest H. Shepard.   E.P. Dutton & Company, Inc.
All ages.

_____ and Lenard, Alexander, translator.   Winnie Ille Pu:
A Latin Edition of Winnie-the-Pooh.   Illustrated by Er-
nest H. Shepard.   E.P. Dutton & Company, Inc., 1960.
Grades 7 up.

Latin lives again in Milne's magnum opus, Winnie-the-
Pooh.   " 'Pooh' has been a classic for so long, it's
about time he showed up in a classical tongue."--New
York Times.

"It won't surprise us if it does more to attract interest
in Latin than Cicero, Caesar and Virgil."--Chicago
Tribune.

MINARIK, Else Holmelund.   Cat and Dog.   Illustrated by
Fritz Siebel.   Harper & Row Publishers, Inc., 1960.
Grades ps-2.

An Early "I Can Read" Book.   "Frisking about, great
friends, [Cat and Dog] perform their little mischiefs,
all in keeping with their particular cat and dog personality.   And in the end, order is restored by a little girl
who loves them both."--Kirkus.

_____.   Father Bear Comes Home.   Illustrated by Mau-
rice Sendak.   Harper & Row Publishers, Inc., 1959.
Grades ps-3.

An "I Can Read" Book.   For beginning readers these
adventures of Little Bear and his friends tell of his fishing trip with Owl, and of Father Bear's homecoming.
Father Bear gives his method for curing hiccups and his
views on mermaids. --H.W. Wilson Company.

_____.   Little Bear.   Illustrated by Maurice Sendak.
Harper & Row Publishers, Inc., 1957.   Grades ps-3.
An "I Can Read" Book.   How Mother Bear copes with
"her Little Bear as he decides what to wear, as he
makes vegetable birthday soup for fear she'll forget to

bake him a cake, and as he makes a brief excursion to
the moon."--Kirkus.
    . Little Bear's Friend. Illustrated by Maurice
Sendak. Harper & Row, Publishers, Inc., 1960. Grades
ps-3.
An "I Can Read" Book. In this story, "Little Bear makes
friends with a child named Emily. With their friends,
a duck, a cat, an owl, and a hen, they play all through
the happy summer.... Only the departure of Emily
brings tears to Little Bear who is consoled by his mother with the thought that, at least, he can write to her."
--Kirkus.
    . Little Bear's Visit. Illustrated by Maurice
Sendak. Harper & Row Publishers, Inc., 1961. Grades
ps-3.
An "I Can Read" Book. Little Bear loved to visit his
grandparents. There was always so much to do, so
much to see, and so much to eat. His grandfather was
never too tired to play (that is, almost never) and his
grandmother told him stories about Mother Bear when
she was a little cub.
    . No Fighting, No Biting! Illustrated by Maurice
Sendak. Harper & Row Publishers, Inc., 1958. Grades
ps-3.
An "I Can Read" Book. "Joan, a quite proper Victorian
young lady, wants to read a book, but little Rosa and
Will will not give her a moment's peace. They push,
they squeeze, and oh, the questions they ask. And so
Joan has no recourse but to tell them an instructive and
entertaining story about two baby alligators who behave
much like the children."--Kirkus.
MINER, Irene S. The True Book of Our Post Office and Its
Helpers. Illustrated by M. Salem. Children's Press,
1955. Grades K-4.
Science and social studies ... these factual books explain so many of the things that puzzle inquisitive young
minds. Students use the True Books for supplementary
work in their classes. They use them to find out about
special things that interest them. They read them to
learn on their own. Each fascinating True Book encourages a child to further his search for the answers he
wants. Easy to read, packed with information, the True
Books are excellent for primary and intermediate grades.
Color illustrations.
    . The True Book of Plants We Know. Illustrated
by K. Murr. Children's Press, 1953. Grades K-4.
See description of author's The True Book of Our Post
Office and Its Helpers.

_____.   The True Book of Policemen and Firemen.   Illus-
trated by M. Salem.   Children's Press, 1954.   Grades
K-4.
See description of author's The True Book of Our Post
Office and Its Helpers.

MOORE, Lilian.   Golden Picture Dictionary.   Illustrated by
Joe and Beth Krush.   Western Publishing Company, Inc.,
1954.   Grades 3-5.

MOORE, Roy.   See: Brownell, Clifford.

MOREY, Walt.   Gentle Ben.   Illustrated by John Schoenherr.
E. P. Dutton & Company, Inc., 1965.   Grades 5-9.
ALA Notable Book, 1965.   Dutton Junior Animal Book
Award.   Sequoyah Award Book.   This tale of Alaska before statehood is "the warm and moving story of the
deep bond of trust and friendship between young Mark
Andersen and Ben, a huge Alaskan brown bear....   Told
with a simplicity and dignity which befits its characters,
human and animal, Gentle Ben is a memorable reading
experience...."--Library Journal.

MOSS, Jeffrey; Raposo, Joe; and Stone, Jon.   The Songs of
Sesame Street (Sesame Street Book and Record Package).
Visuals by Brian Cranner.   Children's Television Workshop.   Manufactured by Columbia Book and Record Li-
brary/CBS, Inc., 1970.   Grade ps.
"A message to parents from the producers of Sesame
Street:   This Sesame Street record book and record
package was created in cooperation with CBS Records to
provide your child with audio-visual material designed
for his entertainment and to further develop his confidence, and those skills and motivations which are en-
couraged on our television show.   The pictures, songs
and printed material in this package have all been prepared under the direct supervision of the staff of Sesame
Street.   If your child watches Sesame Street, he will
recognize many of the elements presented here, but it
is not necessary for him to watch Sesame Street to be
able to enjoy the contents in this package."
Titles and singers of the songs:   "Sesame Street," the
entire cast; "ABC-DEF-GHI," Big Bird; "I've Got Two,"
Big Bird and Oscar plus everybody including Mr. Hopper;
"Goin' for a Ride," Anything People; "What are Kids
Called," Bob and Susan; "Everybody Wash," Ernie and
Bert; "One of These Things," Bob and Susan; "Up and
Down," Two Monsters; "Green," Kermit; "Somebody
Come and Play," the Kids; "I Love Trash," Oscar; "A
Face," Bob; "J-Jump," the Kids; "People in Your Neigh-
borhood," Bob and the Anything People; "Rub Your Tum-

my," Gordon; "Number 5," the Kids; "Five People in
My Family," Anything People; "Nearly Missed," Susan;
"Rubber Duckie," Ernie.
MOTHER GOOSE.   Big Book of Mother Goose.   Illustrated
by Alice Schlesinger.   Grosset & Dunlap, Inc.   Original-
ly published about 1760.   Grade ps.
A giant-size favorite for the youngest reader, with glow-
ing full-color illustrations on every page.
        .   Mother Goose.   Illustrated by Gyo Fujikawa.
Grosset & Dunlap, Inc.   Grades ps-1.
        .   Mother Goose:   The Classic Volland Edition.
Edited by Eulalie O. Grover.   Illustrated by Frederick
Richardson.   Hubbard Press, 1971; originally 1915.
Grades ps-3.
This classic has been in print continuously since 1915
and is the oldest and most respected Mother Goose book
in the U.S.   The full-color reproductions of Frederick
Richardson's famed original paintings present the whole
delightful cast of nursery rhyme characters from Jack
and Jill to Humpty Dumpty.   Selected as one of the ten
outstanding picture books of the year for 1971 by the
New York Times Book Review.   The new edition has
160 pages with 108 full-color plates and 140 additional
rhymes.   Yolanda Federici, Director of Children's Books,
Chicago Public Library, has written a new introduction
for this printing.
        .   Mother Goose Rhymes.   Platt & Munk Company.
Grades ps-2.
Acclaimed as America's favorite collection of Mother
Goose rhymes, this colorful, charming edition delights
the youngest reader with its jolly illustrations.   A peren-
nially fast-selling favorite.
        .   The Real Mother Goose.   Illustrated by Blanche
Fisher Wright.   Rand McNally & Company, 1916.   Grades
ps-1.
Old Mother Goose is still the reigning favorite among
youngsters and this famous edition is the perfect intro-
duction to her charms.   All the lilting verses, charming-
ly illustrated in full color.
        .   The Tall Book of Mother Goose.   Illustrated by
Feodor Rojankovsky.   Harper & Row Publishers, Inc.,
1942.   Grades ps-1.
Color pictures.
        .   The Tenggren Mother Goose.   Illustrated by
Gustav Tenggren.   Little, Brown and Company, 1940.
Grades 1-3.
The Mother Goose that children love.   With pictures in
full color.

⸱ The Very Young Mother Goose. Edited and illustrated by Margot Austin (pseud.). Platt & Munk Company, 1963. Grades ps-3.
Mother Goose rhymes delightfully illustrated in full color
by Margot Austin to make a most appealing book for the
very young.

MUELLER, Virginia. King's Invitation. Illustrated. Concordia Publishing House, 1968. Grades 3-4.
An Arch Book, presenting a Bible story in colorful, easy-
to-read form.

⸱ Secret Journey. Illustrated by B. Wind. Concordia Publishing House, 1968. Grades 4-6.
An Arch Book, presenting a Bible story in colorful, easy-
to-read form.

MUKERJI, Dhan Gopal. Gay Neck: The Story of a Pigeon.
Illustrated by Boris Artzybasheff. E. P. Dutton & Company, Inc. Originally published 1927. Grades 7 up.
A moving story of a carrier pigeon in India whose young
master sends him to serve in World War I. "The 1928
Newbery winner has been effectively redesigned, retain-
ing the original Artzybasheff decorations at the beginning
and end of each chapter; the jacket is joyous."--The
Kirkus Reviews.

MYERS, Caroline Clark, compiler. Holiday (Craft) Handbook
No. 1. Illustrated. Highlights For Children, Inc., 1965.
Grades K-6.
This handbook presents 186 creative suggestions for the
leading holidays and seasons of the school year. "Most
of the features are suited for use in several different
grades, recognizing the wide individual differences, interests, art skills, and creative talents among children of
any grade.... The aim has been to keep material costs
down and teacher-effort at a minimum."--From Foreword.

MYERS, Garry Cleveland. Creative Thinking Activities; A
Highlights Handbook. Illustrated. Highlights For Children, Inc., 1965. Grades K-6.
"A handbook of mental exercises planned to enable children
of every age and ability level to think creatively. It is
not based on book knowledge but on what is in the child's
head. Children will have fun in learning to observe, re-
call, imagine, judge, compare, classify, arrive at con-
clusions, and see causal relations. They will quickly
discover that there may be many answers to these exercises, depending on their experiences and reasoning power.... This volume has been compiled from features ap-
pearing in Highlights For Children, most of which were
originally created by Dr. Garry Cleveland Myers, Ph.D."
--From Foreword.

MYRICK, Mildred. The Secret Three. Illustrated by Arnold Lobel. Harper & Row Publishers, Inc., 1963. Grades ps-3.
An "I Can Read" Book. Two boys find a message in a bottle on the beach, and answer it, and finally meet and form a secret club with their correspondent.--J.K.

NESS, Evaline. Sam, Bangs and Moonshine. Illustrated by the author. Holt, Rinehart and Winston, Inc., 1966. Grades ps-2.
Samantha (known as Sam) is a fisherman's daughter who dreams rich and lovely dreams--moonshine, her father says. But when her tall stories nearly bring disaster to her friend Thomas and her cat Bangs, Sam learns to distinguish between moonshine and reality. Illustrated in 3 colors. An ALA Notable Book. Horn Book Honor List, 1967. The Caldecott Medal, 1967.
NEUFELD, John. Edgar Allan. Illustrated by Loren Dunlap. S.G. Phillips, Inc., 1968. Grades 5-8.
A novel about a white family that adopts a Negro child. "A serious work of art...."--New York Times
_____ . Lisa, Bright and Dark. S.G. Phillips, Inc., 1969. Grades 7 up.
"Compassionate and tragic, an indictment of adults who refuse to get involved, this novel follows three teenagers as they try 'group therapy' in order to help a mentally ill girl friend."--New York Times, Outstanding Books of the Year.
NEVILLE, Emily Cheney. It's Like This, Cat. Illustrated by Emil Weiss. Harper & Row Publishers, Inc., 1963. Grades 5 up.
1964 Newbery Medal Award Winner. Told in the first person, this is a record of "the adventures and family affairs of [Dave Mitchell], a teen-age New York City boy who befriends a homeless tomcat."--Book Buyer's Guide.
NEWBERRY, Clare Turlay. April's Kittens. Illustrated by the author. Harper & Row Publishers, Inc., 1940. Grades ps-3.
The tale of a "one-cat apartment," and of what happened when the pet cat had kittens.
_____ . Marshmallow. Illustrated by the author. Harper & Row Publishers, Inc., 1942. Grades ps-2.
"A true story, with all the pictures done from life, about Mrs. Newberry's pet cat, Oliver, and her rabbit, Marshmallow. The illustrations, in 2 colors, are reproduced by photogravure."--Huntting.

NEWELL, Hope.  The Little Old Woman Who Used Her Head.
Illustrated by Margaret Ruse.  Thomas Nelson Inc.,
1935.  Grades ps-3.
Ten short stories about a little old woman who solves
her problems the hard way, turning simple situations
into complicated ones--logical foolishness.  Ideal for
reading aloud.
NICHOLSON, Thomas D.  See:  Chamberlain, Joseph M.
NOBLE, Iris.  Joseph Pulitzer, Front Page Pioneer.  Julian
Messner Division of Simon & Schuster, Inc., 1957.
Grades 6 up.
Biography of Pulitzer (1847-1911), U.S. journalist and
publisher born in Hungary, who established the Pulitzer
Prize.
_____.  Megan.  Julian Messner Division of Simon &
Schuster, Inc., 1965.  Grades 7 up.
"A good picture of immigrant life and of the various
nationalities which, despite differences and prejudice,
came to regard themselves and each other as Canadians."
--ALA Booklist.
NORTH, Sterling.  Rascal:  A Memoir of a Better Era.  Il-
lustrated by John Schoenherr.  E.P. Dutton & Company,
Inc., 1963.  Grades 6 up.
Runner-up, Newbery Medal, 1964.  Aurianne Award,
1965.  ALA Notable Book, 1963.  Sequoyah Award, 1966.
William Allen White Award, 1966.  Dorothy Canfield
Fisher Award, 1965.  Dutton Animal Book Award, 1963.
Autobiographical.  The warm, delightful story of one
year in the life of a young boy at the close of World
War I, and of his companion, the beguiling little raccoon
who made that year memorable.  "A vibrant picture of
a bygone age, flavored with a generous pinch of nostal-
gia, this book will be loved by those who want a gentle
reminiscence of the past."--Library Journal.
_____.  The Wolfling.  Illustrated by John Schoenherr.
E.P. Dutton & Company, Inc., 1969.  Grades 7 up.
Subtitle:  "A documentary novel of the eighteen-seven-
ties."
NORTHRUP, Marguerite, editor.  The Christmas Story.
Illustrated.  The Metropolitan Museum of Art, 1966.
Grades 3 up.
The familiar accounts from the Gospels of Matthew and
Luke are combined with paintings and woodcuts of the
XV and early XVI centuries.  Among the artists are Fra
Angelico, Robert Campin, Sassetta, Giovanni di Paolo,
Dieric Bouts, Hieronymus Bosch, and Gerard David.
Almost all of the plates were made directly from the
originals.  28 illustrations, 12 in color.

O'DELL, Scott. <u>Island of the Blue Dolphins</u>. Illustrated by
Milton Johnson. Houghton Mifflin Company, 1960.
Grades 7-12.
Winner of the Newbery Medal; ALA Notable Book. "A
haunting and unusual story based on the fact that in the
early 1800's an Indian girl spent 18 years alone on a
rocky island far off the coast of California ... a quiet
acceptance of fate characterizes her ordeal."--Library
Journal.

O'HARA, Mary. <u>My Friend Flicka</u>. J.B. Lippincott Company, 1941; Dell Publishing Company, Inc. Grades 5-9.
Set against the panoramic beauty of the Wyoming green-
grass country, this sympathetic novel introduces us to
Ken McLaughlin, his family, and the stormy wild-tem-
pered filly he named Flicka. "A beautiful book.... It
will pass into that borderland where some of the best-
loved books in the English tongue hold their immortality,
on the shelf with Treasure Island and Dumas and Dickens...."--New York Herald Tribune.

OLDS, Helen. <u>Miss Hattie and the Monkey</u>. Illustrated by
Dorothy Marino. Follett Publishing Company, 1958.
Grades 1-3.
"All children's libraries need this type of book ... to
provide pleasurable and successful experiences to the
beginning reader."--School Library Journal.

OLIPHANT, David D., Jr. <u>Backyard Bandits--Including
California Raccoons and Other Exciting Patio Visitors</u>.
Illustrated. Naturegraph Books, 1968. Grades 4 up.
About thirty-five years of the adventures of a man and
his wife with many wild animals in their own backyard.
Raccoons and their intriguing antics cover most of the
book, but there are vivid chapters on skunks, opossums,
deer and others.

O'NEILL, Mary. <u>Hailstones and Halibut Bones</u>. Illustrated
by Leonard Weisgard. Doubleday & Company, Inc.,
1961. Grades K-5.
Adventures in Color. Twelve children's poems. "The
twelve poems make vivid every sense and dimension of
color--sound, taste, smell, feel, as well as sight."--
Huntting.

OTTO, J.R. "Bob." <u>Football</u>. Illustrated. Creative Educational Society, Inc., 1962. Grades 4 up.
When a boy plays football in school, he soon discovers
that the game he is now playing is a great deal different
from unorganized games. This book is written specifically for that boy, who is generally of elementary or high
school age. The author provides a complete guide to

football:   How Football Began, Fundamental Techniques,
Plays and Play Situations, Football Comes of Age, Sports-
manship, Test Your Knowledge.


PAPE, Donna Lugg.   King Robert the Resting Ruler.   Illustrated by Lola Edick Frank.   Oddo Publishing, Inc.,
1968.   Grades 2-5.
A speech improvement book.   For the (R) sound.   Poor
Queen Grace has quite a problem.   King Robert cannot
be aroused to rule his kingdom.   When she offers re-
wards for arousing King Robert, many try unusual things
to wake the resting king.   But, as the reader will learn,
it is often the simplest thing that is the solution to a
big problem.   Full-color illustrations.
_____.   Liz Dearly's Silly Glasses.   Illustrated by Lola
Edick Frank.   Oddo Publishing, Inc., 1968.   Grades 2-5.
A speech improvement book.   For the (L) sound.   Lovable Liz Dearly needs glasses, but buys some bargain
glasses for her eyes instead of seeing Doctor Loo.   The
glasses she buys from Peddler Luke Plass turn out to
be not such a bargain.   Children will chuckle at the situations Liz gets into with her silly glasses, and will
agree with Liz who learns at the end of the story that
a bargain is not always a bargain.   Full-color Illustrations.
_____.   Professor Fred and the Fid-Fuddlephone.   Illus-
trated by Lola Edick Frank.   Oddo Publishing, Inc.,
1968.   Grades 2-5.
A speech improvement book.   For the (F) sound.   Flute-
tooting musician, Professor Fred, is a fine flute player,
but when his flute becomes damaged he decides to try a
new instrument.   He succeeds in finding a very odd instrument, a fid-fuddlephone, but forgets an important
thing--to do anything well takes practice--which he learns
the hard way when he tries to give a fid-fuddlephone
concert in Farmagie Hall.   Full-color illustrations.
_____.   Scientist Sam.   Illustrated by Lola Edick Frank.
Oddo Publishing, Inc., 1968.   Grades 2-5.
A speech improvement book.   For the (S) sound.   When
Scientist Sam takes off into outer space hoping to find
more unusual species of insects for a collection to enter
in the World's Fair, he finds out-of-this-world speci-
mens.   His hilarious adventures cause a bit of trouble
in his rocket take-off to return home.   He learns that
it isn't quantity, but quality that counts.   Full-color illustrations.

_____. Shoemaker Fooze. Illustrated by Lola Edick
Frank. Oddo Publishing, Inc., 1968. Grades 2-5.
A speech improvement book. For the (Sh) sound. What
a sad shoemaker is Shoemaker Fooze for nobody comes
to buy his shoes! All attempts to improve his business
fail, and finally Shoemaker Fooze comes up with a unique
shoe that wins him fame--a real surprise and an amusing climax. Full-color illustrations.

_____. The Three Thinkers of Thay-Lee. Illustrated by
Lola Edick Frank. Oddo Publishing, Inc., 1968. Grades
2-5.
A speech improvement book. For the (Th) sound, un-
voiced. Thimp, Thamp and Thone become tired of doing
King Thorro's thinking for him. They come up with a
clever idea to give the king confidence in his own ability
to think, a valuable lesson for the reader as well as an
amusing story. Full-color illustrations.

PARKER, Bertha Morris. Golden Book of Science. Illustrated by Harry McNaught. Western Publishing Company,
Inc., 1963; originally published 1952 by Golden Press.
Contains short sections on many science topics of popular
interest, such as: "How old is old?" "A million kinds of
animals"; "Seeds that go traveling"; "The food we eat";
"Grand Canyon"; "Storms"; "Light"; "Building blocks";
etc. Illustrated in color.--J.K.

PATTERSON, Lillie. Frederick Douglass, Freedom Fighter.
Illustrated. Garrard Publishing Company, 1965. Grades
2-5.
An escaped slave himself, Douglass (1817-1895) spent
much of his life trying to free others. This is a portrait of a truly great American. A Discovery Book,
with more than 18 full-page, 3-color illustrations.

PAYNE, Emmy. Katy No-Pocket. Illustrated by H.A. Rey.
Houghton Mifflin Company, 1944. Grades K-3.
A Junior Literary Guild Selection. "A kangaroo mother
without a pouch is in a quandary. Katy asked other
animal mothers what to do, but their methods didn't fit.
The owl helps solve the difficulty.... Truly amusing
pictures...."--Library Journal.

PECK, Richard. See: Hoopes, Ned E.

PEMBERTON, Lois Loyd. The Stork Didn't Bring You. Illustrated by S. Lodico. Thomas Nelson Inc., 1966;
original edition 1948. Grades 4-9.
Presents the facts of life for teen-agers in a language
and style which they can appreciate. The author levels
with the young adult and writes good common sense without covering up unpleasant topics or repeating worn-out
sermons.

PÉNE DU BOIS, William. Bear Party. Illustrated by the
author. The Viking Press Inc., 1963; paperback, 1969.
Grades K-3.
Runner-up, Caldecott Medal Award. "There is fun and
wisdom and friendliness; there are colors and costumes
and merriment; there are bears in fancy dress in the
most delightful combinations and contrasts. A beautiful
piece of bookmaking."--Christian Science Monitor.
_____. The Horse in the Camel Suit. Illustrated by the
author. Harper & Row Publishers, Inc., 1967. Grades
1-5.
A mystery story book.
_____. The Twenty-One Balloons. Illustrated by the au-
thor. The Viking Press Inc., 1947. Grades 4-6.
Winner of the Newbery Award. "When Professor William
Waterman Sherman was found adrift in the Atlantic cling-
ing to the debris of twenty balloons, all America was
rocked with curiosity. Much of this story, we are informed, is based on scientific principles. We'll leave
that to the boys for proof and enjoy the tale for its dead-
pan humor which mingles extravaganza with the smallest
practicalities."--New York Times.
PETERSHAM, Maud and Miska. The Christ Child. Illustrated. Doubleday & Company, Inc., 1931. Grades 1-6.
Bible verses.
PETERSON, Edward C. See: Bullock, Henry M.
PIPER, Watty (pseud.), editor. The Bumper Book. Illustrated. Platt & Munk Company, 1946. Grades ps-3.
A rich harvest of stories and poems with such favorites
as "The Owl and the Pussycat," "Christopher Robin Is
Saying His Prayers," "The Easter Rabbit," and many
more, illustrated in full color.
_____, editor. The Gateway to Storyland. Illustrated.
Platt & Munk Company, 1954. Grades ps-3.
Stories and poems every child should know, from "Peter
Rabbit" to "The Gingerbread Boy," with appealing full-
color illustrations on each page.
_____. The Little Engine That Could. Illustrated by
George and Doris Hauman. Platt & Munk Company,
1954; originally 1929. Grades ps-2.
The complete, original text, illustrated in full color.
One of the all-time classics in children's literature. An
appealing little tale of the courageous little blue engine
who wouldn't give up without trying. "I think I can, I
think I can, I think I can ...," she said as she pulled
a load of food and toys over the mountains for good girls
and boys. Selected as a Notable Children's Book by the

ALA. "Will be going strong, years after today's adult best-seller has gone into literary limbo."--Life Magazine.
_____, editor. Stories That Never Grow Old. Illustrated. Platt & Munk Company. Grades ps-3.
An all-time favorite edition of 15 classic tales--"The Ugly Duckling," "The Lion and the Mouse," "The Bremen Town Musicians," and others--in a book that overflows with color and charm.

PLATT & MUNK Company. Junior Crossword Puzzle Book. Platt & Munk Company. Grades 3-7.
More puzzles, using a specially selected vocabulary.
_____. My First Crossword Puzzle Book. Platt & Munk Company. Grades 3-7.
Fascinating puzzles conveniently arranged in order of difficulty.
_____. 1001 Riddles. Platt & Munk Company. Grades 3-7.
A jumbo harvest of intriguing riddles.

PODENDORF, Illa. The True Book of Animal Babies. Illustrated by P. Adams. Children's Press, 1955. Grades K-4.
Science and social studies ... these factual books explain so many of the things that puzzle inquisitive young minds. Students use the True Books for supplementary work in their classes. They use them to find out about special things that interest them. They read them to learn on their own. Each fascinating True Book encourages a child to further his search for the answers he wants. Easy to read, packed with information, the True Books are excellent for primary and intermediate grades. Color illustrations.
_____. The True Book of Insects. Illustrated by C. Maltman. Children's Press, 1954. Grades K-4.
See description of author's The True Book of Animal Babies.
_____. The True Book of Moon, Sun and Stars. Illustrated by L. Fisher. Children's Press, 1954. Grades K-4.
See description of author's The True Book of Animal Babies.
_____. The True Book of Pebbles and Shells. Illustrated by M. Gehr. Children's Press, 1954. Grades K-4.
See description of author's The True Book of Animal Babies.
_____. The True Book of Science Experiments. Illustrated by M. Salem. Children's Press, 1954. Grades K-4.

See description of author's The True Book of Animal
Babies.
_____. The True Book of Seasons. Illustrated by M.
Gehr. Children's Press, 1955. Grades K-4.
See description of author's The True Book of Animal
Babies.
POLITI, Leo. Song of the Swallows. Illustrated by the au-
thor. Charles Scribner's Sons, 1949. Grades K-3.
Story of the swallows and their return to the Mission at
San Juan Capistrano each year at the same time.
Awarded the Caldecott Medal, 1950.
PRATT, Fletcher. The Civil War. Illustrated by Lee J.
Ames. Doubleday & Company, Inc., 1955. Grades 3-9.
Highlights of battles.
PRICE, Roger. Droodles. Illustrated. Price, Stern,
Sloan, Publishers, Inc., 1965.
A collection of hilarious Droodle classics.
_____ and Stern, Leonard. Mad Libs. Price, Stern,
Sloan, Publishers, Inc., 1958.
Each Mad Libs book contains stories in which key words
are left out. One person asks others for words to fill
in blanks. When the spaces are filled, a fantastic,
idiotic, titillating, or philosophical Mad Lib is born.
_____ and Stern, Leonard. Mad Libs No. 5. Price,
Stern, Sloan, Publishers, Inc., 1968.
See description of the authors' Mad Libs.
_____ and Stern, Leonard. Mad Libs Six. Price, Stern,
Sloan, Publishers, Inc., 1970.
See description of the authors' Mad Libs.
_____ and Stern, Leonard. Monster Mad Libs. Price,
Stern, Sloan, Publishers, Inc., 1965.
See description of the authors' Mad Libs.
_____ and Stern, Leonard. Son of Mad Libs. Price,
Stern, Sloan, Publishers, Inc., 1959.
See description of the authors' Mad Libs.
_____ and Stern, Leonard. Sooper Mad Libs. Price,
Stern, Sloan, Publishers, Inc., 1962.
See description of the authors' Mad Libs.
_____ ; Stern, Leonard; and Sloan, Larry. Elephants,
Grapes & Pickles. Price, Stern, Sloan, Publishers,
Inc., 1964.
More elephant jokes, combined with additional non sequitur
humor.
_____ ; Stern, Leonard; and Sloan, Larry. M Is For Mon-
ster. Price, Stern, Sloan, Publishers, Inc., 1965.
A collection of werewolf, vampire and other invaluable
monster jokes.

_____ ; Stern, Leonard; Sloan, Larry; and Weinrib, Lennie.
The Elephant Book. Price, Stern, Sloan, Publishers,
Inc., revised 1968.
The book that fostered the national elephant joke craze;
a humor classic.

PRICE, Stern, Sloan, Publishers. The World's Worst Jokes,
by the Editors. Price, Stern, Sloan, Publishers, Inc.,
1969.
The craziest, classic non sequitur jokes.

PRIOR, Brenda. Little Sleeping Beauty. Illustrated. Concordia Publishing House, 1969.
An Arch Book, presenting a Bible story in colorful,
easy-to-read form.

PURCELL, John W. The True Book of Holidays. Illustrated
by A. Kohn. Children's Press, 1955. Grades K-5.
These factual books explain so many of the things that
puzzle inquisitive young minds. Students use the True
Books for supplementary work in their classes; to find
out about special things that interest them; and to learn
on their own. Each fascinating True Book encourages
a child to further his search for the answers he wants.
Easy to read, packed with information, the True Books
are excellent for primary and intermediate grades. Col-
or illustrations.

PYLE, Howard. Men of Iron. Illustrated by the author.
Harper & Row Publishers, Inc. Originally published
1891. Grades 5-11.
"How Miles wins his spurs and vanquishes his own and
his father's enemy. A splendid portrayal of life in the
great castles and of the training of young nobles for
knighthood in the days of Henry IV of England."--Toron-
to.

_____ . Pepper and Salt. Illustrated by the author.
Harper & Row Publishers, Inc., 1885. Grades 1-5.
A book of stories. Contents: "The Skillful Huntsman,"
"Claus and His Wonderful Staff," "How Dame Margery
Twist Saw More Than Was Good for Her," "Clever Peter
and the Two Bottles," "Hans Hecklemann's Luck,"
"Farmer Griggs's Boggart," "The Bird in the Linden
Tree," "The Apple of Contentment."

_____ . Some Merry Adventures of Robin Hood of Great
Renown in Nottinghamshire. Illustrated by the author.
Charles Scribner's Sons, 1954. First published about
1490. Grades 4-6.
Contains twelve stories of Robin Hood and his followers.

PYRNELLE, Louise Clarke. Diddie, Dumps and Tot. Pelican Publishing Company, 1963. Originally published
1882.

Reprint of children's classic of life on old Southern Plantation. First published by Harper's in 1882; later published by Grosset & Dunlap; reissued by Pelican in 1963 (the 21st edition).

RANKIN, Louise S. Daughter of the Mountains. Illustrated by Kurt Wiese. The Viking Press Inc., 1948. Grades 4-6.
Prizewinner, New York Herald Tribune's Children's Spring Book Festival. Runner-up, Newbery Medal Award. "This is a story of Tibet and of a journey to the plains of India that was taken by Momo, in search of her little dog, Pempa. The story of her adventures flows along easily with mounting suspense."--Saturday Review.

RANSOME, Arthur. Old Peter's Russian Tales. Thomas Nelson Inc. Originally published 1916. Grades 5-8.
Twenty fairy tales told by a master storyteller. A classic of children's literature.

RAPOSO, Joe. See: Moss, Jeffrey.

RAVIELLI, Anthony. Wonders of the Human Body. Illustrated by the author. The Viking Press Inc., 1954. Grades 4-6.
An ALA Notable Book. "The artist's generously illustrated introduction to anatomy--bones, muscles, nerves, digestive and circulatory system--will serve better than most existing material to explain many of the miracles of the human body. Its text is clear and imaginative." --Horn Book.

RAWLINGS, Marjorie Kinnan. The Yearling. Illustrated by N. C. Wyeth. Charles Scribner's Sons, 1938; 1967. Grades 9 up.
Story of Jody Baxter and his orphan fawn in the scrub forest of Florida. Pulitzer Prize Award, 1939.

REID, John Calvin. Bird Life in Wington. Illustrated. William B. Eerdmans Publishing Company. Grades 3-6.
Over 50 birds, such as "Bing" Canary, Mr. Pelican of the Great A & P Sea Food Company, Mr. Buzzard, Billy Gerty Goose, the Fuller Grass Salesman, and Pastor Penguin, in 30 object lessons depict important lessons in Christian living.

REIDY, John P. See: Richards, Norman.

RESS, Etta Schneider. Field and Meadow. Illustrated. Creative Educational Society, Inc. in cooperation with the National Audubon Society, 1967. Grades 4-8.
This book integrates earth science, ecology and conservation. It "points out the role of plants in sustaining all

other life, nature's adaptation to the seasons, the characteristics of warm and cold-blooded animals, man's
use and abuse of the land, and his increasing attempts
to control and utilize the natural bounty that he has in-
herited."--The Booklist.
Text is by an authority in the subject, and the photographs by top-notch specialists.

REY, H.A.   Anybody at Home?   Illustrated by the author.
Houghton Mifflin Company, 1942.   Grades K-3.
This little paperbound book is a longtime favorite of
very young children.   Each page has a picture that contains a secret.   Open the flap and the mystery is revealed.

_____.   Curious George.   Illustrated by the author.
Houghton Mifflin Company, 1941.   Grades K-3.
ALA Notable Book.   "This satisfyingly funny book is
about a monkey whose curiosity led him into all sorts
of adventures....   Small children will wear the book out
with affection ... jolly bright pictures in the French
manner."--Horn Book.

_____.   Curious George Gets a Medal.   Illustrated by the
author.   Houghton Mifflin Company, 1957.   Grades K-3.
"In popularity, Curious George seems to be running a
close second to the much-loved elephant, Babar, and
children will welcome with great delight this fourth book
about the engaging little monkey who is as good at getting
out of trouble as he is at getting into it...."--Horn Book.

_____.   Curious George Learns the Alphabet.   Illustrated
by the author.   Houghton Mifflin Company, 1963.   Grades
K-3.
"Curious George is as mischievous as ever, as the man
with the yellow hat attempts to teach him the alphabet....
The text is both informative and amusing....   A delightful way to meet the alphabet."--Library Journal.

_____.   Curious George Rides a Bike.   Illustrated by the
author.   Houghton Mifflin Company, 1952.   Grades K-3.
"To his great delight, George is presented with a small
bike; agrees to help a boy with his paper route; and is,
again, because of his curiosity, led into a fascinating
adventure...."--Horn Book.

_____.   Curious George Takes a Job.   Illustrated by the
author.   Houghton Mifflin Company, 1947.   Grades K-3.
"That indefatigable little monkey George, who was captured in Africa in an earlier book because he was curious ... continues his career in a tale of rippling fun
and absurd color-pictures...."--New York Herald Tribune.

_____. Feed the Animals. Illustrated by the author.
Houghton Mifflin Company, 1944. Grades K-3.
This little paperbound book is a longtime favorite of very
young children. Each page has a picture that contains
a secret. Open the flap and the mystery is revealed.
_____. Where's My Baby? Illustrated by the author.
Houghton Mifflin Company, 1943. Grades K-3.
This little paperbound book is a longtime favorite of very
young children. Each page has a picture that contains
a secret. Open the flap and the mystery is revealed.
REY, Margret and H.A. Curious George Flies a Kite. Il-
lustrated by H.A. Rey. Houghton Mifflin Company, 1958.
Grades K-3.
"All the boys and girls who never tire of hearing about
George will be delighted with this new book they can
read by themselves. Only 218 different words have been
used.... Amazing that it can be made so interesting
... sure-fire stuff...."--Library Journal.
RICHARDS, Norman, and Reidy, John P. John F. Kennedy.
Illustrated. Children's Press, 1967. Grades 6 up.
A book in the People of Destiny series on 20th-century
leaders who have shaped the future. These are excellent
biographies, lavishly illustrated with newspaper photographs that capture the importance of some of the greatest events in the 20th century. Each book is a vibrant
portrait of an outstanding person. Objective and accurate,
all manuscripts were read and approved by the subjects
themselves or by someone close to them. Each book
opens on a vivid moment of destiny--then flashes back to
re-create each person's intriguing life story.
ROBBIN, Irving. The How and Why Wonder Book of Explorations and Discoveries. Illustrated by Darrell Sweet.
Wonder-Treasure Books, Inc. Grades 2-7.
Questions most commonly asked by boys and girls are
answered in this authoritative and handsome volume of
easy-to-understand information. Illustrated in full color
and black and white. Edited under the supervision of
Dr. Paul Blackwood, U.S. Office of Education. All text
and art are checked for accuracy by Oakes White of the
Brooklyn Children's Museum.
ROBERTSON, Keith. Henry Reed, Inc. Illustrated by Robert McCloskey. The Viking Press Inc., 1958. Grades
4-6.
William Allen White Award, 1961. An ALA Notable
Book. This is the journal of Henry Reed, son of an
American diplomat. "Hilarious situations which are be-
wildering to their elders, disconcerting to themselves,
and fun for the reader."--Saturday Review.

_____. Henry Reed's Baby-Sitting Service. Illustrated
by Robert McCloskey. The Viking Press Inc., 1966.
Grades 4-6.
William Allen White Award, 1969. "The reason that the
Henry Reed books are so effectively funny is that Henry's
narrative is so calm, straightforward and unexaggerated,
and that he and Midge walk into uproars so naturally and
logically. This time it's a baby-sitting service."--The
Kirkus Service.
_____. Henry Reed's Journey. Illustrated by Robert
McCloskey. The Viking Press Inc., 1963. Grades 4-6.
"From San Francisco across the continent to Grover's
Corner, New Jersey, Henry Reed travels with Midge
Glass and her family in this second book about two irre-
pressible young people...."--Library Journal.
ROBINSON, Tom. Buttons. Illustrated by Peggy Bacon.
The Viking Press Inc., 1938; paperback, 1968. Grades
K-3.
"In all the long gallery of cat characters Buttons is des-
tined to a pre-eminent position. His story is told by
Tom Robinson in short, hard-hitting sentences, and by
Peggy Bacon, who does the best illustrating of her ca-
reer."--New York Times.
ROGERS, Lou. The First Thanksgiving. Illustrated by
Michael Lowenbein. Follett Publishing Company, 1963.
Grades 2-4.
Tells why the Pilgrims came to America, how they lived
their first year at Plymouth, and how they celebrated
their first Thanksgiving.
ROJANKOVSKY, Feodor, editor. The Tall Book of Nursery
Tales. Illustrated by the editor. Harper & Row Pub-
lishers, Inc., 1944. Grades ps-1.
Color pictures.
ROMANO, Louis. See: Georgiady, Nicholas.
ROOD, Ronald N. The How and Why Wonder Book of Ants
and Bees. Illustrated by Cynthia and Alvin Koehler.
Wonder-Treasure Books, Inc. Grades 2-7.
Questions most commonly asked by boys and girls are
answered in this authoritative and handsome volume of
easy-to-understand information. Illustrated in full color
and black and white. Edited under the supervision of
Dr. Paul Blackwood, U.S. Office of Education. All text
and art are checked for accuracy by Oakes White of the
Brooklyn Children's Museum.
_____. The How and Why Wonder Book of Insects. Illus-
trated by Cynthia Koehler. Wonder-Treasure Books,
Inc., 1960. Grades 2-7.

See description of author's The How and Why Wonder
Book of Ants and Bees.
ROSS, David, editor. Illustrated Treasury of Poetry for
Children. Illustrated by Burmah Burris et al. Grosset
& Dunlap, Inc., 1970. Grades 4 up.
A collection of the best-loved and best-known poems in
the English language, and many poems less well known.
There are poems for children to read alone or among
themselves and poems for adults and children to read
together.... Included are works by such great masters
as Shakespeare and Milton, by Walt Whitman, Carl Sandburg, and Langston Hughes ... excerpts from the majes-
tic King James Version of the Bible as well as rollicking songs, limericks, and light verse by such as W. S.
Gilbert, Edward Lear, Charles E. Carryl, and Oliver
Wendell Holmes. The poems are illustrated in color by
a variety of artists both classic and modern.--From book
jacket.
RUSKIN, Ariane. The Pantheon Story of Art for Young People. Illustrated. Pantheon Books, 1964. Grades 7-8.
Illustrated with 68 full-color and 90 black-and-white
plates. "An excellent brief survey of art traces the
development of painting and sculpture from cave to modern.... The text is informative and pleasantly informal
and the more than 150 illustrations of works of art, half
of which are in color, are well chosen and well reproduced."--ALA Booklist.
RYAN, Betty Molgard. Sally Alligator. Illustrated by Howard Lindberg. T. S. Denison & Company, Inc. Grades
2-3.
A nature study about the habits and life span of alligators. Sally is a baby alligator which grows up to learn
how to cope with the hazards of the water and to forage
for her own food. The narrative is developed with suspense and reveals many of the characteristics of alligators that are informative. Three-color illustrations.


SALESKA, Edward J. See: Gockel, Herman W.
SALTEN, Felix. Bambi: A Life in the Woods. Illustrated
by Barbara Cooney. Simon & Schuster, Inc., 1970;
originally published 1929. Grades 3-7.
The unforgettable story of a deer, from his first care-
free days in the meadow when he was filled with bound-
less curiosity and the thrill of discovery, to his maturity
as a handsome and noble stag--a leader of the herd.
"Just lovely--a dappled green jacket and, here and there,

bits of drawings or bigger drawings in russet and char-
coal ... an auspicious entry."--The Kirkus Reviews.

SAUER, Julia. Mike's House. Illustrated by Don Freeman.
The Viking Press Inc., 1954; paperback, 1970. Grades
K-3.
"A real and spontaneous little story that will be loved
especially by the adventurous pre-school child, who, like
its young hero, makes his way in all kinds of weather
to the library Picture Book Hour."--Horn Book.

SAUNDERS, Doris E., editor. The Day They Marched. Illustrated. Johnson Publishing Company, Inc. (Chicago),
1963.
The story of the March on Washington in August 1963
told in pictures by Ebony Magazine photographers. The
brief text carries an introduction by Lerone Bennett, Jr.,
and reprints the full text of Martin Luther King's "I
have a dream" speech and President Kennedy's state-
ment about the March.

_____. See also: Kennedy, John F.

SAUNDERS, Lowell. The Kitten Who Was Different. Illustrated by June Talarcyzk. T.S. Denison & Company,
Inc. Grades 1-6.
A story teaching respect for the handicapped which lends
encouragement to children who differ physically from
others. A kitten named Feelee has sixteen front toes
and is ridiculed by other kittens on the farm for being
different. He runs away to the forest where he encounters a wise owl who teaches Feelee that he must accept
himself and live with his handicap. Four-color illustrations.

SAUNDERS, Marshall. Beautiful Joe. Grosset & Dunlap,
Inc., 1920. Grades 4-6.
This prize-winning book is based on the author's experiences with a real dog who lived the first part of his life
with a cruel master and after being rescued from him,
lived in a happy home.

SAWYER, Ruth. Journey Cake, Ho! Illustrated by Robert
McCloskey. The Viking Press Inc., 1953; paperback,
1970. Grades K-3.
Runner-up, Caldecott Medal Award. "The remarkable
skill of both author and artist is combined in this old
favorite which will delight both old and young...."--Li-
brary Journal.

_____. and Seredy, Kate. Roller Skates. Illustrated by
Valenti Angelo. The Viking Press Inc., 1936; Dell Pub-
lishing Company, Inc. Grades 4-6.
Awarded the Newbery Medal. "For one never-to-be-for-

gotten year Lucinda Wyman (ten years old) was free to
explore New York on roller skates.  She made friends
with Patrick Gilligan and his hansom cab, with Policeman M'Gonegal, with the fruit vendor, Vittore Coppioco,
and with many others.  All Lucinda's adventures are
true and happened to the author herself.  A zestful book
of a warm rich personality to delight old and young."--
Horn Book.

SCHARFF, Robert.  The How and Why Wonder Book of
Oceanography.  Illustrated by Robert Doremus.  Wonder-
Treasure Books, Inc., 1964.  Grades 2-7.
Questions most commonly asked by boys and girls are
answered in this authoritative and handsome volume of
easy-to-understand information.  Illustrated in full color
and black and white.  Edited under the supervision of
Dr. Paul Blackwood, U. S. Office of Education.  All text
and art are checked for accuracy by Oakes White of the
Brooklyn Children's Museum.

SCHECK, Joann.  Three Men Who Walked in Fire.  Illustrated.  Concordia Publishing House, 1967.
An Arch Book, presenting a Bible story in colorful,
easy-to-read form.

_____.  Two Men in the Temple.  Illustrated by J. Rob-
erts.  Concordia Publishing House, 1968.
An Arch Book, presenting a Bible story in colorful,
easy-to-read form.

_____.  Water That Caught on Fire.  Illustrated.  Con-
cordia Publishing House, 1969.
An Arch Book, presenting a Bible story in colorful,
easy-to-read form.

SCHNEIDER, Herman and Nina.  How Big Is Big?  Illustrated by Symeon Shimin.  Addison-Wesley Publishing
Company, 1946.  Grades 2-4.
This book introduces and explores the concept of relative
size, and shows the child his relationship to all sizes of
things in the world--elephants, skyscrapers, mountains,
and planets, then puppies, mice, protozoa.  Well sup-
ported by imaginative three-color illustrations by Symeon
Shimin, this book explains where we fit into the scale
of the universe.

_____.  Let's Find Out about Heat, Water and Air.  Illus-
trated by Jeanne Bendick.  Addison-Wesley Publishing
Company, 1946.  Grades 2-4.
Curiosity and experimentation, basic tools of science,
are stimulated in this early science picture book.  The
many experiments (requiring only simple household materials and objects) demonstrate interesting physical

principles involving heat, water, and air.  Illustrated in
3 colors.

SCHOOLLAND, Marian M.  Marian's Big Book of Bible
Stories; 226 Simply Told Stories for Ages 5 to 9.  Illus-
trated.  William B. Eerdmans Publishing Company, 1947.
Grades K-4.
Even the very young child understands these stories of
unsurpassed simplicity, clarity and dignity.  Exciting
original color pictures are especially designed for the
young child.
_____. Marian's Favorite Bible Stories; A First Bible
Reader for the Young Child.  Illustrated.  William B.
Eerdmans Publishing Company, 1948.  Grades ps-1.
Captures the heart of every young child between 3 and
6 years of age.  The 63 Old and New Testament stories
are short, simple, direct and always true to the Bible.
Twelve full-page full-color pictures are full of action,
and instructive.

SCHOOR, Gene.  The Jim Thorpe Story; America's Greatest
Athlete.  Illustrated.  Julian Messner Division of Simon
& Schuster, Inc., 1951.  Grades 6 up.
Illustrated with photos; contains playing records.

SCHULZ, Charles M.  Happiness Is a Warm Puppy.  Illustrated by the author.  Determined Productions, Inc.,
1962.  Grades K-6.

SECHRIST, Elizabeth Hough, editor.  One Thousand Poems
for Children.  Illustrated by Henry C. Pitz.  Macrae
Smith Company, 1946.  Grades K-8.
A comprehensive collection of the best poetry for children of all ages.  Recently revised.

SEEGER, Ruth Crawford.  American Folk Songs for Children.
Illustrated by Barbara Cooney.  Doubleday & Company,
Inc., 1948.  Grades 1-6.
Intended for use "in home, school and nursery school;
a book for children, parents and teachers."  A big book
of 90 folk songs from all parts of the country that may
be sung and acted out with many variations.  The tunes
and piano accompaniments are simple enough for most
adults to play and there are many suggestions given for
musical play with children.  It is a source book for
family fun.--H. W. Wilson Company.

SELSAM, Millicent Ellis.  Seeds and More Seeds.  Illustrated by Tomi Ungerer.  Harper & Row Publishers,
Inc., 1959.  Grades ps-3.
Benny finds out what seeds are, some different kinds of
seeds, where they come from, what they grow into, and
how they get fertilized and grow.--J. K.

SENDAK, Maurice. Nutshell Library. Illustrated by the author. Harper & Row Publishers, Inc., 1962. All ages.
Includes: Alligators All Around; Chicken Soup with Rice;
One Was Johnny; Pierre.
_____ . Where the Wild Things Are. Illustrated by the
author. Harper & Row Publishers, Inc., 1963. Grades
ps-3.
Winner of the Caldecott Medal, 1964. "A little boy,
dressed in a wolf suit, is sent to his room for behaving
ferociously. Suddenly the walls disappear and he finds
himself in a magic forest [of wild creatures]."--Huntting.
SEREDY, Kate. The Good Master. Illustrated by the au-
thor. The Viking Press Inc., 1935. Grades 4-6.
Runner-up, Newbery Medal Award. "From the time
Cousin Kate arrives from Budapest, having been packed
off by her father because he simply couldn't put up with
her wild antics any longer, the story is agog with unexpected happenings."--Christian Science Monitor.
_____ . The Singing Tree. Illustrated by the author.
The Viking Press Inc., 1939; Dell Publishing Company,
Inc., 1971. Grades 4-6.
Life was good on the great Hungarian plains in the years
before World War I. Kate and Jancsi rode their horses
over miles of fertile land while they planned for the future: Jancsi wanted to breed the highest-stepping horses
in Europe and Kate began to think of going to dances.
Then came the war and the farm became a haven for
refugees and prisoners from the war-torn countries.
With adult responsibilities suddenly thrust on their shoul-
ders, Kate and Jancsi put the old ways behind them as
they courageously faced the future. This warm and
stirring story, a sequel to The Good Master, was a runner-up for the Newbery Medal.
"This is a great book, as lively and amusing as The
Good Master, but with a different theme: peace through
a sense of brotherhood."--Childhood Education.
_____ . The White Stag. Illustrated by the author. The
Viking Press Inc., 1937. Grades 7 up.
Winner of the Newbery Award, 1938. "The wonder of a
fairy tale, the stirring romance of heroic legend ...
rounded out with the color, atmosphere, and poetry of
this artist's retelling of the story of Atilla."--New York
Times.
_____ . See also: Sawyer, Ruth.
SERRAILLIER, Ian. The Silver Sword. Illustrated by C.
Walter Hodges. S.G. Phillips, Inc., 1959. Grades 5-9.
A virtual classic, Boys' Club of America Junior Book

Award and New York Herald Tribune Honor book. Three
Polish children trek across Europe during World War II
in search of their lost father. "A true war story full of
excitement and adventure."--Herald Tribune.

SESAME STREET writers. See: Moss, Jeffrey.

SETON, Ernest Thompson. Wild Animals I Have Known.
Illustrated by the author. Charles Scribner's Sons,
1898. Grades 5-11.
Animals' biographies contained in eight short stories.

SEUSS, Dr. (pseud.). And To Think That I Saw It on Mul-
berry Street. Illustrated by the author. Vanguard Press,
Inc., 1937; E.M. Hale and Company. Grades K-3.
A "nonsense story in verse true to a child's imagination.
In a small boy's mind a plain horse and cart on Mulberry
Street gradually grow into a circus bandwagon drawn by
an elephant and two spirited giraffes."--New York Librar-
ies.
_____ . The Cat in the Hat. Illustrated by the author.
Random House, Inc., 1957. Grades K-3.
A nonsense story in verse about an unusual cat and his
tricks which he displayed for the children one rainy day.
Only 223 different words are used in this story.
_____ . The Cat in the Hat Comes Back. Illustrated by
the author. Beginner Books Division of Random House,
Inc., 1958. Grades K-3.
"A top-notch sequel to The Cat in the Hat, providing de-
lightful fare for beginning readers. Using only 252 dif-
ferent words, the cat comes back and wreaks havoc in
the house of Sally and the teller of the story. But of
course, all is eventually put right."--Library Journal.
_____ . Dr. Seuss's ABC. Illustrated by the author.
Beginner Books Division of Random House, Inc., 1963.
Grades K-3.
_____ . The 500 Hats of Bartholomew Cubbins. Illustrated by the author. Vanguard Press, Inc., 1938.
Grades K-3.
Bartholomew never suspected there was anything strange
about his hat until the day when he took it off respect-
fully as the king passed down the street in his grand
carriage. He snatched it off and another appeared, and
another and another. The Hatmaker, the Grand Duke
Wilfred, the wise men, and the magicians (and also their
cats) were unable to solve the mystery of Bartholomew's
hats.
_____ . Green Eggs and Ham. Illustrated by the author.
Beginner Books Division of Random House, Inc., 1960.
Grades 1-2.

This nonsense story, written in rhymed verse and with
a limited vocabulary, tells of how Sam uses persistence
to prove how good green eggs and ham can be.--H. W.
Wilson Company.

_____. Hop on Pop. Illustrated by the author. Begin-
ner Books Division of Random House, Inc., 1963.
Grades 1-2.
Nonsense rhymes and pictures that teach very simple
words in a funny way. --J. K.

_____. One Fish, Two Fish, Red Fish, Blue Fish. Il-
lustrated by the author. Beginner Books Division of
Random House, Inc., 1960. Grades 1-2.
Another Dr. Seuss book of pictures and rhymes telling
about "from there to here, from here to there, funny
things are everywhere."--the author.

_____. Yertle the Turtle, and Other Stories. Illustrated
by the author. Random House, Inc., 1958. Grades K-3.
Contents: "Yertle the Turtle," "Gertrude McFuzz,"
"The Big Brag." These stories, written in rhymed
verse, appeared originally in Redbook Magazine.

SEWELL, Anna. Black Beauty. Dell Publishing Company,
Inc. Originally published 1877. Grades 3-7.
The adventures of a spirited thoroughbred horse, who,
beginning life as the favorite in a gentleman's stable,
faces a succession of misfortunes when his knees are
broken by a careless groom.

SEYTON, Marion. The Hole in the Hill. Illustrated by
Leonard Shortall. Follett Publishing Company, 1960.
Grades 1-3.
"The adventures of the prehistoric Stone family in their
search for a pet.... Cartoon-type illustrations lend a
delightful element of humor."--School Library Journal.

SHAPIRO, Milton J. Jackie Robinson of the Brooklyn Dodg-
ers. Illustrated. Julian Messner Division of Simon &
Schuster, Inc., 1966. Grades 6 up.
Illustrated with photos.

SHARP, Adda Mai. Daffy. Illustrated by Elizabeth Rice.
Steck-Vaughn Company, 1950. Grades ps-2.
Four-color art. "A first reader about Daffy, the baby
elephant who lets the other animals out of their cages to
cause subsequent confusion. Very simple text explains
each accompanying gay illustration."--Library Journal.

_____. Where is Cubby Bear? Illustrated by Elizabeth
Rice. Steck-Vaughn Company, 1950. Grades ps-2.
Four-color art. "A bright, charming little book with
pleasant, rhythmic prose for young children, and large
type and first-year words for first readers. All about

the adventures of frisky Cubby Bear and Mama Bear,
Topsy and Tubby Bear, Little Deer, and Skippy Rabbit
who try to keep up with him."--Virginia Kirkus Service.

SHARP, William, editor. The Tall Book of Fairy Tales.
Illustrated by the editor. Harper & Row Publishers,
Inc., 1947. Grades ps-3.

SHUTE, Henry A. The Real Diary of a Real Boy. Illustrated by Tasha Tudor. William L. Bauhan, Inc., 1967.
Originally published 1902. Grades 5-8.
In the winter of 1901-02, while rummaging in the shed-
chamber of his father's house, Judge Henry A. Shute
unearthed a salt-box containing: a popgun of pith elder
and hoopskirt wire, a six-inch bean blower for school
use, a frog's hind leg (extra dry), and a horde of other
treasures--among them, a manuscript marked "Diry."
The diary was written--or so its author alleged--when
he was an eleven-year-old boy growing up in the 1860's
in Exeter, New Hampshire. From the moment of its
publication in 1902, The Real Diary of a Real Boy won
immediate popularity, and for years to come was a favorite of readers, young and old alike. Now the lively
adventures of "Plupy," the real boy, are re-issued in
this new edition with delightful illustrations by Tasha
Tudor.
Plupy Shute's "Diry" makes up in wit all that it loses
in spelling. It is also an authentic chronicle of a boy's
world a century ago. That world may have vanished,
but boys still grow up, and they do it with much the
same gusto and spirit, humor and imagination, as Plupy
Shute.
The first through seventh editions of this book were published by Everett Press, Boston; the 18th through 25th
editions by Reilly and Lee, Chicago; it was re-issued by
William L. Bauhan, Inc. in 1967 with new illustrations
by Tasha Tudor.

SIEBERT, Dick. Learning How Baseball. Illustrated.
Creative Educational Society, Inc., 1968. Grades 7 up.
This practical step-by-step text is complemented by over
500 photographs. One of the finest instructional books
on baseball ever published.

SIMON, Martin P. See: Jahsmann, Allan H.

SIMON, Solomon. The Wise Men of Helm and Their Merry
Tales. Illustrated by Lillian Fischel. Behrman House,
Inc., 1945. Grades 3-7.
The New York Times hailed this "rollicking tale, a
classic of its kind, full of merriment and wisdom."
You'll agree with the Mayor of Helm when he says: "It's

not that we Helmites are fools; it's just that foolish
things are always happening to us!" "Rich in humor,
folklore quality and in the underlying truths of life."--
ALA Booklist.  Illustrated in 2 colors.

SLOAN, Larry.  See:  Price, Roger.

SLOBODKINA, Esphyr.  Caps For Sale.  Illustrated by the
author.  Addison-Wesley Publishing Company, 1947.
Grades ps-1.
"Caps for sale," calls the peddler as he walks along,
his caps piled high on his head.  But, while he takes a
nap in a quiet field, the caps are stolen by a treeful of
monkeys.  How he finally gets them back is the amusing
climax of this dramatic old tale.  Easy to act out, with
as many parts as there are children.  Four-color illustrations.

SMITH, Dodie.  The Hundred and One Dalmations.  Illustrated by Janet and Anne Grahame-Johnstone.  The Viking
Press Inc., 1957.  Grades 4-6.
"Pongo and Missis and their fifteen puppies live happily
with their human pets, the Dearlys, until the pups are
stolen.  The rescue of their own and other pups is told
with humor and suspense in an irresistible fantasy."--
ALA Booklist.

SMITH, Dorothy Hall, editor.  The Tall Book of Christmas.
Illustrated by Gertrude Elliott Espenscheid.  Harper &
Row Publishers, Inc., 1954.  Grades ps-3.

SMITHER, Ethel L.  A Picture Book of Palestine.  Illustrated by Ruth King.  Abingdon Press, 1947.  Grades 5-7.
A treasure of everyday information on the Palestine of
Bible days, authenticated by Christian and Jewish schol-
ars.

SOBOL, Donald J.  Encyclopedia Brown and the Case of the
Secret Pitch.  Illustrated by Leonard Shortall.  Thomas
Nelson Inc., 1965.  Grades 2-6.
America's Sherlock Holmes in sneakers solves ten new
mysteries in each book by commonsense methods, challenging the reader to reach the proper solution with him.
Each story is amusing and puzzling but not tricky.  The
reader can find the clues with Encyclopedia or turn to the
solutions if he is stumped.  Illustrated with black-and-
white drawings.

_____.  Encyclopedia Brown, Boy Detective.  Illustrated
by Leonard Shortall.  Thomas Nelson Inc., 1963.
Grades 2-6.
See description of the author's Encyclopedia Brown and
the Case of the Secret Pitch.

    . Encyclopedia Brown Finds the Clues. Illustrated
by Leonard Shortall. Thomas Nelson Inc., 1966.
Grades 2-6.
See description of the author's Encyclopedia Brown and
the Case of the Secret Pitch.
    . Encyclopedia Brown Gets His Man. Illustrated
by Leonard Shortall. Thomas Nelson Inc., 1967.
Grades 2-6.
See description of the author's Encyclopedia Brown and
the Case of the Secret Pitch.
    . Encyclopedia Brown Keeps the Peace. Illustrated
by Leonard Shortall. Thomas Nelson Inc., 1969.
Grades 2-6.
See description of the author's Encyclopedia Brown and
the Case of the Secret Pitch.
    . Encyclopedia Brown Saves the Day. Illustrated
by Leonard Shortall. Thomas Nelson Inc., 1970.
Grades 2-6.
See description of the author's Encyclopedia Brown and
the Case of the Secret Pitch.
    . Encyclopedia Brown Solves Them All. Illustrated
by Leonard Shortall. Thomas Nelson Inc., 1971.
Grades 2-6.
See description of the author's Encyclopedia Brown and
the Case of the Secret Pitch.
SPANGLER, Earl. The Negro in America. Lerner Publications Company. Grades 5-11.
SPAR, Jerome. The Way of the Weather. Illustrated.
Creative Educational Society, Inc. in cooperation with
the American Museum of Natural History, 1967. Grades
5-9.
In this basic volume of modern meteorology the author
describes the physical principles that govern the atmosphere and relates them to various weather phenomena.
The reader is shown how to identify many of the different weather phenomena. Text and pictures provide him
with instructions on how to make simple weather observations and how to prepare local forecasts. He is encour-
aged to apply the principles he has learned to the fascinating, ever-changing moods of the atmosphere.
SPEARE, Elizabeth George. The Bronze Bow. Houghton
Mifflin Company, 1961. Grades 7-12.
Winner of the Newbery Medal. "The book is remarkable
in its integration of setting and reality of characters--
especially Daniel and Leah, in the strength of the message without preaching, and in the holding power of the
plot.... Mrs. Speare writes with compassion and re-
straint...."--Horn Book.

_____. The Witch of Blackbird Pond. Houghton Mifflin
Company, 1958. Grades 7-12.
Winner of Newbery Medal; ALA Notable Book. "Strong
plot, fully-realized characters, and convincing atmosphere distinguish this historical narrative of a girl whose
rebellion against bigotry and her Puritan surroundings
culminates in a witch hunt and trial."--Booklist.
SPIEGELMAN, Judith. UNICEF Festival Book. Illustrated
by Audrey Preissler. United States Committee for
UNICEF, 1966.
SPILHAUS, Athelstan. The Ocean Laboratory. Illustrated.
Creative Educational Society, Inc. in cooperation with
the American Museum of Natural History, 1967. Grades
5-9.
"The author has written an outstanding beginner's introduction to the sea: its origin and structure, the terrain
of the ocean floor, the zones of the sea and their rela-
tion to climate, the life in the sea, modern methods of
oceanographic research, and the resources of the sea
and man's dependence on them. Complete with excellent
drawings and photographs, a glossary of oceanographic
terms, and an index, this exciting book should find favor
with young people."--Science Books/AAAS.
SPINK, Reginald, translator. See: Andersen, Hans Christian.
SPYRI, Johanna. Heidi. Illustrated by Vincent O. Cohen.
E.P. Dutton & Company, Inc. Another version illustrated by William Sharp. Grosset & Dunlap, Inc. Originally published 1884. Grades 3-6.
This famous story of a Swiss child and her life among
the beauties of the Alps has brought love of the mountains and mountain folk to children everywhere.
STAFFORD, Jean. Elephi, the Cat with the High I.Q. Illus-
trated by Erik Blegvad. Dell Publishing Company, Inc.,
1966. Grades 2-6.
A terribly smart and sophisticated cat, Elephi ingeniously
rescues a small car from a snowdrift and hides it in the
New York apartment where he lives.
STEIG, William. Sylvester and the Magic Pebble. Illustrated by the author. Simon & Schuster, Inc., 1969.
Grades ps-3.
Four-color illustrations. Winner of the 1970 Caldecott
Medal. "If you're not moved by Sylvester's predicament,
by the lion's bewilderment, by moods forlorn and joyous,
if you don't take to the logical, easy stance of the ani-
mal friends ... if you don't appreciate the fair beauty of
Steig's landscapes, well, then one will know for sure
who's the donkey."--New York Times.

STEINBERG, Phillip Orso.    George, the Discontented Giraffe.
Illustrated by Earl W. Moline, Jr.    T.S. Denison &
Company, Inc.    Grades K-4.
A warm tale of fact and fancy of a young giraffe and his
animal friends.    This story tells how the giraffe acquired
its long neck; for zoologists substantiate the fact that the
giraffe was once a short-necked animal, much like the
okapi that roams the arid plains of Africa.    A fine
thread of tender humor is interwoven throughout this
suspense story.    Four-color illustrations.
STERN, Leonard.    See:  Price, Roger.
STEVENS, Carla.    Rabbit and Skunk and the Scary Rock.
Illustrated by Robert Kraus.    Addison-Wesley Publishing
Company, 1962.    Grades ps-1.
A scary mystery story for beginning readers in which
Rabbit and Skunk encounter a rock that makes all kinds
of strange and spooky noises.    Their reaction to this
noisy rock and how they finally solve the mystery make
for a funny story.    Illustrated in 2 colors.
STEVENSON, Robert Louis.    The Black Arrow.    Illustrated
by Lionel Edwards.    E.P. Dutton & Company, Inc.,
1958; Dell Publishing Company, Inc.    Originally published 1888.    Grades 6-10.
Against the background of the Wars of the Roses in 15th-
century England, Dick Shelton, in a series of swift-
paced adventures, outwits his scheming guardian and
overcomes bandits and seamen to win at last the orphaned
heiress, Joanna Sedley.
          .  A Child's Garden of Verses.    Illustrated by Mary
Shillabeer.    E.P. Dutton & Company, Inc.    Another
version illustrated by Gyo Fujikawa.    Grosset & Dunlap,
Inc., 1957.    Another version published by Platt & Munk
Company.    Originally published 1885.    Grades ps-3.
From the world of childhood, which he, as few others,
could miraculously re-enter, Stevenson created these
verses of undiminishing appeal.    First published in England in 1885 under the title Penny Whistles.
          .  Kidnapped.    Illustrated by George Oakley.    E.P.
Dutton & Company, Inc., 1959; Dell Publishing Company,
Inc.    Originally published 1886.    Grades 6-10.
The tale of David Balfour, first shanghaied and shipwrecked, then--with Alan Breck--hunted by fellow Scots
as traitors to the crown.    He finally returns to Scotland
to claim his rightful inheritance from his unscrupulous
uncle.
          .  Treasure Island.    Illustrated by S. Van Abbé.
E.P. Dutton & Company, Inc.; Dell Publishing Company,

Inc.   Originally published 1883.   Grades 6-10.
A masterpiece of adventure, the story of piracy and con-
cealed treasure, set in the middle eighteenth century.
This story of Jim's discovery of a treasure map and his
subsequent voyage to Captain Kidd's former hideout presents a host of characters--including Long John Silver--
who engage in murder and mutiny before the conclusion
of the adventure.

STOLZ, Mary.   The Bully of Barkham Street.   Illustrated
by Leonard Shortall.   Harper & Row Publishers, Inc.,
1963; Dell Publishing Company, Inc., 1968.   Grades 3-7.
Martin Hastings, the bully of the block, didn't care if
he had any friends.   Large and mean, Martin was hate-
ful and irresponsible.   But was he?   A rare view
emerges of an 11-year-old boy's lonely world.   1964
Junior Books Award Medal: Boys' Club of America.

_____.   Emmett's Pig.   Illustrated by Garth Williams.
Harper & Row Publishers, Inc., 1959.   Grades ps-3.
An "I Can Read" Book.   Emmett's room in the apartment
house was filled with pigs--pig banks, glass pigs, a
stuffed pig, pictures of pigs and books about pigs.   But
he had never once seen a live pig.   And of course, a pig
was what Emmett wanted more than anything in the world.
And on his birthday he got a perfect present.

STONE, Jon.   See:  Moss, Jeffrey.

SUTTON, Felix.   The How and Why Wonder Book of Deserts.
Illustrated by Robert Doremus.   Wonder-Treasure Books,
Inc., 1965.   Grades 2-7.
Questions most commonly asked by boys and girls are
answered in this authoritative and handsome volume of
easy-to-understand information.   Illustrated in full color
and black and white.   Edited under the supervision of
Dr. Paul Blackwood, U.S. Office of Education.   All text
and art are checked for accuracy by Oakes White of the
Brooklyn Children's Museum.

SWIFT, Jonathan.   Gulliver's Travels.   Illustrated by Arthur
Rackham.   E. P. Dutton & Company, Inc., 1952.   Orig-
inally published 1726.   Grades 6 up.
A tale of imaginative voyages into places where Gulliver
encounters the tiny people of Lilliput, the giants of
Brobdingnag, and many other amazing creatures.


TALBOT, Winifred.   Happy Hospital Surprises.   Illustrated
by Lawrence Spiegel.   T.S. Denison & Company, Inc.
Grades K-4.
A story to prepare children for a hospital stay.   Larry

is going to the hospital for an operation.  In this story,
his parents prepare him by suggesting the surprises that
are in store for him.   The result is that he is happy
about his stay in the hospital because he has been alerted
about what to expect.  Four-color illustrations.

TARKINGTON, Booth.  Penrod.  Illustrated by Gordon Grant.
Doubleday & Company, Inc., 1914.  Grades 7-9.
Twelve-year-old Penrod Schofield, typical boy in a middle-class midwestern family, has trying experiences in
growing up that inspire both laughs and sympathy.

_____. Seventeen.  Grosset & Dunlap, Inc., 1970.  Orig-
inally published 1916.  Grades 5-11.
Subtitle: "A tale of youth and summer time and the
Baxter family, especially William."  Mabel Dodge Holmes
states in her introduction to the 1944 Harper edition:
"You will not fail to find funny the things that happen to
William Baxter, the just-growing-up hero of this book.
Perhaps you will even suspect at times that in laughing
at William you are laughing at yourself.  You will sym-
pathize with his trials and mourn over his disappoint-
ments and humiliations.  You will rejoice in his all-too-
few triumphs.  For Mr. Tarkington seems to understand
the struggles involved in the process of turning from
child into adult...."

TAYLOR, Sydney.  All-of-a-Kind Family.  Illustrated by
Helen John.  Follett Publishing Company, 1951; Dell
Publishing Company, Inc., 1966.  Grades 2-6.
Five high-spirited little girls have simple but happy times
together growing up on New York's Lower East Side at
the turn of the century in a family rich in kindness
though poor in money.

TAZEWELL, Charles.  The Littlest Angel.  Illustrated by
S. Leone.  Children's Press, 1966.  Grades K-3.
Classic story of a boy angel--his troubles, his triumphs,
and the "perfect" gift he brings the Christ Child.  Full
color.  Primary grade children respond to this captivating Easy Reading Picture Story Book as they reinforce
their newly acquired reading skills.

TELLANDER, Marian.  Space.  Illustrated by Robert Hedgell.
Follett Publishing Company, 1960.  Grades 2-4.
An introduction to the solar system and the universe.

TERHUNE, Albert Payson.  Lad: A Dog.  Illustrated by
Sam Savitt.  E. P. Dutton & Company, Inc., 1959.  Originally published 1919.  Grades 5 up.
Handsome Anniversary Edition of the now classic story
of Sunnybank Lad, the collie comrade of the author, first
published in 1919.  "Written with an affectionate insight

into dog character that will delight dog lovers."--Book-
list.

THOMAS, Joan Gale. If Jesus Came to My House. Illustrated by the author. Lothrop, Lee & Shepard Company,
1951. Grades K-3.
Illustrated in color. "In enchanting rhyme ... a small
boy imagines the adventures of an afternoon spent with
Jesus.... But since Jesus really can't visit him, he'll
do nice things for somebody else instead."--Chicago
Tribune.

THOMPSON, Kay. Eloise. Illustrated by Hilary Knight.
Simon & Schuster, Inc., 1955. Grades K-6.
The story of a little girl who lives at the Plaza Hotel
in New York, who has Inner Resources and is interested
in people when they are not boring, and who knows everything about the Plaza.

TRAPP, Maria Augusta. Story of the Trapp Family Singers.
Illustrated. J.B. Lippincott Company, 1949; Dell Publishing Company, Inc. Grades 5 up.
This true story tells how Maria--a young student from
an Austrian convent--became governess to the seven
children of the widowed Baron Trapp and how she later
became his wife. This book was the inspiration for the
musical and movie The Sound of Music.

TRAVERS, Pamela. Mary Poppins. See: Chase, Alice.

TRESSELT, Alvin. Rain Drop Splash. Illustrated by Leonard Weisgard. Lothrop, Lee & Shepard Company, 1946.
Grades K-3.
Caldecott Award Runner-Up, 1946. ALA Notable Book,
1946. "Striking pictures in tones of yellow and brown
and simple text, poetic in mood, describe a rainstorm
in terms a small child can understand."--ALA Booklist.
_____. White Snow, Bright Snow. Illustrated by Roger
Duvoisin. Lothrop, Lee & Shepard Company, 1947.
Grades K-3.
Illustrated in color. Caldecott Medal, 1947. ALA Notable Book, 1947. "A revelation to children who have
never known the wonder and excitement of a first snow-
fall--a miracle to those who watch for it every year that
its mystery, magic and fun have at last been captured."
--Horn Book.

TWAIN, Mark (pseud.). Huckleberry Finn. Illustrated by
C. Walter Hodges. E.P. Dutton & Company, Inc.,
1955. Originally published 1884. Grades 5-9.
The waif Huck, escaping his would-be civilizers, and the
runaway slave Jim journey by raft down the Mississippi
into varied and exciting adventures.

_____.  The Prince and the Pauper.  Illustrated by Robert Hodgson.  E. P. Dutton & Company, Inc., 1968. Originally published 1882.  Grades 5 up.
Edward was Prince; Tom was a beggar; but they happened to look exactly alike.  When they exchanged places, their strange, unconventional ways brought them endless trouble--until they were reunited.

_____.  Tom Sawyer.  Illustrated by C. Walter Hodges. E. P. Dutton & Company, Inc.  Originally published 1878. Grades 5-9.
The escapades of a mischievous boy, based on reminiscences of the author's boyhood in Missouri, full of incident and fun.

UDRY, Janice May.  A Tree Is Nice.  Illustrated by Marc Simont.  Harper & Row Publishers, Inc., 1956.  Grades ps-1.
Caldecott Award Winner, 1957.  This picture book describes the delights to be had in, with, or under a tree, and tells why it is good to have trees around.

_____.  What Mary Jo Shared.  Illustrated by Eleanor Mill.  Albert Whitman & Company, 1966.  Grades K-2. Illustrated in full color.  Mary Jo shares her father at Show and Tell.  "The Woods are Negroes and they are neither idealized nor exaggerated.  Negroes who look like Negroes are rare enough;  Negroes shown living through a universal experience are even rarer."--Kirkus.

_____.  What Mary Jo Wanted.  Illustrated by Eleanor Mill.  Albert Whitman & Company, 1968.  Grades K-3. Illustrations in full color.  A quiet story of a Negro girl who longs for a dog, gets one, and takes full responsibility for its care.  "The theme has appeal, writing style is adequate, and the illustrations show a very attractive middle-class Negro family."--U. C. Bulletin. "Ordinary childhood experiences that emphasize similarity rather than disparity between the aspirations and reactions of white and Negro children, and that's something of value to school and public library collections."--Library Journal.

VERNE, Jules.  Around the Moon.  Illustrated by W. F. Phillips.  E. P. Dutton & Company, Inc., 1970.  Grades 3-7.
Translated by Jacqueline and Robert Baldick.  Sequel to: From the Earth to the Moon.

_____    . Around the World in Eighty Days.  Illustrated
by W. F. Phillips.  E. P. Dutton & Company, Inc., 1968.
Originally published 1873.  Grades 7 up.
New translation by Jacqueline and Robert Baldick.  A
bright and free flowing translation of quixotic adventures
and ingenious methods of travel employed by Phineas
Fogg, his manservant, Passepartout, and the assiduous
detective, Fix, as they journey around the world in
eighty days to settle a wager.

_____    . From the Earth to the Moon.  Illustrated by W. F.
Phillips.  E. P. Dutton & Company, Inc., 1970.  Origi-
nally published 1865.  Grades 3-7.
Edited by Robert Baldick.

_____    . Journey to the Centre of the Earth.  Illustrated
by W. F. Phillips.  E. P. Dutton & Company, Inc., 1970.
Originally published 1864.  Grades 3-7.
Translated from the French by Robert Baldick.

_____    . Twenty Thousand Leagues Under the Sea.  Illustrated by William McLaren.  E. P. Dutton & Company,
Inc.  Originally published 1869.  Grades 5-9.
A handsome new edition of the famous 19th-century science fiction tale of Captain Nemo, the Nautilus, and adventures as exciting today as they were a century ago.

VOIGHT, Nila.  Adventures in the Neighborhood.  Illustrated.
Lawrence Publishing Company.  Grades 1-6.
A high motivation reader for encouraging interest and a
positive attitude in the slower reader, and for extending
the basic vocabulary of children in all grades.  Edited
by Ida Mulock.

_____    . Exploring around the House.  Illustrated.  Lawrence Publishing Company.  Grades 1-6.
A high motivation reader for encouraging interest and a
positive attitude in the slower reader, and for extending
the basic vocabulary of children in all grades.  Edited
by Ida Mulock.

VOS, Catherine F.  The Child's Story Bible.  Illustrated by
Betty Beeby.  William B. Eerdmans Publishing Company,
1967; originally 1949.  Grades 3-5.
Revised by Marianne Vos Radius.  The fifty original
full-color paintings by Betty Beeby, and additional art-
work and original maps, meet the highest standards of
artistic excellence and biblical accuracy.

VREEKEN, Elizabeth.  The Boy Who Would Not Say His
Name.  Illustrated by Leonard Shortall.  Follett Publishing Company, 1959.  Grades 1-3.
Bobby will tell no one his right name until he gets lost
and wants to go home.

WACKERBARTH, Marjorie.  Bobby Discovers Bird Watching.
   Illustrated by Lawrence Spiegel.  T.S. Denison & Company, Inc., 1962.  Grades 2-6.
   This is a book of bird lore that will lead a reader into
   a greater interest in the birds about him.  The reader
   learns to identify birds by the feet, flight patterns, as
   well as shape and color.  He discovers that birds stake
   out territory claims where other birds may not trespass
   during the nesting season.  He is tricked by the mimicry
   of a mockingbird.  He learns about bird flyways as well
   as many other pertinent facts.  Four-color illustrations.
   _____.  Bobby Learns about Butterflies.  Illustrated by
   Lawrence Spiegel.  T.S. Denison & Company, Inc.,
   1963.  Grades 2-6.
   A nature study about the habits, growth and development
   of butterflies.  On a fluttering golden tree in Grandpa's
   yard Bobby discovers the migrating Monarch butterfly.
   He learns about its habits, growth and development.  He
   learns the difference between moths and butterflies and
   sees some of the most interesting moths.  Four-color
   illustrations.
   _____.  Bobby Learns about Squirrels.  Illustrated by
   Lawrence Spiegel.  T.S. Denison & Company, Inc.,
   1966.  Grades 2-6.
   A nature study about the characteristics of squirrels.
   Bobby becomes interested in squirrels.  He meets the
   saucy red squirrel, the interesting albino squirrel, the
   melanistic (all black) and the erythritic (all red) squirrels.  He discovers that flying squirrels really glide
   instead of fly.  Four-color illustrations.
   _____.  Bobby Learns about Woodland Babies.  Illustrated
   by Lawrence Spiegel.  T.S. Denison & Company, Inc.
   Grades 2-6.
   A nature study about the babyhood of wild animals.  Together Bobby and his grandfather, a self-trained naturalist, roam, hike, and observe seven different wild babies
   of the woods.  From their experiences and by study in
   the library, Bobby finds out what each young animal
   must learn before it leaves its mother, about self-pres-
   ervation, home building, hunting food, and defense
   against its natural enemies.  Four-color illustrations.
   _____. and Graham, Lillian S.  Bobby Discovers Garden
   Friends.  Illustrated.  T.S. Denison & Company, Inc.,
   1960.  Grades 2-6.
   A nature study of the various wild insect life that can be
   found in the average home yard.  When Bobby becomes
   acquainted with Mr. Centipede who introduces him to all

the wild insect life in his own garden, he is given pertinent information about the life and habits of the ladybug,
the wasp, grasshopper and many other insects. Four-
color illustrations.

WAGNER, Jane. J.T. Illustrated by Gordon Parks, Jr.
Van Nostrand Reinhold Company, 1969; Dell Publishing
Company, Inc., 1971. Grades 3-8.
Illustrated with black-and-white photographs. Different
people get turned on by different things. With J.T. Gam-
ble it was a cat--an old, one-eyed, near-dead alley cat.
To hear the talk that went around, you wouldn't have
thought a kid like J.T. would have given the time of day
for anything as no-good as this cat--but he did.
The story takes place in Harlem at Christmastime.
You'll like it because it's about a boy with real feelings
and problems who is having a hard time letting people
know what he's all about. As it turns out, J.T. is a
pretty special guy. Even the grownups who had about
given up on him think so. Maybe the best thing about
this story is that everybody gets just a little closer to
what is real--and it wouldn't have happened if it hadn't
been for J.T. and his cat.--book jacket.

WALPOLE, Ellen Wales, editor. The Golden Dictionary.
Illustrated by Gertrude Elliott. Western Publishing Company, Inc., 1944. Grades 2-4.
Contains 1030 words and more than 1500 pictures in
color.

WARBURG, Sandol Stoddard. I Like You. Illustrated by
Jacqueline Chwast. Houghton Mifflin Company, 1965.
Grades K-3.
"A small book with a single message amplified and illus-
trated with cartoon-style drawings, the text an enjoyable
rambling catalogue."--Chicago Bulletin.

WARD, Lynd. The Biggest Bear. Illustrated by the author.
Houghton Mifflin Company, 1952. Grades K-3.
A Caldecott Medal Winner and ALA Notable Book. "Mr.
Ward has told a story full of action, suspense, and humor, in the fewest possible words (not another word is
needed and not one should be left out). Some of his
best pictures supplement the story.... An outstanding
book in every way."--Horn Book.

WARNER, Gertrude Chandler. The Boxcar Children. Illustrated. Albert Whitman & Company, 1950. Grades 3-8.
How can four children make a home for themselves in
an old boxcar? They do in this, their first adventure.
Miss Warner has proved ... that nothing outdoes the
appeal of an easy-to-read mystery. Good readers at an

early age enjoy her books; reluctant readers of many
ages often have their first successful reading experience
when they commence with the Alden Family series.
_____. Surprise Island. Illustrated. Albert Whitman &
Company, 1949. Grades 3-8.
Summer vacation on an almost private island brings many
surprises to the Aldens and a chance to play detectives.
An easy-to-read mystery in the Alden Family series.
(See description of author's The Boxcar Children.)
WARREN, Mary P. Boy with a Sling. Illustrated by S.
Mathews. Concordia Publishing House, 1965.
An Arch Book. Children, parents, and teachers are
still discovering these colorful and easy-to-read little
treasures. They're long enough to tell a whole Bible
story in bouncy verse or prose, and short enough to be
interesting.
_____. Great Escape. Illustrated by Roberts. Concordia
Publishing House, 1966.
An Arch Book, presenting a Bible story in colorful, easy-
to-read form.
_____. Great Surprise. Illustrated by Betty Wind. Con-
cordia Publishing House, 1964. Grades 5 up.
An Arch Book, presenting a Bible story in colorful, easy-
to-read form.
_____. Lame Man Who Walked Again. Illustrated by
Betty Wind. Concordia Publishing House, 1966.
An Arch Book, presenting a Bible story in colorful, easy-
to-read form.
_____. Little Boat That Almost Sank. Illustrated by
Rada. Concordia Publishing House, 1965.
An Arch Book, presenting a Bible story in colorful, easy-
to-read form.
WARRINGTON, John. See: Aesop.
WASSERMANN, Selma and Jack. Sailor Jack. Illustrated by
Don Loehle. Benefic Press, 1960. Grades ps-2.
The Sailor Jack series of books, which relates exciting
adventures aboard an atomic submarine, is especially
suited to individualized reading programs and offers am-
ple opportunity for self-directed learning. The books,
effective in fostering attitudes of sympathy, humor, and
group responsibility, are phrased in practical, easy-to-
read vocabularies. Reluctant readers become avid ship-
mates, for the authors are specialists in the study of
corrective reading. Their stories provide special appeal
in the combination of real-life sea experiences, adult
characters, and fast-moving action with anecdotal humor
to attract reluctant readers. Reading level of this book:
ps.

_____. Sailor Jack and Bluebell. Illustrated by Jack
Faulkner. Benefic Press, 1960. Grades K-3.
Reading level: K. See description of the authors' Sailor
Jack.
_____. Sailor Jack and Bluebell's Dive. Illustrated by
Marita Root. Benefic Press, 1961. Grades K-3.
Reading level: K. See description of the authors' Sailor
Jack.
_____. Sailor Jack and Eddy. Illustrated by Robert S.
Robison. Benefic Press, 1961. Grades ps-2.
Reading level: ps. See description of the authors'
Sailor Jack.
_____. Sailor Jack and Homer Pots. Illustrated by Bob
Jones. Benefic Press, 1961. Grades ps-2.
Reading level: ps. See description of the authors'
Sailor Jack.
_____. Sailor Jack and the Ball Game. Illustrated by
William Lackey. Benefic Press, 1962. Grades 1-4.
Reading level: grade 1. See description of the authors'
Sailor Jack.
_____. Sailor Jack and the Jet Plane. Illustrated by
Robert S. Robison. Benefic Press, 1962. Grades K-3.
Reading level: K. See description of the authors' Sailor
Jack.
_____. Sailor Jack and the Target Ship. Illustrated by
Bob Jones. Benefic Press, 1960. Grades 2-5.
Reading level: grade 2. See description of the authors'
Sailor Jack.
_____. Sailor Jack Goes North. Illustrated by Bob
Jones. Benefic Press, 1961. Grades 3-6.
Reading level: grade 3. See description of the authors'
Sailor Jack.
_____. Sailor Jack's New Friend. Illustrated by Don
Loehle. Benefic Press, 1960. Grades 1-4.
Reading level: grade 1. See description of the authors'
Sailor Jack.
WATTERS, Garnette. See: Courtis, Stuart A.
WEBB, Addison. Birds in Their Homes. Illustrated by
Sabra Mallett Kimball. Doubleday & Company, Inc.,
1947. Grades 3-7.
How birds live.
WEBBER, Irma E. Up Above and Down Below. Illustrated
by the author. Addison-Wesley Publishing Company,
1943. Grades 2-4.
A young science book showing how plants look, both
above the ground where you can see them, and under the
ground where you can't see them. About plants with

roots, tubers, and bulbs; how they get their food, and
their importance as a source of food for animals and
people.   Three-color illustrations.

WEINRIB, Lennie.   See:  Price, Roger.

WEISS, Harvey.  Clay, Wood and Wire.  Illustrated by the
author.   Addison-Wesley Publishing Company, 1956.
Grades 7 up.
Sculpture for beginners with step-by-step directions for
making all kinds of three-dimensional forms, using many
different materials.   The reader is urged to experiment
and express his own creative feelings.   The book also
gives an excellent historical view of sculpture with more
than fifty photographs.   Diagrams in two colors.

_____.  Pencil, Pen and Brush.  Illustrated by the author.
Addison-Wesley Publishing Company, 1961.   Grades 7
up.
Explains simply and graphically the basic techniques of
drawing and, at the same time, suggests ways for the
reader to develop his own individuality and style through
experimentation.   Generously illustrated with drawings
by the world's masters, from Leonardo to Paul Klee.
Diagrams in two colors by the author.

WEISS, M. Jerry, editor.  Ten Short Plays.  Dell Publish-
ing Company, Inc.   Grades 7 up.
Contents:  William Saroyan, "Coming Through the Rye";
Tennessee Williams, "The Case of the Crushed Petuni-
as"; Thornton Wilder, "The Happy Journey to Trenton
and Camden"; Susan Glaspell, "Suppressed Desires";
Sherwood Anderson, "The Triumph of the Egg"; Maxwell
Anderson, "The Feast of the Ortolans"; Paul Green,
"Quare Medicine"; M. Jerry Weiss, "Parents Are Peo-
ple" (a guidance play); Norman Corwin, "My Client
Curley" (a radio play); Gore Vidal, "Visit to a Small
Planet" (a television play).

WESSELS, Katharine Tyler.  Golden Song Book.  Illustrated
by Gertrude Elliott.   Western Publishing Company, 1945.
Grades 1-2.
Favorite songs and singing games.

WEST, Jerry (pseud.).  The Happy Hollisters.  Illustrated
by Helen B. Hamilton.   Doubleday & Company, Inc.,
1953.   Grades 4-6.
The Happy Hollister Adventure Series consists of stories
of a happy family of five lively boys and girls.

_____.  The Happy Hollisters at Sea Gull Beach.  Illus-
trated by Helen B. Hamilton.   Doubleday & Company,
Inc., 1953.   Grades 4-6.
See description of author's The Happy Hollisters.

_____ . The Happy Hollisters on a River Trip. Illus-
trated by Helen B. Hamilton. Doubleday & Company,
Inc., 1953. Grades 4-6.
See description of author's The Happy Hollisters.
WHITE, Anne H. Junket. Illustrated by Robert McCloskey.
The Viking Press Inc., 1955; paperback, 1969. Grades
4-6.
"Junket, a busy Airedale who liked everything just so,
returned from a late spring jaunt to find the farm animals gone and the people replaced by the McDonegals,
a family grossly inept at country living."--ALA Booklist.
WHITE, E. B. Charlotte's Web. Illustrated by Garth Wil-
liams. Harper & Row Publishers, Inc., 1952; Dell Pub-
lishing Company, Inc., 1967. Grades 2-6.
The endearing story of a little girl Fern and her friends
in the barn, Wilbur the Pig and Charlotte A. Cavatica,
a beautiful gray spider who spins her gossamer web and
saves Wilbur's life. An ALA Distinguished Children's
Book 1952; an ALA Notable Children's Book 1940-54;
Runner-up for the Newbery Medal.
_____ . Stuart Little. Illustrated by Garth Williams.
Harper & Row Publishers, Inc., 1945; Dell Publishing
Company, Inc., 1967. Grades 2-6.
"The adventures of a youngster of a normal family who
was no bigger than a mouse and looked just like one."
--American News or Books.
An inventive and debonair mouse, Stuart has a great ad-
venture when he leaves New York and heads for Boston
in search of his friend Margalo, a beautiful little bird.
"An endearing book for young and old, full of wit and
wisdom and amusement, and Garth Williams' drawings
make a perfect accompaniment."--Horn Book.
_____ . The Trumpet of the Swan. Illustrated by Edward
Frascino. Harper & Row Publishers, Inc., 1970. All
ages.
Knowing how to read and write is not enough for Louis,
a voiceless Trumpeter Swan; his determination to learn
to play a stolen trumpet takes him far from his wilderness home.--H.W. Wilson Company.
WHITEHEAD, Robert J. See: Bamman, Henry A.
WIGGIN, Kate Douglas. The Birds' Christmas Carol. Illustrated by Jessie Gillespie. Houghton Mifflin Company,
1886. Grades 4-6.
"A well-known Christmas story ... which has both humor
and pathos. Nearly every page of this edition is illustrated in color or in black and white."--Wilson Children's
Catalog.

_____ . Rebecca of Sunnybrook Farm. Illustrated by
Helen Mason Grose. Houghton Mifflin Company, 1903.
Grades 4-7.
"Kate Douglas Wiggin has received literary immortality
for her famous Rebecca of Sunnybrook Farm and other
favorite books for children ... in Rebecca she created
'the nicest child in American literature.' "--book
jacket. This classic is in the Houghton Mifflin Riv-
erside Bookshelf Series.
WILDE, Oscar. The Happy Prince and Other Stories. Illus-
trated by Peggy Fortnum. E.P. Dutton & Company,
Inc., 1968. Originally published 1888, 1891. Grades
3-7.
Fairy tales, written with 'delicate, poetic charm,' including: "The Happy Prince," "The Nightingale and the
Rose," "The Selfish Giant," "The Devoted Friend," "The
Remarkable Rocket," "The Young King," "The Birthday
of the Infanta," "The Fisherman and His Soul," and
"The Star-Child."
WILDER, Laura Ingalls. By the Shores of Silver Lake.
Illustrated by Garth Williams. Harper & Row Publishers, Inc., 1939. Grades 4-8.
In this book the family spends the winter on a Dakota
homestead miles from the nearest neighbor. Runner-
up for the Newbery Medal.
The "Little House" Books are classic stories of pioneer
life. "One of the phenomenal achievements in modern
literature for children, a genuine chronicle of American
life and of family life at their equal best. Through
these books young Laura Ingalls of the 1870's and 1880's
has stepped from pages of the past into the flesh and
blood reality of a chosen friend."--Horn Book.
_____ . Farmer Boy. Illustrated by Garth Williams.
Harper & Row Publishers, Inc., 1933. Grades 3-7.
A "Little House" Book (See description of the author's
By the Shores of Silver Lake). Almanzo Wilder's boyhood on his father's farm in upper New York state, a
century ago.
_____ . Little House in the Big Woods. Illustrated by
Garth Williams. Harper & Row Publishers, Inc., 1932.
Grades 3-7.
A "Little House" Book (See description of the author's
By the Shores of Silver Lake). The Ingalls family is
snug and safe in their Wisconsin log house, in spite of
blizzards, wolves, and the lonely forest. Runner-up
for Newbery Medal.

_____.  Little House on the Prairie.  Illustrated by Garth
Williams.  Harper & Row Publishers, Inc., 1935.
Grades 3-7.
In the second "Little House" book, Laura and her family
journey by covered wagon into Indian territory.
_____.  Little Town on the Prairie.  Illustrated by Garth
Williams.  Harper & Row Publishers, Inc., 1941.
Grades 4-8.
The little settlement of The Long Winter becomes a
frontier town, and Laura, at 15, receives a "certificate"
to teach school.  Runner-up for the Newbery Medal.
(A "Little House" Book.)
_____.  On the Banks of Plum Creek.  Illustrated by
Garth Williams.  Harper & Row Publishers, Inc., 1937.
Grades 3-7.
The Ingalls family, after moving to Minnesota, encounters
a terrible blizzard and a grasshopper plague.  Runner-up
for the Newbery Medal.  (A "Little House" Book.)
WILKIE, Katharine E.  Daniel Boone Taming the Wilds.
Illustrated.  Garrard Publishing Company, 1960.  Grades
2-5.
Here is true adventure as a fearless frontiersman opens
the way westward for many thousands of settlers.  A
Discovery Book.  More than 18 full-page, 3-color illus-
trations.
WILLARD, Barbara.  A Dog and a Half.  Illustrated by Jane
Paton.  Thomas Nelson Inc., 1971.  Grades 3-5.
A St. Bernard dog is adopted by Jill and her friend
Limpet, who encounter some humorous complications in
this charming younger level novel.
WILLIAMS, Beryl.  See: Epstein, Samuel.
WILLIAMS, Eric, editor.  The Will to Be Free: Great Es-
cape Stories.  Thomas Nelson Inc., 1971.  Grades 6 up.
Eleven true stories of daring escapes from war-time
enemies or tyrannical governments, told in their own
words by the escapers themselves and collected by a
famous World War II escaper.
WILLIAMS, Garth, editor.  The Tall Book of Make-Believe.
Illustrated by the editor.  Harper & Row, Publishers,
Inc., 1950.  Grades K-5.
WILLIAMS, Margery.  The Velveteen Rabbit.  Illustrated
by William Nicholson.  Doubleday & Company, Inc.,
1926.  Grades 3-5.
About a toy rabbit who wanted to be real.
WILLIAMS, Ursula Moray.  The Three Toymakers.  Illus-
trated by Shirley Hughes.  Thomas Nelson Inc., 1971.
Grades 3-5.

A prize-winning modern old-fashioned tale about the
King's Contest for the best toy and about two good toymakers who compete against an evil one.   Honor Book,
1971 Children's Spring Festival.

WILSON, Holly.  Snowbound in Hidden Valley.  Illustrated
by Dorothy Bayley Morse.  Julian Messner Division of
Simon & Schuster, Inc., 1957.  Grades 3-6.
"Set in Henry's Bend, a small town in Upper Michigan,
this story of the friendship that is sparked between Jo
Shannon and Onota, a Chippewa Indian girl, when Jo is
snowbound with an Indian family, is natural and exciting."--Michigan State Library.

WIND, Gerhard L.  My Bible Story Book.  Illustrated.
Concordia Publishing House, 1956.  Grades ps-2.
The reality and central message of the Bible presented
in a simple manner for children ages 3 to 7.   Each of
the 46 stories from the Old and New Testaments is just
one page long.  Colorful, full-page illustrations.

WITTY, Paul, and Kohler, J.  You and the Constitution of
the United States.  Illustrated by L. Fisher.  Children's
Press, 1948.  Grades 5-8.
Illustrated in color and in black and white.

WOJCIECHOWSKA, Maia.  Tuned Out.  Harper & Row Publishers, Inc., 1968; Dell Publishing Company, Inc.
Grades 7 up.
Summer turns into a nightmare for Jim when his brother
returns from his first year at college drastically changed.
He has become full of doubts, with urgent needs--one of
which is drugs.  Horn Book Honor List.  CSA Book of
the Year.  ALA Notable Book.
"No recent novel or factual treatment succeeds as well
in showing the self-deception, the sense of alienation,
the bitterness against the established order today...."--
Horn Book.

WOODS, Ruth.  Little Quack.  Illustrated by Mel Pekarsky.
Follett Publishing Company, 1961.  Grades 1-3.
Who's afraid?  Not Little Quack, though his brothers
begin the day thinking he is timid.

WRIGHT, Dare.  The Lonely Doll.  Illustrated.  Doubleday
& Company, Inc., 1957.  Grades ps-3.
Illustrated with photographs.

WRIGHT, Wendell W., editor.  The Rainbow Dictionary.
Illustrated.  World Publishing Company, 1959; originally
1947.  Grades K-6.

WYLER, Rose.  See: Ames, Gerald.

WYNDHAM, Lee.  Candy Stripers.  Julian Messner Division
of Simon & Schuster, Inc., 1958.  Grades 6-9.

"Although 15-year-old Bonnie Schuyler became a junior
volunteer nurse's aide because she had nothing better to
do that summer, it wasn't long before she was caught
up in the tempo and heartbreak of a hospital and found
herself wanting to be a dedicated Candy Striper."--New
York Times.

WYSS, Johann R.  The Swiss Family Robinson.  Illustrated
by Charles Folkard.  E.P. Dutton & Company, Inc.;
Dell Publishing Company, Inc.  Originally published 1813.
Grades 5-9.
The story of a shipwrecked family--a minister, his wife
and four sons, Fritz, Ernest, Francis and Jack--who
are cast up on a desert island, build a house in a tree,
and survive cleverly and happily.  Translated by Audrey
Clark.


YASHIMA, Taro.  Crow Boy.  Illustrated by the author.
The Viking Press Inc., 1955; paperback, 1969.  Grades
K-3.
Runner-up, Caldecott Medal Award.  "About a shy moun-
tain boy in Japan who leaves his home at dawn and re-
turns there at sunset to go to the village school.  Pic-
tures and text of moving and harmonious simplicity."--
Saturday Review.
_____.  Umbrella.  Illustrated by the author.  The Viking
Press Inc., 1958; paperback, 1970.  Grades K-3.
Runner-up, Caldecott Medal Award.  "The anticipation,
impatience, and joy of a little girl who waits for a rainy
day to use her birthday umbrella are sensitively portrayed in a beautiful picture book."--ALA Booklist.

YATES, Elizabeth.  Amos Fortune, Free Man.  Illustrated
by Nora S. Unwin.  E.P. Dutton & Company, Inc.,
1950; Dell Publishing Company, Inc., 1971.  Grades 5
up.
Winner of the Newbery Medal.  In 1710, At-Mun, a
young African prince, was captured by slave traders and
brought to Massachusetts.  In a land where enslaved
blacks soon forgot their African identities, At-Mun began
a new life as Amos Fortune.  Even as a slave, his hon-
esty and competence won him the respect of many.  When,
at the age of sixty he bought his freedom, he began a
journey that was to bring the same fortune to many of
the black people whose lives he touched.
"Based on fact, this is a sensitively written and moving
story of a life dedicated to the fight for freedom and
service to others."--Booklist.

YOUNG, Bob and Jan. Good-Bye, Amigos. Julian Messner
  Division of Simon & Schuster, Inc., 1963. Grades 7
  up.
  "Well-written story in which the high school Spanish Club
  takes on the responsibility of improving the recreation
  facilities of the local migrant labor camp. The problems
  of both the ranchers and the workers are brought out."--
  Los Angeles County Board of Education.


ZAFFO, George J. Airplanes & Trucks & Trains, Fire En-
  gines, Boats & Ships, & Building & Wrecking Machines.
  Illustrated by the author. Grosset & Dunlap, Inc., 1968.
  Grades K-3.
  A beautiful large-size book resplendent with color illus-
  trations throughout.
  _____. Big Book of Building and Wrecking Machines.
  Illustrated by the author. Grosset & Dunlap, Inc., 1951.
  Grades K-3.
  For parents to read aloud and for young readers to read
  for themselves. Illustrated in 4 colors.
ZIM, Herbert S. Dinosaurs. Illustrated by James Gordon
  Irving. William Morrow and Company, Inc., 1954.
  Grades 3-7.
  Illustrations on every page. "Here is everything young
  readers want to know about dinosaurs. The writing is
  simple, vivid, and direct."--Library Journal.
  _____. Snakes. Illustrated by James Gordon Irving.
  William Morrow and Company, Inc., 1949. Grades 3-7.
  Illustrations on almost every page. "All the facts about
  United States snakes are arrestingly covered. Each fact
  is charmingly illustrated."--Scientific Monthly.
ZINDEL, Paul. The Pigman. Harper & Row Publishers,
  Inc., 1968; Dell Publishing Company, Inc., 1970.
  Grades 7 up.
  Two lonely high school students meet a strange old man,
  Mr. Pignati. For a short while the three find unexpected
  love and laughter with one another. But the unreal
  world they create out of their zaniness is soon tragically
  shattered and the young people are left to confront the
  harsh reality of their lives.
  "A 'now' book ... thoroughly contemporary, sensitive--
  and shocking,"--Horn Book; "An intensely moving story
  of believably alienated young people,"--Library Journal.
ZION, Gene. Harry and the Lady Next Door. Illustrated
  by Margaret Bloy Graham. Harper & Row Publishers,
  Inc., 1960. Grades ps-3.

An "I Can Read" Book. "Harry, the white dog with black spots, attempts to silence the lady singer who lives next door. His valiant attempts repeatedly fail when he enlists the help of a cow, a parade musician, and even the wind, to repress the enthusiastic vocalist. But finally his persistence gets him his way, and the lady next door is removed from hearing distance."--Kirkus.

_____. Harry the Dirty Dog. Illustrated by Margaret Bloy Graham. Harper & Row Publishers, Inc., 1956. Grades ps-3.

"Harry was a black-and-white dog who disliked getting a bath. After running away and playing in all the dirtiest places possible, Harry returned home to find himself in a most unexpected ... difficulty."--Retail Bookseller.

Chapter Three

BEST SELLERS BY TITLE

This chapter lists the 958 best sellers alphabetically by title, giving the author, the original date of publication of each book, and the publisher(s) who reported the book as a best seller in this survey.

Abraham Lincoln. Ingri and Edgar Parin D'Aulaire. 1940. Doubleday.
Abraham Lincoln. Clara Ingram Judson. 1961. Follett.
Abraham Lincoln: For the People. Anne Colver. 1960. Garrard; Dell.
Across Five Aprils. Irene Hunt. 1964. Follett.
Adam of the Road. Elizabeth Janet Gray. 1942. Viking.
Adventures in the Neighborhood. Nila Voight. Lawrence.
The Adventures of Odysseus. Andrew Lang. 1879. Dutton.
Adventures of Peter Cottontail. Thornton W. Burgess. Grosset & Dunlap.
Aesop's Fables. John Warrington, editor. Dutton.
Aesop's Stories. Edward W. and M.P. Dolch. 1951. Garrard.
Afro-American Contributors to American Life. John M. Franco. 1971. Benefic.
Afro-Americans Then and Now. Doris Haynes and Jane Hurley. 1969. Benefic.
Airplanes & Trucks & Trains, Fire Engines, Boats & Ships, & Building & Wrecking Machines. George Zaffo. 1968. Grosset & Dunlap.
Albert Einstein. Elma Ehrlich Levinger. 1949. Julian Messner.
Album of Horses. Marguerite Henry. 1951. Rand McNally.
Alice's Adventures in Wonderland and Through the Looking Glass. Lewis Carroll (pseud.). 1865 and 1872 respectively. Dutton.
All-of-a-Kind Family. Sydney Taylor. 1951. Follett; Dell.
America and Its Presidents. Earl S. Miers. 1959. Grosset & Dunlap.

American Folk Songs for Children.   Ruth Crawford Seeger.
    1948.   Doubleday.
Amos Fortune, Free Man.   Elizabeth Yates.   1950.   Dutton;
    Dell.
And Now Miguel.   Joseph Krumgold.   1953.   Thomas Y.
    Crowell; Apollo Editions.
And To Think That I Saw It on Mulberry Street.   Dr. Seuss
    (pseud.).   1937.   Vanguard; Hale.
Andy and the Lion.   James Daugherty.   1938.   Viking.
Angelo the Naughty One.   Helen Garrett.   1944.   Viking.
Angus and the Cat.   Marjorie Flack.   1931.   Doubleday.
Angus and the Ducks.   Marjorie Flack.   1930.   Doubleday.
Angus Lost.   Marjorie Flack.   1932.   Doubleday.
Animal Industry.   Boy Scouts of America.   1944.   Boy
    Scouts of America.
Animal Stories.   Edward W. and M. P. Dolch.   1952.   Gar-
    rard.
Animals Everywhere.   Ingri and Edgar Parin D'Aulaire.
    1954.   Doubleday.
The Answer Book.   Mary Elting.   1959.   Grosset & Dunlap.
The Answer Book of Sports.   Bill Mazer.   1969.   Grosset
    & Dunlap.
Answers and More Answers.   Mary Elting.   1961.   Grosset
    & Dunlap.
Anybody At Home?   H. A. Rey.   1942.   Houghton Mifflin.
April's Kittens.   Clare Turlay Newberry.   1940.   Harper &
    Row.
Archery.   Boy Scouts of America.   1964.   Boy Scouts of
    America.
Around and About.   Marchette Chute.   1957.   Dutton.
Around the Moon.   Jules Verne.   1865.   Dutton.
Around the World in Eighty Days.   Jules Verne.   1873.
    Dutton; Dell.
Art.   Boy Scouts of America.   1968.   Boy Scouts of Amer-
    ica.
Astronomy.   Boy Scouts of America.   1971.   Boy Scouts
    of America.
At the Back of the North Wind.   George MacDonald.   1871.
    Dutton.
Athletics.   Boy Scouts of America.   1964.   Boy Scouts of
    America.
Atlas of the Presidents.   Donald E. Cooke.   1964.   Ham-
    mond.
Atoms, Energy, and Machines.   Jack McCormick.   1967.
    Creative Educational Society.
Automotive Safety.   Boy Scouts of America.   1962.   Boy
    Scouts of America.

Aviation. Boy Scouts of America. 1968. Boy Scouts of
America.


Baby Born in a Stable. A.H. Kramer. Concordia.
Backyard Bandits--Including California Raccoons and Other
Exciting Patio Visitors. David D. Oliphant, Jr. 1968.
Naturegraph.
Bambi: A Life in the Woods. Felix Salten. 1929. Simon
& Schuster.
Barney's Adventure. Margot Austin. 1941. Dutton.
Baseball. Frank F. DeClemente. 1962. Creative Educa-
tional Society.
Basketball. Joe Hutton and Vern B. Hoffman. 1962. Crea-
tive Educational Society.
Basketry. Boy Scouts of America. 1968. Boy Scouts of
America.
A Bear Called Paddington. Michael Bond. 1960. Houghton
Mifflin; Dell.
Bear Cub Scout Book. Boy Scouts of America. 1967. Boy
Scouts of America.
Bear Party. William Pene Du Bois. 1963. Viking.
The Bears on Hemlock Mountain. Alice Dalgliesh. 1952.
Scribner.
Beautiful Joe. Marshall Saunders. 1920. Grosset & Dun-
lap.
Becky Lou in Grandmother's Days. Hazel Craig. Denison.
Beggar's Greatest Wish. Alyce Bergey. 1969. Concordia.
Ben and Me. Robert Lawson. 1939. Little, Brown.
Benjamin Franklin. Ingri and Edgar Parin D'Aulaire. 1950.
Doubleday.
Benjamin Franklin: Man of Ideas. Charles P. Graves.
1960. Garrard.
Benny and the Bear. Barbee Carleton. 1960. Follett.
Bessie, the Messy Penguin. Joyce Holland. 1960. Denison.
Better Homes and Gardens Junior Cook Book. Better Homes
And Gardens Editors. 1955. Meredith.
Better Homes and Gardens Story Book. Better Homes And
Gardens Editors. 1950. Meredith.
Between Planets. Robert A. Heinlein. 1951. Scribner.
Bible Stories. Mary Alice Jones. 1952. Rand McNally.
Big Book of Airplanes. Charles L. Black. 1951. Grosset
& Dunlap.
Big Book of Building and Wrecking Machines. George J.
Zaffo. 1951. Grosset & Dunlap.
Big Book of Mother Goose. Alice Schlesinger, illustrator.
Grosset & Dunlap.

Big Book of Real Trains. Doris Duenewald, editor. 1970.
    Grosset & Dunlap.
Big Book of Real Trucks. Elizabeth Cameron; originally by
    George J. Zaffo. 1950. Grosset & Dunlap.
Big Book of Submarines. Grosset & Dunlap.
Big New School. Evelyn Hastings. 1959. Follett.
The Big Wave. Pearl S. Buck. 1948. John Day.
The Biggest Bear. Lynd Ward. 1952. Houghton Mifflin.
Bird Life in Wington. John Calvin Reid. Eerdmans.
Bird Study. Boy Scouts of America. 1967. Boy Scouts of
    America.
The Birds' Christmas Carol. Kate Douglas Wiggin. 1886.
    Houghton Mifflin.
Birds in Their Homes. Addison Webb. 1947. Doubleday.
The Black Arrow. Robert Louis Stevenson. 1888. Dutton;
    Dell.
Black Beauty. Anna Sewell. 1877. Dell.
Black Gold. Marguerite Henry. 1957. Rand McNally.
Blink, the Patchwork Bunny. Matthew V. Howard. 1959.
    Denison.
Blue Willow. Doris Gates. 1940. Viking.
Blueberries For Sal. Robert McCloskey. 1948. Viking.
The Boats on the River. Marjorie Flack. 1946. Viking.
Bobby Bear and the Bees. Marilyn Olear Helmrath and Janet
    LaSpisa Bartlett. 1968. Oddo.
Bobby Bear Finds Maple Sugar. Marilyn Olear Helmrath
    and Janet LaSpisa Bartlett. 1968. Oddo.
Bobby Bear Goes Fishing. Marilyn Olear Helmrath and
    Janet LaSpisa Bartlett. 1968. Oddo.
Bobby Bear in the Spring. Marilyn Olear Helmrath and Janet
    LaSpisa Bartlett. 1968. Oddo.
Bobby Bear's Halloween. Marilyn O. Helmrath and Janet
    L. Bartlett. 1968. Oddo.
Bobby Bear's Rocket Ride. Marilyn O. Helmrath and Janet
    L. Bartlett. 1968. Oddo.
Bobby Discovers Bird Watching. Marjorie Wackerbarth.
    1962. Denison.
Bobby Discovers Garden Friends. Marjorie Wackerbarth and
    Lillian S. Graham. 1960. Denison.
Bobby Learns About Butterflies. Marjorie Wackerbarth.
    1963. Denison.
Bobby Learns About Squirrels. Marjorie Wackerbarth. 1966.
    Denison.
Bobby Learns About Woodland Babies. Marjorie Wackerbarth.
    Denison.
The Book of Marvels. Richard Halliburton. 1937. Bobbs-
    Merrill.

Book of Nursery & Mother Goose Rhymes.  Marguerite De
  Angeli.  1954.  Doubleday.
The Book of the Ancient Greeks.  Dorothy Mills.  1925.
  Putnam.
The Book of the Ancient Romans.  Dorothy Mills.  1927.
  Putnam.
The Book of the Ancient World for Younger Readers.  Doro-
  thy Mills.  1923.  Putnam.
Born to Trot.  Marguerite Henry.  1950.  Rand McNally.
The Boxcar Children.  Gertrude Chandler Warner.  1950.
  Albert Whitman.
The Boy Scout Encyclopedia.  Bruce Grant.  1952.  Rand
  McNally.
Boy Scout Handbook.  Boy Scouts of America.  1910.  Boy
  Scouts of America.
Boy Scout Songbook.  Boy Scouts of America.  1971.  Boy
  Scouts of America.
Boy Who Gave His Lunch Away.  Dave Hill.  1967.  Con-
  cordia.
Boy Who Ran Away.  Irene Elmer.  1964.  Concordia.
Boy Who Saved His Family.  Alyce Bergey.  1966.
  Concordia.
The Boy Who Would Not Say His Name.  Elizabeth Vreeken.
  1959.  Follett.
Boy With a Sling.  Mary P. Warren.  1965.  Con-
  cordia.
Braggy King of Babylon.  Yvonne McCall.  1969.  Concordia.
Bright April.  Marguerite Lofft De Angeli.  1946.  Double-
  day.
Brighty of the Grand Canyon.  Marguerite Henry.  1956.
  Rand McNally.
The Bronze Bow.  Elizabeth George Speare.  1961.  Houghton
  Mifflin.
The Bully of Barkham Street.  Mary Stolz.  1963.  Harper
  & Row; Dell.
The Bumper Book.  Watty Piper, editor.  1946.  Platt &
  Munk.
Buttons.  Tom Robinson.  1938.  Viking.
By the Shores of Silver Lake.  Laura Ingalls Wilder.  1939.
  Harper & Row.


The Call of the Wild.  Jack London.  1903.  Macmillan;
  Dutton.
Camping.  Boy Scouts of America.  1966.  Boy Scouts of
  America.

Candy Stripers. Lee Wyndham. 1958. Julian Messner.
Canoeing. Boy Scouts of America. 1968. Boy Scouts of
    America.
Caps For Sale. Esphyr Slobodkina. 1947. Addison-Wesley.
Careers Outdoors. James Joseph. 1962. Thomas Nelson.
Carry On, Mr. Bowditch. Jean Lee Latham. 1955. Hough-
    ton Mifflin.
The Case of the Cat's Meow. Crosby Newell Bonsall. 1965.
    Harper & Row.
The Case of the Hungry Stranger. Crosby Newell Bonsall.
    1963. Harper & Row.
Casey, the Utterly Impossible Horse. Anita Feagles. 1960.
    Addison-Wesley.
Casper, the Caterpillar. Celeste K. Foster. Denison.
Cat and Dog. Else Holmelund Minarik. 1960. Harper &
    Row.
The Cat in the Hat. Dr. Seuss. 1957. Random House.
The Cat in the Hat Beginner Book Dictionary. Phillip D.
    Eastman. 1964. Random House.
The Cat in the Hat Comes Back. Dr. Seuss. 1958. Ran-
    dom House.
Centerburg Tales. Robert McCloskey. 1951. Viking.
Chapbook 2. 1966. Bethany.
Charlie and the Chocolate Factory. Roald Dahl. 1964.
    Knopf.
Charlotte's Web. E.B. White. 1952. Harper & Row; Dell.
Chemistry. Boy Scouts of America. 1962. Boy Scouts of
    America.
Chicken Little Count-to-Ten. Margaret Friskey. 1946.
    Children's.
A Child's Book of Poems. Gyo Fujikawa. 1969. Grosset
    & Dunlap.
A Child's Garden of Bible Stories. Arthur W. Gross. 1948.
    Concordia.
A Child's Garden of Prayer. Herman W. Gockel and Ed-
    ward J. Saleska, compilers. 1948. Concordia.
A Child's Garden of Verses. Robert Louis Stevenson. 1885.
    Dutton; Grosset & Dunlap; Platt & Munk.
The Child's Story Bible. Catherine F. Vos; revised by
    Marianne Vos Radius. 1967. Eerdmans.
The Christ Child. Maud and Miska Petersham. 1931. Dou-
    bleday.
Christmas; A Book of Stories Old and New. Alice Dalgliesh,
    compiler. 1934. Scribner.
A Christmas Carol and The Cricket on the Hearth. Charles
    Dickens. 1843. Dutton.
Christmas Nutshell Library. Hilary Knight. 1963. Harper
    & Row.

The Christmas Story. Marguerite Northrup, editor. 1966.
Metropolitan Museum of Art.

Christopher Columbus. Clara Ingram Judson. 1964. Follett.

Circus Stories. Edward W. and M. P. Dolch. 1956. Garrard.

Citizen of the Galaxy. Robert A. Heinlein. 1957. Scribner.

Citizenship. Boy Scouts of America. 1966. Boy Scouts of America.

City Beneath the Sea. Henry A. Bauman and Robert J. Whitehead. 1964. Benefic.

The Civil War. Fletcher Pratt. 1955. Doubleday.

Clay, Wood and Wire. Harvey Weiss. 1956. Addison-Wesley.

Coin Collecting. Boy Scouts of America. 1966. Boy Scouts of America.

Colonial Williamsburg Coloring Book. Marian Cannon. 1948. Colonial Williamsburg Foundation.

Color Me Brown. Lucille Giles. Johnson (Chicago).

Columbus. Ingri and Edgar Parin D'Aulaire. 1955. Doubleday.

Come and Have Fun. Edith Thacher Hurd. 1962. Harper & Row.

Conservation of Natural Resources. Boy Scouts of America. 1967. Boy Scouts of America.

Cooking. Boy Scouts of America. 1967. Boy Scouts of America.

Corduroy. Don Freeman. 1968. Viking.

Cotton In My Sack. Lois Lenski. 1949. Lippincott; Dell.

The Country Bunny and the Little Gold Shoes. Dubose Heyward. 1939. Houghton Mifflin.

The Courage of Sarah Noble. Alice Dalgliesh. 1954. Scribner.

Courtis-Watters Illustrated Golden Dictionary for Young Readers. Stuart A. Courtis and Garnette Watters. 1952. Western.

Cowboy Sam. Edna Walker Chandler. 1960. Benefic.

Cowboy Sam and Big Bill. Edna W. Chandler. 1970. Benefic.

Cowboy Sam and Dandy. Edna W. Chandler. 1962. Benefic.

Cowboy Sam and Flop. Edna W. Chandler. 1971. Benefic.

Cowboy Sam and Freckles. Edna W. Chandler. 1971. Benefic.

Cowboy Sam and Freddy. Edna W. Chandler. 1970. Benefic.

Cowboy Sam and Miss Lily. Edna W. Chandler. 1971. Benefic.

Cowboy Sam and Porky. Edna W. Chandler. 1971. Benefic.

Cowboy Sam and Sally.  Edna W. Chandler.  1959.  Benefic.
Cowboy Sam and Shorty.  Edna W. Chandler.  1962.  Benefic.
Cowboy Sam and the Airplane.  Edna W. Chandler.  1959.
    Benefic.
Cowboy Sam and the Fair.  Edna W. Chandler.  1970.
    Benefic.
Cowboy Sam and the Indians.  Edna W. Chandler.  1971.
    Benefic.
Cowboy Sam and the Rodeo.  Edna W. Chandler.  1959.
    Benefic.
Cowboy Sam and the Rustlers.  Edna W. Chandler.  1970.
    Benefic.
Creative Art Activities for Home and School.  Doris V.
    Brown and Pauline McDonald.  1966.  Lawrence.
Creative Thinking Activities;  A Highlights Handbook.  Garry
    Cleveland Myers.  1965.  Highlights For Children.
Creative Writing Activities; A Highlights Handbook.  Walter
    B. Barbe, compiler.  1965.  Highlights For Children.
The Cricket on the Hearth.  Charles Dickens.  1845.  Dut-
    ton.
Crow Boy.  Taro Yashima.  1955.  Viking.
Cub Scout Fun Book.  Boy Scouts of America.  1967.  Boy
    Scouts of America.
Cub Scout Magic.  Boy Scouts of America.  1960.  Boy
    Scouts of America.
Cub Scout Songbook.  Boy Scouts of America.  1969.  Boy
    Scouts of America.
The Curious Cow.  Esther Meeks.  1960.  Follett.
Curious George.  H.A. Rey.  1941.  Houghton Mifflin.
Curious George Flies a Kite.  Margret and H.A. Rey.  1958.
    Houghton Mifflin.
Curious George Gets a Medal.  H.A. Rey.  1957.  Houghton
    Mifflin.
Curious George Learns the Alphabet.  H.A. Rey.  1963.
    Houghton Mifflin.
Curious George Rides a Bike.  H.A. Rey.  1952.  Houghton
    Mifflin.
Curious George Takes a Job.  H.A. Rey.  1947.  Houghton
    Mifflin.
Cycling.  Boy Scouts of America.  1971.  Boy Scouts of
    America.


Daffy.  Adda Mai Sharp.  1950.  Steck-Vaughn.
Dan Frontier.  William J. Hurley.  1959.  Benefic.
Dan Frontier and the Big Cat.  William J. Hurley.  1961.
    Benefic.

Dan Frontier and the New House. William J. Hurley. 1961.
Benefic.
Dan Frontier and the Wagon Train. William J. Hurley.
1959. Benefic.
Dan Frontier Goes Exploring. William J. Hurley. 1963.
Benefic.
Dan Frontier Goes Hunting. William J. Hurley. 1959.
Benefic.
Dan Frontier Goes to Congress. William J. and Jane Hurley.
1964. Benefic.
Dan Frontier Scouts with the Army. William J. Hurley.
1962. Benefic.
Dan Frontier, Sheriff. William J. Hurley. 1960. Benefic.
Dan Frontier, Trapper. William J. Hurley. 1962. Benefic.
Dan Frontier with the Indians. William J. Hurley. 1959.
Benefic.
Dandelion. Don Freeman. 1964. Viking.
Dandy, the Dime. James S. Kerr. Denison.
Daniel Boone. James Daugherty. 1939. Viking.
Daniel Boone Taming the Wilds. Katharine E. Wilkie. 1960.
Garrard.
Daniel in the Lion's Den. Jane Latourette and Mathews.
1966. Concordia.
Danny and the Dinosaur. Syd Hoff. 1958. Harper & Row.
The Dark Frigate. Charles Boardman Hawes. 1934. Little,
Brown.
Dash and Dart: Two Fawns. Mary and Conrad Buff. 1942.
Viking.
Daughter of the Mountains. Louise S. Rankin. 1948. Vik-
ing.
D'Aulaires' Book of Greek Myths. Ingri and Edgar Parin
D'Aulaire. 1962. Doubleday.
The Day They Marched. Doris E. Saunders, editor. 1963.
Johnson (Chicago).
The Day We Saw the Sun Come Up. Alice E. Goudey. 1961.
Scribner.
Den Chief's Denbook. Boy Scouts of America. 1968. Boy
Scouts of America.
The Desert. Alexander and Elsie Klots. 1967. Creative
Educational Society.
Did You Ever See? Walter Einsel. 1962. Addison-Wesley.
Diddie, Dumps and Tot. Louise Clarke Pyrnelle. 1882.
Pelican.
Dinosaurs. Herbert S. Zim. 1954. William Morrow.
Dinosaurs and Other Prehistoric Animals. Darlene Geis.
1959. Grosset & Dunlap.
Dipper of Copper Creek. John and Jean George. 1956.
Dutton.

Dr. George Washington Carver, Scientist. Shirley Graham and George D. Lipscomb. 1944. Messner.

Dr. Seuss's ABC. Dr. Seuss. 1963. Random House.

A Dog and a Half. Barbara Willard. 1971. Thomas Nelson.

Dog Care. Boy Scouts of America. 1969. Boy Scouts of America.

Dog Stories. Edward W. and M. P. Dolch. 1954. Garrard.

Donkey Daniel in Bethlehem. Janice Kramer. 1970. Concordia.

Don't Take Teddy. Babbis Friis-Baastad. 1967. Scribner.

The Door in the Wall. Marguerite Lofft De Angeli. 1949. Doubleday.

Dot To Dot. Isobel R. Beard. 1969. Follett.

Down, Down the Mountain. Ellis Credle. 1934. Thomas Nelson.

Drag Strip. William Campbell Gault. 1959. Dutton.

The Dragon Fish. Pearl S. Buck. 1944. John Day; Dell.

Draw With Dots. Isobel R. Beard. Follett.

Droodles. Roger Price. 1965. Price/Stern/Sloan.

Durango Street. Frank Bonham. 1965. Dutton.


The Earth's Story. Gerald Ames and Rose Wyler. 1967. Creative Educational Society.

Edgar Allan. John Neufeld. 1968. S. G. Phillips.

Edge of Awareness. Ned E. Hoopes and Richard Peck. 1966. Dell.

Egermeier's Bible Story Books. Elsie E. Egermeier. 1923. Warner.

The Egg Tree. Katherine Milhous. 1950. Scribner.

Eight Bags of Gold. Janice Kramer and Mathews. 1964. Concordia.

Electricity. Boy Scouts of America. 1964. Boy Scouts of America.

Electronics Pioneer, Lee De Forest. I. E. Levine. 1964. Messner.

The Elephant Book. Roger Price; Leonard Stern; Larry Sloan; and Lennie Weinrib. 1968. Price/Stern/Sloan.

Elephants, Grapes & Pickles. Roger Price; Leonard Stern; and Larry Sloan. 1964. Price/Stern/Sloan.

Elephi, The Cat With the High I.Q. Jean Stafford. 1966. Dell.

Ellen Tebbits. Beverly Cleary. 1951. William Morrow.

Eloise. Kay Thompson. 1955. Simon & Schuster.

Emmett's Pig. Mary Stolz. 1959. Harper & Row.

The Empty Schoolhouse. Natalie Savage Carlson. 1965. Harper & Row; Dell.

Encyclopedia Brown and the Case of the Secret Pitch. Donald J. Sobol. 1965. Thomas Nelson.

Encyclopedia Brown, Boy Detective.  Donald J. Sobol.  1963.
   Thomas Nelson.
Encyclopedia Brown Finds the Clues.  Donald J. Sobol.
   1966.  Thomas Nelson.
Encyclopedia Brown Gets His Man.  Donald J. Sobol.  1967.
   Thomas Nelson.
Encyclopedia Brown Keeps the Peace.  Donald J. Sobol.
   1969.  Thomas Nelson.
Encyclopedia Brown Saves the Day.  Donald J. Sobol.  1970.
   Thomas Nelson.
Encyclopedia Brown Solves Them All.  Donald J. Sobol.
   1971.  Thomas Nelson.
English Folk and Fairy Tales.  Joseph Jacobs, editor.  1904.
   Putnam.
The Enormous Egg.  Oliver Butterworth.  1956.  Little,
   Brown.
Explorer Member's Guide.  Boy Scouts of America.  1969.
   Boy Scouts of America.
Exploring Around the House.  Nila Voight.  Lawrence.
The Extra Egg.  Edna A. Anderson.  Denison.


Facts of Life and Love for Teenagers.  Evelyn Millis Duvall
   and Sylvanus Duvall.  1950.  Association.
Fairy Tales and Fables.  Doris Duenewald, editor.  1970.
   Grosset & Dunlap.
Famous American Indians.  Edmond L. Leipold.  Denison.
Famous American Negroes.  Edmond L. Leipold.  Denison.
Famous Paintings:  An Introduction to Art.  Alice Elizabeth
   Chase.  1951.  Platt & Munk.
Farmer Boy.  Laura Ingalls Wilder.  1933.  Harper & Row.
Farmer in the Sky.  Robert A. Heinlein.  1950.  Scribner;
   Dell.
Father Bear Comes Home.  Else Holmelund Minarik.  1959.
   Harper & Row.
Favorite Poems Old and New.  Helen Josephine Ferris,
   editor.  1957.  Doubleday.
Feed the Animals.  H.A. Rey.  1944.  Houghton Mifflin.
Field and Meadow.  Etta Schneider Ress.  1967.  Creative
   Educational Society.
Fieldbook.  Boy Scouts of America.  1967.  Boy Scouts of
   America.
Fifteen.  Beverly Cleary.  1956.  Morrow.
Fingerprinting.  Boy Scouts of America.  1964.  Boy Scouts
   of America.
The Fire Cat.  Esther Averill.  1960.  Harper & Row.

Fire on the Mountain. Henry A. Bamman and Robert J.
    Whitehead. 1963. Benefic.
Firemanship. Boy Scouts of America. 1968. Boy Scouts
    of America.
First Aid. Boy Scouts of America. 1960. Boy Scouts of
    America.
First Aid to Animals. Boy Scouts of America. 1963. Boy
    Scouts of America.
The First Thanksgiving. Lou Rogers. 1963. Follett.
The First Woman Doctor: The Story of Elizabeth Blackwell,
    M. D. Rachel Baker. 1944. Messner.
Fishermen's Surprise. Alyce Bergey. 1967. Concordia.
Fishing. Boy Scouts of America. 1954. Boy Scouts of
    America.
The Five Chinese Brothers. Claire Huchet Bishop. 1938.
    Coward McCann; Hale.
The Five Hundred Hats of Bartholomew Cubbins. Dr. Seuss.
    1938. Vanguard.
Flags of American History. David D. Crouthers. 1964.
    Hammond.
Flicka, Ricka, Dicka and the New Dotted Dresses. Maj
    Lindman. 1939. Albert Whitman.
Flicka, Ricka, Dicka and the Three Kittens. Maj Lindman.
    1941. Albert Whitman.
Flight to the South Pole. Henry A. Bamman and Robert J.
    Whitehead. 1965. Benefic.
Flip. Wesley Dennis. 1941. Viking.
Flip and the Morning. Wesley Dennis. 1951. Viking.
Florence Nightingale: War Nurse. Anne Colver. 1961.
    Garrard; Dell.
Folk Stories. Edward W. and M. P. Dolch. 1952. Garrard.
Follett Beginning-To-Read Picture Dictionary. Alta McIntire.
    1959. Follett.
Food and Life. Gerald Ames and Rose Wyler. 1966. Crea-
    tive Educational Society.
Football. J. R. "Bob" Otto. 1962. Creative Educational
    Society.
Forest and Woodland. Stephen Collins. 1967. Creative Ed-
    ucational Society.
Forestry. Boy Scouts of America. 1971. Boy Scouts of
    America.
The Four Friends. Carol Hoff. 1955. Follett.
The Four-Story Mistake. Elizabeth Enright. 1942. Holt,
    Rinehart & Winston; Dell.
Frederick Douglass, Freedom Fighter. Lillie Patterson.
    1965. Garrard.

Fresh and Salt Water. B. Bartram Cadbury. 1967. Creative Educational Society.
A Friend Is Someone Who Likes You. Joan Walsh Anglund. 1958. Harcourt Brace Jovanovich.
From the Earth to the Moon. Jules Verne. 1865. Dutton.
Fun With Dots. Madeline May. 1969. Follett.


Gardening. Boy Scouts of America. 1971. Boy Scouts of America.
The Gateway to Storyland. Watty Piper, editor. 1954. Platt & Munk.
Gay-Neck: The Story of a Pigeon. Dhan Gopal Mukerji. 1927. Dutton.
Gentle Ben. Walt Morey. 1965. Dutton.
Geology. Boy Scouts of America. 1953. Boy Scouts of America.
George, the Discontented Giraffe. Phillip Orso Steinberg. Denison.
George Washington. Ingri and Edgar Parin D'Aulaire. 1936. Doubleday.
George Washington. Clara Ingram Judson. 1961. Follett.
George Washington Carver, Negro Scientist. Sam and Beryl Epstein. 1960. Garrard.
George Washington: Father of Freedom. Stewart Graff. 1964. Garrard; Dell.
Gertie the Duck. Nicholas Georgiady and Louis Romano. 1959. Follett.
Gilberto and the Wind. Marie Hall Ets. 1963. Viking.
The Gingham Dog and the Calico Cat. Eugene Field. 1956. Follett.
Gobble, Gobble, Gobble. Mary Jackson Ellis. Denison.
Golden Book of Science. Bertha Morris Parker. 1952. Western.
The Golden Dictionary. Ellen Wales Walpole, editor. 1944. Western.
The Golden Egg Book. Margaret Wise Brown. 1947. Western.
Golden Picture Dictionary. Lilian Moore. 1954. Western.
Golden Song Book. Katharine Tyler Wessels. 1945. Western.
Goldilocks and the Three Bears. 1831. Grosset & Dunlap.
Golf, Swimming and Tennis. Otis J. Dypwick and Helen Hull Jacobs. 1962. Creative Educational Society.
The Good Master. Kate Seredy. 1935. Viking.
Good Samaritan. Janice Kramer. 1964. Concordia.

Good-Bye, Amigos.  Bob and Jan Young.  1963.  Messner.
Goodnight Moon.  Margaret Wise Brown.  1947.  Harper &
   Row.
Great Escape.  Mary P. Warren.  1966.  Con-
   cordia.
The Great Houdini, Magician Extraordinary.  Samuel Epstein
   and Beryl Williams.  1950.  Messner.
Great Promise.  Alyce Bergey.  1968.  Concordia.
Great Surprise.  Warren and Wind.  1964.  Concordia.
Greek Gods and Heroes.  Robert Graves.  1960.  Double-
   day; Dell.
Green Eggs and Ham.  Dr. Seuss.  1960.  Random.
Grimm's Fairy Tales.  Jakob and Wilhelm Grimm.  1812-
   1815.  Dutton.
Gulliver's Travels.  Jonathan Swift.  1726.  Dutton.


Hailstones and Halibut Bones.  Mary O'Neill  1961.  Dou-
   bleday.
Handbook of Nature Study.  Anna Botsford Comstock.  1939.
   Cornell.
Hans Andersen's Fairy Tales.  Hans Christian Andersen.
   1835.  Dutton.
Hans Brinker: Or The Silver Skates.  Mary Mapes Dodge.
   1865.  Dutton.
Happiness Is a Warm Puppy.  Charles M. Schulz.  1962.
   Determined.
Happiness Is Smiling.  Katherine Gehm.  Denison.
The Happy Birthday Present.  Joan Heilbroner.  1961.
   Harper & Row.
The Happy Hollisters.  Jerry West (pseud. ).  1953.  Dou-
   bleday.
The Happy Hollisters at Sea Gull Beach.  Jerry West
   (pseud. ).  1953.  Doubleday.
The Happy Hollisters on a River Trip.  Jerry West (pseud. ).
   1953.  Doubleday.
Happy Hospital Surprises.  Winifred Talbot.  Denison.
The Happy Prince and Other Stories.  Oscar Wilde.  1888.
   Dutton.
Harold and the Purple Crayon.  Crockett Johnson (pseud. ).
   1955.  Harper & Row.
Harriet The Spy.  Louise Fitzhugh.  1964.  Harper & Row;
   Dell.
Harry and the Lady Next Door.  Gene Zion.  1960.  Harper
   & Row.
Harry the Dirty Dog.  Gene Zion.  1956.  Harper & Row.
Harvey Hopper.  Bernice M. Chappel.  Denison.

Have Space Suit--Will Travel.  Robert A. Heinlein.  1958.
    Scribner.
Have You Seen My Brother?  Elizabeth Guilfoile.  1962.
    Follett.
Heidi.  Johanna Spyri.  1884.  Dutton; Grosset & Dunlap.
Helen Keller:  Toward the Light.  Stewart and Polly Anne
    Graff.  1965.  Garrard; Dell.
Henny Penny.  Paul Galdone.  1860.  Seabury.
Henry and Beezus.  Beverly Cleary.  1952.  Morrow.
Henry and Ribsy.  Beverly Cleary.  1954.  Morrow.
Henry and the Clubhouse.  Beverly Cleary.  1962.  Morrow.
Henry and the Paper Route.  Beverly Cleary.  1957.  Mor-
    row.
Henry Huggins.  Beverly Cleary.  1950.  Morrow.
Henry Reed, Inc.  Keith Robertson.  1958.  Viking.
Henry Reed's Baby-Sitting Service.  Keith Robertson.  1966.
    Viking.
Henry Reed's Journey.  Keith Robertson.  1963.  Viking.
Here Comes the Strikeout.  Leonard Kessler.  1965.  Harper
    & Row.
Hiking.  Boy Scouts of America.  1962.  Boy Scouts of
    America.
Hold Fast to Your Dreams.  Catherine Blanton.  1955.  Mes-
    sner.
The Hole in the Hill.  Marion Seyton.  1960.  Follett.
The Hole in the Tree.  Jean Craighead George.  1957.  Dut-
    ton.
A Hole Is To Dig:  A First Book of First Definitions.  Ruth
    Krauss.  1952.  Harper & Row.
Holiday (Craft) Handbook No. 1.  Caroline Clark Myers,
    compiler.  1965.  Highlights For Children.
Holiday (Craft) Handbook No. 4.  The Editors of Highlights.
    1965.  Highlights For Children.
Home Repairs.  Boy Scouts of America.  1961.  Boy Scouts
    of America.
Homer Price.  Robert McCloskey.  1943.  Viking.
Hop On Pop.  Dr. Seuss.  1963.  Random.
The Horse in the Camel Suit.  William Pene du Bois.  1967.
    Harper & Row.
A Horse of Her Own.  Selma Hudnut.  1963.  Van Nostrand
    Reinhold.
Horse Stories.  Edward W. and M. P. Dolch.  1958.  Gar-
    rard.
Horsemanship.  Boy Scouts of America.  1969.  Boy Scouts
    of America.
Hot Rod.  Henry Gregor Felsen.  1950.  Dutton.
The House at Pooh Corner.  A. A. Milne.  1928.  Dutton; Dell.

House on the Rock. Jane Latourette and Mathews. 1966.
Concordia.
Houses From the Sea. Alice E. Goudey. 1959. Scribner.
The How and Why Wonder Book of Ants and Bees. Ronald
N. Rood. Wonder-Treasure Books.
The How and Why Wonder Book of Birds. Robert Mathewson.
1960. Wonder-Treasure Books.
The How and Why Wonder Book of Deserts. Felix Sutton.
1965. Wonder-Treasure Books.
The How and Why Wonder Book of Ecology. Shelly and
Mary Louise Grossman. 1971. Wonder-Treasure Books.
The How and Why Wonder Book of Explorations and Discov-
eries. Irving Robbin. Wonder-Treasure Books.
The How and Why Wonder Book of Insects. Ronald N. Rood.
1960. Wonder-Treasure Books.
The How and Why Wonder Book of Oceanography. Robert
Scharff. 1964. Wonder-Treasure Books.
The How and Why Wonder Book of Reptiles and Amphibians.
Robert Mathewson. 1960. Wonder-Treasure Books.
The How and Why Wonder Book of Sea Shells. Donald F.
Low. Wonder-Treasure Books.
The How and Why Wonder Book of the Human Body. Martin
L. Keen. Wonder-Treasure Books.
How Big Is Big? Herman and Nina Schneider. 1946. Ad-
dison-Wesley.
How Maps and Globes Help Us. David Hackler. 1962.
Benefic.
Huckleberry Finn. Mark Twain. 1884. Dutton; Dell.
The Hundred and One Dalmations. Dodie Smith. 1957. Vik-
ing.
Hunting Grizzly Bears. Henry A. Bamman and Robert J.
Whitehead. 1963. Benefic.
Hurlbut's Story of the Bible. Jesse Lyman Hurlbut. 1966.
Zondervan.


I Like You. Sandol Stoddard Warburg. 1965. Houghton
Mifflin.
I Want To Be a Nurse. Carla Greene. 1957. Children's.
If Jesus Came To My House. Joan Gale Thomas. 1951.
Lothrop, Lee & Shepard.
Illustrated Atlas for Young America. Hammond Inc. 1967.
Hammond Inc.
Illustrated Treasury of Children's Literature. Margaret E.
Martignoni, editor. 1955. Grosset & Dunlap.
Illustrated Treasury of Poetry for Children. David Ross,
editor. 1970. Grosset & Dunlap.

I'm Really Dragged But Nothing Gets Me Down.   Nat Hentoff.
    1968.   Simon & Schuster; Dell.
In John's Back Yard.   Esther Meeks.   1957.   Follett.
In My Mother's House.   Ann Nolan Clark.   1941.   Viking.
In the Forest.   Marie Hall Ets.   1944.   Viking.
The Incredible Journey.   Sheila Burnford.   1961.   Little,
    Brown.
Indian Lore.   Boy Scouts of America.   1959.   Boy Scouts
    of America.
The Indians of New Jersey:   Dickon Among the Lenapes.
    Mark Raymond Harrington.   Rutgers.
Insect Life.   Boy Scouts of America.   1963.   Boy Scouts of
    America.
Invincible Louisa.   Cornelia Meigs.   1933.   Little, Brown.
Island of the Blue Dolphins.   Scott O'Dell.   1960.   Houghton
    Mifflin.
It's Like This, Cat.   Emily Cheney Neville.   1963.   Harper
    & Row.


J.T.   Jane Wagner.   1969.   Van Nostrand Reinhold; Dell.
Jackie Robinson of the Brooklyn Dodgers.   Milton J. Shapiro.
    1966.   Messner.
James and the Giant Peach.   Roald Dahl.   1961.   Knopf.
Jazz Country.   Nat Hentoff.   1965.   Harper & Row; Dell.
Jeanne-Marie Counts Her Sheep.   Francoise.   1951.   Scrib-
    ner.
Jesus, the Little New Baby.   Mary Edna Lloyd.   1951.
    Abingdon.
The Jim Thorpe Story; America's Greatest Athlete.   Gene
    Schoor.   1951.   Messner.
Jimmy, a Little Pup.   Clarence Jonk.   Denison.
John F. Kennedy.   Norman Richards and John P. Reidy.
    1967.   Children's.
John F. Kennedy:   New Frontiersman.   Charles P. Graves.
    1965.   Garrard; Dell.
Johnny Tremain.   Esther Forbes.   1943.   Houghton Mifflin;
    Dell.
Join the Dots.   Isobel R. Beard.   1969.   Follett.
Jokes and Riddles.   George Carlson.   Platt & Munk.
Jon and the Little Lost Lamb.   Jan Latourette.   1965.
    Concordia.
Jonathan and the Octopus.   Celeste K. Foster.   Denison.
Jo's Boys.   Louisa May Alcott.   1886.   Little, Brown.
Joseph Pulitzer, Front Page Pioneer.   Iris Noble.   1957.
    Messner.
Journey Cake, Ho!   Ruth Sawyer.   1953.   Viking.

Journey to the Centre of the Earth.    Jules Verne.   1864.
    Dutton.
Julius.   Syd Hoff.   1959.   Harper & Row.
The Jungle Books.   Rudyard Kipling.   1894.   Doubleday;
    Dell.
Junior Crossword Puzzle Book.   Platt & Munk.
Junior Illustrated Encyclopedia of Sports.   Herbert Kamm.
    1960.   Bobbs-Merrill.
Junior Miss.   Sally Benson.   1941.   Doubleday.
Junior Science Book of Icebergs and Glaciers.   Patricia
    Lauber.   1961.   Garrard.
Junior Science Book of Penguins.   Patricia Lauber.   1963.
    Garrard.
Junior Science Book of Rain, Hail, Sleet, and Snow.   Nancy
    Larrick.   1961.   Garrard.
Junior Science Book of Volcanoes.   Patricia Lauber.   1965.
    Garrard.
Junket.   Anne H. White.   1955.   Viking.
Just Follow Me.   Phoebe Erickson.   1960.   Follett.
Just Me.   Marie Hall Ets.   1965.   Viking.
Just So Stories.   See:   New Illustrated Just So Stories.
Justin Morgan Had a Horse.   Marguerite Henry.   1954.
    Rand McNally.


Katy and the Big Snow.   Virginia Lee Burton.   1943.   Hough-
    ton Mifflin.
Katy No-Pocket.   Emmy Payne.   1944.   Houghton Mifflin.
Keer-Loo.   Laura Louise Foster.   1965.   Naturegraph.
The Kennedy Years and the Negro.   John F. Kennedy.   Doris
    E. Saunders, editor.   1964.   Johnson (Chicago).
Kidnapped.   Robert Louis Stevenson.   1886.   Dutton.
Kim.   Rudyard Kipling.   1901.   Doubleday; Dell.
King Arthur and the Round Table.   A. M. Hadfield.   1953.
    Dutton.
King of the Wind.   Marguerite Henry.   1948.   Rand McNally.
King Robert the Resting Ruler.   Donna Lugg Pape.   1968.
    Oddo.
King Solomon's Mines.   H. Rider Haggard.   1886.   Dutton.
King's Invitation.   Virginia Mueller.   1968.   Concordia.
The Kitten Who Was Different.   Lowell Saunders.   Denison.
Kon-Tiki For Young People.   Thor Heyerdahl.   1960.   Rand
    McNally.


Lad:   A Dog.   Albert Payson Terhune.   1926.   Dutton.
Lame Man Who Walked Again.   Mary P. Warren.   1966.
    Concordia.

Landslide!  Veronique Day.  1963.  Dell.
Lassie Come-Home.  Eric Knight.  1941.  Holt, Rinehart
and Winston.
Last One Home Is a Green Pig.  Edith Thacher Hurd.  1959.
Harper & Row.
Learning Begins at Home--A Stimulus for a Child's I. Q.
Doris V. Brown and Pauline McDonald.  Lawrence.
Learning How Baseball.  Dick Siebert.  1968.  Creative Edu-
cational Society.
Leatherwork.  Boy Scouts of America.  1970.  Boy Scouts
of America.
Lentil.  Robert McCloskey.  1940.  Viking.
Let's Find Out About Heat, Water and Air.  Herman and
Nina Schneider.  1946.  Addison-Wesley.
Let's Go Outdoors.  Harriet E. Huntington.  1939.  Double-
day.
Lifesaving.  Boy Scouts of America.  1965.  Boy Scouts of
America.
Link the Dots.  Isobel R. Beard.  1969.  Follett.
Lisa, Bright and Dark.  John Neufeld.  1969.  S. G. Phillips.
Little Bear.  Else Holmelund Minarik.  1957.  Harper &
Row.
Little Bear's Friend.  Else Holmelund Minarik.  1960.
Harper & Row.
Little Bear's Visit.  Else Holmelund Minarik.  1961.  Harper
& Row.
Little Benjamin and the First Christmas.  Betty Forell.
1964.  Concordia.
Little Black Sambo.  Helen Bannerman.  1900.  Platt &
Munk.
Little Boat That Almost Sank.  Mary P. Warren.  1965.
Concordia.
Little Book About God (Protestant).  Lauren Ford.  1934.
Doubleday.
Little Chief.  Syd Hoff.  1961.  Harper & Row.
Little Eddie.  Carolyn Haywood.  1947.  Morrow.
The Little Engine That Could.  Watty Piper (pseud. ).  1929.
Platt & Munk.
The Little Family.  Lois Lenski.  1932.  Doubleday.
Little Folded Hands.  A. Jahsmann, reviser.  1959.  Con-
cordia.
The Little House.  Virginia Lee Burton.  1942.  Houghton
Mifflin.
Little House in the Big Woods.  Laura Ingalls Wilder.  1932.
Harper & Row.
Little House on the Prairie.  Laura Ingalls Wilder.  1935.
Harper & Row.

The Little Island.   Golden MacDonald.   1946.   Doubleday.
Little Lord Fauntleroy.   Frances Hodgson Burnett.   1886.
    Dutton.
Little Men.   Louisa May Alcott.   1871.   Dutton; Little,
    Brown.
The Little Old Woman Who Used Her Head.   Hope Newell.
    1935.   Thomas Nelson.
Little Quack.   Ruth Woods.   1961.   Follett.
The Little Rabbit Who Wanted Red Wings.   Carolyn Sherwin
    Bailey.   1945.   Platt & Munk.
Little Red Riding Hood.   Jakob and Wilhelm Grimm.   1812.
    Grosset & Dunlap.
Little Sleeping Beauty.   Brenda Prior.   1969.   Concordia.
Little Toot.   Hardie Gramatky.   1939.   Putnam.
Little Town on the Prairie.   Laura Ingalls Wilder.   1941.
    Harper & Row.
Little Vic.   Doris Gates.   1951.   Viking.
Little Visits With God.   Allan H. Jahsmann and Martin P.
    Simon.   1957.   Concordia.
Little Women.   Louisa May Alcott.   1868.   Little, Brown;
    Dutton.
The Littlest Angel.   Charles Tazewell.   1966.   Children's.
Liz Dearly's Silly Glasses.   Donna Lugg Pape.   1968.   Oddo.
The Lonely Doll.   Dare Wright.   1957.   Doubleday.
Lorna Doone.   Richard Doddridge Blackmore.   1869.   Dutton.
The Lost Kingdom.   Chester Bryant.   1951.   Messner.
The Lost Princess: A Double Story.   George MacDonald.
    Dutton.
Lost Uranium Mine.   Henry A. Bamman and Robert J. White-
    head.   1964.   Benefic.
Lots More Tell Me Why.   Arkady Leokum.   1971.   Grosset
    & Dunlap.
Love Is a Special Way of Feeling.   Joan Walsh Anglund.
    1960.   Harcourt Brace Jovanovich.


M Is For Monster.   Roger Price; Leonard Stern; and Larry
    Sloan.   1965.   Price/Stern/Sloan.
Mable the Whale.   Patricia King.   1958.   Follett.
Mad Libs.   Roger Price and Leonard Stern.   1958.   Price/
    Stern/Sloan.
Mad Libs No. 5.   Roger Price and Leonard Stern.   1968.
    Price/Stern/Sloan.
Mad Libs Six.   Roger Price and Leonard Stern.   1970.
    Price/Stern/Sloan.
Madeline.   Ludwig Bemelmans.   1939.   Viking.
Madeline and the Bad Hat. Ludwig Bemelmans.   1957.   Viking.

Madeline and the Gypsies.  Ludwig Bemelmans.  1959.  Viking.

Madeline in London.  Ludwig Bemelmans.  1961.  Viking.

Madeline's Rescue.  Ludwig Bemelmans.  1953.  Viking.

The Magic Wishbone.  Sister Adele Marie, C. S. J.  Lawrence.

Make It Yourself!  Bernice Wells Carlson.  1950.  Abingdon.

Make Way for Ducklings.  Robert McCloskey.  1941.  Viking.

Man Caught by a Fish.  M. M. Brem.  1967.  Concordia.

Marco Polo.  Manuel Komroff.  1952.  Messner.

Marian's Big Book of Bible Stories.  Marian M. Schoolland.
     1947.  Eerdmans.

Marian's Favorite Bible Stories.  Marian M. Schoolland.
     1948.  Eerdmans.

Marshmallow.  Clare Turlay Newberry.  1942.  Harper &
     Row.

Martin Luther King Jr., 1929-1968; An Ebony Picture Biography.  Dr. Martin Luther King, Jr.  1969.  Johnson
     (Chicago).

Mary Poppins.  See: Walt Disney's Mary Poppins.

Mary's Story.  M. M. Brem.  1967.  Concordia.

Megan.  Iris Noble.  1965.  Messner.

Mei Li.  Thomas Handforth.  1938.  Doubleday.

Melindy's Medal.  Georgene Faulkner and John Becker.
     1945.  Messner.

Men of Iron.  Howard Pyle.  1891.  Harper & Row.

The Middle Ages.  Dorothy Mills.  1935.  Putnam.

Mike Mulligan and His Steam Shovel.  Virginia Lee Burton.
     1939.  Houghton Mifflin.

Mike's House.  Julia Sauer.  1954.  Viking.

Minn of the Mississippi.  Holling C. Holling.  1951.  Houghton Mifflin.

Miracles:  Poems by Children of the English-Speaking World.
     Richard Lewis, editor.  1966.  Simon & Schuster.

Miss Hattie and the Monkey.  Helen Olds.  1958.  Follett.

Miss Hickory.  Carolyn Sherwin Bailey.  1946.  Viking.

Mr. Mighty.  M. Worden Kidder and Barbara Kidder.  Denison.

Mr. Popper's Penguins.  Richard and Florence Atwater.
     1938.  Little, Brown.

Mr. Revere and I.  Robert Lawson.  1953.  Little, Brown.

Mr. Wizard's Experiments for Young Scientists.  Don Herbert.  1959.  Doubleday.

Mr. Wonderful.  Barbara Kidder.  Denison.

Misty of Chincoteague.  Marguerite Henry.  1947.  Rand
     McNally.

Moby Dick.  Herman Melville.  1851.  Grosset & Dunlap.

The Monkey and the Crocodile:  A Jataka Tale from India.
   Paul Galdone.  Seabury.
Monster Mad Libs.  Roger Price and Leonard Stern.  1965.
   Price/Stern/Sloan.
Mop Top.  Don Freeman.  1955.  Viking.
More Little Visits with God.  Allan H. Jahsmann and Martin
   P. Simon.  1961.  Concordia.
More Tell Me Why.  Arkady Leokum.  1967.  Grosset &
   Dunlap.
Most Wonderful King.  Dave Hill.  1968.  Concordia.
Mother Goose.  Gyo Fujikawa, illustrator.  Grosset & Dun-
   lap.
Mother Goose; The Classic Volland Edition.  Eulalie O.
   Grover, editor.  1915.  Hubbard.
Mother Goose Rhymes.  Platt & Munk.
Motorboating.  Boy Scouts of America.  1962.  Boy Scouts
   of America.
Mouse House.  Rumer Godden.  1957.  Viking.
Music.  Boy Scouts of America.  1968.  Boy Scouts of
   America.
Mustang, Wild Spirit of the West.  Marguerite Henry.  1966.
   Rand McNally.
My Bible Story Book.  Gerhard L. Wind.  1956.  Concordia.
My Brimful Book.  Dana Bruce, editor.  1960.  Platt &
   Munk.
My First Crossword Puzzle Book.  Platt & Munk.
My Friend Flicka.  Mary O'Hara.  1941.  Lippincott; Dell.
My Own Little House.  Merriman Kaune.  1957.  Follett.
My Picture Story Bible.  Dena Korfker.  Zondervan.
My Side of the Mountain.  Jean Craighead George.  1959.
   Dutton.
Mythology.  Edith Hamilton.  1942.  Little, Brown.


"National Velvet."  Enid Bagnold.  1949.  Morrow.
Nature.  Boy Scouts of America.  1952.  Boy Scouts of
   America.
Nature Atlas of America.  Emil L. Jordan.  1952.  Ham-
   mond.
The Negro in America.  Earl Spangler.  Lerner.
New Illustrated Just So Stories.  Rudyard Kipling.  1912.
   Doubleday.
Nine Days to Christmas.  Marie Hall Ets and Aurora La-
   bastida.  1959.  Viking.
The Nitty Gritty.  Frank Bonham.  1968.  Dutton; Dell.
No Fighting, No Biting!  Else Holmelund Minarik.  1958.
   Harper & Row.

Nobody Listens to Andrew.  Elizabeth Guilfoile.  1957.  Fol-
lett.
Norman the Doorman.  Don Freeman.  1959.  Viking.
Now We Are Six.  A.A. Milne.  1927.  Dutton; Dell.
Nutshell Library.  Maurice Sendak.  1962.  Harper & Row.


The Ocean Laboratory.  Athelstan Spilhaus.  1967.  Creative
Educational Society.
Old Peter's Russian Tales.  Arthur Ransome.  1916.  Thom-
as Nelson.
Oliver.  Syd Hoff.  1960.  Harper & Row.
On the Banks of Plum Creek.  Laura Ingalls Wilder.  1937.
Harper & Row.
On Two Wheels: An Anthology About Men and Motorcycles.
Don McKay, editor.  1971.  Dell.
Once a Mouse: A Fable Cut in Wood.  Marcia Brown.
1961.  Scribner.
One Fish, Two Fish, Red Fish, Blue Fish.  Dr. Seuss.
1960.  Random.
One God: The Ways We Worship Him.  Florence Mary
Fitch.  1944.  Lothrop, Lee & Shepard.
One Hundred Bible Stories.  1966.  Concordia.
One Morning in Maine.  Robert McCloskey.  1952.  Viking.
1001 Riddles.  Platt & Munk.
One Thousand Poems for Children.  Elizabeth Hough Sechrist,
editor.  1946.  Macrae Smith.
Onion John.  Joseph Krumgold.  1959.  Thomas Y. Crowell;
Apollo Editions.
The Otters' Tale.  Gavin Maxwell.  See: Ring of Bright
Water.
The Outnumbered.  Charlotte Brooks, editor.  1967.  Dell.
The Outsiders.  S.E. Hinton.  1967.  Viking; Dell.


Paddle-to-the-Sea.  Holling C. Holling.  1941.  Houghton
Mifflin.
The Pantheon Story of Art for Young People.  Ariane Ruskin.
1964.  Pantheon.
Parks and Gardens.  Robert S. Lemmon.  1967.  Creative
Educational Society.
Patrol Leader's Handbook.  Boy Scouts of America.  1967.
Boy Scouts of America.
Paul Bunyan Swings His Axe.  Dell J. McCormick.  1936.
Caxton.
Pecos Bill.  James Cloyd Bowman.  1937.  Albert Whitman.
Pelle's New Suit.  Elsa Maartman Beskow.  1929.  Harper &
Row.

Pencil, Pen and Brush. Harvey Weiss. 1961. Addison-Wesley.

Penrod. Booth Tarkington. 1914. Doubleday.

Pepper and Salt. Howard Pyle. 1885. Harper & Row.

Personal Fitness. Boy Scouts of America. 1968. Boy Scouts of America.

Peter Churchmouse. Margot Austin. 1941. Dutton.

Peter Pan. James M. Barrie. 1949. Scribner.

The Peter Pan Bag. Lee Kingman. 1970. Houghton Mifflin; Dell.

Peter's Policeman. Anne Lattin. 1958. Follett.

Pets. Boy Scouts of America. 1969. Boy Scouts of America.

Photography. Boy Scouts of America. 1960. Boy Scouts of America.

A Picture Book of Palestine. Ethel L. Smither. 1947. Abingdon.

The Pigman. Paul Zindel. 1968. Harper & Row; Dell.

Pilgrim's Progress. John Bunyan. 1678; 1684. Dutton.

Pinocchio: The Story of a Puppet. Carlo Collodi. 1881. Dutton.

Pioneering. Boy Scouts of America. 1967. Boy Scouts of America.

Pippi Goes on Board. Astrid Lindgren. 1957. Viking.

Pippi in the South Seas. Astrid Lindgren. 1959. Viking.

Pippi Longstocking. Astrid Lindgren. 1950. Viking.

Planets, Stars and Space. Joseph M. Chamberlain and Thomas D. Nicholson. 1962. Creative Educational Society.

Play With Me. Marie Hall Ets. 1955. Viking.

Poems for Youth: An American Anthology. William Rose Benet, compiler. 1923. Dutton.

Point of Departure. Robert S. Gold, editor. Dell.

Pony Engine. F. M. Ford. Grosset & Dunlap.

The Poppy Seed Cakes. Margery Clark (pseud.). 1924. Doubleday.

The Presidents in American History. Charles A. Beard and William Beard. 1948. Messner.

The Prince and the Pauper. Mark Twain. 1882. Dutton.

Princess and the Baby. Janice Kramer. 1969. Concordia.

Professor Fred and the Fid-Fuddlephone. Donna Lugg Pape. 1968. Oddo.

Public Health. Boy Scouts of America. 1969. Boy Scouts of America.

Public Speaking. Boy Scouts of America. 1969. Boy Scouts of America.

The Pushcart War. Jean Merrill. 1964. Addison-Wesley.

Puzzles and Riddles.   Isobel R. Beard.   Follett.
Puzzles for Pleasure.   Isobel R. Beard.   Follett.


Queenie Peavy.   Robert Burch.   1966.   Viking.


Rabbit and Skunk and the Scary Rock.   Carla Stevens.   1962.
    Addison-Wesley.
Rabbit Hill.   Robert Lawson.   1944.   Viking; Dell.
Radio.   Boy Scouts of America.   1965.   Boy Scouts of
    America.
Rain Drop Splash.   Alvin Tresselt.   1946.   Lothrop, Lee
    & Shepard.
The Rainbow Dictionary.   Wendell W. Wright, editor.   1947.
    World.
Rascal: A Memoir of a Better Era.   Sterling North.   1963.
    Dutton.
Reading.   Boy Scouts of America.   1965.   Boy Scouts of
    America.
The Real Diary of a Real Boy.   Henry A. Shute.   1902.
    William L. Bauhan.
The Real Mother Goose.   Blanche Fisher Wright, illustrator.
    1916.   Rand McNally.
Rebecca of Sunnybrook Farm.   Kate Douglas Smith Wiggin.
    1903.   Houghton Mifflin.
Recreational Sports.   Clifford Brownell and Roy Moore.
    1962.   Creative Educational Society.
The Red Badge of Courage.   Stephen Crane.   1895.   Dutton.
The Red Balloon.   Albert Lamourisse.   1956.   Doubleday.
Red Light Green Light.   Golden MacDonald.   1944.   Double-
    day.
Red Planet; A Colonial Boy on Mars.   Robert A. Heinlein.
    1949.   Scribner.
Renaissance and Reformation Times.   Dorothy Mills.   1939.
    Putnam.
Reptile Study.   Boy Scouts of America.   1971.   Boy Scouts
    of America.
The Rich Fool.   Janice Kramer.   1964.   Concordia.
Rifle and Shotgun Shooting.   Boy Scouts of America.   1967.
    Boy Scouts of America.
Ring of Bright Water.   Gavin Maxwell.   1961.   Dutton.
Robin Deer.   Olga Cossi.   1968.   Naturegraph.
Robinson Crusoe.   Daniel Defoe.   1719.   Dutton; Dell.
Rocket Ship Galileo.   Robert A. Heinlein.   1947.   Scribner.
Rocky, the Rocket Mouse.   Alyce Bergey.   Denison.

Roller Skates.  Ruth Sawyer and Kate Seredy.  1936.  Vi-
    king; Dell.
The Rolling Stones.  Robert A. Heinlein.  1952.  Scribner.
Rowing.  Boy Scouts of America.  1964.  Boy Scouts of
    America.
The Runaway Bunny.  Margaret Wise Brown.  1942.  Harper
    & Row.


Sacred Well of Sacrifice.  Henry A. Bamman and Robert J.
    Whitehead.  1964.  Benefic.
Safety.  Boy Scouts of America.  1971.  Boy Scouts of
    America.
Sailor Jack.  Selma and Jack Wassermann.  1960.  Benefic.
Sailor Jack and Bluebell.  Selma and Jack Wassermann.
    1960.  Benefic.
Sailor Jack and Bluebell's Dive.  Selma and Jack Wasser-
    mann.  1961.  Benefic.
Sailor Jack and Eddy.  Selma and Jack Wassermann.  1961.
    Benefic.
Sailor Jack and Homer Pots.  Selma and Jack Wassermann.
    1961.  Benefic.
Sailor Jack and the Ball Game.  Selma and Jack Wasser-
    mann.  1962.  Benefic.
Sailor Jack and the Jet Plane.  Selma and Jack Wassermann.
    1962.  Benefic.
Sailor Jack and the Target Ship.  Selma and Jack Wasser-
    mann.  1960.  Benefic.
Sailor Jack Goes North.  Selma and Jack Wassermann.  1961.
    Benefic.
Sailor Jack's New Friend.  Selma and Jack Wassermann.
    1960.  Benefic.
Sally Alligator.  Betty Molgard Ryan.  Denison.
Sam, Bangs and Moonshine.  Evaline Ness.  1966.  Holt,
    Rinehart and Winston.
Sam Houston:  Hero of Texas.  Jean Lee Latham.  1965.
    Garrard.
Sammy the Seal.  Syd Hoff.  1959.  Harper & Row.
The Saturdays.  Elizabeth Enright.  1941.  Holt, Rinehart
    & Winston; Dell.
Scholarship.  Boy Scouts of America.  1970.  Boy Scouts of
    America.
Scientist Sam.  Donna Lugg Pape.  1968.  Oddo.
Scout How Book.  Boy Scouts of America.  1969.  Boy
    Scouts of America.
Sea Star, Orphan of Chincoteague.  Marguerite Henry.  1949.
    Rand McNally.

The Search for Piranha. Henry A. Bamman and Robert J.
    Whitehead. 1964. Benefic.
The Secret Garden. Frances Hodgson Burnett. 1912.
    Lippincott; Dell.
Secret Journey. Virginia Mueller. 1968. Concordia.
Secret of the Andes. Ann Nolan Clark. 1952. Viking.
Secret of the Star. Hill and Roberts. 1966. Concordia.
The Secret Three. Mildred Myrick. 1963. Harper & Row.
Seeds and More Seeds. Millicent Ellis Selsam. 1959.
    Harper & Row.
Sensible Kate. Doris Gates. 1943. Viking.
Sesame Street. See: The Songs of Sesame Street.
Seventeen. Booth Tarkington. 1916. Harper; Grosset &
    Dunlap.
Shan's Lucky Knife. Jean Merrill. 1960. Addison-Wesley.
Shoemaker Fooze. Donna Lugg Pape. 1968. Oddo.
Show and Tell. Patricia Miles Martin. 1962. Putnam.
Sigmund Freud. Rachel Baker. 1952. Messner.
Signaling. Boy Scouts of America. 1940. Boy Scouts of
    America.
The Silver Sword. Ian Serraillier. 1959. S.G. Phillips.
Simeon's Secret. Janice Kramer. 1969. Concordia.
The Singing Tree. Kate Seredy. 1939. Viking; Dell.
Sitting Bull, Champion of His People. Shannon Garst. 1946.
    Messner.
Skip, the Pioneer Boy. Gwendolen L. Hayden. Denison.
Small-Boat Sailing. Boy Scouts of America. 1965. Boy
    Scouts of America.
Small Rain: Verses from the Bible. Jessie Orton Jones,
    editor. 1943. Viking.
The Smallest Boy in the Class. Jerrold Beim. 1949. Mor-
    row.
Smoky, the Cow Horse. Will James. 1926. Scribner.
Snakes. Herbert S. Zim. 1949. Morrow.
Snipp, Snapp, Snurr and the Big Surprise. Maj Lindman.
    1937. Albert Whitman.
Snipp, Snapp, Snurr and the Buttered Bread. Maj Lindman.
    1934. Albert Whitman.
Snipp, Snapp, Snurr and the Gingerbread. Maj Lindman.
    1936. Albert Whitman.
Snipp, Snapp, Snurr and the Magic Horse. Maj Lindman.
    1933. Albert Whitman.
Snipp, Snapp, Snurr and the Red Shoes. Maj Lindman.
    1932. Albert Whitman.
Snipp, Snapp, Snurr and the Yellow Sled. Maj Lindman.
    1936. Albert Whitman.
Snow Treasure. Marie McSwigan. 1942. Dutton.

Snowbound in Hidden Valley. Holly Wilson. 1957. Messner.
The Snowy Day. Ezra Jack Keats. 1962. Viking.
Soil and Water Conservation. Boy Scouts of America. 1968.
    Boy Scouts of America.
Some Merry Adventures of Robin Hood of Great Renown in
    Nottinghamshire. Howard Pyle. 1954. Scribner.
Something New at the Zoo. Esther Meeks. 1957. Follett.
Son of Mad Libs. Roger Price and Leonard Stern. 1959.
    Price/Stern/Sloan.
The Song of Hiawatha. Henry Wadsworth Longfellow. 1855.
    Dutton.
Song of the Swallows. Leo Politi. 1949. Scribner.
The Songs of Sesame Street. Jeffrey Moss; Joe Raposo;
    and Jon Stone. 1970. Children's Television Workshop,
    Columbia Book and Record Library, CBS, Inc.
Sooper Mad Libs. Roger Price and Leonard Stern. 1962.
    Price/Stern/Sloan.
The Soul Brothers and Sister Lou. Kristin Hunter. 1968.
    Scribner.
Space. Marian Tellander. 1960. Follett.
Space Cadet. Robert A. Heinlein. 1948. Scribner.
Spaghetti Eddie. Mary Jackson Ellis. Denison.
Spooks and Spirits and Shadowy Shapes. Emma L. Brock
    et al. 1949. Dutton.
Springtime for Jeanne-Marie. Francoise. 1955. Scribner.
Stamp Collecting. Boy Scouts of America. 1966. Boy
    Scouts of America.
The Star Beast. Robert A. Heinlein. 1954. Scribner.
Starman Jones. Robert A. Heinlein. 1953. Scribner; Dell.
Starship Troopers. Robert A. Heinlein. 1959. Putnam.
The Steadfast Tin Soldier. Hans Christian Andersen. Scrib-
    ner.
Still More Answers. Mary Elting and Franklin Folsom.
    1970. Grosset & Dunlap.
Still More Tell Me Why. Arkady Leokum. 1968. Grosset
    & Dunlap.
Stone Soup; An Old Tale. Marcia Brown. 1947. Scribner.
Stories of Champions: Baseball Hall of Fame. Sam and
    Beryl Epstein. 1965. Garrard.
Stories That Never Grow Old. Watty Piper, editor. Platt
    & Munk.
The Stork Didn't Bring You. Lois Loyd Pemberton. 1948.
    Thomas Nelson.
Stormy, Misty's Foal. Marguerite Henry. 1963. Rand
    McNally.
The Story About Ping. Marjorie Flack. 1933. Viking.

The Story of Doctor Dolittle. Hugh Lofting. 1920. Lippincott; Dell.

The Story of Ferdinand. Munro Leaf. 1936. Viking.

The Story of Linda Lookout. Keith Lundy Hoofnagle. Naturegraph.

The Story of Little Black Sambo. Helen Bannerman. 1899. Lippincott.

The Story of Mount Vernon. Natalie M. Miller. 1965. Children's.

Story of Noah's Ark. Jane Latourette. 1965. Concordia.

Story of the Bible World. Nelson Beecher Keyes. 1962. Hammond.

The Story of the Jew. Harry Gersh and Elma E. and Lee J. Levinger. Behrman.

The Story of the Liberty Bell. Natalie Miller. 1965. Children's.

The Story of the Lincoln Memorial. Natalie Miller. 1966. Children's.

The Story of the Star-Spangled Banner. Natalie Miller. 1965. Children's.

The Story of the Statue of Liberty. Natalie Miller. 1965. Children's.

Story of the Trapp Family Singers. Maria Augusta Trapp. 1949. Lippincott; Dell.

Strawberry Girl. Lois Lenski. 1945. Lippincott; Dell.

Stuart Little. E. B. White. 1945. Harper & Row; Dell.

The Summer of the Swans. Betsy Byars. 1970. Viking.

The Superlative Horse. Jean Merrill. 1961. Addison-Wesley.

Surprise Island. Gertrude Chandler Warner. 1949. Albert Whitman.

Swimmer Is a Hopper. Mary Jackson Ellis. Denison.

Swimming. Boy Scouts of America. 1960. Boy Scouts of America.

Swimmy. Leo Lionni. 1963. Pantheon.

The Swiss Family Robinson. Johann R. Wyss. 1813. Dutton; Dell.

Sylvester and the Magic Pebble. William Steig. 1969. Simon & Schuster.


Tales from a Finnish Tupa. James Cloyd Bowman and Margery Bianco. 1936. Albert Whitman.

Tales from Shakespeare. Charles and Mary Lamb. 1807. Dutton.

Tales of the Sea Foam. Lisette G. Brown. 1969. Naturegraph.

The Tall Book of Bible Stories. Katherine Gibson, editor.
    1957. Harper & Row.
The Tall Book of Christmas. Dorothy Hall Smith, editor.
    1954. Harper & Row.
The Tall Book of Fairy Tales. William Sharp. 1947.
    Harper & Row.
The Tall Book of Make-Believe. Garth Williams. 1950.
    Harper & Row.
The Tall Book of Mother Goose. Feodor Rojankowsky, illus-
    trator. 1942. Harper & Row.
The Tall Book of Nursery Tales. Feodor Rojankovsky.
    1944. Harper & Row.
Tall Tales from the High Hills. Ellis Credle. 1957. Thom-
    as Nelson.
Tanglewood Tales. Nathaniel Hawthorne. 1853. Dutton.
The Tasha Tudor Book of Fairy Tales. Dana Bruce, editor.
    1961. Platt & Munk.
Tell Me a Joke. Dana Bruce, editor. 1966. Platt &
    Munk.
Tell Me a Riddle. Dana Bruce, editor. 1966. Platt &
    Munk.
Tell Me about Christmas. Mary Alice Jones. 1958. Rand
    McNally.
Tell Me about God. Mary Alice Jones. 1943. Rand Mc-
    Nally.
Tell Me about Heaven. Mary Alice Jones. 1956. Rand
    McNally.
Tell Me about Jesus. Mary Alice Jones. 1944. Rand Mc-
    Nally.
Tell Me about Prayer. Mary Alice Jones. 1948. Rand
    McNally.
Tell Me about the Bible. Mary Alice Jones. 1945. Rand
    McNally.
Tell Me Some More. Crosby Newell Bonsall. 1961. Harper
    & Row.
Tell Me Why. Arkady Leokum. 1969. Grosset & Dunlap.
Ten Short Plays. M. Jerry Weiss, editor. Dell.
The Tenggren Mother Goose. Gustav Tenggren, illustrator.
    1940. Little, Brown.
Thee, Hannah! Marguerite De Angeli. 1940. Doubleday.
They Were Strong and Good. Robert Lawson. 1940. Viking.
The Thirty-Nine Steps. John Buchan. 1915. Dutton.
Three Fox Fables. Paul Galdone. Seabury.
The Three Little Pigs. Paul Galdone. Seabury.
The Three Little Pigs. Margaret Hillert. Follett.
Three Men Who Walked in Fire. Joann Scheck. 1967. Con-
    cordia.

The Three Thinkers of Thay-Lee. Donna Lugg Pape. 1968.
Oddo.
The Three Toymakers. Ursula Moray Williams. 1971.
Thomas Nelson.
Through the Looking Glass. Lewis Carroll. 1872. Dutton.
Thunder Road. William Campbell Gault. 1952. Dutton.
Tim Tadpole and the Great Bullfrog. Marjorie Flack. 1934.
Doubleday.
Time for the Stars. Robert A. Heinlein. 1956. Scribner.
Time of Wonder. Robert McCloskey. 1957. Viking.
Timothy Turtle. Al Graham. 1949. Viking.
Tom Brown's School Days. Thomas Hughes. 1857. Dutton.
Tom Sawyer. Mark Twain. 1878. Dutton; Dell.
Too Many Dogs. Ramona Dupre. 1960. Follett.
The Tough Winter. Robert Lawson. 1954. Viking.
Track and Field. Earl "Bud" Meyers and Rich Hacker.
1962. Creative Educational Society.
Treasure Island. Robert Louis Stevenson. 1883. Dutton;
Dell.
Tree in the Trail. Holling C. Holling. 1942. Houghton
Mifflin.
A Tree Is Nice. Janice May Udry. 1956. Harper & Row.
Tricks and Teasers; A Highlights Handbook. The Editors
of Highlights. 1965. Highlights For Children.
The True Book of Air Around Us. Margaret Friskey. 1953.
Children's.
The True Book of Animal Babies. Illa Podendorf. 1955.
Children's.
The True Book of Birds We Know. Margaret Friskey.
1954. Children's.
The True Book of Dinosaurs. Mary L. Clark. 1955. Chil-
dren's.
The True Book of Farm Animals. John Lewellen. 1954.
Children's.
The True Book of Holidays. John W. Purcell. 1955. Chil-
dren's.
The True Book of Indians. Teri Martini. 1954. Children's.
The True Book of Insects. Illa Podendorf. 1954. Chil-
dren's.
The True Book of Moon, Sun and Stars. Illa Podendorf.
1954. Children's.
The True Book of Our Post Office and Its Helpers. Irene
S. Miner. 1955. Children's.
The True Book of Pebbles and Shells. Illa Podendorf. 1954.
Children's.
The True Book of Plants We Know. Irene S. Miner. 1953.
Children's.

The True Book of Policemen and Firemen.    Irene S. Miner.
    1954.    Children's.
The True Book of Science Experiments.    Illa Podendorf.
    1954.    Children's.
The True Book of Seasons.    Illa Podendorf.    1955.    Chil-
    dren's.
The Trumpet of the Swan.    E.B. White.    1970.    Harper &
    Row.
Tuned Out.    Maia Wojciechowska.    1968.    Harper & Row;
    Dell.
Tunnel in the Sky.    Robert A. Heinlein.    1955.    Scribner.
The Twenty-One Balloons.    William Pene du Bois.    1947.
    Viking; Dell.
Twenty-Seven Cats Next Door.    Anita Feagles.    1965.    Ad-
    dison-Wesley.
Twenty Thousand Leagues Under the Sea.    Jules Verne.
    1869.    Dutton.
Two Men in the Temple.    Joan Scheck.    1968.    Concordia.


Umbrella.    Taro Yashima.    1958.    Viking.
Uncle Remus Stories.    See:    Walt Disney's Uncle Remus
    Stories.
Understood Betsy.    Dorothy Canfield Fisher.    1916.    Holt,
    Rinehart and Winston.
Unforgiving Servant.    Janice Kramer.    1968.    Concordia.
UNICEF Festival Book.    Judith Spiegelman.    1966.    United
    States Committee for UNICEF.
Up a Road Slowly.    Irene Hunt.    1966.    Follett.
Up Above and Down Below.    Irma E. Webber.    1943.    Addi-
    son-Wesley.


The Velveteen Rabbit.    Margery Williams.    1926.    Double-
    day.
The Very Young Mother Goose.    Margot Austin (pseud.),
    editor.    1963.    Platt & Munk.
Viking Treasure.    Henry A. Bamman and Robert J. White-
    head.    1965.    Benefic.
The Voyages of Doctor Dolittle.    Hugh Lofting.    1922.
    Lippincott; Dell.


Walls Came Tumbling Down.    Dave Hill.    1967.    Concordia.
Walt Disney's Mary Poppins.    Alice Chase.    1964.    Western.
Walt Disney's Uncle Remus Stories.    Joel Chandler Harris.
    1946.    Western.

The Water-Buffalo Children and The Dragon Fish. Pearl
Sydenstricker Buck. 1943; 1944. John Day; Dell.
Water That Caught on Fire. Joann Scheck. 1969. Con-
cordia.
The Way of the Weather. Jerome Spar. 1967. Creative
Educational Society.
Weather. Boy Scouts of America. 1963. Boy Scouts of
America.
Webelos Scout Book. Boy Scouts of America. 1967. Boy
Scouts of America.
Webster's Elementary Dictionary. G. & C. Merriam Com-
pany. 1966. Merriam.
Wee Gillis. Munro Leaf. 1938. Viking.
What Do You Say, Dear? Sesyle Joslin. 1958. Addison-
Wesley.
What Mary Jo Shared. Janice May Udry. 1966. Albert
Whitman.
What Mary Jo Wanted. Janice May Udry. 1968. Albert
Whitman.
What's Inside the Egg? May Garelick. 1955. Addison-
Wesley.
The Wheel on the School. Meindert DeJong. 1954. Harper
& Row.
When We Were Very Young. A.A. Milne. 1924. Dutton;
Dell.
Where Does the Butterfly Go When It Rains? May Garelick.
1961. Addison-Wesley.
Where Is Cubby Bear? Adda Mai Sharp. 1950. Steck-
Vaughn.
Where Is Everybody? Remy Charlip. 1957. Addison-Wes-
ley.
Where the Wild Things Are. Maurice Sendak. 1963.
Harper & Row.
Where's My Baby? H.A. Rey. 1943. Houghton Mifflin.
Whistle For Willie. Ezra Jack Keats. 1964. Viking.
White Snow, Bright Snow. Alvin Tresselt. 1947. Lothrop,
Lee & Shepard.
The White Stag. Kate Seredy. 1937. Viking.
White Stallion of Lipizza. Marguerite Henry. 1964. Rand
McNally.
Who Will Be My Friends? Syd Hoff. 1960. Harper &
Row.
Who's a Pest? Crosby Newell Bonsall. 1962. Harper &
Row.
"Why" Stories. Edward W. and M.P. Dolch. 1958. Gar-
rard.
Why the Chimes Rang. Raymond MacDonald Alden. Bobbs-
Merrill.

Wild Animals I Have Known. Ernest Thompson Seton. 1898.
Scribner.
Wild Wheels. Don McKay, editor. 1969. Dell.
Wildlife Management. Boy Scouts of America. 1952. Boy
Scouts of America.
The Will To Be Free: Great Escape Stories. Eric Williams,
editor. 1971. Thomas Nelson.
Wind in the Willows. Kenneth Grahame. 1908. Scribner;
Dell.
Winnie Ille Pu: A Latin Edition of Winnie-the-Pooh. Alan
Alexander Milne. 1960. Dutton.
Winnie-the-Pooh. Alan Alexander Milne. 1926. Dutton;
Dell.
Winnie-the-Pooh's Calendar Book. A. A. Milne. Dutton.
Winter on the Johnny Smoker. Mildred H. Comfort. Deni-
son.
The Wise Men of Helm and Their Merry Tales. 1945.
Behrman.
The Witch of Blackbird Pond. Elizabeth George Speare.
1958. Houghton Mifflin; Dell.
The Wizard of Oz. L. Frank Baum. 1900. Bobbs-Merrill.
Wolf Cub Scout Book. Boy Scouts of America. 1967. Boy
Scouts of America.
The Wolfling. Sterling North. Dutton.
A Wonder Book. Nathaniel Hawthorne. 1851. Dutton.
The Wonderful Wizard of Oz. L. Frank Baum. 1900.
Bobbs-Merrill; Dutton.
Wonderful World of Horses. Ned Hoopes, editor. 1966.
Dell.
Wonders of the Human Body. Anthony Ravielli. 1954. Vi-
king.
Wood Carving. Boy Scouts of America. 1966. Boy Scouts
of America.
Woodwork. Boy Scouts of America. 1970. Boy Scouts of
America.
World God Made. Alyce Bergey. 1965. Con-
cordia.
A World Explorer: Marco Polo. Charles P. Graves. 1963.
Garrard.
World's Worst Jokes. Price Stern Editors. 1969. Price/
Stern/Sloan.
Would You Believe? Don Adams. 1966. Price/Stern/
Sloan.
A Wrinkle in Time. Madeleine L'Engle. 1962. Farrar,
Straus & Giroux.

The Yearling.   Marjorie Kinnan Rawlings.   1938.   Scribner.
Yertle the Turtle, and Other Stories.   Dr. Seuss.   1958.
   Random.
Yo-Ho and Kim.   Ruth Jaynes.   Lawrence.
Yo-Ho and Kim at Sea.   Ruth Jaynes.   Lawrence.
You and the Constitution of the United States.   Paul Witty
   and J. Kohler.   1948.   Children's.
You and the United Nations.   Lois Fisher.   1958.   Children's.
You Come Too.   Robert Frost.   1959.   Holt, Rinehart and
   Winston.
Young Readers Bible.   Henry M. Bullock and Edward C.
   Peterson, editors.   1968.   Abingdon.

Chapter Four

BEST SELLERS BY ILLUSTRATOR

This chapter lists alphabetically by illustrator those best sellers for which an illustrator was named by the publisher(s) reporting the book as a best seller in this survey. The author, publisher, and date of the edition by that publisher illustrated by the named illustrator, are given for each title.

Adams, Adrienne. Houses from the Sea, by Alice E. Goudey. Scribner, 1959.
_____. Mouse House, by Rumer Godden. Viking, 1957.
Adams, P. The True Book of Animal Babies, by Illa Podendorf. Children's, 1955.
Alexander, Martha. Understood Betsy, by Dorothy Canfield Fisher. Holt, 1972.
Andrew, Mary Stevens. Have You Seen My Brother? by Elizabeth Guilfoile. Follett, 1962.
Ames, Lee J. The Civil War, by Fletcher Pratt. Doubleday, 1955.
Angelo, Valenti. Roller Skates, by Ruth Sawyer and Kate Seredy. Viking, 1936.
Anglund, Joan Walsh. A Friend Is Someone Who Likes You, by Joan Walsh Anglund. Harcourt, 1958.
_____. Love Is a Special Way of Feeling, by Joan Walsh Anglund. Harcourt, 1960.
Ardizzone, Edward. The Thirty-Nine Steps, by John Buchan. Dutton, 1964.
Artzybasheff, Boris. Gay Neck: The Story of a Pigeon, by Dhan Gopal Mukerji. Dutton, 1927.
Austin, Margot (pseud.). Barney's Adventure, by Margot Austin. Dutton, 1941.
_____. Peter Churchmouse, by Margot Austin. Dutton, 1941.
_____. The Very Young Mother Goose, edited by Margot Austin. Platt & Munk, 1963.

_____. and others.  My Brimful Book, edited by Dana
Bruce.  Platt & Munk, 1960.
Averill, Esther.  The Fire Cat, by Esther Averill.  Harper
& Row, 1960.
Ayer, Margaret.  The Lost Kingdom, by Chester Bryant.
Messner, 1951.
Ayton-Symington, J.  Robinson Crusoe, by Daniel Defoe.
Dutton, 1954.


Bacon, Peggy.  Buttons, by Tom Robinson.  Viking, 1938.
Baer, Howard.  Too Many Dogs, by Ramona Dupre.  Follett,
1960.
Bannerman, Helen.  The Story of Little Black Sambo, by
Helen Bannerman.  Lippincott, 1923.
Bannon, Laura.  Pecos Bill, by James Cloyd Bowman.  Al-
bert Whitman, 1937.
_____. Tales from a Finnish Tupa, by James Cloyd
Bowman and Margery Bianco.  Albert Whitman, 1936.
Barnum, Jay Hyde.  The Boats on the River, by Marjorie
Flack.  Viking, 1946.
Batten, John D.  English Folk and Fairy Tales, edited by
Joseph Jacobs.  Putnam, 1904.
Baumhauer, Hans.  Hans Andersen's Fairy Tales, by Hans
Christian Andersen; translated by Reginald Spink.  Dut-
ton, 1953.
_____. Hans Brinker: Or The Silver Skates, by Mary
Mapes Dodge.  Dutton, 1956.
Beeby, Betty.  The Child's Story Bible, by Catherine F.
Vos; revised by Marianne Vos Radius.  Eerdmans, 1967.
Behm, B.  Great Promise, by Alyce Bergey.  Concordia,
1968.
Bemelmans, Ludwig.  Madeline, by Ludwig Bemelmans.
Viking, 1939.
_____. Madeline and the Bad Hat, by Ludwig Bemelmans.
Viking, 1957.
_____. Madeline and the Gypsies, by Ludwig Bemelmans.
Viking, 1959.
_____. Madeline in London, by Ludwig Bemelmans.  Vi-
king, 1961.
_____. Madeline's Rescue, by Ludwig Bemelmans.  Vi-
king, 1953.
Bendick, Jeanne.  Let's Find Out about Heat, Water and
Air, by Herman and Nina Schneider.  Addison-Wesley,
1946.
Bennett, Richard.  Tall Tales from the High Hills, by Ellis
Credle.  Nelson, 1957.

Berta, Hugh.  Jimmy, a Little Pup, by Clarence Jonk.
    Denison.
Beskow, Elsa.  Pelle's New Suit, by Elsa Beskow.  Harper,
    1929.
Biro, B. S.  The Wonderful Wizard of Oz, by L. Frank
    Baum.  Dutton.
Blegvad, Erik.  Elephi, the Cat with the High I. Q., by Jean
    Stafford.  Dell, 1966.
Bolognese, Don.  Lassie Come-Home, by Eric Knight.  Holt,
    1941.
Bonsall, Crosby Newell.  The Case of the Cat's Meow, by
    Crosby Newell Bonsall.  Harper, 1965.
_____.  The Case of the Hungry Stranger, by Crosby
    Newell Bonsall.  Harper, 1963.
_____.  Who's a Pest? by Crosby Newell Bonsall.  Harper,
    1962.
Boyd, Jack.  Dan Frontier, by William J. Hurley.  Benefic,
    1959.
_____.  Dan Frontier and the Big Cat, by William J.
    Hurley.  Benefic, 1961.
_____.  Dan Frontier and the Wagon Train, by William
    J. Hurley.  Benefic, 1959.
_____.  Dan Frontier Goes Exploring, by William J.
    Hurley.  Benefic, 1963.
_____.  Dan Frontier Goes Hunting, by William J. Hurley.
    Benefic, 1959.
_____.  Dan Frontier Scouts with the Army, by William
    J. Hurley.  Benefic, 1962.
_____.  Dan Frontier, Sheriff, by William J. Hurley.
    Benefic, 1960.
_____.  Dan Frontier, Trapper, by William J. Hurley.
    Benefic, 1962.
_____.  Dan Frontier with the Indians, by William J.
    Hurley.  Benefic, 1959.
Brock, C. E.  A Christmas Carol and The Cricket on the
    Hearth, by Charles Dickens.  Dutton, 1963.
Brophy, Ruth.  Happiness Is Smiling, by Katherine Gehm.
    Denison.
_____.  Harvey Hopper, by Bernice M. Chappel.  Denison.
Brown, Marcia.  Once a Mouse; A Fable Cut in Wood, by
    Marcia Brown.  Scribner, 1961.
_____.  The Steadfast Tin Soldier, by Hans Christian
    Andersen; translated by M. R. James.  Scribner, 1953.
_____.  Stone Soup; An Old Tale, by Marcia Brown.
    Scribner, 1947.
Brown, Paul.  "National Velvet," by Enid Bagnold.  Morrow,
    1949.

Bruce, Lucile.   The Extra Egg, by Edna A. Anderson.
   Denison.
Buff, Conrad.   Dash and Dart: Two Fawns, by Mary and
   Conrad Buff.   Viking, 1942.
Burger, Carl.   The Incredible Journey, by Sheila Burnford.
   Little, 1961.
_____.   The Story of Mount Vernon, by Natalie M. Miller.
   Children's, 1965.
Burkert, Nancy Ekholm.   James and the Giant Peach, by
   Roald Dahl.   Knopf, 1961.
Burris, Burmah, et al.   Illustrated Treasury of Poetry for
   Children, edited by David Ross.   Grosset, 1970.
Burton, Virginia Lee.   Katy and the Big Snow, by Virginia
   Lee Burton.   Houghton, 1943.
_____.   The Little House, by Virginia Lee Burton.
   Houghton, 1942.
_____.   Mike Mulligan and His Steam Shovel, by Virginia
   Lee Burton.   Houghton, 1939.
Busoni, R.   Why the Chimes Rang, by Raymond MacDonald
   Alden.   Bobbs-Merrill, 1954.


Cady, Harrison, and Kerr, George.   Adventures of Peter
   Cottontail, by Thornton W. Burgess.   Grosset.
Cammell, Donald S.   King Arthur and the Round Table, by
   A. M. Hadfield.   Dutton, 1953.
Cannon, Marian.   Colonial Williamsburg Coloring Book, by
   Marian Cannon.   Colonial Williamsburg Foundation, 1948.
Chaiko, Ted.   The Tall Book of Bible Stories, edited by
   Katherine Gibson.   Harper, 1957.
Chalmers, Mary.   The Happy Birthday Present, by Joan
   Heilbroner.   Harper, 1961.
Chappell, Warren.   The Dark Frigate, by Charles Boardman
   Hawes.   Little, 1971.
Charlip, Remy.   Where Is Everybody? by Remy Charlip.
   Addison-Wesley, 1957.
Charlot, Jean.   And Now Miguel, by Joseph Krumgold.
   Thomas Y. Crowell, 1953; Apollo, 1970.
_____.   Secret of the Andes, by Ann Nolan Clark.   Viking,
   1952.
Sister Charlotte Anne, C. S. J.   The Magic Wishbone, by
   Sister Adele Marie, C. S. J.   Lawrence.
Chwast, Jacqueline.   I Like You, by Sandol Stoddard War-
   burg.   Houghton, 1965.
Chute, Marchette.   Around and About, by Marchette Chute.
   Dutton, 1957.
Cirlin, Edgard.   Marco Polo, by Manuel Komroff.   Messner,
   1952.

Clark, Grace.   Walt Disney's Mary Poppins, by Alice Chase;
    edited by Annie N. Bedford.   Western, 1964.
Cohen, Vincent O.   Heidi, by Johanna Spyri.   Dutton.
Cooney, Barbara.   American Folk Songs for Children, by
    Ruth Crawford Seeger.   Doubleday, 1948.
_____.   Bambi:   A Life in the Woods, by Felix Salten.
    Simon & Schuster, 1970.
Cooper, Marjorie.   Tell Me about Christmas, by Mary Alice
    Jones.   Rand McNally, 1958.
_____.   Tell Me About Heaven, by Mary Alice Jones.
    Rand McNally, 1956.
Copelman, Evelyn.   The Wizard of Oz, by L. Frank Baum.
    Bobbs-Merrill.
Cosgrave, John O'Hara II.   Carry On, Mr. Bowditch, by
    Jean Lee Latham.   Houghton, 1955.
Craig, Sam.   Becky Lou in Grandmother's Days, by Hazel
    Craig.   Denison.
Cranner, Brian.   The Songs of Sesame Street (Sesame Street
    Book and Record Package), written by Jeffrey Moss, Joe
    Raposo, and Jon Stone.
Credle, Ellis.   Down, Down the Mountain, by Ellis Credle.
    Nelson, 1934.


Darling, Louis.   Ellen Tebbits, by Beverly Cleary.   Morrow,
    1951.
_____.   The Enormous Egg, by Oliver Butterworth.   Little,
    Brown, 1956.
_____.   Henry and Beezus, by Beverly Cleary.   Morrow,
    1952.
_____.   Henry and Ribsy, by Beverly Cleary.   Morrow,
    1954.
_____.   Henry and the Clubhouse, by Beverly Cleary.
    Morrow, 1962.
_____.   Henry and the Paper Route, by Beverly Cleary.
    Morrow, 1957.
_____.   Henry Huggins, by Beverly Cleary.   Morrow,
    1950.
Daugherty, James.   Andy and the Lion, by James Daugherty.
    Viking, 1938.
_____.   Daniel Boone, by James Daugherty.   Viking,
    1939.
D'Aulaire, Ingri and Edgar Parin.   Abraham Lincoln, by
    Ingri and Edgar Parin D'Aulaire.   Doubleday, 1940.
_____.   Animals Everywhere, by Ingri and Edgar Parin
    D'Aulaire.   Doubleday, 1954.

_____. Benjamin Franklin, by Ingri and Edgar Parin D'Aulaire.  Doubleday, 1950.

_____. Columbus, by Ingri and Edgar Parin D'Aulaire. Doubleday, 1955.

_____. D'Aulaires' Book of Greek Myths, by Ingri and Edgar Parin D'Aulaire.  Doubleday, 1962.

_____. George Washington, by Ingri and Edgar Parin D'Aulaire.  Doubleday, 1936.

Davis, Dimitris.  Greek Gods and Heroes, by Robert Graves. Doubleday, 1960; Dell.

De Angeli, Marguerite.  Book of Nursery and Mother Goose Rhymes, by Marguerite De Angeli.  Doubleday, 1954.

_____. Bright April, by Marguerite De Angeli.  Doubleday, 1946.

_____. The Door in the Wall, by Marguerite De Angeli. Doubleday, 1949.

_____. Thee, Hannah! by Marguerite De Angeli.  Doubleday. 1940.

Dempster, Al, and Justice, Bill.  Walt Disney's Uncle Remus Stories, by Joel Chandler Harris; edited by Marion Palmer.  Western, 1946.

Dennis, Wesley.  Album of Horses, by Marguerite Henry. Rand McNally, 1951.

_____. Black Gold, by Marguerite Henry.  Rand McNally, 1957.

_____. Born to Trot, by Marguerite Henry.  Rand McNally, 1950.

_____. Brighty of the Grand Canyon, by Marguerite Henry.  Rand McNally, 1956.

_____. Flip, by Wesley Dennis.  Viking, 1941.

_____. Flip and the Morning, by Wesley Dennis.  Viking, 1951.

_____. Justin Morgan Had a Horse, by Marguerite Henry. Rand McNally, 1954.

_____. King of the Wind, by Marguerite Henry.  Rand McNally, 1948.

_____. Misty of Chincoteague, by Marguerite Henry. Rand McNally, 1947.

_____. Sea Star, Orphan of Chincoteague, by Marguerite Henry.  Rand McNally, 1949.

_____. Stormy, Misty's Foal, by Marguerite Henry. Rand McNally, 1963.

_____. White Stallion of Lipizza, by Marguerite Henry. Rand McNally, 1964.

_____. and others.  My Brimful Book, edited by Dana Bruce.  Platt & Munk, 1960.

Denslow, W. W.   The Wonderful Wizard of Oz, by L. Frank
    Baum.  Bobbs-Merrill.
Dersh, Stanley.   America and Its Presidents, by Earl S.
    Miers.  Grosset & Dunlap, 1970.
Doane, Pelagie.   Tell Me about the Bible, by Mary Alice
    Jones.  Rand McNally, 1945.
Doremus, Robert.   George Washington:  Father of Freedom,
    by Stewart Graff.  Garrard, 1964; Dell, 1966.
_____.  The How and Why Wonder Book of Deserts, by
    Felix Sutton.  Wonder-Treasure, 1965.
_____.  The How and Why Wonder Book of Oceanography,
    by Robert Scharff.  Wonder-Treasure, 1964.
_____.  Spooks and Spirits and Shadowy Shapes, by Emma
    L. Brock et al.  Dutton, 1949.
Dunlap, Loren.   Edgar Allan, by John Neufeld.  Phillips,
    1968.
Dunnington, Tom.   The Story of the Lincoln Memorial, by
    Natalie Miller.  Children's, 1966.
Duvoisin, Roger.   White Snow, Bright Snow, by Alvin Tres-
    selt.  Lothrop, 1947.


Edwards, Lionel.   The Black Arrow, by Robert Louis Ste-
    venson.  Dutton, 1958; Dell.
_____.  Lorna Doone, by Richard Doddridge Blackmore.
    Dutton.
Einsel, Walter.   Did You Ever See? by Walter Einsel.
    Addison-Wesley, 1962.
Elkin, Frank.   Tell Me a Riddle, edited by Dana Bruce.
    Platt & Munk, 1966.
Elliott, Gertrude.   The Golden Dictionary, edited by Ellen
    Wales Walpole.  Western, 1944.
_____.  Golden Song Book, by Katharine Tyler Wessels.
    Western, 1945.
Enright, Elizabeth.   The Four-Story Mistake, by Elizabeth
    Enright.  Holt, Rinehart & Winston, 1942; Dell, 1967.
_____.  The Saturdays, by Elizabeth Enright.  Holt, Rine-
    hart & Winston, 1941; Dell, 1966.
Erickson, Phoebe.   Adventures of Peter Cottontail, by
    Thornton W. Burgess.  Grosset & Dunlap.
_____.  Just Follow Me, by Phoebe Erickson.  Follett,
    1960.
Espenschied, Gertrude.   Peter's Policeman, by Anne Lattin.
    Follett, 1958.
_____.  The Tall Book of Christmas, edited by Dorothy
    Hall Smith.  Harper & Row, 1954.

Ets, Marie Hall. Gilberto and the Wind, by Marie Hall Ets.
Viking, 1963.
_____. In the Forest, by Marie Hall Ets. Viking, 1944.
_____. Just Me, by Marie Hall Ets. Viking, 1965.
_____. Nine Days to Christmas, by Marie Hall Ets and
Aurora Labastida. Viking, 1959.
_____. Play with Me, by Marie Hall Ets. Viking, 1955.
Evans, Katherine. Chicken Little Count-to-Ten, by Margaret
Friskey. Children's, 1946.
_____. Mable the Whale, by Patricia King. Follett,
1958.
_____. The True Book of Air Around Us, by Margaret
Friskey. Children's, 1953.


Faulkner, Jack. Sailor Jack and Bluebell, by Selma and
Jack Wassermann. Benefic, 1960.
Fax, Elton C. Dr. George Washington Carver, Scientist,
by Shirley Graham and George D. Lipscomb. Messner,
1944.
_____. Melindy's Medal, by Georgene Faulkner and John
Becker. Messner, 1945.
_____. Sitting Bull, Champion of His People, by Shannon
Garst. Messner, 1946.
Ferguson, Walter. The How and Why Wonder Book of Birds,
by Robert Mathewson. Wonder-Treasure, 1960.
Fischel, Lillian. The Wise Men of Helm and Their Merry
Tales, by Solomon Simon. Behrman, 1945.
Fisher, Lois. The True Book of Moon, Sun and Stars, by
Illa Podendorf. Children's, 1954.
_____. You and the Constitution of the United States, by
Paul Witty and J. Kohler. Children's, 1948.
_____. You and the United Nations, by Lois Fisher.
Children's, 1951.
Fitzhugh, Louise. Harriet the Spy, by Louise Fitzhugh.
Harper & Row, 1964; Dell, 1967.
Flack, Marjorie. Angus and the Cat, by Marjorie Flack.
Doubleday, 1931.
_____. Angus and the Ducks, by Marjorie Flack. Dou-
bleday, 1930.
_____. Angus Lost, by Marjorie Flack. Doubleday,
1932.
_____. The Country Bunny and the Little Gold Shoes, by
Dubose Heyward. Houghton Mifflin, 1939.
_____. Tim Tadpole and the Great Bullfrog, by Marjorie
Flack. Doubleday, 1934.

Fleischmann, Glen.  Still More Answers, by Mary Elting
and Franklin Folsom.  Grosset, 1970.
Folkard, Charles.  Grimm's Fairy Tales, by Jakob and
Wilhelm Grimm.  Dutton, 1949.
————————.  Pinocchio: The Story of a Puppet, by Carlo Col-
lodi.  Dutton, 1952.
————————.  The Swiss Family Robinson, by Johann R. Wyss.
Dutton; Dell.
Ford, Lauren.  Little Book about God (Protestant), by Lau-
ren Ford.  Doubleday, 1934.
Fortnum, Peggy.  A Bear Called Paddington, by Michael
Bond.  Houghton Mifflin, 1960; Dell, 1968.
————————.  The Happy Prince and Other Stories, by Oscar
Wilde.  Dutton, 1968.
Foster, Celeste K.  Casper, the Caterpillar, by Celeste K.
Foster.  Denison.
————————.  Jonathan and the Octopus, by Celeste K. Foster.
Denison.
Foster, Laura Louise.  Keer-Loo, by Laura Louise Foster.
Naturegraph, 1965.
Frame, Paul.  Helen Keller: Toward the Light, by Stewart
and Polly Anne Graff.  Garrard, 1965; Dell, 1966.
————————.  John F. Kennedy: New Frontiersman, by Charles
P. Graves.  Garrard, 1965; Dell, 1966.
Francoise.  Jeanne-Marie Counts Her Sheep, by Francoise.
Scribner, 1951.
————————.  Springtime for Jeanne-Marie, by Francoise.
Scribner, 1955.
Frank, Lola Edick.  King Robert the Resting Ruler, by
Donna Lugg Pape.  Oddo, 1968.
————————.  Liz Dearly's Silly Glasses, by Donna Lugg Pape.
Oddo, 1968.
————————.  Professor Fred and the Fid-Fuddlephone, by
Donna Lugg Pape.  Oddo, 1968.
————————.  Scientist Sam, by Donna Lugg Pape.  Oddo, 1968.
————————.  Shoemaker Fooze, by Donna Lugg Pape.  Oddo,
1968.
————————.  The Three Thinkers of Thay-Lee, by Donna Lugg
Pape.  Oddo, 1968.
Frascino, Edward.  The Trumpet of the Swan, by E. B.
White.  Harper & Row, 1970.
Freeman, Don.  Corduroy, by Don Freeman.  Viking, 1968.
————————.  Dandelion, by Don Freeman.  Viking, 1964.
————————.  Mike's House, by Julia Sauer.  Viking, 1954.
————————.  Mop Top, by Don Freeman.  Viking, 1955.
————————.  Norman the Doorman, by Don Freeman.  Viking,
1959.

Fujikawa, Gyo.   A Child's Book of Poems, compiled by Gyo
    Fujikawa.   Grosset, 1969.
_____ .  A Child's Garden of Verses, by Robert Louis
    Stevenson.   Grosset, 1957.
_____ .  Fairy Tales and Fables, edited by Doris Duene-
    wald.   Grosset, 1970.
_____ .  Mother Goose.   Grosset.


Galdone, Paul.   Henny Penny, by Paul Galdone.   Seabury,
    1968.
_____ .  The Monkey and the Crocodile:  A Jataka Tale
    from India, by Paul Galdone.   Seabury, 1969.
_____ .  Three Fox Fables (adapted from Aesop), by Paul
    Galdone.   Seabury, 1971.
_____ .  The Three Little Pigs, by Paul Galdone.   Sea-
    bury, 1970.
Gannett, Ruth.   Miss Hickory, by Carolyn Sherwin Bailey.
    Viking, 1946.
Geary, Clifford.   Between Planets, by Robert A. Heinlein.
    Scribner, 1951.
_____ .  Farmer in the Sky, by Robert A. Heinlein.
    Scribner, 1950.
_____ .  Red Planet; A Colonial Boy on Mars, by Robert
    A. Heinlein.   Scribner, 1949.
_____ .  The Rolling Stones, by Robert A. Heinlein.
    Scribner, 1952.
_____ .  Space Cadet, by Robert A. Heinlein.   Scribner,
    1948.
_____ .  Starman Jones, by Robert A. Heinlein.   Scribner,
    1953.
Gehr, M.   The True Book of Pebbles and Shells, by Illa
    Podendorf.   Children's, 1954.
_____ .  The True Book of Seasons, by Illa Podendorf.
    Children's, 1955.
George, Jean.   Dipper of Copper Creek, by John and Jean
    George.   Dutton, 1956.
_____ .  The Hole in the Tree, by Jean Craighead George.
    Dutton, 1957.
_____ .  My Side of the Mountain, by Jean Craighead
    George.   Dutton, 1959.
Gillespie, Jessie.   The Birds' Christmas Carol, by Kate
    Douglas Wiggin.   Houghton Mifflin.
Glanzman, Louis S.   Pippi Goes on Board, by Astrid Lind-
    gren.   Viking, 1957.
_____ .  Pippi in the South Seas, by Astrid Lindgren.
    Viking, 1959.

_____.  Pippi Longstocking, by Astrid Lindgren.  Viking, 1950.

Graham, Margaret Bloy.  Harry and the Lady Next Door, by Gene Zion.  Harper & Row, 1960.

_____.  Harry the Dirty Dog, by Gene Zion.  Harper & Row, 1956.

Grahame-Johnstone, Janet and Anne.  The Hundred and One Dalmations, by Dodie Smith.  Viking, 1957.

Gramatky, Hardie.  Little Toot, by Hardie Gramatky.  Putnam, 1939.

Grant, Gordon.  Penrod, by Booth Tarkington.  Doubleday, 1914.

Grider, Dorothy.  The Little Rabbit Who Wanted Red Wings, by Carolyn Sherwin Bailey.  Platt & Munk, 1945.

_____.  Tell Me about God, by Mary Alice Jones.  Rand McNally, 1943.

_____.  Tell Me about Jesus, by Mary Alice Jones.  Rand McNally, 1944.

_____.  Tell Me about Prayer, by Mary Alice Jones.  Rand McNally, 1948.

Grose, Helen Mason.  Rebecca of Sunnybrook Farm, by Kate Douglas Wiggin.  Houghton Mifflin, 1903.

Grossman, Shelly.  The How and Why Wonder Book of Ecology, by Shelly and Mary Louise Grossman.  Wonder-Treasure, 1971.


Hamil, Tom.  Show and Tell, by Patricia Miles Martin.  Putnam, 1962.

Hamilton, Helen B.  The Happy Hollisters, by Jerry West (pseud.).  Doubleday, 1953.

_____.  The Happy Hollisters at Sea Gull Beach, by Jerry West (pseud.).  Doubleday, 1953.

_____.  The Happy Hollisters on a River Trip, by Jerry West (pseud.).  Doubleday, 1953.

Hansens, Aline.  Make It Yourself! by Bernice Wells Carlson.  Abingdon, 1950.

Hauman, George and Doris.  The Little Engine That Could, by Watty Piper (pseud.).  Platt & Munk, 1929.

Hawkinson, John and Lucy.  The Story of the Statue of Liberty, by Natalie Miller.  Children's, 1965.

Haywood, Carolyn.  Little Eddie, by Carolyn Haywood.  Morrow, 1947.

Herrera, Velino.  In My Mother's House, by Ann Nolan Clark.  Viking, 1941.

Heston, C.  The True Book of Indians, by Teri Martini.  Children's, 1954.

Hiroshige and Hokusai. The Big Wave, by Pearl S. Buck.
    John Day, 1948.
Hodgell, Robert. Space, by Marian Tellander. Follett,
    1960.
Hodges, C. Walter. Huckleberry Finn, by Mark Twain
    (pseud.). Dutton, 1955.
————. The Silver Sword, by Ian Serraillier. Phillips,
    1959.
————. Tom Sawyer, by Mark Twain (pseud.). Dutton.
Hodgson, Robert. The Prince and the Pauper, by Mark
    Twain (pseud.). Dutton, 1968.
Hoecke, Hazel. Something New at the Zoo, by Esther Meeks.
    Follett, 1957.
Hoff, Syd. Danny and the Dinosaur, by Syd Hoff. Harper
    & Row, 1958.
————. Julius, by Syd Hoff. Harper & Row, 1959.
————. Little Chief, by Syd Hoff. Harper & Row, 1961.
————. Oliver, by Syd Hoff. Harper & Row, 1960.
————. Sammy the Seal, by Syd Hoff. Harper & Row,
    1959.
————. Who Will Be My Friends? by Syd Hoff. Harper
    & Row, 1960.
Hokusai and Hiroshige. The Big Wave, by Pearl S. Buck.
    John Day, 1948.
Holling, Holling C. Minn of the Mississippi, by Holling C.
    Holling. Houghton Mifflin, 1951.
————. Paddle-to-the-Sea, by Holling C. Holling.
    Houghton Mifflin, 1941.
————. Tree in the Trail, by Holling C. Holling.
    Houghton Mifflin, 1942.
Holmes, Louis F. Color Me Brown, by Lucille Giles.
    Johnson (Chicago).
Holmes, Rosinda, and Westover, Ned. Robin Deer, by Olga
    Cossi. Naturegraph, 1968.
Hook, F. Little Folded Hands, revised by Allan H. Jahs-
    mann. Concordia, 1959.
Hughes, Shirley. The Three Toymakers, by Ursula Moray
    Williams. Nelson, 1971.
Hurd, Clement. Come and Have Fun, by Edith Thacher
    Hurd. Harper & Row, 1962.
————. Goodnight Moon, by Margaret Wise Brown.
    Harper & Row, 1947.
————. Last One Home Is a Green Pig, by Edith Thacher
    Hurd. Harper & Row, 1959.
————. The Runaway Bunny, by Margaret Wise Brown.
    Harper & Row, 1942.

Irving, James Gordon.  Dinosaurs, by Herbert S. Zim.
    Morrow, 1954.
_____.  Snakes, by Herbert S. Zim.  Morrow, 1949.


Jackson, Polly.  Abraham Lincoln, by Clara Ingram Judson.
    Follett, 1961.
_____.  Big New School, by Evelyn Hastings.  Follett,
    1959.
_____.  Christopher Columbus, by Clara Ingram Judson.
    Follett, 1964.
Jakobsen, Rena.  What's Inside the Egg? by May Garelick.
    Addison-Wesley, 1955.
James, Will.  Smoky, the Cow Horse, by Will James.
    Scribner, 1926.
John, Helen.  All-of-a-Kind Family, by Sydney Taylor.
    Follett, 1951; Dell, 1966.
Johnson, Crockett (pseud.).  Harold and the Purple Crayon,
    by Crockett Johnson.  Harper & Row, 1955.
Johnson, Milton.  Island of the Blue Dolphins, by Scott
    O'Dell.  Houghton Mifflin, 1960.
Jones, Bob.  Sailor Jack and Homer Pots, by Selma and
    Jack Wassermann.  Benefic, 1961.
_____.  Sailor Jack and the Target Ship, by Selma and
    Jack Wassermann.  Benefic, 1960.
_____.  Sailor Jack Goes North, by Selma and Jack Was-
    sermann.  Benefic, 1961.
Jones, Elizabeth Orton.  Small Rain:  Verses from the Bi-
    ble, edited by Jessie Orton Jones.  Viking, 1943.
Justice, Bill.  Walt Disney's Uncle Remus Stories, by Joel
    Chandler Harris; edited by Marion Palmer.  Western,
    1946.


Kaufmann, John.  The Empty Schoolhouse, by Natalie Savage
    Carlson.  Harper & Row, 1965; Dell, 1968.
Kaune, Merriman.  My Own Little House, by Merriman
    Kaune.  Follett, 1957.
Keats, Ezra Jack.  The Snowy Day, by Ezra Jack Keats.
    Viking, 1962.
_____.  Whistle for Willie, by Ezra Jack Keats.  Viking,
    1964.
Kerr, George, and Cady, Harrison.  Adventures of Peter
    Cottontail, by Thornton W. Burgess.  Grosset & Dunlap.
Kessler, Leonard.  Here Comes the Strikeout, by Leonard
    Kessler.  Harper & Row, 1965.
Kiddell-Monroe, Joan.  The Adventures of Odysseus, by
    Andrew Lang.  Dutton.

_____ . Aesop's Fables, edited by John Warrington.
Dutton.
_____ . The Song of Hiawatha, by Henry Wadsworth Long-
fellow. Dutton, 1959.
Kidder, Barbara. Mr. Mighty, by M. Worden Kidder and
Barbara Kidder. Denison.
_____ . Mr. Wonderful, by Barbara Kidder. Denison.
Kimball, Sabra Mallett. Birds in Their Homes, by Addison
Webb. Doubleday, 1947.
King, Ruth. A Picture Book of Palestine, by Ethel L.
Smither. Abingdon, 1947.
Knight, Hilary. Christmas Nutshell Library, by Hilary
Knight. Harper & Row, 1963.
_____ . Eloise, by Kay Thompson. Simon & Schuster,
1955.
Koehler, Cynthia. The How and Why Wonder Book of In-
sects, by Ronald N. Rood. Wonder-Treasure, 1960.
Koehler, Cynthia and Alvin. The How and Why Wonder
Book of Ants and Bees, by Ronald N. Rood. Wonder-
Treasure.
_____ . The How and Why Wonder Book of Sea Shells,
by Donald F. Low. Wonder-Treasure.
_____ . Lots More Tell Me Why, by Arkady Leokum.
Grosset & Dunlap, 1971.
_____ . More Tell Me Why, by Arkady Leokum. Grosset
& Dunlap, 1967.
_____ . Still More Tell Me Why, by Arkady Leokum.
Grosset & Dunlap, 1968.
_____ . Tell Me Why, by Arkady Leokum. Grosset &
Dunlap, 1969.
Kohn, A. The True Book of Holidays, by John W. Purcell.
Children's, 1955.
Kraus, Robert. Rabbit and Skunk and the Scary Rock, by
Carla Stevens. Addison-Wesley, 1962.
Krehbiel, B. and E. I Want to Be a Nurse, by Carla
Greene. Children's, 1957.
Krush, Joe and Beth. Courtis-Watters Illustrated Golden
Dictionary for Young Readers, by Stuart A. Courtis and
Garnette Watters. Western, 1952.
_____ . Fifteen, by Beverly Cleary. Morrow, 1956.
_____ . Golden Picture Dictionary, by Lilian Moore.
Western, 1954.


Lackey, William. Sailor Jack and the Ball Game, by Selma
and Jack Wassermann. Benefic, 1962.
Lampher. Baby Born in a Stable, by A.H. Kramer. Concordia.

Lantz, Paul. Blue Willow, by Doris Gates. Viking, 1940.
LaSalle, Janet. Follett Beginning-to-Read Picture Dictionary, by Alta McIntire. Follett, 1959.
Lawson, Robert. Adam of the Road, by Elizabeth Janet Gray. Viking, 1942.
_____. Ben and Me, by Robert Lawson. Little Brown, 1939.
_____. Mr. Popper's Penguins, by Richard and Florence Atwater. Little, Brown, 1938.
_____. Mr. Revere and I, by Robert Lawson. Little, Brown, 1953.
_____. Rabbit Hill, by Robert Lawson. Viking, 1944; Dell, 1968.
_____. The Story of Ferdinand, by Munro Leaf. Viking, 1936.
_____. They Were Strong and Good, by Robert Lawson. Viking, 1940.
_____. The Tough Winter, by Robert Lawson. Viking, 1954.
_____. Wee Gillis, by Munro Leaf. Viking, 1938.
Lazare, Jerry. Queenie Peavy, by Robert Burch. Viking, 1966.
Lee, Carvel. Bessie, the Messy Penguin, by Joyce Holland. Denison, 1960.
Lenski, Lois. Cotton in My Sack, by Lois Lenski. Lippincott, 1949; Dell, 1966.
_____. The Little Family, by Lois Lenski. Doubleday, 1932.
_____. Strawberry Girl, by Lois Lenski. Lippincott, 1945; Dell, 1967.
Leone, S. The Littlest Angel, by Charles Tazewell. Children's, 1966.
Lindberg, Howard. Sally Alligator, by Betty Molgard Ryan. Denison.
Lindman, Maj. Flicka, Ricka, Dicka and the New Dotted Dresses, by Maj Lindman. Albert Whitman, 1939.
_____. Flicka, Ricka, Dicka and the Three Kittens, by Maj Lindman. Albert Whitman, 1941.
_____. Snipp, Snapp, Snurr and the Big Surprise, by Maj Lindman. Albert Whitman, 1937.
_____. Snipp, Snapp, Snurr and the Buttered Bread, by Maj Lindman. Albert Whitman, 1934.
_____. Snipp, Snapp, Snurr and the Gingerbread, by Maj Lindman. Albert Whitman, 1936.
_____. Snipp, Snapp, Snurr and the Magic Horse, by Maj Lindman. Albert Whitman, 1933.
_____. Snipp, Snapp, Snurr and the Red Shoes, by Maj Lindman. Albert Whitman, 1932.

_____ . Snipp, Snapp, Snurr and the Yellow Sled, by Maj
Lindman.  Albert Whitman, 1936.

Lionni, Leo.  Swimmy, by Leo Lionni.  Pantheon, 1963.

Lobel, Arnold.  The Secret Three, by Mildred Myrick.  Harper
& Row, 1963.

Lodico, S.  The Stork Didn't Bring You, by Lois Loyd Pemberton.  Nelson, 1966.

Loehle, Don.  Sailor Jack, by Selma and Jack Wassermann.
Benefic, 1960.

_____ . Sailor Jack's New Friend, by Selma and Jack
Wassermann.  Benefic, 1960.

Lofting, Hugh.  The Story of Doctor Dolittle, by Hugh Lofting.
Lippincott, 1920.

_____ . The Voyages of Doctor Dolittle, by Hugh Lofting.
Lippincott, 1922.

Lougheed, Robert.  Mustang, Wild Spirit of the West, by
Marguerite Henry.  Rand McNally, 1966.

Lowenbein, Michael.  The First Thanksgiving, by Lou
Rogers.  Follett, 1963.


Maltman, C.  The True Book of Dinosaurs, by Mary L.
Clark.  Children's, 1955.

_____ . The True Book of Insects, by Illa Podendorf.
Children's, 1954.

Malvern, Corinne.  The First Woman Doctor: The Story of
Elizabeth Blackwell, M. D. , by Rachel Baker.  Messner,
1944.

Marilue.  Bobby Bear and the Bees, by Marilyn Olear Helmrath and Janet LaSpisa Bartlett.  Oddo, 1968.

_____ . Bobby Bear Finds Maple Sugar, by Marilyn O.
Helmrath and Janet L. Bartlett.  Oddo, 1968.

_____ . Bobby Bear Goes Fishing, by Marilyn O. Helmrath and Janet L. Bartlett.  Oddo, 1968.

_____ . Bobby Bear in the Spring, by Marilyn O. Helmrath and Janet L. Bartlett.  Oddo, 1968.

_____ . Bobby Bear's Halloween, by Marilyn O. Helmrath and Janet L. Bartlett.  Oddo, 1968.

_____ . Bobby Bear's Rocket Ride, by Marilyn O. Helmrath and Janet L. Bartlett.  Oddo, 1968.

Marino, Dorothy.  Miss Hattie and the Monkey, by Helen
Olds.  Follett, 1958.

Mastri, F. and J.  The Boy Scout Encyclopedia, by Bruce
Grant.  Rand McNally, 1952.

Mathews, S.  Boy Who Ran Away, by Irene Elmer.  Concordia, 1964.

_____ . Boy with a Sling, by Mary P. Warren. Concordia, 1965.

_____ . Daniel in the Lion's Den, by Jane Latourette.
Concordia, 1966.

_____ . Eight Bags of Gold, by Janice Kramer. Concordia, 1964.

_____ . Good Samaritan, by Janice Kramer. Concordia,
1964.

_____ . House on the Rock, by Jane Latourette. Concordia, 1966.

_____ . The Rich Fool, by Janice Kramer. Concordia,
1964.

_____ . Story of Noah's Ark, by Jane Latourette. Concordia, 1965.

_____ . Unforgiving Servant, by Janice Kramer. Concordia, 1968.

Mathews, S. Schofer. Dandy, the Dime, by James S. Kerr.
Denison.

Mawicke, J. Answers and More Answers, by Mary Elting.
Grosset & Dunlap, 1961.

Mawicke, Tram. The Answer Book, by Mary Elting. Grosset & Dunlap, 1959.

McCann, Gerald. Florence Nightingale, War Nurse, by
Anne Colver. Garrard, 1961; Dell, 1966.

McCloskey, Robert. Blueberries for Sal, by Robert Mc-
Closkey. Viking, 1948.

_____ . Centerburg Tales, by Robert McCloskey. Viking,
1951.

_____ . Henry Reed, Inc., by Keith Robertson. Viking,
1958.

_____ . Henry Reed's Baby-Sitting Service, by Keith
Robertson. Viking, 1966.

_____ . Henry Reed's Journey, by Keith Robertson. Viking, 1963.

_____ . Homer Price, by Robert McCloskey. Viking,
1943.

_____ . Journey Cake, Ho! by Ruth Sawyer. Viking,
1953.

_____ . Junket, by Anne H. White. Viking, 1955.

_____ . Lentil, by Robert McCloskey. Viking, 1940.

_____ . Make Way for Ducklings, by Robert McCloskey.
Viking, 1941.

_____ . One Morning in Maine, by Robert McCloskey.
Viking, 1952.

_____ . Time of Wonder, by Robert McCloskey. Viking,
1957.

McConis, Ted. The Summer of the Swans, by Betsy Byars.
Viking, 1970.

McCormick, Dell J.   Paul Bunyan Swings His Axe, by Dell
J. McCormick.   Caxton, 1936.
McLaren, William.   Twenty Thousand Leagues under the
Sea, by Jules Verne.   Dutton.
McNaught, Harry.   Golden Book of Science, by Bertha Mor-
ris Parker.   Western, 1952.
Merryweather, Jack.   Cowboy Sam, by Edna Walker Chandler.
Benefic, 1960.
————.   Cowboy Sam and Big Bill, by Edna W. Chandler.
Benefic, 1970.
————.   Cowboy Sam and Dandy, by Edna W. Chandler.
Benefic, 1962.
————.   Cowboy Sam and Flop, by Edna W. Chandler.
Benefic, 1971.
————.   Cowboy Sam and Freckles, by Edna W. Chandler.
Benefic, 1971.
————.   Cowboy Sam and Freddy, by Edna W. Chandler.
Benefic, 1970.
————.   Cowboy Sam and Miss Lily, by Edna W. Chandler.
Benefic, 1971.
————.   Cowboy Sam and Porky, by Edna W. Chandler.
Benefic, 1971.
————.   Cowboy Sam and Sally, by Edna W. Chandler.
Benefic, 1959.
————.   Cowboy Sam and Shorty, by Edna W. Chandler.
Benefic, 1962.
————.   Cowboy Sam and the Airplane, by Edna W.
Chandler.   Benefic, 1959.
————.   Cowboy Sam and the Fair, by Edna W. Chandler.
Benefic, 1970.
————.   Cowboy Sam and the Indians, by Edna W. Chand-
ler.   Benefic, 1971.
————.   Cowboy Sam and the Rodeo, by Edna W. Chandler.
Benefic, 1959.
————.   Cowboy Sam and the Rustlers, by Edna W.
Chandler.   Benefic, 1970.
Milhous, Katherine.   The Egg Tree, by Katherine Milhous.
Scribner, 1950.
Mill, Eleanor.   What Mary Jo Shared, by Janice May Udry.
Albert Whitman, 1966.
————.   What Mary Jo Wanted, by Janice May Udry.
Albert Whitman, 1968.
Moline, Earl W., Jr.   Blink, the Patchwork Bunny, by
Matthew V. Howard.   Denison, 1959.
————.   George, the Discontented Giraffe, by Phillip
Orso Steinberg.   Denison.
————.   Swimmer Is a Hopper, by Mary Jackson Ellis.
Denison.

Morse, Dorothy Bayley.  Snowbound in Hidden Valley, by
    Holly Wilson.  Messner, 1957.
Moyers, William.  Abraham Lincoln: For the People, by
    Anne Colver.  Garrard, 1960; Dell, 1966.
Mozley, Charles.  The Red Badge of Courage, by Stephen
    Crane.  Dutton.
Mullin, Willard.  Junior Illustrated Encyclopedia of Sports,
    by Herbert Kamm.  Bobbs-Merrill, 1960.
Murr, K.  The True Book of Plants We Know, by Irene S.
    Miner.  Children's, 1953.
Mutchler, D.  The True Book of Farm Animals, by John
    Lewellen.  Children's, 1954.
Myers, Sylvia.  Spaghetti Eddie, by Mary Jackson Ellis.
    Denison.


Nason, Thomas W.  You Come Too, by Robert Frost.  Holt,
    Rinehart & Winston, 1959.
Ness, Evaline.  Sam, Bangs and Moonshine, by Evaline
    Ness.  Holt, Rinehart & Winston, 1966.
Newberry, Clare Turlay.  April's Kittens, by Clare Turlay
    Newberry.  Harper & Row, 1940.
_____.  Marshmallow, by Clare Turlay Newberry.
    Harper & Row, 1942.
Nicholas.  New Illustrated Just So Stories, by Rudyard
    Kipling.  Doubleday, 1952.
Nicholson, William.  The Velveteen Rabbit, by Margery Wil-
    liams.  Doubleday, 1926.
Noonan, Dan.  Mr. Wizard's Experiments for Young Scien-
    tists, by Don Herbert.  Doubleday, 1959.


Oakley, George.  Kidnapped, by Robert Louis Stevenson.
    Dutton, 1959.
Obata.  World God Made, by Alyce Bergey.  Concordia,
    1965.


Page, Helen.  The Gingham Dog and the Calico Cat, by
    Eugene Field.  Follett, 1956.
Palazzo, Tony.  Timothy Turtle, by Al Graham.  Viking,
    1949.
Pape, Frank G.  Pilgrim's Progress, by John Bunyan.  Dut-
    ton.
Parks, Gordon, Jr.  J.T., by Jane Wagner.  Van Nostrand
    Reinhold, 1969; Dell, 1971.
Paton, Jane.  A Dog and a Half, by Barbara Willard.  Nel-
    son, 1971.

Patterson, Bob.  George Washington, by Clara Ingram Judson.  Follett, 1961.

Paull, Grace.  Jesus, the Little New Baby, by Mary Edna Lloyd.  Abingdon, 1951.

Pekarsky, Mel.  The Curious Cow, by Esther Meeks.  Follett, 1960.

————.  Little Quack, by Ruth Woods.  Follett, 1961.

Pene du Bois, William.  Bear Party, by William Pene du Bois.  Viking, 1963.

————.  The Horse in the Camel Suit, by William Pene du Bois.  Harper & Row, 1967.

————.  The Twenty-One Balloons, by William Pene du Bois.  Viking, 1947.

Petersham, Maud and Miska.  The Poppy Seed Cakes, by Margery Clark (pseud.).  Doubleday, 1924.

Peterson, Russell F.  Dinosaurs and Other Prehistoric Animals, by Darlene Geis.  Grosset & Dunlap, 1959.

Phillips, W. F.  Around the Moon, by Jules Verne.  Dutton, 1970.

————.  Around the World in Eighty Days, by Jules Verne.  Dutton, 1968.

————.  From the Earth to the Moon, by Jules Verne.  Dutton, 1970.

————.  Journey to the Centre of the Earth, by Jules Verne.  Dutton, 1970.

Pickard, Charles.  The Call of the Wild, by Jack London.  Dutton, 1968.

Pistorius, A.  The True Book of Birds We Know, by Margaret Friskey.  Children's, 1954.

Pitz, Henry C.  One Thousand Poems for Children, edited by Elizabeth Hough Sechrist.  Macrae Smith, 1946.

————.  Winter on the Johnny Smoker, by Mildred H. Comfort.  Denison.

Politi, Leo.  Angelo the Naughty One, by Helen Garrett.  Viking, 1944.

————.  Song of the Swallows, by Leo Politi.  Scribner, 1949.

Porter, Jim.  The Four Friends, by Carol Hoff.  Follett, 1955.

Preissler, Audrey.  UNICEF Festival Book, by Judith Spiegelman.  United States Committee for UNICEF, 1966.

Prestopino, George.  Pony Engine, by F. M. Ford.  Grosset & Dunlap.

Pyle, Howard.  Men of Iron, by Howard Pyle.  Harper, 1891.

————.  Pepper and Salt, by Howard Pyle. Harper, 1885.

_____. Some Merry Adventures of Robin Hood of Great
Renown in Nottinghamshire, by Howard Pyle. Scribner,
1954.


Rackham, Arthur. Gulliver's Travels, by Jonathan Swift.
Dutton, 1952.
_____. Tales from Shakespeare, by Charles and Mary
Lamb. Dutton.
Rada. Little Boat That Almost Sank, by Mary P. Warren.
Concordia, 1965.
Ravielli, Anthony. Wonders of the Human Body, by Anthony
Ravielli. Viking, 1954.
Reardon, Mary. Snow Treasure, by Marie McSwigan. Dut-
ton, 1942.
Rey, H.A. Anybody at Home? by H.A. Rey. Houghton
Mifflin, 1942.
_____. Curious George, by H.A. Rey. Houghton Mif-
flin, 1941.
_____. Curious George Flies a Kite, by Margret and
H.A. Rey. Houghton Mifflin, 1958.
_____. Curious George Gets a Medal, by H.A. Rey.
Houghton Mifflin, 1957.
_____. Curious George Learns the Alphabet, by H.A.
Rey. Houghton Mifflin, 1963.
_____. Curious George Rides a Bike, by H.A. Rey.
Houghton Mifflin, 1952.
_____. Curious George Takes a Job, by H.A. Rey.
Houghton Mifflin, 1947.
_____. Feed the Animals, by H.A. Rey. Houghton Mif-
flin, 1944.
_____. Katy No-Pocket, by Emmy Payne. Houghton
Mifflin, 1944.
_____. Where's My Baby? by H.A. Rey. Houghton
Mifflin, 1943.
Rice, Elizabeth. Daffy, by Adda Mai Sharp. Steck-Vaughn,
1950.
_____. Where Is Cubby Bear? by Adda Mai Sharp.
Steck-Vaughn, 1950.
Richardson, Frederick. Mother Goose; The Classic Volland
Edition, edited by Eulalie O. Grover. Hubbard, 1971.
Roberts, J. Great Escape, by Mary P. Warren. Concordia,
1966.
_____. Secret of the Star, by Dave Hill. Concordia,
1966.
_____. Two Men in the Temple, by Joann Scheck. Con-
cordia, 1968.

Robison, Robert S.   Sailor Jack and Eddy, by Selma and
     Jack Wassermann.   Benefic, 1961.
_____.   Sailor Jack and the Jet Plane, by Selma and
     Jack Wassermann.   Benefic, 1962.
Rohrer, George.   Dan Frontier Goes to Congress, by Wil-
     liam J. and Jane Hurley.   Benefic, 1964.
Rojankovsky, Feodor.   The Tall Book of Mother Goose.
     Harper & Row, 1942.
_____.   The Tall Book of Nursery Tales.   Harper &
     Row, 1944.
Root, Marita.   Sailor Jack and Bluebell's Dive, by Selma
     and Jack Wassermann.   Benefic, 1961.
Ruse, Margaret.   The Little Old Woman Who Used Her
     Head, by Hope Newell.   Nelson, 1935.


Salem, M.   The True Book of Our Post Office and Its Help-
     ers, by Irene S. Miner.   Children's, 1955.
_____.   The True Book of Policemen and Firemen, by
     Irene S. Miner.   Children's, 1954.
_____.   The True Book of Science Experiments, by Illa
     Podendorf.   Children's, 1954.
Savage, Steele.   Mythology, by Edith Hamilton.   Little,
     Brown, 1942.
Savitt, Sam.   Lad: A Dog, by Albert Payson Terhune.
     Dutton, 1959.
Schindelman, Joseph.   Charlie and the Chocolate Factory,
     by Roald Dahl.   Knopf, 1964.
Schlesinger, Alice.   Big Book of Mother Goose.   Grosset
     & Dunlap.
Schoenherr, John.   Gentle Ben, by Walt Morey.   Dutton,
     1965.
_____.   Rascal: A Memoir of a Better Era, by Sterling
     North.   Dutton, 1963.
_____.   The Wolfling, by Sterling North.   Dutton, 1969.
Schulz, Charles M.   Happiness Is a Warm Puppy, by
     Charles M. Schulz.   Determined, 1962.
Sears, Jewel.   Gobble, Gobble, Gobble, by Mary Jackson
     Ellis.   Denison.
Sendak, Maurice.   Father Bear Comes Home, by Else H.
     Minarik.   Harper & Row, 1959.
_____.   A Hole Is To Dig, by Ruth Krauss.   Harper,
     1952.
_____.   Little Bear, by Else H. Minarik.   Harper, 1957.
_____.   Little Bear's Friend, by Else H. Minarik.
     Harper, 1960.
_____.   Little Bear's Visit, by Else H. Minarik.   Harper,
     1961.

_____. No Fighting, No Biting! by Else H. Minarik. Harper, 1958.

_____. Nutshell Library, by Maurice Sendak. Harper, 1962.

_____. What Do You Say, Dear? by Sesyle Joslin. Addison-Wesley, 1958.

_____. The Wheel on the School, by Meindert DeJong. Harper, 1954.

_____. Where the Wild Things Are, by Maurice Sendak. Harper, 1963.

Seredy, Kate. The Good Master, by Kate Seredy. Viking, 1935.

_____. Little Vic, by Doris Gates. Viking, 1951.

_____. The Singing Tree, by Kate Seredy. Viking, 1939.

_____. The White Stag, by Kate Seredy. Viking, 1937.

Seton, Ernest Thompson. Wild Animals I Have Known, by Ernest Thompson Seton. Scribner, 1898.

Seuss, Dr. (pseud.). And To Think That I Saw It on Mulberry Street, by Dr. Seuss. Vanguard, 1937; Hale.

_____. The Cat in the Hat, by Dr. Seuss. Random, 1957.

_____. The Cat in the Hat Comes Back, by Dr. Seuss. Beginner Books, 1958.

_____. Dr. Seuss's ABC, by Dr. Seuss. Beginner Books, 1963.

_____. The 500 Hats of Bartholomew Cubbins, by Dr. Seuss. Vanguard, 1938.

_____. Green Eggs and Ham, by Dr. Seuss. Beginner Books, 1960.

_____. Hop on Pop, by Dr. Seuss. Beginner Books, 1963.

_____. One Fish, Two Fish, Red Fish, Blue Fish, by Dr. Seuss. Beginner, 1960.

_____. Yertle the Turtle, and Other Stories, by Dr. Seuss. Random, 1958.

Sewell, Helen. The Bears on Hemlock Mountain, by Alice Dalgliesh. Scribner, 1952.

Sharp, William. Heidi, by Johanna Spyri. Grosset.

_____. The Tall Book of Fairy Tales, edited by William Sharp. Harper, 1947.

Shepard, Ernest H. At the Back of the North Wind, by George MacDonald. Dutton.

_____. The House at Pooh Corner, by A.A. Milne. Dutton, 1928; Dell, 1970.

_____. Now We Are Six, by A.A. Milne. Dutton, 1927; Dell, 1970.

_____. When We Were Very Young, by A.A. Milne. Dutton, 1924; Dell, 1970.

_____. The Wind in the Willows, by Kenneth Grahame. Scribner, 1961.

_____. Winnie Ille Pu, by A.A. Milne and Alexander Lenard, translator. Dutton, 1960.

_____. Winnie-the-Pooh, by A.A. Milne. Dutton, 1926; Dell, 1970.

_____. Winnie-the-Pooh's Calendar Book, by A.A. Milne. Dutton.

Shillabeer, Mary. A Child's Garden of Verses, by Robert Louis Stevenson. Dutton.

Shimin, Symeon. How Big Is Big? by Herman and Nina Schneider. Addison-Wesley, 1946.

_____. Onion John, by Joseph Krumgold. T.Y. Crowell, 1959; Apollo, 1970.

Shipman, Robert. Twenty-Seven Cats Next Door, by Anita Feagles. Addison-Wesley, 1965.

Shortall, Leonard. The Boy Who Would Not Say His Name, by Elizabeth Vreeken. Follett, 1959.

_____. The Bully of Barkham Street, by Mary Stolz. Harper, 1963; Dell, 1968.

_____. Encyclopedia Brown and the Case of the Secret Pitch, by Donald J. Sobol. Nelson, 1965.

_____. Encyclopedia Brown, Boy Detective, by Donald J. Sobol. Nelson, 1963.

_____. Encyclopedia Brown Finds the Clues, by Donald J. Sobol. Nelson, 1966.

_____. Encyclopedia Brown Gets His Man, by Donald J. Sobol. Nelson, 1967.

_____. Encyclopedia Brown Keeps the Peace, by Donald J. Sobol. Nelson, 1969.

_____. Encyclopedia Brown Saves the Day, by Donald J. Sobol. Nelson, 1970.

_____. Encyclopedia Brown Solves Them All, by Donald J. Sobol. Nelson, 1971.

_____. The Hole in the Hill, by Marion Seyton. Follett, 1960.

Siebel, Fritz. Cat and Dog, by Else H. Minarik. Harper, 1960.

_____. Tell Me Some More, by Crosby Newell Bonsall. Harper, 1961.

Simmons, Don. Dan Frontier and the New House, by William J. Hurley. Benefic.

Simon, Martin P. Little Visits with God, by Allan H. Jahsmann. Concordia, 1957.

Simont, Marc. A Tree Is Nice, by Janice May Udry. Harper, 1956.

Slobodkina, Esphyr.  Caps for Sale, by Esphyr Slobodkina.
    Addison-Wesley, 1947.
Smith, Alvin.  The Nitty Gritty, by Frank Bonham.  Dutton,
    1968; Dell, 1971.
Smith, Jessie Willcox.  Little Women, by Louisa May Alcott.
    Little, Brown, 1968.
Smith, William A. and Bird, Esther.  The Water-Buffalo
    Children and The Dragon Fish, by Pearl S. Buck.  John
    Day, 1943 and 1944; Dell, 1966.
Sokol, Bill.  Tell Me a Joke, edited by Dana Bruce.  Platt
    & Munk, 1966.
Solbert, Ronni.  The Pushcart War, by Jean Merrill.  Ad-
    dison-Wesley, 1964.
_____.  Shan's Lucky Knife, by Jean Merrill.  Addison-
    Wesley, 1960.
_____.  The Superlative Horse, by Jean Merrill.  Addison-
    Wesley, 1961.
Spiegel, Lawrence.  Bobby Discovers Bird Watching, by
    Marjorie Wackerbarth.  Denison, 1962.
_____.  Bobby Discovers Garden Friends, by Marjorie
    Wackerbarth and Lillian S. Graham.  Denison, 1960.
_____.  Bobby Learns about Butterflies, by Marjorie
    Wackerbarth.  Denison, 1963.
_____.  Bobby Learns about Squirrels, by Marjorie
    Wackerbarth.  Denison, 1966.
_____.  Bobby Learns about Woodland Babies, by Marjorie
    Wackerbarth.  Denison.
_____.  Happy Hospital Surprises, by Winifred Talbot.
    Denison.
_____.  Rocky, the Rocket Mouse, by Alyce Bergey.
    Denison.
Stanley, Diana and Tenniel, John.  Alice's Adventures in
    Wonderland and Through the Looking Glass, by Lewis
    Carroll (pseud.).  Dutton, 1954.
Steig, William.  Sylvester and the Magic Pebble, by William
    Steig.  Simon & Schuster, 1969.
Stevens, Mary.  Nobody Listens to Andrew, by Elizabeth
    Guilfoile.  Follett, 1957.
Sweet, Allen D.  The How and Why Wonder Book of Reptiles
    and Amphibians, by Robert Mathewson.  Wonder-Treasure,
    1960.
Sweet, Darrell.  The How and Why Wonder Book of Explora-
    tions and Discoveries, by Irving Robbin.  Wonder-Treas-
    ure.
_____.  The How and Why Wonder Book of the Human
    Body, by Martin L. Keen.  Wonder-Treasure.

Talarcyzk, June.  The Kitten Who Was Different, by Lowell
    Saunders.  Denison.
Tanis, William.  How Maps and Globes Help Us, by David
    Hackler.  Benefic, 1962.
Tenggren, Gustav.  The Tenggren Mother Goose.  Little,
    Brown, 1940.
Tenniel, John, and Stanley, Diana.  Alice's Adventures in
    Wonderland and Through the Looking Glass, by Lewis
    Carroll (pseud.).  Dutton, 1954.
Thomas, Joan Gale.  If Jesus Came to My House, by Joan
    Gale Thomas.  Lothrop, 1951.
Timmins, William, and Mastri, F. and J.  The Boy Scout
    Encyclopedia, by Bruce Grant.  Rand McNally, 1952.
Tomes, Margot.  Landslide! by Veronique Day.  Coward-Mc-
    Cann, 1963; Dell, 1966.
Toothill, Harry.  Little Lord Fauntleroy, by Frances Hodgson
    Burnett.  Dutton.
_____.  Little Men, by Louisa May Alcott.  Dutton, 1957.
Torrey, Marjorie.  Sensible Kate, by Doris Gates.  Viking,
    1943.
Townsend, Virginia.  Tales of the Sea Foam, by Lisette G.
    Brown.  Naturegraph, 1969.
Tudor, Tasha.  The Real Diary of a Real Boy, by Henry A.
    Shute.  Bauhan, 1967.
_____.  The Secret Garden, by Frances Hodgson Burnett.
    Lippincott, 1962.
_____.  The Tasha Tudor Book of Fairy Tales, edited by
    Dana Bruce.  Platt & Munk, 1961.
_____.  and others.  My Brimful Book, edited by Dana
    Bruce.  Platt & Munk, 1960.


Ungerer, Tomi.  Seeds and More Seeds, by Millicent Ellis
    Selsam.  Harper, 1959.
Unwin, Nora S.  Amos Fortune, Free Man, by Elizabeth
    Yates.  Dutton, 1950.
_____.  Peter Pan, by James M. Barrie.  Scribner, 1949.
Uptton, Clive.  Egermeier's Bible Story Books, by Elsie E.
    Egermeier.  Warner, 1923.


Van Abbe, S.  Little Women, by Louisa May Alcott.  Dutton,
    1948.
_____.  Tanglewood Tales, by Nathaniel Hawthorne.  Dut-
    ton, 1952.
_____.  Tom Brown's Schooldays, by Thomas Hughes.
    Dutton.

_____. Treasure Island, by Robert Louis Stevenson.
Dutton.

_____. A Wonder Book, by Nathaniel Hawthorne.  Dutton.
Voter, Thomas W.  Rocket Ship Galileo, by Robert A. Heinlein.  Scribner, 1947.


Ward, Lynd.  The Biggest Bear, by Lynd Ward.  Houghton,
1952.

_____. Johnny Tremain, by Esther Forbes.  Houghton,
1943; Dell.
Warren, Betsy.  The Story of the Liberty Bell, by Natalie
Miller.  Children's, 1965.
Watkins-Pitchford, D.J.  The Lost Princess: A Double
Story, by George MacDonald.  Dutton, 1965.
Webber, Irma E.  Up Above and Down Below, by Irma E.
Webber.  Addison-Wesley, 1943.
Weisgard, Leonard.  The Courage of Sarah Noble, by Alice
Dalgliesh.  Scribner, 1954.

_____. Favorite Poems Old and New, edited by Helen
Josephine Ferris.  Doubleday, 1957.

_____. The Golden Egg Book, by Margaret Wise Brown.
Western, 1963.

_____. Hailstones and Halibut Bones, by Mary O'Neill.
Doubleday, 1961.

_____. The Little Island, by Golden MacDonald.  Double-
day, 1946.

_____. Rain Drop Splash, by Alvin Tresselt.  Lothrop,
1946.

_____. Red Light Green Light, by Golden MacDonald.
Doubleday, 1944.

_____. Where Does the Butterfly Go When It Rains? by
May Garelick.  Addison-Wesley, 1961.
Weiss, Emil.  It's Like This, Cat, by Emily Cheney Neville.
Harper, 1963.
Weiss, Harvey.  Clay, Wood and Wire, by Harvey Weiss.
Addison-Wesley, 1956.

_____. Pencil, Pen and Brush, by Harvey Weiss.  Ad-
dison-Wesley, 1961.
Westover, Ned, and Holmes, Rosinda.  Robin Deer, by Olga
Cossi.  Naturegraph, 1968.
Whitear, A.R.  King Solomon's Mines, by H. Rider Haggard.
Dutton.
Wiese, Kurt.  Daughter of the Mountains, by Louise S.
Rankin.  Viking, 1948.

_____. The Five Chinese Brothers, by Claire Huchet
Bishop.  Coward-McCann, 1938; Hale.

_____. The Story about Ping, by Marjorie Flack. Viking, 1933.

Wilde, G. The Story of the Star-Spangled Banner, by Natalie Miller. Children's, 1965.

Wilde, Irma. The Three Little Pigs, by Margaret Hillert. Follett, 1963.

Williams, Garth. By the Shores of Silver Lake, by Laura Ingalls Wilder. Harper, 1939.

_____. Charlotte's Web, by E. B. White. Harper, 1952; Dell, 1967.

_____. Emmett's Pig, by Mary Stolz. Harper, 1959.

_____. Farmer Boy, by Laura Ingalls Wilder. Harper, 1933.

_____. Little House in the Big Woods, by Laura Ingalls Wilder. Harper, 1932.

_____. Little House on the Prairie, by Laura Ingalls Wilder. Harper, 1935.

_____. Little Town on the Prairie, by Laura Ingalls Wilder. Harper, 1941.

_____. On the Banks of Plum Creek, by Laura Ingalls Wilder. Harper, 1937.

_____. Stuart Little, by E. B. White. Harper, 1945; Dell, 1967.

_____. The Tall Book of Make-Believe, edited by Garth Williams. Harper, 1950.

Wilson, Dagmar. Benny and the Bear, by Barbee Carleton. Follett, 1960.

_____. Casey, the Utterly Impossible Horse, by Anita Feagles. Addison-Wesley, 1960.

_____. Gertie the Duck, by Nicholas Georgiady and Louis Romano. Follett, 1959.

Wind, Betty. Boy Who Saved His Family, by Alyce Bergey. Concordia, 1966.

_____. Great Surprise, by Mary P. Warren. Concordia, 1964.

_____. Jon and the Little Lost Lamb, by Jane Latourette. Concordia, 1965.

_____. Lame Man Who Walked Again, by Mary P. Warren. Concordia, 1966.

_____. Little Benjamin and the First Christmas, by Betty Forell. Concordia, 1964.

_____. Most Wonderful King, by Dave Hill. Concordia, 1968.

_____. Secret Journey, by Virginia Mueller. Concordia, 1968.

Wohlberg, Meg. The Smallest Boy in the Class, by Jerrold Beim. Morrow, 1949.

Woodward, Hildegard.   Christmas; A Book of Stories Old and
    New, compiled by Alice Dalgliesh.   Scribner, 1934.
Wright, Blanche Fisher.   The Real Mother Goose.   Rand
    McNally, 1916.
Wyeth, N.C.   The Yearling, by Marjorie Kinnan Rawlings.
    Scribner, 1938.


Yashima, Taro.   Crow Boy, by Taro Yashima.   Viking,
    1955.
_____.   Umbrella, by Taro Yashima.   Viking, 1958.


Zaffo, George J.   Airplanes & Trucks & Trains, Fire En-
    gines, Boats & Ships, & Building & Wrecking Machines,
    by George J. Zaffo.   Grosset & Dunlap, 1968.
_____.   Big Book of Airplanes, by Charles L. Black.
    Grosset, 1951.
_____.   Big Book of Building and Wrecking Machines, by
    George J. Zaffo.   Grosset, 1951.
_____.   Big Book of Real Trucks, by Elizabeth Cameron.
    Grosset, 1950.
Zemsky, Jessica.   In John's Back Yard, by Esther Meeks.
    Follett, 1957.

Chapter Five

BEST SELLERS BY YEAR OF ORIGINAL PUBLICATION

This chapter lists the best sellers chronologically by the date of their original publication. Those books first published before 1940 appear in a continuous listing, the symbol "NF" designating nonfiction. The books first published from 1940 on are divided into yearly listings of "Fiction" and "Nonfiction," naming the original publishers. Nearly all of the in-print best sellers on this list that were published before 1939 are fiction; the few in-print nonfiction best sellers published before 1939 are outstanding books of their respective fields--including biography, ancient history, religion, poetry and verse, and even some nature study--that, on the whole, contain a minimum of outdated material.

The ratio of nonfiction to fiction best sellers appears to increase rather steadily year by year in recent decades. This apparent trend may be somewhat deceiving, for books that sold 100,000 copies or more but are now out of print are not included in this survey. There also appears to be a rather steady increase in the number of best sellers published from year to year; this trend, too, may appear greater than it really is because of the exclusion of out-of-print best sellers from this survey.

| | |
|---|---|
| c. 1490 | Some Merry Adventures of Robin Hood of Great Renown in Nottinghamshire. |
| 1678, 1684 | Pilgrim's Progress, by John Bunyan. |
| 1719 | Robinson Crusoe, by Daniel Defoe. |
| 1726 | Gulliver's Travels, by Jonathan Swift. |
| 1760 | Mother Goose. |
| 1807 | Tales from Shakespeare, by Charles and Mary Lamb. |
| 1812, 1815 | Grimm's Fairy Tales, by Jakob and Wilhelm Grimm. |
| 1812 | Little Red Riding Hood, by Jakob and Wilhelm Grimm. |

| 1813 |    | The Swiss Family Robinson, by Johann R. Wyss. |
|------|----|------|
| 1831 |    | Goldilocks and the Three Bears. |
| 1835 |    | Hans Andersen's Fairy Tales, by Hans Christian Andersen. |
| 1835 |    | The Steadfast Tin Soldier, by Hans Christian Andersen. |
| 1843 |    | A Christmas Carol, by Charles Dickens. |
| 1845 |    | The Cricket on the Hearth, by Charles Dickens. |
| 1851 |    | Moby Dick, by Herman Melville. |
| 1851 |    | A Wonder Book for Boys and Girls, by Nathaniel Hawthorne. |
| 1853 |    | Tanglewood Tales, by Nathaniel Hawthorne. |
| 1855 | NF | The Song of Hiawatha, by Henry Wadsworth Longfellow. |
| 1857 |    | Tom Brown's Schooldays, by Thomas Hughes. |
| 1860 |    | Henny Penny. |
| 1864 |    | Journey to the Centre of the Earth, by Jules Verne. |
| 1865 |    | Alice's Adventures in Wonderland, by Lewis Carroll. |
| 1865 |    | Around the Moon, by Jules Verne. |
| 1865 |    | From the Earth to the Moon, by Jules Verne. |
| 1865 |    | Hans Brinker:  Or The Silver Skates, by Mary Mapes Dodge. |
| 1868 |    | Little Women, by Louisa May Alcott. |
| 1869 |    | Lorna Doone, by Richard Doddridge Blackmore. |
| 1869 |    | Twenty Thousand Leagues under the Sea, by Jules Verne. |
| 1871 |    | At the Back of the North Wind, by George MacDonald. |
| 1871 |    | Little Men, by Louisa May Alcott. |
| 1872 |    | Through the Looking Glass, by Lewis Carroll. |
| 1873 |    | Around the World in Eighty Days, by Jules Verne. |
| 1877 |    | Black Beauty, by Anna Sewell. |
| 1878 |    | The Adventures of Tom Sawyer, by Mark Twain. |
| 1879 | NF | The Adventures of Odysseus, by Andrew Lang. |
| 1881 |    | Pinocchio:  The Story of a Puppet, by Carlo Collodi. |
| 1882 |    | Diddie, Dumps and Tot, by Louise Clarke Pyrnelle. |
| 1882 |    | The Prince and the Pauper, by Mark Twain. |
| 1883 |    | Treasure Island, by Robert Louis Stevenson. |
| 1884 |    | The Adventures of Huckleberry Finn, by Mark Twain. |
| 1884 |    | Heidi, by Johanna Spyri. |
| 1885 | NF | A Child's Garden of Verses, by Robert Louis Stevenson. |

| | |
|---|---|
| 1885 | Pepper and Salt, by Howard Pyle. |
| 1886 | The Birds' Christmas Carol, by Kate Douglas Wiggin. |
| 1886 | Jo's Boys, by Louisa May Alcott. |
| 1886 | Kidnapped, by Robert Louis Stevenson. |
| 1886 | King Solomon's Mines, by H. Rider Haggard. |
| 1886 | Little Lord Fauntleroy, by Frances Hodgson Burnett. |
| 1888, 1891 | The Happy Prince and Other Stories, by Oscar Wilde. |
| 1888 | The Black Arrow, by Robert Louis Stevenson. |
| 1891 | Men of Iron, by Howard Pyle. |
| 1894 | The Jungle Books, by Rudyard Kipling. |
| 1895 | The Red Badge of Courage, by Stephen Crane. |
| 1898   NF | Wild Animals I Have Known, by Ernest Thompson Seton. |
| 1900 | The Story of Little Black Sambo, by Helen Bannerman. |
| 1900 | The Wonderful Wizard of Oz, by L. Frank Baum. |
| 1901 | Kim, by Rudyard Kipling. |
| 1902   NF | The Real Diary of a Real Boy, by Henry A. Shute. |
| 1903 | The Call of the Wild, by Jack London. |
| 1903 | Rebecca of Sunnybrook Farm, by Kate Douglas Wiggin. |
| 1904 | English Folk and Fairy Tales, edited by Joseph Jacobs. |
| 1908 | The Wind in the Willows, by Kenneth Grahame. |
| 1910   NF | Boy Scout Handbook, by The Boy Scouts of America. |
| 1912 | Just So Stories, by Rudyard Kipling. |
| 1912 | The Secret Garden, by Frances Hodgson Burnett. |
| 1914 | Penrod, by Booth Tarkington. |
| 1915 | Mother Goose: The Classic Volland Edition, edited by Eulalie O. Grover. |
| 1915 | The Thirty-Nine Steps, by John Buchan. |
| 1916 | Old Peter's Russian Tales, by Arthur Ransome. |
| 1916 | The Real Mother Goose.   Rand McNally. |
| 1916 | Seventeen, by Booth Tarkington. |
| 1916 | Understood Betsy, by Dorothy Canfield Fisher. |
| 1919 | Lad: A Dog, by Albert Payson Terhune. |
| 1920 | Beautiful Joe, by Marshall Saunders. |
| 1920 | The Story of Doctor Dolittle, by Hugh Lofting. |
| 1922 | The Voyages of Doctor Dolittle, by Hugh Lofting. |
| 1923   NF | The Book of the Ancient World for Younger Readers, by Dorothy Mills. |

1923  NF   Egermeier's Bible Story Books, by Elsie E. Egermeier.

1923  NF   Poems for Youth: An American Anthology, compiled by William Rose Benet.

1924       The Dark Frigate, by Charles Boardman Hawes.

1924       The Poppy Seed Cakes, by Margery Clark.

1924       When We Were Very Young, by A.A. Milne.

1925  NF   The Book of the Ancient Greeks, by Dorothy Mills.

1926       Smoky, the Cow Horse, by Will James.

1926       The Velveteen Rabbit, by Margery Williams.

1926       Winnie-the-Pooh, by A.A. Milne.

1927  NF   The Book of the Ancient Romans, by Dorothy Mills.

1927       Gay Neck: The Story of a Pigeon, by Dhan Gopal Mukerji.

1927  NF   Now We Are Six, by A.A. Milne.

1928       The House at Pooh Corner, by A.A. Milne.

1929       Bambi: A Life in the Woods, by Felix Salten.

1929       The Little Engine That Could, by Watty Piper.

1929       Pelle's New Suit, by Elsa Beskow.

1930       Angus and the Ducks, by Marjorie Flack.

1931       Angus and the Cat, by Marjorie Flack.

1931  NF   The Christ Child, by Maud and Miska Petersham.

1932       Angus Lost, by Marjorie Flack.

1932       The Little Family, by Lois Lenski

1932       Little House in the Big Woods, by Laura Ingalls Wilder.

1932       Snipp, Snapp, Snurr and the Red Shoes, by Maj Lindman.

1933       Farmer Boy, by Laura Ingalls Wilder.

1933  NF   Invincible Louisa, by Cornelia Meigs.

1933       Snipp, Snapp, Snurr and the Magic Horse, by Maj Lindman.

1933       The Story about Ping, by Marjorie Flack.

1934       Christmas: A Book of Stories Old and New, compiled by Alice Dalgliesh.

1934       Down, Down the Mountain, by Ellis Credle.

1934  NF   Little Book about God (Protestant), by Lauren Ford.

1934       Snipp, Snapp, Snurr and the Buttered Bread, by Maj Lindman.

1934       Tim Tadpole and the Great Bullfrog, by Marjorie Flack.

1935       The Good Master, by Kate Seredy.

1935       Little House on the Prairie, by Laura Ingalls Wilder.

1935          The Little Old Woman Who Used Her Head, by
              Hope Newell.
1935   NF     The Middle Ages, by Dorothy Mills.
1936   NF     George Washington, by Ingri and Edgar Parin
              D'Aulaire.
1936          Paul Bunyan Swings His Axe, by Dell J. Mc-
              Cormick.
1936          Roller Skates, by Ruth Sawyer and Kate Seredy.
1936          Snipp, Snapp, Snurr and the Gingerbread, by
              Maj Lindman.
1936          Snipp, Snapp, Snurr and the Yellow Sled, by
              Maj Lindman.
1936          The Story of Ferdinand, by Munro Leaf.
1936          Tales from a Finnish Tupa, by James Cloyd
              Bowman and Margery Bianco.
1937          And To Think That I Saw It on Mulberry Street,
              by Dr. Seuss.
1937   NF     The Book of Marvels, by Richard Halliburton.
1937          On the Banks of Plum Creek, by Laura Ingalls
              Wilder.
1937          Pecos Bill, by James Cloyd Bowman.
1937          Snipp, Snapp, Snurr and the Big Surprise, by
              Maj Lindman.
1937          The White Stag, by Kate Seredy.
1938          Andy and the Lion, by James Daugherty.
1938          Buttons, by Tom Robinson.
1938          The Five Chinese Brothers, by Claire Bishop.
1938          The 500 Hats of Bartholomew Cubbins, by Dr.
              Seuss.
1938          Mei Li, by Thomas Handforth.
1938          Mr. Popper's Penguins, by Richard and Florence
              Atwater.
1938          Wee Gillis, by Munro Leaf.
1938          The Yearling, by Marjorie Kinnan Rawlings.
1939   NF     Ben and Me, by Robert Lawson.
1939          By the Shores of Silver Lake, by Laura Ingalls
              Wilder.
1939          The Country Bunny and the Little Gold Shoes,
              by Dubose Heyward.
1939   NF     Daniel Boone, by James Daugherty.
1939          Flicka, Ricka, Dicka and the New Dotted
              Dresses, by Maj Lindman.
1939   NF     Handbook of Nature Study, by Anna Botsford
              Comstock.
1939   NF     Let's Go Outdoors, by Harriet E. Huntington.
1939          Little Toot, by Hardie Gramatky.
1939          Madeline, by Ludwig Bemelmans.

1939              Mike Mulligan and His Steam Shovel, by Virginia
                  Lee Burton.
1939    NF        Renaissance and Reformation Times, by Dorothy
                  Mills.
1939              The Singing Tree, by Kate Seredy.

## 1940

Fiction
April's Kittens, by Clare Turlay Newberry.   Harper.
Blue Willow, by Doris Gates.   Viking.
Lentil, by Robert McCloskey.   Viking.
The Tenggren Mother Goose, illustrated by Gustav Tenggren.
    Little, Brown.
Thee, Hannah! by Marguerite De Angeli.   Doubleday.

Nonfiction
Abraham Lincoln, by Ingri and Edgar Parin D'Aulaire.   Dou-
    bleday.
Signaling.   Boy Scouts of America.
They Were Strong and Good, by Robert Lawson.   Viking.

## 1941

Fiction
Barney's Adventure, by Margot Austin.   Dutton.
Curious George, by H. A. Rey.   Houghton Mifflin.
Flicka, Ricka, Dicka and the Three Kittens, by Maj Lind-
    man.   Albert Whitman.
Flip, by Wesley Dennis.   Viking.
In My Mother's House, by Ann Nolan Clark.   Viking.
Junior Miss, by Sally Benson.   Random.
Lassie Come-Home, by Eric Knight.   Winston.
Little Town on the Prairie, by Laura Ingalls Wilder.   Harper.
Make Way for Ducklings, by Robert McCloskey.   Viking.
My Friend Flicka, by Mary O'Hara.   Lippincott.
Peter Churchmouse, by Margot Austin.   Dutton.
The Saturdays, by Elizabeth Enright.   Rinehart.

Nonfiction
Paddle-to-the-Sea, by Holling Clancy Holling.   Houghton
    Mifflin.

## 1942

Fiction
Adam of the Road, by Elizabeth Janet Gray.   Viking.
Anybody at Home? by H. A. Rey.   Houghton Mifflin.
Dash and Dart: Two Fawns, by Mary and Conrad Buff.   Vi-
    king.

The Four-Story Mistake, by Elizabeth Enright.   Rinehart.
The Little House, by Virginia Lee Burton.   Houghton Mifflin.
Marshmallow, by Clare Turlay Newberry.   Harper.
The Runaway Bunny, by Margaret Wise Brown.   Harper.
Snow Treasure, by Marie McSwigan.   Dutton.
The Tall Book of Mother Goose, illustrated by Feodor Rojan-
    kovsky.   Harper.

Nonfiction
Mythology, by Edith Hamilton.   Little, Brown.
Tree in the Trail, by Holling Clancy Holling.   Houghton Mif-
    flin.

## 1943

Fiction
Homer Price, by Robert McCloskey.   Viking.
Johnny Tremain, by Esther Forbes.   Houghton Mifflin.
Katy and the Big Snow, by Virginia Lee Burton.   Houghton
    Mifflin.
Sensible Kate, by Doris Gates.   Viking.
The Water-Buffalo Children, by Pearl Sydenstricker Buck.
    John Day.
Where's My Baby? by H.A. Rey.   Houghton Mifflin.

Nonfiction
Small Rain:  Verses from the Bible, edited by Jessie Orton
    Jones.   Viking.
Tell Me about God, by Mary Alice Jones.   Rand McNally.
Up Above and Down Below, by Irma E. Webber.   Addison-
    Wesley.

## 1944

Fiction
Angelo the Naughty One, by Helen Garrett.   Viking.
The Dragon Fish, by Pearl S. Buck.   John Day.
Feed the Animals, by H.A. Rey.   Houghton Mifflin.
In the Forest, by Marie Hall Ets.   Viking.
Katy No-Pocket, by Emmy Payne.   Houghton Mifflin.
Rabbit Hill, by Robert Lawson.   Viking.
The Tall Book of Nursery Tales, edited by Feodor Rojankov-
    sky.   Harper.

Nonfiction
Animal Industry.   Boy Scouts of America.
Dr. George Washington Carver, Scientist, by Shirley Graham
    and George D. Lipscomb.   Messner.
The First Woman Doctor:  The Story of Elizabeth Blackwell,
    M.D., by Rachel Baker.   Messner.

The Golden Dictionary, edited by Ellen Wales Walpole.  Golden.
One God:  The Ways We Worship Him, by Florence Mary
    Fitch.  Lothrop.
Red Light Green Light, by Golden MacDonald.  Doubleday.
Tell Me about Jesus, by Mary Alice Jones.  Rand McNally.

## 1945

### Fiction

The Little Rabbit Who Wanted Red Wings, by Carolyn Sherwin
    Bailey.  Platt & Munk.
Melindy's Medal, by Georgene Faulkner and John Becker.
    Messner.
Strawberry Girl, by Lois Lenski.  Lippincott.
Stuart Little, by E. B. White.  Harper.
The Wise Men of Helm and Their Merry Tales, by Solomon
    Simon.  Behrman.

### Nonfiction

Golden Song Book, by Katharine Tyler Wessels.  Golden.
Tell Me about the Bible, by Mary Alice Jones.  Rand Mc-
    Nally.

## 1946

### Fiction

Bright April, by Marguerite De Angeli.  Doubleday.
The Bumper Book, edited by Watty Piper.  Platt & Munk.
Miss Hickory, by Carolyn Sherwin Bailey.  Viking.
Walt Disney's Uncle Remus Stories, by Joel Chandler Harris.
    Golden.

### Nonfiction

The Boats on the River, by Marjorie Flack.  Viking.
Chicken Little Count-to-Ten, by Margaret Friskey.  Chil-
    dren's.
How Big Is Big? by Herman and Nina Schneider.  Addison-
    Wesley.
Let's Find Out about Heat, Water and Air, by Herman and
    Nina Schneider.  Addison-Wesley.
The Little Island, by Golden MacDonald.  Doubleday.
One Thousand Poems for Children, edited by Elizabeth Hough
    Sechrist.  Macrae Smith.
Rain Drop Splash, by Alvin Tresselt.  Lothrop.
Sitting Bull, Champion of His People, by Shannon Garst.
    Messner.

## 1947

Fiction

Caps for Sale, by Esphyr Slobodkina.  Addison-Wesley.
Curious George Takes a Job, by H.A. Rey.  Houghton Mifflin.
Goodnight Moon, by Margaret Wise Brown.  Harper.
Little Eddie, by Carolyn Haywood.  Morrow.
Misty of Chincoteague, by Marguerite Henry.  Rand McNally.
Rocket Ship Galileo, by Robert A. Heinlein.  Scribner.
Stone Soup: An Old Tale, by Marcia Brown.  Scribner.
The Tall Book of Fairy Tales, edited by William Sharp.
     Harper.
The Twenty-One Balloons, by William Pène du Bois.  Viking.

Nonfiction

Birds in Their Homes, by Addison Webb.  Doubleday.
The Golden Egg Book, by Margaret Wise Brown.  Simon &
     Schuster.
Marian's Big Book of Bible Stories, by Marian M. Schoolland.
     Eerdmans.
A Picture Book of Palestine, by Ethel L. Smither.  Abingdon.
The Rainbow Dictionary, edited by Wendell W. Wright.
     World.
White Snow, Bright Snow, by Alvin Tresselt.  Lothrop.

## 1948

Fiction

The Big Wave, by Pearl Sydenstricker Buck.  John Day.
Blueberries for Sal, by Robert McCloskey.  Viking.
Daughter of the Mountains, by Louise S. Rankin.  Viking.
King of the Wind, by Marguerite Henry.  Rand McNally.
Space Cadet, by Robert A. Heinlein.  Scribner.

Nonfiction

American Folk Songs for Children, by Ruth Seeger.  Doubleday.
A Child's Garden of Bible Stories, by Arthur W. Gross.
     Concordia.
A Child's Garden of Prayer, compiled by Herman W. Gockel
     and Edward J. Saleska.  Concordia.
Colonial Williamsburg Coloring Book, by Marian Cannon.
     Colonial Williamsburg Foundation.
Marian's Favorite Bible Stories, by Marian M. Schoolland.
     Eerdmans.
The Presidents in American History, by Charles A. Beard.
     Messner.

The Stork Didn't Bring You, by Lois Loyd Pemberton.  Nelson.
Tell Me about Prayer, by Mary Alice Jones.  Rand McNally.
You and the Constitution of the United States, by Paul Witty and J. Kohler.  Children's.

## 1949

Fiction
Cotton in My Sack, by Lois Lenski.  Lippincott.
The Door in the Wall, by Marguerite De Angeli.  Doubleday.
"National Velvet," by Enid Bagnold.  Morrow.
Peter Pan, by James M. Barrie.  Scribner.
Red Planet:  A Colonial Boy on Mars, by Robert A. Heinlein.  Scribner.
Sea Star, Orphan of Chincoteague, by Marguerite Henry.  Rand McNally.
The Smallest Boy in the Class, by Jerrold Beim.  Morrow.
Song of the Swallows, by Leo Politi.  Scribner.
Spooks and Spirits and Shadowy Shapes, by Emma L. Brock et al.  Dutton.
Surprise Island, by Gertrude Chandler Warner.  Albert Whitman.
Timothy Turtle, by Al Graham.  Viking.

Nonfiction
Albert Einstein, by Elma Ehrlich Levinger.  Messner.
The Child's Story Bible, by Catherine F. Vos.  Eerdmans.
Snakes, by Herbert S. Zim.  Morrow.
Story of the Trapp Family Singers, by Maria Augusta Trapp.  Lippincott.

## 1950

Fiction
Better Homes and Gardens Story Book.  Meredith.
Born to Trot, by Marguerite Henry.  Rand McNally.
The Boxcar Children, by Gertrude Chandler Warner.  Albert Whitman.
Daffy, by Adda Mai Sharp.  Steck-Vaughn.
The Egg Tree, by Katherine Milhous.  Scribner.
Farmer in the Sky, by Robert A. Heinlein.  Scribner.
Henry Huggins, by Beverly Cleary.  Morrow.
Hot Rod, by Henry Gregor Felsen.  Dutton.
Pippi Longstocking, by Astrid Lindgren.  Viking.
The Tall Book of Make-Believe, edited by Garth Williams.  Harper.
Where is Cubby Bear? by Adda Mai Sharp.  Steck-Vaughn.

Nonfiction
Amos Fortune, Free Man, by Elizabeth Yates. Dutton.
Benjamin Franklin, by Ingri and Edgar Parin D'Aulaire. Dou-
    bleday.
Big Book of Real Trucks, by George J. Zaffo. Grosset &
    Dunlap.
Facts of Life and Love for Teenagers, by Evelyn Millis
    Duvall and Sylvanus Duvall. Association.
The Great Houdini, Magician Extraordinary, by Samuel Ep-
    stein and Beryl Williams. Messner.
Make It Yourself! by Bernice Wells Carlson. Abingdon-
    Cokesbury.

## 1951

Fiction
Aesop's Stories, by Edward W. and M. P. Dolch. Garrard.
All-of-a-Kind Family, by Sydney Taylor. Follett.
Between Planets, by Robert A. Heinlein. Scribner.
Centerburg Tales, by Robert McCloskey. Viking.
Ellen Tebbits, by Beverly Cleary. Morrow.
Flip and the Morning, by Wesley Dennis. Viking.
If Jesus Came to My House, by Joan Gale Thomas. Lothrop.
Jeanne-Marie Counts Her Sheep, by Francoise. Scribner.
Little Vic, by Doris Gates. Viking.
The Lost Kingdom, by Chester Bryant. Messner.

Nonfiction
Album of Horses, by Marguerite Henry. Rand McNally.
Big Book of Airplanes, by Charles L. Black. Grosset &
    Dunlap.
Big Book of Building and Wrecking Machines, by George J.
    Zaffo. Grosset & Dunlap.
Famous Paintings: An Introduction to Art, by Alice Elizabeth
    Chase. Platt & Munk.
Jesus, the Little New Baby, by Mary Edna Lloyd. Abingdon.
The Jim Thorpe Story: America's Greatest Athlete, by Gene
    Schoor. Messner.
Minn of the Mississippi, by Holling Clancy Holling. Houghton
    Mifflin.
You and the United Nations, by Lois Fisher. Children's.

## 1952

Fiction
Animal Stories, by Edward W. and M. P. Dolch. Garrard.
The Bears on Hemlock Mountain, by Alice Dalgliesh. Scrib-
    ner.
The Biggest Bear, by Lynd Ward. Houghton Mifflin.

Charlotte's Web, by E.B. White. Harper.
Curious George Rides a Bike, by H.A. Rey. Houghton Mifflin.
Folk Stories, by Edward W. and M.P. Dolch. Garrard.
Henry and Beezus, by Beverly Cleary. Morrow.
One Morning in Maine, by Robert McCloskey. Viking.
The Rolling Stones, by Robert A. Heinlein. Scribner.
Secret of the Andes, by Ann Nolan Clark. Viking.
Thunder Road, by William Campbell Gault. Dutton.

Nonfiction
Bible Stories, by Mary Alice Jones. Rand McNally.
The Boy Scout Encyclopedia, by Bruce Grant. Rand McNally.
Courtis-Watters Illustrated Golden Dictionary for Young Readers, by Stuart A. Courtis and Garnette Watters. Golden.
Golden Book of Science, by Bertha Morris Parker. Golden.
A Hole Is To Dig, by Ruth Krauss. Harper.
Marco Polo, by Manuel Komroff. Messner.
Nature. Boy Scouts of America.
Nature Atlas of America, by Emil L. Jordan. Hammond.
Sigmund Freud, by Rachel Baker. Messner.
Wildlife Management. Boy Scouts of America.

## 1953

Fiction
And Now Miguel, by Joseph Krumgold. T.Y. Crowell.
The Happy Hollisters, by Jerry West. Doubleday.
The Happy Hollisters at Sea Gull Beach, by Jerry West. Doubleday.
The Happy Hollisters on a River Trip, by Jerry West. Doubleday.
Journey Cake, Ho! by Ruth Sawyer. Viking.
King Arthur and the Round Table, by A.M. Hadfield. Dutton.
Madeline's Rescue, by Ludwig Bemelmans. Viking.
Starman Jones, by Robert A. Heinlein. Scribner.

Nonfiction
Geology. Boy Scouts of America.
Mr. Revere and I, by Robert Lawson. Little, Brown.
The True Book of Air Around Us, by Margaret Friskey. Children's.
The True Book of Plants We Know, by Irene S. Miner. Children's.

## 1954

Fiction
Book of Nursery and Mother Goose Rhymes, by Marguerite De Angeli. Doubleday.

Dog Stories, by Edward W. and M.P. Dolch. Garrard.
The Gateway to Storyland, edited by Watty Piper. Platt &
Munk.
Henry and Ribsy, by Beverly Cleary. Morrow.
Justin Morgan Had a Horse, by Marguerite Henry. Rand Mc-
Nally.
Mike's House, by Julia Sauer. Viking.
The Star Beast, by Robert A. Heinlein. Scribner.
The Tall Book of Christmas, edited by Dorothy Hall Smith.
Harper.
The Tough Winter, by Robert Lawson. Viking.
The Wheel on the School, by Meindert DeJong. Harper.

Nonfiction
Animals Everywhere, by Ingri and Edgar Parin D'Aulaire.
Doubleday.
The Courage of Sarah Noble, by Alice Dalgliesh. Scribner.
Dinosaurs, by Herbert S. Zim. Morrow.
Fishing. Boy Scouts of America.
Golden Picture Dictionary, by Lilian Moore. Golden.
The True Book of Birds We Know, by Margaret Friskey.
Children's.
The True Book of Farm Animals, by John Lewellen. Chil-
dren's.
The True Book of Indians, by Teri Martini. Children's.
The True Book of Insects, by Illa Podendorf. Children's.
The True Book of Moon, Sun and Stars, by Illa Podendorf.
Children's.
The True Book of Pebbles and Shells, by Illa Podendorf.
Children's.
The True Book of Policemen and Firemen, by Irene S. Miner.
Children's.
The True Book of Science Experiments, by Illa Podendorf.
Children's.
Wonders of the Human Body, by Anthony Ravielli. Viking.

## 1955

Fiction
Crow Boy, by Taro Yashima. Viking.
Eloise, by Kay Thompson. Simon & Schuster.
The Four Friends, by Carol Hoff. Follett.
Harold and the Purple Crayon, by Crockett Johnson. Harper.
Hold Fast to Your Dreams, by Catherine Blanton. Messner.
Illustrated Treasury of Children's Literature, edited by Mar-
garet E. Martignoni. Grosset & Dunlap.
Junket, by Anne H. White. Viking.
Mop Top, by Don Freeman. Viking.

Play with Me, by Marie Hall Ets. Viking.
Springtime for Jeanne-Marie, by Francoise. Scribner.
Tunnel in the Sky, by Robert A. Heinlein. Scribner.

Nonfiction
Better Homes and Gardens Junior Cook Book. Meredith.
Carry On, Mr. Bowditch, by Jean Lee Latham. Houghton
    Mifflin.
The Civil War, by Fletcher Pratt. Doubleday.
Columbus, by Ingri and Edgar Parin D'Aulaire. Doubleday.
The True Book of Animal Babies, by Illa Podendorf. Chil-
    dren's.
The True Book of Dinosaurs, by Mary L. Clark. Children's.
The True Book of Holidays, by John W. Purcell. Children's.
The True Book of Our Post Office and Its Helpers, by Irene
    S. Miner. Children's.
The True Book of Seasons, by Illa Podendorf. Children's.
What's Inside the Egg? by May Garelick. Addison-Wesley.

## 1956
Fiction
Brighty of the Grand Canyon, by Marguerite Henry. Rand
    McNally.
Circus Stories, by Edward W. and M. P. Dolch. Garrard.
Dipper of Copper Creek, by John and Jean George. Dutton.
The Enormous Egg, by Oliver Butterworth. Little, Brown.
Fifteen, by Beverly Cleary. Morrow.
The Gingham Dog and the Calico Cat, by Eugene Field. Fol-
    lett.
Harry the Dirty Dog, by Gene Zion. Harper.
The Red Balloon, by Albert Lamourisse. Doubleday.
Time for the Stars, by Robert A. Heinlein. Scribner.

Nonfiction
Clay, Wood and Wire, by Harvey Weiss. Addison-Wesley.
My Bible Story Book, by Gerhard L. Wind. Concordia.
Tell Me about Heaven, by Mary Alice Jones. Rand McNally.
A Tree Is Nice, by Janice May Udry. Harper.

## 1957
Fiction
Around and About, by Marchette Chute. Dutton.
Black Gold, by Marguerite Henry. Rand McNally.
The Cat in the Hat, by Dr. Seuss. Random.
Citizen of the Galaxy, by Robert A. Heinlein. Scribner.
Curious George Gets a Medal, by H. A. Rey. Houghton Mif-
    flin.

Henry and the Paper Route, by Beverly Cleary.   Morrow.
The Hundred and One Dalmations, by Dodie Smith.   Viking.
In John's Back Yard, by Esther Meeks.   Follett.
Little Bear, by Else H. Minarik.   Harper.
The Lonely Doll, by Dare Wright.   Doubleday.
Madeline and the Bad Hat, by Ludwig Bemelmans.   Viking.
Mouse House, by Rumer Godden.   Viking.
My Own Little House, by Merriman Kaune.   Follett.
Nobody Listens to Andrew, by Elizabeth Guilfoile.   Follett.
Pippi Goes on Board, by Astrid Lindgren.   Viking.
Snowbound in Hidden Valley, by Holly Wilson.   Messner.
Something New at the Zoo, by Esther Meeks.   Follett.
Tall Tales from the High Hills, by Ellis Credle.   Nelson.
Time of Wonder, by Robert McCloskey.   Viking.
Where Is Everybody? by Remy Charlip.   Addison-Wesley.

Nonfiction
Favorite Poems Old and New, edited by Helen Josephine
    Ferris.   Doubleday.
The Hole in the Tree, by Jean Craighead George.   Dutton.
I Want to Be a Nurse, by Carla Greene.   Children's.
Joseph Pulitzer, Front Page Pioneer, by Iris Noble.   Messner.
Little Visits with God, by Allan H. Jahsmann.   Concordia.
The Tall Book of Bible Stories, edited by Katherine Gibson.
    Harper.

## 1958

Fiction
A Bear Called Paddington, by Michael Bond.
Candy Stripers, by Lee Wyndham.   Messner.
The Cat in the Hat Comes Back, by Dr. Seuss.   Random.
Curious George Flies a Kite, by Margret and H.A. Rey.
    Houghton Mifflin.
Danny and the Dinosaur, by Syd Hoff.   Harper.
Have Space Suit--Will Travel, by Robert A. Heinlein.   Scrib-
    ner.
Henry Reed, Inc., by Keith Robertson.   Viking.
Horse Stories, by Edward W. and M.P. Dolch.   Garrard.
Mable the Whale, by Patricia King.   Follett.
Mad Libs, by Roger Price and Leonard Stern.   Price, Stern,
    Sloan.
Miss Hattie and the Monkey, by Helen Olds.   Follett.
No Fighting, No Biting! by Else H. Minarik.   Harper.
Peter's Policeman, by Anne Lattin.   Follett.
Umbrella, by Taro Yashima.   Viking.
"Why" Stories, by Edward W. and M.P. Dolch.   Garrard.

The Witch of Blackbird Pond, by Elizabeth George Speare.
   Houghton Mifflin.
Yertle the Turtle, and Other Stories, by Dr. Seuss.   Random.

Nonfiction
A Friend Is Someone Who Likes You, by Joan Walsh Anglund.
   Harcourt, Brace.
Tell Me about Christmas, by Mary Alice Jones.   Rand Mc-
   Nally.
What Do You Say, Dear? by Sesyle Joslin.   Addison-Wesley.

## 1959

Fiction
Big New School, by Evelyn Hastings.   Follett.
Blink, the Patchwork Bunny, by Matthew V. Howard.   Deni-
   son.
The Boy Who Would Not Say His Name, by Elizabeth Vreeken.
   Follett.
Cowboy Sam and Sally, by Edna Walker Chandler.   Benefic.
Cowboy Sam and the Airplane, by Edna Walker Chandler.
   Benefic.
Cowboy Sam and the Rodeo, by Edna Walker Chandler.
   Benefic.
Dan Frontier, by William J. Hurley.   Benefic.
Dan Frontier and the Wagon Train, by William J. Hurley.
   Benefic.
Dan Frontier Goes Hunting, by William J. Hurley.   Benefic.
Dan Frontier with the Indians, by William J. Hurley.   Benefic.
Drag Strip, by William Campbell Gault.   Dutton.
Emmett's Pig, by Mary Stolz.   Harper.
Father Bear Comes Home, by Else H. Minarik.   Harper.
Gertie the Duck, by Nicholas Georgiady and Louis Romano.
   Follett.
Julius, by Syd Hoff.   Harper.
Last One Home Is a Green Pig, by Edith Thacher Hurd.
   Harper.
Madeline and the Gypsies, by Ludwig Bemelmans.   Viking.
My Side of the Mountain, by Jean Craighead George.   Dutton.
Nine Days to Christmas, by Marie Hall Ets and Aurora
   Labastida.   Viking.
Norman the Doorman, by Don Freeman.   Viking.
Onion John, by Joseph Krumgold.   T.Y. Crowell.
Pippi in the South Seas, by Astrid Lindgren.   Viking.
Sammy the Seal, by Syd Hoff.   Harper.
Son of Mad Libs, by Roger Price and Leonard Stern.   Price,
   Stern, Sloan.
Starship Troopers, by Robert A. Heinlein.   Putnam.

## Nonfiction

America and Its Presidents, by Earl S. Miers.  Grosset
    & Dunlap.
The Answer Book, by Mary Elting.  Grosset & Dunlap.
Dinosaurs and Other Prehistoric Animals, by Darlene Geis.
    Grosset & Dunlap.
Follett Beginning-to-Read Picture Dictionary, by Alta Mc-
    Intire.  Follett.
Houses from the Sea, by Alice E. Goudey.  Scribner.
Indian Lore.  Boy Scouts of America.
Little Folded Hands, by Allan H. Jahsmann.  Concordia.
Mr. Wizard's Experiments for Young Scientists, by Don Her-
    bert.  Doubleday.
Seeds and More Seeds, by Millicent E. Selsam.  Harper.
The Silver Sword, by Ian Serraillier.  Phillips.
You Come Too, by Robert Frost.  Holt, Rinehart.

## 1960

## Fiction

Benny and the Bear, by Barbee Carleton.  Follett.
Bessie, the Messy Penguin, by Joyce Holland.  Denison.
Casey, the Utterly Impossible Horse, by Anita Feagles.  Ad-
    dison-Wesley.
Cat and Dog, by Else H. Minarik.  Harper.
Cowboy Sam, by Edna Walker Chandler.  Benefic.
Dan Frontier, Sheriff, by William J. Hurley.  Benefic.
The Fire Cat, by Esther Averill.  Harper.
Green Eggs and Ham, by Dr. Seuss.  Beginner.
The Curious Cow, by Esther Meeks.  Follett.
Harry and the Lady Next Door, by Gene Zion.  Harper.
The Hole in the Hill, by Marion Seyton.  Follett.
Island of the Blue Dolphins, by Scott O'Dell.  Houghton Mif-
    flin.
Just Follow Me, by Phoebe Erickson.  Follett.
Little Bear's Friend, by Else H. Minarik.  Harper.
My Brimful Book, edited by Dana Bruce.  Platt & Munk.
Oliver, by Syd Hoff.  Harper.
One Fish, Two Fish, Red Fish, Blue Fish, by Dr. Seuss.
    Beginner.
Sailor Jack, by Selma and Jack Wassermann.  Benefic.
Sailor Jack and Bluebell, by Selma and Jack Wassermann.
    Benefic.
Sailor Jack and the Target Ship, by Selma and Jack Wasser-
    mann.  Benefic.
Sailor Jack's New Friend, by Selma and Jack Wassermann.
    Benefic.
Shan's Lucky Knife, by Jean Merrill.  Addison-Wesley.

Too Many Dogs, by Ramona Dupre.  Follett.
Who Will Be My Friends? by Syd Hoff.  Harper.
Winnie Ille Pu, by A.A. Milne and Alexander Lenard, trans-
    lator.  Dutton.

Nonfiction

Abraham Lincoln:  For the People, by Anne Colver.  Gar-
    rard.
Benjamin Franklin:  Man of Ideas, by Charles P. Graves.
    Garrard.
Bobby Discovers Garden Friends, by Marjorie Wackerbarth
    and Lillian S. Graham.
Cub Scout Magic.  Boy Scouts of America.
Daniel Boone Taming the Wilds, by Katharine E. Wilkie.
    Garrard.
First Aid.  Boy Scouts of America.
George Washington Carver, Negro Scientist, by Sam and
    Beryl Epstein.  Garrard.
Greek Gods and Heroes, by Robert Graves.  Doubleday.
The How and Why Wonder Book of Birds, by Robert Mathew-
    son.  Wonder-Treasure.
The How and Why Wonder Book of Insects, by Ronald N.
    Rood.  Wonder-Treasure.
The How and Why Wonder Book of Reptiles and Amphibians,
    by Robert Mathewson.  Wonder-Treasure.
Junior Illustrated Encyclopedia of Sports, edited by Willard
    Mullin.  Bobbs-Merrill.
Kon-Tiki for Young People, by Thor Heyerdahl.  Rand Mc-
    Nally.
Love Is a Special Way of Feeling, by Joan Walsh Anglund.
    Harcourt Brace.
Photography.  Boy Scouts of America.
Space, by Marian Tellander.  Follett.
Swimming.  Boy Scouts of America.

## 1961

Fiction

The Bronze Bow, by Elizabeth George Speare.  Houghton
    Mifflin.
Dan Frontier and the Big Cat, by William J. Hurley.  Benefic.
Dan Frontier and the New House, by William J. Hurley.
    Benefic.
The Happy Birthday Present, by Joan Heilbroner.  Harper.
The Incredible Journey, by Sheila Burnford.  Little, Brown.
James and the Giant Peach, by Roald Dahl.  Knopf.
Little Bear's Visit, by Else H. Minarik.  Harper.
Little Chief, by Syd Hoff.  Harper & Row.

Little Quack, by Ruth Woods.  Follett.
Madeline in London, by Ludwig Bemelmans.  Viking.
Once a Mouse, by Marcia Brown.  Scribner.
Sailor Jack and Bluebell's Dive, by Selma and Jack Wasser-
    mann.  Benefic.
Sailor Jack and Eddy, by Selma and Jack Wassermann.
    Benefic.
Sailor Jack and Homer Pots, by Selma and Jack Wassermann.
    Benefic.
Sailor Jack Goes North, by Selma and Jack Wassermann.
    Benefic.
The Superlative Horse, by Jean Merrill.  Addison-Wesley.
The Tasha Tudor Book of Fairy Tales, edited by Dana Bruce.
    Platt & Munk.
Tell Me Some More, by Crosby Newell Bonsall.  Harper.

Nonfiction
Abraham Lincoln, by Clara Ingram Judson.  Follett.
Answers and More Answers, by Mary Elting.  Grosset &
    Dunlap.
The Day We Saw the Sun Come Up, by Alice E. Goudey.
    Scribner.
Florence Nightingale:  War Nurse, by Anne Colver.  Garrard.
George Washington, by Clara Ingram Judson.  Follett.
Hailstones and Halibut Bones, by Mary O'Neill.  Doubleday.
Home Repairs.  Boy Scouts of America.
Junior Science Book of Icebergs and Glaciers, by Patricia
    Lauber.  Garrard.
Junior Science Book of Rain, Hail, Sleet, and Snow, by Nancy
    Larrick.  Garrard.
More Little Visits with God, by Allan H. Jahsmann.  Con-
    cordia.
Pencil, Pen and Brush, by Harvey Weiss.  Addison-Wesley.
Ring of Bright Water, by Gavin Maxwell.  Dutton.
Where Does the Butterfly Go When It Rains? by May Gare-
    lick.  Addison-Wesley.

## 1962

Fiction
Come and Have Fun, by Edith Thacher Hurd.  Harper &
    Row.
Cowboy Sam and Dandy, by Edna Walker Chandler.  Benefic.
Cowboy Sam and Shorty, by Edna Walker Chandler.  Benefic.
Dan Frontier Scouts with the Army, by William J. Hurley.
    Benefic.
Dan Frontier, Trapper, by William J. Hurley.  Benefic.
Have You Seen My Brother? by Elizabeth Guilfoile.  Follett.

Henry and the Clubhouse, by Beverly Cleary.  Morrow.
Nutshell Library, by Maurice Sendak.  Harper & Row.
Rabbit and Skunk and The Scary Rock, by Carla Stevens.
    Addison-Wesley.
Sailor Jack and the Ball Game, by Selma and Jack Wasser-
    mann.  Benefic.
Sailor Jack and the Jet Plane, by Selma and Jack Wasser-
    mann.  Benefic.
Show and Tell, by Patricia Miles Martin.  Putnam.
The Snowy Day, by Ezra Jack Keats.  Viking.
Sooper Mad Libs, by Roger Price and Leonard Stern.  Price,
    Stern, Sloan.
Who's a Pest? by Crosby Newell Bonsall.  Harper & Row.
A Wrinkle in Time, by Madeleine L'Engle.  Farrar, Straus.

Nonfiction
Automotive Safety.  Boy Scouts of America.
Baseball, by Frank F. DeClemente.  Creative Educational
    Society.
Basketball, by Joe Hutton and Vern B. Hoffman.  Creative
    Educational Society.
Bobby Discovers Bird Watching, by Marjorie Wackerbarth.
    Denison.
Careers Outdoors, by James Joseph.  Nelson.
Chemistry.  Boy Scouts of America.
D'Aulaires' Book of Greek Myths, by Ingri and Edgar Parin
    D'Aulaire.  Doubleday.
Did You Ever See? by Walter Einsel.  Addison-Wesley.
Football, by J. R. "Bob" Otto.  Creative Educational Society.
Golf, Swimming and Tennis, by Otis J. Dypwick and Helen
    Hull Jacobs.  Creative Educational Society.
Happiness Is a Warm Puppy, by Charles M. Schulz.  Deter-
    mined.
Hiking.  Boy Scouts of America.
How Maps and Globes Help Us, by David Hackler.  Benefic.
Motorboating.  Boy Scouts of America.
Planets, Stars and Space, by Joseph M. Chamberlain and
    Thomas D. Nicholson.  Creative Educational Society.
Recreational Sports, by Clifford Brownell and Roy Moore.
    Creative Educational Society.
Story of the Bible World, by Nelson Beecher Keyes.  Ham-
    mond.
Track and Field, by Earl "Bud" Meyers and Rich Hacker.
    Creative Educational Society.

## 1963

Fiction

Bear Party, by William Pene du Bois. Viking.

The Bully of Barkham Street, by Mary Stolz. Harper &
Row.

The Case of the Hungry Stranger, by Crosby N. Bonsall.
Harper & Row.

Christmas Nutshell Library, by Hilary Knight. Harper &
Row.

Curious George Learns the Alphabet, by H.A. Rey. Houghton
Mifflin.

Dan Frontier Goes Exploring, by William J. Hurley. Benefic.

Encyclopedia Brown, Boy Detective, by Donald J. Sobol.
Nelson.

Fire on the Mountain, by Henry A. Bamman and Robert J.
Whitehead. Benefic.

Gilberto and the Wind, by Marie Hall Ets. Viking.

Good-Bye, Amigos, by Bob and Jan Young. Messner.

Henry Reed's Journey, by Keith Robertson. Viking.

Hop on Pop, by Dr. Seuss. Beginner Books.

Hunting Grizzly Bears, by Henry A. Bamman and Robert J.
Whitehead. Benefic.

It's Like This, Cat, by Emily Cheney Neville. Harper &
Row.

Landslide! by Veronique Day. Coward-McCann.

Rascal: A Memoir of a Better Era, by Sterling North. Dutton.

The Secret Three, by Mildred Myrick. Harper & Row.

Stormy, Misty's Foal, by Marguerite Henry. Rand McNally.

Swimmy, by Leo Lionni. Pantheon.

The Three Little Pigs, by Margaret Hillert. Follett.

The Very Young Mother Goose, edited by Margot Austin.

Where the Wild Things Are, by Maurice Sendak. Harper
& Row.


Nonfiction

Bobby Learns about Butterflies, by Marjorie Wackerbarth.
Denison.

The Day They Marched, edited by Doris E. Saunders. Johnson (Chicago).

Dr. Seuss's ABC, by Dr. Seuss. Beginner.

First Aid to Animals. Boy Scouts of America.

The First Thanksgiving, by Lou Rogers. Follett.

The Indians of New Jersey: Dickon among the Lenapes, by
Mark Raymond Harrington. Rutgers University.

Insect Life. Boy Scouts of America.

Junior Science Book of Penguins, by Patricia Lauber. Garrard.

Weather.  Boy Scouts of America.
A World Explorer:  Marco Polo, by Charles P. Graves.
    Garrard.


## 1964

### Fiction

Across Five Aprils, by Irene Hunt.  Follett.
Charlie and the Chocolate Factory, by Roald Dahl.  Knopf.
City Beneath the Sea, by Henry A. Bamman and Robert J.
    Whitehead.  Benefic.
Dan Frontier Goes to Congress, by William J. and Jane
    Hurley.  Benefic.
Dandelion, by Don Freeman.  Viking.
Harriet the Spy, by Louise Fitzhugh.  Harper & Row.
Lost Uranium Mine, by Henry A. Bamman and Robert J.
    Whitehead.  Benefic.
The Pushcart War, by Jean Merrill.  Addison-Wesley.
Sacred Well of Sacrifice, by Henry A. Bamman and Robert
    J. Whitehead.  Benefic.
The Search for Piranha, by Henry A. Bamman and Robert
    J. Whitehead.  Benefic.
Walt Disney's Mary Poppins, by Alice Chase.  Golden.
Whistle for Willie, by Ezra Jack Keats.  Viking.
White Stallion of Lipizza, by Marguerite Henry.  Rand Mc-
    Nally.


### Nonfiction

Archery.  Boy Scouts of America.
Athletics.  Boy Scouts of America.
Atlas of the Presidents, by Donald E. Cooke.  Hammond.
Boy Who Ran Away, by Irene Elmer.  Concordia.
The Cat in the Hat Beginner Book Dictionary, by Phillip D.
    Eastman.  Random.
Christopher Columbus, by Clara Ingram Judson.  Follett.
Eight Bags of Gold, by Janice Kramer.  Concordia.
Electricity.  Boy Scouts of America.
Electronics Pioneer, Lee De Forest, by I. E. Levine.  Mess-
    ner.
Elephants, Grapes & Pickles, by Roger Price, Leonard
    Stern, and Larry Sloan.  Price, Stern, Sloan.
Fingerprinting.  Boy Scouts of America.
Flags of American History, by David D. Crouthers.  Ham-
    mond.
George Washington:  Father of Freedom, by Stewart Graff.
    Garrard.
Good Samaritan, by Janice Kramer.  Concordia.
Great Surprise, by Mary P. Warren.  Concordia.

The How and Why Wonder Book of Oceanography, by Robert Scharff. Wonder-Treasure.
The Kennedy Years and the Negro, edited by Doris E. Saunders. Johnson (Chicago).
Little Benjamin and the First Christmas, by Betty Forell. Concordia.
The Pantheon Story of Art for Young People, by Ariane Ruskin. Pantheon.
The Rich Fool, by Janice Kramer. Concordia.
Rowing. Boy Scouts of America.

## 1965

### Fiction
The Case of the Cat's Meow, by Crosby N. Bonsall. Harper & Row.
Durango Street, by Frank Bonham. Dutton.
The Empty Schoolhouse, by Natalie S. Carlson. Harper & Row.
Encyclopedia Brown and the Case of the Secret Pitch, by Donald J. Sobol. Nelson.
Flight to the South Pole, by Henry A. Bamman and Robert J. Whitehead. Benefic.
Gentle Ben, by Walt Morey. Dutton.
Here Comes the Strikeout, by Leonard Kessler. Harper & Row.
I Like You, by Sandol Stoddard Warburg. Houghton Mifflin.
Jazz Country, by Nat Hentoff. Harper & Row.
Just Me, by Marie Hall Ets. Viking.
Keer-Loo, by Laura Louise Foster. Naturegraph.
Megan, by Iris Noble. Messner.
Monster Mad Libs, by Roger Price and Leonard Stern. Price, Stern, Sloan.
Twenty-Seven Cats Next Door, by Anita Feagles. Addison-Wesley.
Viking Treasure, by Henry A. Bamman and Robert J. Whitehead. Benefic.

### Nonfiction
Boy with a Sling, by Mary P. Warren. Concordia.
Creative Thinking Activities: A Highlights Handbook, by Garry Cleveland Myers. Highlights.
Creative Writing Activities: A Highlights Handbook, compiled by Walter B. Barbe. Highlights.
Droodles, by Roger Price. Price Stern Sloan.
Frederick Douglass, Freedom Fighter, by Lillie Patterson. Garrard.
Helen Keller: Toward the Light, by Stewart and Polly Anne Graff. Garrard.

Holiday (Craft) Handbook No. 1, compiled by Caroline Clark
    Myers.  Highlights.
Holiday (Craft) Handbook No. 4.  Highlights.
The How and Why Wonder Book of Deserts, by Felix Sutton.
    Wonder-Treasure.
John F. Kennedy:  New Frontiersman, by Charles P. Graves.
    Garrard.
Jon and the Little Lost Lamb, by Jane Latourette.  Con-
    cordia.
Junior Science Book of Volcanoes, by Patricia Lauber.  Gar-
    rard.
Lifesaving.  Boy Scouts of America.
Little Boat That Almost Sank, by Mary P. Warren.  Con-
    cordia.
M Is for Monster, by Roger Price, Leonard Stern, and
    Larry Sloan.  Price, Stern, Sloan.
Radio.  Boy Scouts of America.
Reading.  Boy Scouts of America.
Sam Houston:  Hero of Texas, by Jean Lee Latham.  Gar-
    rard.
Small-Boat Sailing.  Boy Scouts of America.
Stories of Champions:  Baseball Hall of Fame, by Sam and
    Beryl Epstein.  Garrard.
The Story of Mount Vernon, by Natalie M. Miller.  Chil-
    dren's.
Story of Noah's Ark, by Jane Latourette.  Concordia.
The Story of the Liberty Bell, by Natalie Miller.  Children's.
The Story of the Star-Spangled Banner, by Natalie Miller.
    Children's.
The Story of the Statue of Liberty, by Natalie Miller.  Chil-
    dren's.
Tricks and Teasers:  A Highlights Handbook.  Highlights.
World God Made, by Alyce Bergey.  Concordia.

## 1966

Fiction
Elephi, the Cat with the High I.Q., by Jean Stafford.  Dell.
Encyclopedia Brown Finds the Clues, by Donald J. Sobol.
    Nelson.
Henry Reed's Baby-Sitting Service, by Keith Robertson.  Vi-
    king.
The Littlest Angel, by Charles Tazewell.  Children's.
Queenie Peavy, by Robert Burch.  Viking.
Sam, Bangs and Moonshine, by Evaline Ness.  Holt, Rine-
    hart.
Up a Road Slowly, by Irene Hunt.  Follett.
What Mary Jo Shared, by Janice May Udry.  Albert Whitman.

Wonderful World of Horses, edited by Ned Hoopes.   Dell.

Nonfiction
Bobby Learns about Squirrels, by Marjorie Wackerbarth.
    Denison.
Boy Who Saved His Family, by Alyce Bergey.   Concordia.
Camping.   Boy Scouts of America.
Chapbook 2.   Bethany.
The Christmas Story, edited by Marguerite Northrup.   Metro-
    politan Museum of Art.
Citizenship.   Boy Scouts of America.
Coin Collecting.   Boy Scouts of America.
Creative Art Activities for Home and School, by Doris V.
    Brown and Pauline McDonald.   Lawrence.
Daniel in the Lion's Den, by Jane Latourette.   Concordia.
Edge of Awareness, edited by Ned E. Hoopes and Richard
    Peck.   Dell.
Food and Life, by Gerald Ames and Rose Wyler.   Creative
    Educational Society.
Great Escape, by Mary P. Warren.   Concordia.
House on the Rock, by Jane Latourette.   Concordia.
Hurlbut's Story of the Bible, by Jesse Lyman Hurlbut.   Revell.
Jackie Robinson of the Brooklyn Dodgers, by Milton J. Shapi-
    ro.   Messner.
Lame Man Who Walked Again, by Mary P. Warren.   Con-
    cordia.
Miracles:   Poems by Children of the English-Speaking World,
    edited by Richard Lewis.   Simon & Schuster.
Mustang, Wild Spirit of the West, by Marguerite Henry.
    Rand McNally.
One Hundred Bible Stories.   Concordia.
Secret of the Star, by Dave Hill.   Concordia.
Stamp Collecting.   Boy Scouts of America.
The Story of the Lincoln Memorial, by Natalie Miller.   Chil-
    dren's.
Tell Me a Joke, edited by Dana Bruce.   Platt & Munk.
Tell Me a Riddle, edited by Dana Bruce.   Platt & Munk.
UNICEF Festival Book, by Judith Spiegelman.   United States
    Committee for UNICEF.
Webster's Elementary Dictionary.   Merriam.
Wood Carving.   Boy Scouts of America.
Would You Believe? by Don Adams.   Price, Stern, Sloan.

## 1967

Fiction
Don't Take Teddy, by Babbis Friis-Baastad; translated by
    Lise Somme McKinnon.   Scribner.

Encyclopedia Brown Gets His Man, by Donald J. Sobol.   Nelson.

The Horse in the Camel Suit, by William Pene du Bois.
Harper & Row.

The Outnumbered, edited by Charlotte Brooks.   Dell.

The Outsiders, by S. E. Hinton.   Viking.

Nonfiction

Atoms, Energy, and Machines, by Jack McCormick.   Creative Educational Society.

Bear Cub Scout Book.   Boy Scouts of America.

Bird Study.   Boy Scouts of America.

Boy Who Gave His Lunch Away, by Dave Hill.   Concordia.

Conservation of Natural Resources.   Boy Scouts of America.

Cooking.   Boy Scouts of America.

Cub Scout Fun Book.   Boy Scouts of America.

The Desert, by Alexander and Elsie Klots.   Creative Educational Society.

The Earth's Story, by Gerald Ames and Rose Wyler.   Creative Educational Society.

Field and Meadow, by Etta Schneider Ress.   Creative Educational Society.

Fieldbook.   Boy Scouts of America.

Fishermen's Surprise, by Alyce Bergey.   Concordia.

Forest and Woodland, by Stephen Collins.   Creative Educational Society.

Fresh and Salt Water, by B. Bartram Cadbury.   Creative Educational Society.

Illustrated Atlas for Young America.   Hammond.

John F. Kennedy, by Norman Richards and John P. Reidy.
Children's.

Man Caught by a Fish, by M. M. Brem.   Concordia.

Mary's Story, by M. M. Brem.   Concordia.

More Tell Me Why, by Arkady Leokum.   Grosset & Dunlap.

The Ocean Laboratory, by Athelstan Spilhaus.   Creative Educational Society.

Parks and Gardens, by Robert S. Lemmon.   Creative Educational Society.

Patrol Leader's Handbook.   Boy Scouts of America.

Pioneering.   Boy Scouts of America.

Rifle and Shotgun Shooting.   Boy Scouts of America.

Three Men Who Walked in Fire, by Joann Scheck.   Concordia.

Walls Came Tumbling Down, by Dave Hill.   Concordia.

The Way of the Weather, by Jerome Spar.   Creative Educational Society.

Webelos Scout Book.   Boy Scouts of America.

Wolf Cub Scout Book.   Boy Scouts of America.

## 1968

### Fiction

Bobby Bear and the Bees, by Marilyn O. Helmrath and Janet
L. Bartlett. Oddo.

Bobby Bear Finds Maple Sugar, by Marilyn O. Helmrath and
Janet L. Bartlett. Oddo.

Bobby Bear Goes Fishing, by Marilyn O. Helmrath and Janet
L. Bartlett. Oddo.

Bobby Bear in the Spring, by Marilyn O. Helmrath and Janet
L. Bartlett. Oddo.

Bobby Bear's Halloween, by Marilyn O. Helmrath and Janet
L. Bartlett. Oddo.

Bobby Bear's Rocket Ride, by Marilyn O. Helmrath and Janet
L. Bartlett. Oddo.

Corduroy, by Don Freeman. Viking.

Edgar Allan, by John Neufeld. Phillips.

I'm Really Dragged But Nothing Gets Me Down, by Nat Hentoff. Simon & Schuster.

King Robert the Resting Ruler, by Donna Lugg Pape. Oddo.

Liz Dearly's Silly Glasses, by Donna Lugg Pape. Oddo.

Mad Libs No. 5, by Roger Price and Leonard Stern. Price,
Stern, Sloan.

The Nitty Gritty, by Frank Bonham. Dutton.

The Pigman, by Paul Zindel. Harper & Row.

Professor Fred and the Fid-Fuddlephone, by Donna Lugg Pape.
Oddo.

Scientist Sam, by Donna Lugg Pape. Oddo.

Shoemaker Fooze, by Donna Lugg Pape. Oddo.

The Soul Brothers and Sister Lou, by Kristin Hunter. Scribner.

The Three Thinkers of Thay-Lee, by Donna L. Pape. Oddo.

Tuned Out, by Maia Wojciechowska. Harper & Row.

What Mary Jo Wanted, by Janice May Udry. Albert Whitman.

### Nonfiction

Airplanes & Trucks & Trains, Fire Engines, Boats & Ships,
& Building & Wrecking Machines, by George J. Zaffo.
Grosset & Dunlap.

Art. Boy Scouts of America.

Aviation. Boy Scouts of America.

Backyard Bandits--Including California Raccoons and Other
Exciting Patio Visitors, by David D. Oliphant, Jr. Naturegraph.

Basketry. Boy Scouts of America.

Canoeing. Boy Scouts of America.

Den Chief's Denbook. Boy Scouts of America.

Firemanship. Boy Scouts of America.

Great Promise, by Alyce Bergey. Concordia.
King's Invitation, by Virginia Mueller. Concordia.
Learning How Baseball, by Dick Siebert. Creative Educational Society.
Most Wonderful King, by Dave Hill. Concordia.
Music. Boy Scouts of America.
Personal Fitness. Boy Scouts of America.
Robin Deer, by Olga Cossi. Naturegraph.
Secret Journey, by Virginia Mueller. Concordia.
Soil and Water Conservation. Boy Scouts of America.
Still More Tell Me Why, by Arkady Leokum. Grosset & Dunlap.
Two Men in the Temple, by Joann Scheck. Concordia.
Unforgiving Servant, by Janice Kramer. Concordia.
Young Readers' Bible, edited by Henry M. Bullock and Edward C. Peterson.

## 1969

### Fiction

Encyclopedia Brown Keeps the Peace, by Donald J. Sobol. Nelson.
J.T., by Jane Wagner. Van Nostrand Reinhold.
Lisa, Bright and Dark, by John Neufeld. Phillips.
The Monkey and the Crocodile: A Jataka Tale from India, by Paul Galdone. Seabury.
Sylvester and the Magic Pebble, by William Steig. Simon & Schuster.
Tales of the Sea Foam, by Lisette G. Brown. Naturegraph.
Wild Wheels, edited by Don McKay. Dell.
The Wolfling, by Sterling North. Dutton.

### Nonfiction

Afro-Americans Then and Now, by Doris Haynes and Jane Hurley. Benefic.
The Answer Book of Sports, by Bill Mazer. Grosset & Dunlap.
Beggar's Greatest Wish, by Alyce Bergey. Concordia.
Braggy King of Babylon, by Yvonne McCall. Concordia.
A Child's Book of Poems, compiled by Gyo Fujikawa. Grosset & Dunlap.
Cub Scout Songbook. Boy Scouts of America.
Dog Care. Boy Scouts of America.
Explorer Member's Guide. Boy Scouts of America.
Horsemanship. Boy Scouts of America.
Join the Dots, by Isobel R. Beard. Follett.
Little Sleeping Beauty, by Brenda Prior. Concordia.
Martin Luther King Jr., 1929-1968: An Ebony Picture Biography. Johnson (Chicago).

Pets.   Boy Scouts of America.
Princess and the Baby, by Janice Kramer.   Concordia.
Public Health.   Boy Scouts of America.
Public Speaking.   Boy Scouts of America.
Scout How Book.   Boy Scouts of America.
Simeon's Secret, by Janice Kramer.   Concordia.
Tell Me Why, by Arkady Leokum.   Grosset & Dunlap.
Water That Caught on Fire, by Joann Scheck.   Concordia.
The World's Worst Jokes.   Price, Stern, Sloan.

## 1970

### Fiction
Cowboy Sam and Big Bill, by Edna Walker Chandler.   Benefic.
Cowboy Sam and Freddy, by Edna Walker Chandler.   Benefic.
Cowboy Sam and the Fair, by Edna Walker Chandler.   Benefic.
Cowboy Sam and the Rustlers, by Edna Walker Chandler.
     Benefic.
Encyclopedia Brown Saves the Day, by Donald J. Sobol.
     Nelson.
Fairy Tales and Fables, edited by Doris Duenewald.   Grosset
     & Dunlap.
Mad Libs Six, by Roger Price and Leonard Stern.   Price,
     Stern, Sloan.
The Peter Pan Bag, by Lee Kingman.   Houghton Mifflin.
The Summer of the Swans, by Betsy Byars.   Viking.
The Three Little Pigs, by Paul Galdone.   Seabury.
The Trumpet of the Swan, by E. B. White.   Harper & Row.

### Nonfiction
Big Book of Real Trains, edited by Doris Duenewald.   Grosset & Dunlap.
Donkey Daniel in Bethlehem, by Janice Kramer.   Concordia.
Illustrated Treasury of Poetry for Children, edited by David
     Ross.   Grosset & Dunlap.
Leatherwork.   Boy Scouts of America.
Scholarship.   Boy Scouts of America.
The Songs of Sesame Street, by Jeffrey Moss, Joe Raposo,
     and Jon Stone.   Children's Television Workshop.
Still More Answers, by Mary Elting and Franklin Folsom.
     Grosset & Dunlap.
Woodwork.   Boy Scouts of America.

## 1971

### Fiction
Cowboy Sam and Flop, by Edna Walker Chandler.   Benefic.
Cowboy Sam and Freckles, by Edna Walker Chandler.
     Benefic.

Cowboy Sam and Miss Lily, by Edna W. Chandler.  Benefic.
Cowboy Sam and Porky, by Edna W. Chandler.  Benefic.
Cowboy Sam and the Indians, by Edna W. Chandler.  Benefic.
A Dog and a Half, by Barbara Willard.  Nelson.
Encyclopedia Brown Solves Them All, by Donald J. Sobol.
    Nelson.
On Two Wheels:  An Anthology about Men and Motorcycles,
    edited by Don McKay.  Dell.
Point of Departure, edited by Robert S. Gold.  Dell.
Three Fox Fables, by Paul Galdone.  Seabury.
The Three Toymakers, by Ursula Moray Williams.  Nelson.

Nonfiction
Afro-American Contributors to American Life, by John M.
    Franco.  Benefic.
Astronomy.  Boy Scouts of America.
Boy Scout Songbook.  Boy Scouts of America.
Cycling.  Boy Scouts of America.
Forestry.  Boy Scouts of America.
Gardening.  Boy Scouts of America.
The How and Why Wonder Book of Ecology, by Shelly and
    Mary Louise Grossman.  Wonder-Treasure.
Lots More Tell Me Why, by Arkady Leokum.  Grosset &
    Dunlap.
Reptile Study.  Boy Scouts of America.
Safety.  Boy Scouts of America.
The Will to Be Free:  Great Escape Stories, edited by Eric
    Williams.  Nelson.

Chapter Six

BEST SELLERS BY NUMBER OF COPIES SOLD

This chapter lists those 304 best sellers for which publishers reported sales figures in this survey, by the total number of hardbound and paperback copies of each book sold since its publication by the publisher named, and gives the original date of publication of each book. Numbers given in parentheses are estimates.

Egermeier's Bible Story Books.  Elsie E. Eger-
    meier.  1923.  Warner Press Publishers...  2,000,000
Encyclopedia Brown and the Case of the Secret
    Pitch.  Donald J. Sobol.  1965.  Thomas
    Nelson Inc.................................  (2,000,000+)
Encyclopedia Brown, Boy Detective.  Donald J.
    Sobol.  1963.  Thomas Nelson Inc.........  (2,000,000+)
Encyclopedia Brown Finds the Clues.  Donald J.
    Sobol.  1966.  Thomas Nelson Inc.........  (2,000,000+)
The Little Engine That Could.  Watty Piper
    (pseud.).  1929.  Platt & Munk Company...  2,000,000+
Abraham Lincoln: For the People.  Anne Colver.
    1960.  Garrard Publishing Company.......  1,687,626
Casey, the Utterly Impossible Horse.  Anita
    Feagles.  1960.  Addison-Wesley Publishing
    Company.................................  1,504,000
Daniel Boone Taming the Wilds.  Katharine E.
    Wilkie.  1960.  Garrard Publishing Com-
    pany....................................  1,428,492
Nature Atlas of America.  Emil L. Jordan.
    1952.  Hammond Incorporated.............  1,385,000
Rabbit and Skunk and the Scary Rock.  Carla
    Stevens.  1962.  Addison-Wesley Publishing
    Company.................................  1,269,000
Story of the Bible World.  Nelson Beecher Keyes.
    1962.  Hammond Incorporated.............  1,190,000
Caps for Sale.  Esphyr Slobodkina.  1947.  Ad-
    dison-Wesley Publishing Company..........  1,163,000

Better Homes and Gardens Story Book. Better
 Homes and Gardens Editors. 1950. Mere-
 dith Corporation........................... 1,105,266
The Great Houdini, Magician Extraordinary.
 Samuel Epstein and Beryl Williams. Julian
 Messner Division of Simon & Schuster, Inc. 1,103,000
Encyclopedia Brown Gets His Man. Donald J.
 Sobol. 1967. Thomas Nelson Inc......... (1,000,000+)
Encyclopedia Brown Keeps the Peace. Donald
 J. Sobol. 1969. Thomas Nelson Inc...... (1,000,000+)
Encyclopedia Brown Saves the Day. Donald J.
 Sobol. 1970. Thomas Nelson Inc......... (1,000,000+)
Encyclopedia Brown Solves Them All. Donald
 J. Sobol. 1971. Thomas Nelson Inc...... (1,000,000+)
Lassie Come-Home. Eric Knight. 1941. Holt,
 Rinehart and Winston, Inc.................. 1,000,000+
Understood Betsy. Dorothy Canfield Fisher.
 1916. Holt, Rinehart and Winston, Inc..... 1,000,000+
What Do You Say, Dear? Sysyle Joslin. 1958.
 Addison-Wesley Publishing Company.......... 905,000
The Tall Book of Nursery Tales. Feodor Rojan-
 kovsky, editor. 1944. Harper & Row Pub-
 lishers, Inc............................... 896,000
Charlotte's Web. E. B. White. 1952. Harper
 & Row Publishers, Inc..................... 892,000
Pencil, Pen and Brush. Harvey Weiss. 1961.
 Addison-Wesley Publishing Company......... 840,000
Paul Bunyan Swings His Axe. Dell J. McCormick.
 1936. The Caxton Printers, Ltd............ 771,158
Better Homes and Gardens Junior Cook Book.
 Better Homes and Gardens Editors. 1955.
 Meredith Corporation....................... 758,236
The Big Wave. Pearl S. Buck. 1948. The John
 Day Company, Inc.......................... 663,906
Let's Find Out About Heat, Water and Air. Her-
 man and Nina Schneider. 1946. Addison-
 Wesley Publishing Company................. 642,000
Junior Science Book of Icebergs and Glaciers.
 Patricia Lauber. 1961. Garrard Publishing
 Company................................... 592,715
The Tall Book of Mother Goose. Feodor Rojan-
 kovsky, illustrator. 1942. Harper & Row
 Publishers, Inc........................... 573,000
Baby Born in a Stable. A. H. Kramer. Con-
 cordia Publishing House.................... 513,934
Junior Science Book of Volcanoes. Patricia
 Lauber. 1965. Garrard Publishing Company. 507,132

Stories of Champions: Baseball Hall of Fame.
Sam and Beryl Epstein. 1965. Garrard
Publishing Company........................ 503, 667
Album of Horses. Marguerite Henry. 1951.
Rand McNally & Company................. 500, 000+
Down, Down the Mountain. Ellis Credle. 1934.
Thomas Nelson Inc........................ (500, 000+)
Misty of Chincoteague. Marguerite Henry. 1947.
Rand McNally & Company................. 500, 000+
The Real Mother Goose. Blanche Fisher Wright,
illustrator. 1916. Rand McNally & Company. 500, 000+
Stuart Little. E.B. White. 1945. Harper & Row
Publishers, Inc............................ 500, 000
Tell Me about God. Mary Alice Jones. 1943.
Rand McNally & Company................. 500, 000+
Tell Me about Jesus. Mary Alice Jones. 1944.
Rand McNally & Company................. 500, 000+
How Big Is Big? Herman and Nina Schneider.
1946. Addison-Wesley Publishing Comapny... 483, 000
Little Benjamin and the First Christmas. Betty
Forell. 1964. Concordia Publishing House.. 462, 633
A Child's Garden of Prayer. Herman W. Gockel
and Edward J. Saleska, compilers. 1948.
Concordia Publishing House................ 450, 272
World God Made. Alyce Bergey. 1965. Concordia
Publishing House.......................... 446, 221
Good Samaritan. Janice Kramer. 1964. Concordia
Publishing House.......................... 442, 940
Did You Ever See? Walter Einsel. 1962. Ad-
dison-Wesley Publishing Company........... 434, 000
Little Folded Hands. Allan H. Jahsmann. 1959.
Concordia Publishing House................ 432, 779
The Child's Story Bible. Catherine F. Vos and
Marianne Vos Radius. 1949. Wm. B. Eerd-
mans Publishing Company.................. 408, 760
A Child's Garden of Bible Stories. Arthur W.
Gross. 1948. Concordia Publishing House.. 397, 205
Story of Noah's Ark. Jane Latourette. 1965. Con-
cordia Publishing House................... 391, 861
The Tall Book of Fairy Tales. William Sharp,
editor. 1947. Harper & Row Publishers,
Inc....................................... 390, 000
Little Bear. Else Holmelund Minarik. 1957.
Harper & Row Publishers, Inc.............. 387, 000
One God: The Ways We Worship Him. Florence
Mary Fitch. 1944. Lothrop, Lee & Shepard
Company................................... 385, 000

Junior Science Book of Rain, Hail, Sleet, and Snow.
　　Nancy Larrick.　1961.　Garrard Publishing
　　Company...................................... 377, 312
Boy Who Ran Away.　Irene Elmer.　1964.　Con-
　　cordia Publishing House...................... 376, 429
Boy with a Sling.　Mary P. Warren.　1965.　Con-
　　cordia Publishing House...................... 373, 333
Great Surprise.　Mary P. Warren.　1964.　Con-
　　cordia Publishing House...................... 355, 953
Jon and the Little Lost Lamb.　Jane Latourette.
　　1965.　Concordia Publishing House............ 355, 670
Little Boat That Almost Sank.　Mary P. Warren.
　　1965.　Concordia Publishing House........... 350, 134
Tricks and Teasers; A Highlights Handbook.　The
　　Editors of Highlights.　1965.　Highlights For
　　Children, Inc................................ 350, 000
Little House in the Big Woods.　Laura Ingalls
　　Wilder.　1932.　Harper & Row Publishers,
　　Inc.......................................... 349, 000
Little Visits with God.　Allan H. Jahsmann.　1957.
　　Concordia Publishing House.................. 342, 539
Eight Bags of Gold.　Janice Kramer.　1964.　Con-
　　cordia Publishing House...................... 326, 366
Chapbook 2.　1966.　The Bethany Press.......... 320, 000
The Rich Fool.　Janice Kramer.　1964.　Con-
　　cordia Publishing House...................... 318, 386
Angus and the Ducks.　Marjorie Flack.　1930.
　　Doubleday & Company, Inc.................... 313, 445
Secret of the Star.　Dave Hill.　1966.　Con-
　　cordia Publishing House...................... 312, 481
Henny Penny.　Paul Galdone.　1860.　The Seabury
　　Press........................................ 305, 000
Little Toot.　Hardie Gramatky.　1939.　G. P. Put-
　　nam's Sons................................... 300, 000+
What's Inside the Egg?　May Garelick.　1955.
　　Addison-Wesley Publishing Company........... 296, 000
Danny and the Dinosaur.　Syd Hoff.　1958.　Harper
　　& Row Publishers, Inc....................... 293, 000
Abraham Lincoln.　Ingri and Edgar Parin D'Aulaire.
　　1940.　Doubleday & Company, Inc............. 284, 499
Boy Who Gave His Lunch Away.　Dave Hill.　1967.
　　Concordia Publishing House.................. 282, 979
Nobody Listens to Andrew.　Elizabeth Guilfoile.
　　1957.　Follett Publishing Company............ 282, 344
Where the Wild Things Are.　Maurice Sendak.
　　1963.　Harper & Row Publishers Inc.......... 272, 000
Mary's Story.　M. M. Brem.　1967.　Concordia
　　Publishing House............................. 270, 004

Little House on the Prairie.  Laura Ingalls Wilder.
   1935.  Harper & Row Publishers, Inc......... 270,000
The Three Little Pigs.  Paul Galdone.  The Sea-
   bury Press.................................. 270,000
The Horse in the Camel Suit.  William Pene du
   Bois.  1967.  Harper & Row Publishers, Inc.. 264,000
New Illustrated Just So Stories.  Rudyard Kipling.
   1912.  Doubleday & Company, Inc............ 263,571
Boy Who Saved His Family.  Alyce Bergey.  1966.
   Concordia Publishing House................. 263,359
The Tall Book of Make-Believe.  Garth Williams,
   editor.  1950.  Harper & Row Publishers, Inc. 262,000
A Horse of Her Own.  Hudnut.  Van Nostrand Rein-
   hold Company............................... 260,000
Twenty-Seven Cats Next Door.  Anita Feagles.  1965.
   Addison-Wesley Publishing Company.......... 260,000
Daniel in the Lion's Den.  Jane Latourette.  1966.
   Concordia Publishing House................. 259,425
House on the Rock.  Jane Latourette.  1966.  Con-
   cordia Publishing House.................... 250,639
The Biggest Bear.  Lynd Ward.  1952.  Houghton
   Mifflin Company............................ 250,000+
Bobby Bear and the Bees.  Marilyn Olear Helm-
   rath and Janet LaSpisa Bartlett.  1968.  Oddo
   Publishing, Inc............................ 250,000+
Bobby Bear Finds Maple Sugar.  Marilyn Olear
   Helmrath and Janet LaSpisa Bartlett.  1968.
   Oddo Publishing, Inc....................... 250,000+
Bobby Bear Goes Fishing.  Marilyn Olear Helm-
   rath and Janet LaSpisa Bartlett.  1968.  Oddo
   Publishing, Inc............................ 250,000+
Bobby Bear in the Spring.  Marilyn Olear Helm-
   rath and Janet LaSpisa Bartlett.  1968.  Oddo
   Publishing, Inc............................ 250,000+
Bobby Bear's Halloween.  Marilyn Olear Helmrath
   and Janet LaSpisa Bartlett.  1968.  Oddo Pub-
   lishing, Inc............................... 250,000+
Bobby Bear's Rocket Ride.  Marilyn Olear Helm-
   rath and Janet LaSpisa Bartlett.  1968.  Oddo
   Publishing, Inc............................ 250,000+
Brighty of the Grand Canyon.  Marguerite Henry.
   1956.  Rand McNally & Company............. 250,000+
The Country Bunny and the Little Gold Shoes.
   Dubose Heyward.  1939.  Houghton Mifflin
   Company.................................... 250,000+
Curious George.  H.A. Rey.  1941.  Houghton
   Mifflin Company............................ 250,000+

Johnny Tremain.  Esther Forbes.  1943.
    Houghton Mifflin Company.................... 250,000+
King of the Wind.  Marguerite Henry.  1948.
    Rand McNally & Company..................... 250,000+
The Little House.  Virginia Lee Burton.  1942.
    Houghton Mifflin Company................... 250,000+
Mike Mulligan and His Steam Shovel.  Virginis Lee
    Burton.  1939.  Houghton Mifflin Company.... 250,000+
Tell Me about the Bible.  Mary Alice Jones.  1945.
    Rand McNally & Company.................... 250,000+
Where's My Baby?  H.A. Rey.  1943.  Houghton
    Mifflin Company............................. 250,000+
Helen Keller:  Toward the Light.  Stewart and
    Polly Anne Graff.  1965.  Garrard Publishing
    Company.................................... 249,388
Lame Man Who Walked Again.  Mary P. Warren.
    1966.  Concordia Publishing House.......... 244,523
The Red Balloon.  Albert Lamourisse.  1956.
    Doubleday & Company, Inc................... 242,941
Man Caught by a Fish.  M.M. Brem.  1967.  Con-
    cordia Publishing House..................... 242,588
Clay, Wood and Wire.  Harvey Weiss.  1956.
    Addison-Wesley Publishing Company.......... 242,000
Great Escape.  Mary P. Warren.  1966.  Con-
    cordia Publishing House..................... 235,954
John F. Kennedy:  New Frontiersman.  Charles P.
    Graves.  1965.  Garrard Publishing Company.. 233,670
Where Is Everybody?  Remy Charlip.  1957.  Ad-
    dison-Wesley Publishing Company............. 229,000
Fishermen's Surprise.  Alyce Bergey.  1967.
    Concordia Publishing House.................. 228,712
Angus and the Cat.  Marjorie Flack.  1931.  Dou-
    bleday & Company, Inc..................... 227,800
Nutshell Library.  Maurice Sendak.  1962.  Harper
    & Row Publishers, Inc...................... 227,000
My Bible Story Book.  Gerhard L. Wind.  1956.
    Concordia Publishing House.................. 226,186
The Tall Book of Christmas.  Dorothy Hall Smith,
    editor.  1954.  Harper & Row Publishers,
    Inc........................................ 225,000
Father Bear Comes Home.  Else Holmelund Min-
    arik.  1959.  Harper & Row Publishers, Inc.  224,000
On the Banks of Plum Creek.  Laura Ingalls
    Wilder.  1937.  Harper & Row Publishers,
    Inc........................................ 223,000
One Hundred Bible Stories; Illustrated King James
    Edition.  Concordia Publishing House......... 216,782

The Happy Hollisters. Jerry West (pseud.).
   1953. Doubleday & Company, Inc............. 214,520
Follett Beginning-To-Read Picture Dictionary.
   Alta McIntire. 1959. Follett Publishing
   Company.................................... 214,235
George Washington. Ingri and Edgar Parin
   D'Aulaire. 1936. Doubleday & Company, Inc. 211,141
Three Men Who Walked in Fire. Joann Scheck.
   1967. Concordia Publishing House........... 211,105
Goodnight Moon. Margaret Wise Brown. 1947.
   Harper & Row Publishers, Inc............... 208,000
Book of Nursery & Mother Goose Rhymes. Mar-
   guerite De Angeli. 1954. Doubleday & Com-
   pany, Inc.................................. 206,396
By the Shores of Silver Lake. Laura Ingalls
   Wilder. 1939. Harper & Row Publishers,
   Inc........................................ 206,000
Little Bear's Friend. Else Holmelund Minarik.
   1960. Harper & Row Publishers, Inc........ 203,000
Walls Came Tumbling Down. Dave Hill. 1967.
   Concordia Publishing House................. 202,368
Little Town on the Prairie. Laura Ingalls Wilder.
   1941. Harper & Row Publishers, Inc........ 201,000
Black Gold. Marguerite Henry. 1957. Rand Mc-
   Nally & Company........................... 200,000+
Born to Trot. Marguerite Henry. 1950. Rand
   McNally & Company........................ 200,000+
Justin Morgan Had a Horse. Marguerite Henry.
   1054. Rand McNally & Company............ 200,000+
Mustang, Wild Spirit of the West. Marguerite
   Henry. 1966. Rand McNally & Company..... 200,000+
Sea Star, Orphan of Chincoteague. Marguerite
   Henry. 1949. Rand McNally & Company..... 200,000+
Stormy, Misty's Foal. Marguerite Henry. 1963.
   Rand McNally & Company................... 200,000+
Tell Me about Prayer. Mary Alice Jones. 1948.
   Rand McNally & Company................... 200,000+
White Stallion of Lipizza. Marguerite Henry. 1964.
   Rand McNally & Company................... 200,000+
Farmer Boy. Laura Ingalls Wilder. 1933. Harper
   & Row Publishers, Inc...................... 197,000
Illustrated Atlas for Young America. 1967. Ham-
   mond Incorporated.......................... 195,000
The Pushcart War. Jean Merrill. 1964. Addison-
   Wesley Publishing Company................. 195,000
Sammy the Seal. Syd Hoff. 1959. Harper & Row
   Publishers, Inc............................ 194,000

A Tree Is Nice.   Janice May Udry.   1956.   Harper
   & Row Publishers, Inc...................... 194,000
If Jesus Came to My House.   Joan Gale Thomas.
   1951.   Lothrop, Lee & Shepard Company...... 190,500
Little Bear's Visit.   Else H. Minarik.   1961.
   Harper & Row Publishers, Inc................ 190,000
The Little Island.   Golden MacDonald.   1946.   Dou-
   bleday & Company, Inc...................... 188,545
The Door in the Wall.   Marguerite De Angeli.   1949.
   Doubleday & Company, Inc.................... 185,891
Secret Journey.   Virginia Mueller.   1968.   Con-
   cordia Publishing House..................... 185,778
The Little Family.   Lois Lenski.   1932.   Double-
   day & Company, Inc......................... 185,593
A World Explorer:   Marco Polo.   Charles P. Graves.
   1963.   Garrard Publishing Company.......... 183,945
The Velveteen Rabbit.   Margery Williams.   1926.
   Doubleday & Company, Inc................... 182,934
Most Wonderful King.   Dave Hill.   1968.   Con-
   cordia Publishing House..................... 180,327
The Christ Child.   Maud and Miska Petersham.   1931.
   Doubleday & Company, Inc................... 180,221
Hailstones and Halibut Bones.   Mary O'Neill.   1961.
   Doubleday & Company, Inc................... 178,386
Men of Iron.   Howard Pyle.   1891.   Harper &
   Row Publishers, Inc........................ 177,000
Flags of American History.   David D. Crouthers.
   1964.   Hammond Incorporated................ 175,000
The Superlative Horse.   Jean Merrill.   1961.
   Addison-Wesley Publishing Company.......... 174,000
White Snow, Bright Snow.   Alvin Tresselt.   1947.
   Lothrop, Lee & Shepard Company............ 174,000
Holiday (Craft) Handbook No. 1.   Caroline Clark
   Myers, compiler.   1965.   Highlights For Chil-
   dren, Inc.................................. 171,000
Harry the Dirty Dog.   Gene Zion.   1956.   Harper
   & Row Publishers, Inc...................... 168,000
The Monkey and the Crocodile:   A Jataka Tale from
   India.   Paul Galdone.   The Seabury Press.... 168,000
The Trumpet of the Swan.   E.B. White.   1970.
   Harper & Row Publishers, Inc.............. 165,000
Florence Nightingale:   War Nurse.   Anne Colver.
   1961.   Garrard Publishing Company.......... 164,933
Marian's Favorite Bible Stories; A First Bible
   Reader for the Young Child.   Marian M.
   Schoolland.   1948.   Wm. B. Eerdmans Pub-
   lishing Company........................... 164,000

Where Does the Butterfly Go When It Rains? May
Garelick. 1961. Addison-Wesley Publishing
Company.................................... 164, 000
Princess and the Baby. Janice Kramer. 1969.
Concordia Publishing House............... 162, 945
The Boy Scout Encyclopedia. Bruce Grant. 1952.
Rand McNally & Company.................. 160, 000+
Three Fox Fables. Paul Galdone. The Seabury
Press..................................... 160, 000
Junior Science Book of Penguins. Patricia Lauber.
1963. Garrard Publishing Company.......... 158, 778
Great Promise. Alyce Bergey. 1968. Con-
cordia Publishing House.................... 157, 965
Little Sleeping Beauty. Brenda Prior. 1969.
Concordia Publishing House................ 157, 458
Beggar's Greatest Wish. Alyce Bergey. 1969.
Concordia Publishing House................ 157, 260
Angus Lost. Marjorie Flack. 1932. Doubleday
& Company, Inc.......................... 157, 011
Braggy King of Babylon. Yvonne McCall. 1969.
Concordia Publishing House................ 156, 838
Favorite Poems Old and New. Helen Josephine
Ferris, editor. 1957. Doubleday & Company,
Inc....................................... 156, 498
Holiday (Craft) Handbook No. 4. 1965. High-
lights for Children, Inc.................... 156, 000
The Fire Cat. Esther Averill. 1960. Harper &
Row Publishers, Inc...................... 154, 000
Unforgiving Servant. Janice Kramer. 1968. Con-
cordia Publishing House.................... 152, 200
It's Like This, Cat. Emily Cheney Neville. 1963.
Harper & Row Publishers, Inc............. 152, 000
Atlas of the Presidents. Donald E. Cooke. 1964.
Hammond Incorporated.................... 150, 000
Atoms, Energy, and Machines. Jack McCormick.
1967. Creative Educational Society, Inc...... 150, 000
Bible Stories. Mary Alice Jones. 1952. Rand
McNally & Company....................... 150, 000+
Creative Writing Activities; A Highlights Handbook.
Walter B. Barbe. 1965. Highlights For Chil-
dren, Inc................................. 150, 000
The Earth's Story. Gerald Ames and Rose Wyler.
1967. Creative Educational Society, Inc...... 150, 000
Planets, Stars and Space. Joseph M. Chamberlain
and Thomas D. Nicholson. 1962. Creative
Educational Society, Inc................... 150, 000

The Way of the Weather. Jerome Spar. 1967.
    Creative Educational Society, Inc............ 150,000
Tim Tadpole and the Great Bullfrog. Marjorie
    Flack. 1934. Doubleday & Company, Inc.... 148,794
Simeon's Secret. Janice Kramer. 1969. Con-
    cordia Publishing House.................... 147,882
Two Men in the Temple. Joann Scheck. 1968.
    Concordia Publishing House.................. 147,082
No Fighting, No Biting! Else Holmelund Minarik.
    1958. Harper & Row Publishers, Inc......... 147,000
King's Invitation. Virginia Mueller. 1968. Con-
    cordia Publishing House..................... 145,977
Pelle's New Suit. Elsa Beskow. 1929. Harper
    & Row Publishers, Inc....................... 145,000
Let's Go Outdoors. Harriet E. Huntington. 1939.
    Doubleday & Company, Inc................... 144,550
April's Kittens. Clare Turlay Newberry. 1940.
    Harper & Row Publishers, Inc............... 144,000
Harry and the Lady Next Door. Gene Zion. 1960.
    Harper & Row Publishers, Inc............... 142,000
The Wheel on the School. Meindert DeJong. 1954.
    Harper & Row Publishers, Inc............... 142,000
Water That Caught on Fire. Joann Scheck. 1969.
    Concordia Publishing House................. 140,128
Birds in Their Homes. Addison Webb. 1947.
    Doubleday & Company, Inc................... 137,911
Shan's Lucky Knife. Jean Merrill. 1960. Addison-
    Wesley Publishing Company................. 135,000
More Little Visits with God. Allan H. Jahsmann
    and Martin P. Simon. 1961. Concordia Pub-
    lishing House.............................. 134,521
George Washington Carver, Negro Scientist. Sam
    and Beryl Epstein. 1960. Garrard Publishing
    Company................................... 134,460
The Jungle Books. Rudyard Kipling. 1894. Dou-
    bleday & Company, Inc..................... 134,085
Julius. Syd Hoff. 1959. Harper & Row Pub-
    lishers, Inc............................... 133,000
The Tall Book of Bible Stories. Katherine Gibson,
    editor. 1957. Harper & Row Publishers, Inc. 133,000
Pepper and Salt. Howard Pyle. 1885. Harper &
    Row Publishers, Inc....................... 132,000
Bright April. Marguerite De Angeli. 1946. Dou-
    bleday & Company, Inc..................... 131,418
Last One Home Is a Green Pig. Edith Thacher
    Hurd. 1959. Harper & Row Publishers, Inc. 131,000
Handbook of Nature Study. Anna Botsford Comstock.
    1939. Cornell University Press............. 130,000+

Learning How Baseball.  Dick Siebert.  1968.
    Creative Educational Society, Inc.............  130,000
George Washington:  Father of Freedom.  Stewart
    Graff.  1964.  Garrard Publishing Company...  129,549
Where Is Cubby Bear?  Adda Mai Sharp.  1950.
    Steck-Vaughn Company.....................  127,750
Little Book about God.  Lauren Ford.  1934.
    Doubleday & Company, Inc..................  126,972
Animal Stories.  Edward W. and M. P. Dolch.
    1952.  Garrard Publishing Company..........  126,832
The Civil War.  Fletcher Pratt.  1955.  Double-
    day & Company, Inc.......................  125,197
The Case of the Hungry Stranger.  Crosby Newell
    Bonsall.  1963.  Harper & Row Publishers,
    Inc......................................  125,000
Colonial Williamsburg Coloring Book.  Marian
    Cannon.  1948.  The Colonial Williamsburg
    Foundation................................  125,000
Diddie, Dumps and Tot.  Louise Clarke Pyrnelle.
    1882.  Pelican Publishing Company..........  125,000+
Here Comes the Strikeout.  Leonard Kessler.  1965.
    Harper & Row Publishers, Inc..............  125,000
Kon-Tiki for Young People.  Thor Heyerdahl.  1960.
    Rand McNally & Company...................  (125,000)
Red Light Green Light.  Golden MacDonald.  1944.
    Doubleday & Company, Inc..................  124,900
Who Will Be My Friends?  Syd Hoff.  1960.
    Harper & Row Publishers, Inc..............  123,000
The Poppy Seed Cakes.  Margery Clark (pseud.).
    1924.  Doubleday & Company, Inc............  122,131
Marian's Big Book of Bible Stories.  Marian M.
    Schoolland.  1947.  Wm. B. Eerdmans Pub-
    lishing Company...........................  121,750
Baseball.  Frank F. DeClemente.  1962.  Creative
    Educational Society, Inc...................  120,000
Basketball.  Joe Hutton and Vern B. Hoffman.
    1962.  Creative Educational Society, Inc......  120,000
Football.  J. R. "Bob" Otto.  1962.  Creative Edu-
    cational Society, Inc......................  120,000
Golf, Swimming and Tennis.  Otis J. Dypwick and
    Helen Hull Jacobs.  1962.  Creative Educational
    Society, Inc..............................  120,000
Recreational Sports.  Clifford Brownell and Roy
    Moore.  1962.  Creative Educational Society,
    Inc......................................  120,000
Track and Field.  Earl "Bud" Meyers and Rich
    Hacker.  1962.  Creative Educational Society,
    Inc......................................  120,000

The Case of the Cat's Meow. Crosby Newell
    Bonsall. 1965. Harper & Row Publishers... 119,000
Rain Drop Splash. Alvin Tresselt. 1946.
    Lothrop, Lee & Shepard Company........... 119,000
Seeds and More Seeds. Millicent Ellis Selsam.
    1959. Harper & Row Publishers, Inc........ 119,000
Tell Me Some More. Crosby Newell Bonsall.
    1961. Harper & Row Publishers, Inc........ 119,000
Donkey Daniel in Bethlehem. Janice Kramer.
    1970. Concordia Publishing House........... 118,350
Cat and Dog. Else H. Minarik. 1960. Harper
    & Row Publishers, Inc..................... 117,000
The Lonely Doll. Dare Wright. 1957. Doubleday
    & Company, Inc........................... 116,671
Oliver. Syd Hoff. 1960. Harper & Row Publishers,
    Inc...................................... 116,000
Christmas Nutshell Library. Hilary Knight. 1963.
    Harper & Row Publishers, Inc.............. 115,000
Thee, Hannah! Marguerite De Angeli. 1940. Dou-
    bleday & Company, Inc.................... 114,785
The Happy Birthday Present. Joan Heilbroner. 1961.
    Harper & Row Publishers, Inc.............. 114,000
The Runaway Bunny. Margaret Wise Brown. 1942.
    Harper & Row Publishers, Inc.............. 114,000
Mei Li. Thomas Handforth. 1938. Doubleday &
    Company, Inc............................. 113,745
Emmett's Pig. Mary Stolz. 1959. Harper &
    Row Publishers, Inc...................... 113,000
Folk Stories. Edward W. and M.P. Dolch. 1952.
    Garrard Publishing Company................ 112,557
Harold and the Purple Crayon. Crockett Johnson
    (pseud.). 1955. Harper & Row Publishers... 112,000
UNICEF Festival Book. Judith Spiegelman. 1966.
    United States Committee for UNICEF........ 112,000
Dog Stories. Edward W. and M.P. Dolch. 1954.
    Garrard Publishing Company................ 111,362
Benjamin Franklin. Ingri and Edgar Parin
    D'Aulaire. 1950. Doubleday & Company,
    Inc...................................... 110,425
The Desert. Alexander and Elsie Klots. 1967.
    Creative Educational Society, Inc............. 110,000
Field and Meadow. Etta Schneider Ress. 1967.
    Creative Educational Society, Inc............. 110,000
Forest and Woodland. Stephen Collins. 1967.
    Creative Educational Society, Inc............. 110,000
Fresh and Salt Water. B. Bartram Cadbury.
    1967. Creative Educational Society, Inc...... 110,000

A Hole Is to Dig. Ruth Krauss. 1952. Harper &
Row Publishers, Inc......................... 110,000
Parks and Gardens. Robert S. Lemmon. 1967.
Creative Educational Society, Inc............. 110,000
Mr. Wizard's Experiments for Young Scientists.
Don Herbert. 1959. Doubleday & Company.. 108,445
Animals Everywhere. Ingri and Edgar Parin
D'Aulaire. 1954. Doubleday & Company...... 107,739
Columbus. Ingri and Edgar Parin D'Aulaire.
1955. Doubleday & Company, Inc............ 107,516
Daffy. Adda Mai Sharp. 1950. Steck-Vaughn
Company.................................... 106,964
The Happy Hollisters at Sea Gull Beach. Jerry
West (pseud.). 1953. Doubleday & Company,
Inc....................................... 106,140
Who's a Pest? Crosby Newell Bonsall. 1962.
Harper & Row Publishers, Inc.............. 106,000
Bird Life in Wington. John Calvin Reid. Wm. B.
Eerdmans Publishing Company.............. 105,400
American Folk Songs for Children. Ruth C.
Seeger. 1948. Doubleday & Company....... 105,399
Junior Miss. Sally Benson. 1941. Doubleday
& Company, Inc........................... 104,945
Circus Stories. Edward W. and M.P. Dolch.
1956. Garrard Publishing Company......... 104,905
The Happy Hollisters on a River Trip. Jerry
West (pseud.). 1953. Doubleday & Company. 104,150
Aesop's Stories. Edward W. and M.P. Dolch.
1951. Garrard Publishing Company......... 103,656
Sam Houston: Hero of Texas. Jean Lee Latham.
1965. Garrard Publishing Company......... 103,268
Horse Stories. Edward W. and M.P. Dolch.
1958. Garrard Publishing Company......... 103,095
Benjamin Franklin: Man of Ideas. Charles P.
Graves. 1960. Garrard Publishing Com-
pany...................................... 102,171
Frederick Douglass, Freedom Fighter. Lillie
Patterson. 1965. Garrard Publishing Com-
pany...................................... 102,142
D'Aulaires' Book of Greek Myths. Ingri and Edgar
Parin D'Aulaire. 1962. Doubleday & Com-
pany, Inc................................. 101,953
"Why" Stories. Edward W. and M.P. Dolch.
1958. Garrard Publishing Company......... 101,290
Creative Thinking Activities; A Highlights Handbook.
Garry Cleveland Myers. 1965. Highlights For
Children, Inc............................. 101,000

The Secret Three.    Mildred Myrick.   1963.
    Harper & Row Publishers, Inc...............    101, 000

Anybody at Home?   H. A. Rey.   1942.   Houghton
    Mifflin Company............................    (100, 000–
                                     250, 000)

The Bronze Bow.    Elizabeth George Speare.
    1961.    Houghton Mifflin Company............    (100, 000–
                                     250, 000)

Carry On,   Mr. Bowditch.    Jean Lee Latham.
    1955.    Houghton Mifflin Company............    (100, 000–
                                     250, 000)

Come and Have Fun.    Edith Thacher Hurd.   1962.
    Harper & Row Publishers, Inc..............    100, 000

Curious George Gets a Medal.    H. A. Rey.   1957.
    Houghton Mifflin Company..................    (100, 000–
                                     250, 000)

Curious George Flies a Kite.    Margret and H.A.
    Rey.   1958.    Houghton Mifflin Company......    (100, 000–
                                     250, 000)

Curious George Learns the Alphabet.    H. A. Rey.
    1963.    Houghton Mifflin Company...........    (100, 000–
                                     250, 000)

Curious George Rides a Bike.    H. A. Rey.   1952.
    Houghton Mifflin Company..................    (100, 000–
                                     250, 000)

Curious George Takes a Job.    H. A. Rey.   1947.
    Houghton Mifflin Company..................    (100, 000–
                                     250, 000)

Feed the Animals.    H. A. Rey.   1944.   Houghton
    Mifflin Company...........................    (100, 000–
                                     250, 000)

Food and Life.    Gerald Ames and Rose Wyler.
    1966.    Creative Educational Society, Inc.....    100, 000

I Like You.    Sandol Stoddard Warburg.   1965.
    Houghton Mifflin Company..................    (100, 000–
                                     250, 000)

Island of the Blue Dolphins.    Scott O'Dell.   1960.
    Houghton Mifflin Company..................    (100, 000–
                                     250, 000)

Katy and the Big Snow.    Virginia Lee Burton.
    1943.    Houghton Mifflin Company............    (100, 000–
                                     250, 000)

Katy No-Pocket.    Emmy Payne.   1944.   Houghton
    Mifflin Company...........................    (100, 000–
                                     250, 000)

King Robert the Resting Ruler.    Donna Lugg Pape.
    1968.    Oddo Publishing, Inc................    100, 000+

Little Chief.  Syd Hoff.  1961.  Harper & Row,
    Publishers, Inc............................ 100, 000
Liz Dearly's Silly Glasses.  Donna Lugg Pape.
    1968.  Oddo Publishing, Inc................. 100, 000+
Marshmallow.  Clare Turlay Newberry.  1942.
    Harper & Row Publishers, Inc............... 100, 000
Minn of the Mississippi.  Holling C. Holling.
    1951.  Houghton Mifflin Company............ (100, 000-
                                                                250, 000)

Mother Goose; The Classic Volland Edition.
    Eulalie O. Grover, editor.  1915.  Hubbard
    Press...................................... 100, 000
The Ocean Laboratory.  Athelstan Spilhaus.  1967.
    Creative Educational Society, Inc............ 100, 000
Paddle-to-the-Sea.  Holling C. Holling.  1941.
    Houghton Mifflin Company................... (100, 000-
                                                                250, 000)

Professor Fred and the Fid-Fuddlephone.  Donna
    Lugg Pape.  1968.  Oddo Publishing, Inc..... 100, 000+
Scientist Sam.  Donna Lugg Pape.  1968.  Oddo
    Publishing, Inc............................ 100, 000+
Shoemaker Fooze.  Donna Lugg Pape.  1968.  Oddo
    Publishing, Inc............................ 100, 000+
Tell Me about Christmas.  Mary Alice Jones.  1958.
    Rand McNally & Company................... 100, 000+
Tell Me about Heaven.  Mary Alice Jones.  1956.
    Rand McNally & Company................... 100, 000+
The Three Thinkers of Thay-Lee.  Donna Lugg
    Pape.  1968.  Oddo Publishing, Inc.......... 100, 000+
Tree in the Trail.  Holling C. Holling.  1942.
    Houghton Mifflin Company................... (100, 000-
                                                                250, 000)

Up Above and Down Below.  Irma E. Webber.
    1943.  Addison-Wesley Publishing Company... 100, 000
The Witch of Blackbird Pond.  Elizabeth George
    Speare.  1958.  Houghton Mifflin Company.... (100, 000-
                                                                250, 000)

Chapter Seven

BEST SELLERS BY TYPE OF BOOK,
SUBJECT CATEGORY, AND AGE LEVEL


This chapter groups the best sellers according to
type of book and general subject category, and divides the
books in each group into three approximate age levels:
preschool-grade 3 (picture books), grades 4-7, and grades
8-12.  The number of best sellers in each category and
age group is as follows [with the page on which each category begins given in brackets]:


| ps-3 | 4-7 | 8-12 | |
|---|---|---|---|
| | | | FICTION |
| 0 | 14 | 13 | Adventure [267] |
| 12 | 22 | 9 | Animal stories [268] |
| 5 | 2 | 0 | Anthologies, miscellaneous [270] |
| 74 | 10 | 0 | Anthropomorphic animals [270] |
| 10 | 3 | 0 | Anthropomorphic inanimate objects [273] |
| 0 | 25 | 16 | Boys growing up [273] |
| 73 | 0 | 0 | Early childhood [275] |
| 15 | 15 | 0 | Fairy tales and fables [277] |
| 10 | 12 | 0 | Fantasy, nonsense stories, and satire [278] |
| 0 | 10 | 0 | Folk tales [279] |
| 0 | 22 | 9 | Girls growing up, and family stories [279] |
| 0 | 19 | 9 | Historical fiction [280] |
| 7 | 6 | 0 | Holiday stories [282] |
| 9 | 0 | 0 | Mother Goose [282] |
| 3 | 11 | 0 | Mysteries [283] |
| 0 | 0 | 6 | Novelty books [283] |
| 0 | 0 | 2 | Plays [284] |
| 23 | 23 | 0 | Remedial reading--adventure stories [284] |
| 0 | 0 | 19 | Science fiction [286] |
| 0 | 6 | 0 | Speech improvement stories [287] |
| 0 | 0 | 1 | Translation [287] |

| ps-3 | 4-7 | 8-12 | |
|---|---|---|---|
| | | | NONFICTION |
| 14 | 2 | 0 | Activity books [287] |
| 0 | 0 | 2 | Anthologies of essays etc. [288] |
| 0 | 4 | 9 | Arts [288] |
| 1 | 32 | 19 | Biographies [289] |
| 4 | 1 | 4 | Careers and occupations [291] |
| 0 | 2 | 1 | Conduct of life, etc. [291] |
| 5 | 2 | 0 | Dictionaries [292] |
| 0 | 0 | 10 | Health, safety, and self improvement [292] |
| 1 | 15 | 13 | History, government and politics [293] |
| 0 | 1 | 10 | Hobbies [294] |
| 0 | 4 | 4 | Jokes and riddles [294] |
| 18 | 10 | 3 | Miscellaneous information and reference [295] |
| 0 | 4 | 2 | Mythology [296] |
| 7 | 5 | 2 | Poems and verses [297] |
| 51 | 16 | 0 | Religion [297] |
| 26 | 46 | 16 | Science [300] |
| 0 | 4 | 5 | Scout handbooks [303] |
| 2 | 3 | 2 | Songbooks and music [304] |
| 0 | 6 | 18 | Sports [304] |

## FICTION

### Adventure

Grades 4-7

The Big Wave, by Pearl S. Buck.   John Day, 1948.
Daughter of the Mountains, by Louise S. Rankin.   Viking, 1948.
The Door in the Wall, by Marguerite De Angeli.   Doubleday, 1949.
The Dragon Fish, by Pearl S. Buck.   John Day, 1944.
The Jungle Books, by Rudyard Kipling.   1894.
Kim, by Rudyard Kipling.   1901.
Landslide! by Veronique Day.   Coward-McCann, 1963.
The Lost Kingdom, by Chester Bryant.   Messner, 1951.
Robinson Crusoe, by Daniel Defoe.   1719.
Secret of the Andes, by Ann Nolan Clark.   Viking, 1952.
Snowbound in Hidden Valley, by Holly Wilson.   Messner, 1957.

Some Merry Adventures of Robin Hood of Great Renown in
    Nottinghamshire.  About 1490.
The Swiss Family Robinson, by Johann R. Wyss.  1813.
The Water-Buffalo Children, by Pearl S. Buck.  John Day,
    1943.

Grades 8-12

The Black Arrow, by Robert Louis Stevenson.  1888.
The Bronze Bow, by Elizabeth George Speare.  Houghton
    Mifflin, 1961.
The Dark Frigate, by Charles Boardman Hawes.  1924.
Island of the Blue Dolphins, by Scott O'Dell.  Houghton
    Mifflin, 1960.
Kidnapped, by Robert Louis Stevenson.  1886.
King Solomon's Mines, by H. Rider Haggard.  1886.
Lorna Doone, by Richard Doddridge Blackmore.  1869.
Moby Dick, by Herman Melville.  1851.
On Two Wheels:  An Anthology about Men and Motorcycles,
    edited by Don McKay.  Dell, 1971.
Pilgrim's Progress, by John Bunyan.  1678 and 1684.
The Thirty-Nine Steps, by John Buchan.  1915.
Treasure Island, by Robert Louis Stevenson.  1883.
Wild Wheels, edited by Don McKay.  Dell, 1969.


Animal Stories

Preschool-grade 3

April's Kittens, by Clare Turlay Newberry.  Harper, 1940.
Dog Stories, by Edward W. and M.P. Dolch.  Garrard,
    1954.
Emmett's Pig, by Mary Stolz.  Harper, 1959.
Feed the Animals, by H.A. Rey.  Houghton Mifflin, 1944.
Flicka, Ricka, Dicka and the Three Kittens, by Maj Lind-
    man.  Albert Whitman, 1941.
Horse Stories, by Edward W. and M.P. Dolch.  Garrard,
    1958.
Make Way for Ducklings, by Robert McCloskey.  Viking,
    1941.
Marshmallow, by Clare Turlay Newberry.  Harper, 1942.
Miss Hattie and the Monkey, by Helen Olds.  Follett, 1958.
Something New at the Zoo, by Esther Meeks.  Follett, 1957.
Twenty-Seven Cats Next Door, by Anita Feagles.  Addison-
    Wesley, 1965.
Where's My Baby? by H.A. Rey.  Houghton Mifflin, 1943.

## Grades 4-7

Bambi: A Life in the Woods, by Felix Salten. Simon &
    Schuster, 1929.
The Bears on Hemlock Mountain, by Alice Dalgliesh. Scrib-
    ner, 1952.
Beautiful Joe, by Marshall Saunders. Grosset & Dunlap,
    1920.
Black Beauty, by Anna Sewell. 1877.
Black Gold, by Marguerite Henry. Rand McNally, 1957.
Born to Trot, by Marguerite Henry. Rand McNally, 1950.
Brighty of the Grand Canyon, by Marguerite Henry. Rand
    McNally, 1956.
A Dog and a Half, by Barbara Willard. Nelson, 1971.
Gentle Ben, by Walt Morey. Dutton, 1965.
A Horse of Her Own, by Hudnut. Van Nostrand Reinhold.
Justin Morgan Had a Horse, by Marguerite Henry. Rand
    McNally, 1954.
King of the Wind, by Marguerite Henry. Rand McNally,
    1948.
Lad: A Dog, by Albert Payson Terhune. 1919.
Lassie Come-Home, by Eric Knight. Winston, 1941.
Little Vic, by Doris Gates. Viking, 1951.
Mr. Popper's Penguins, by Richard and Florence Atwater.
    Little, Brown, 1938.
Misty of Chincoteague, by Marguerite Henry. Rand McNally,
    1947.
My Friend Flicka, by Mary O'Hara. Lippincott, 1941.
Sea Star, Orphan of Chincoteague, by Marguerite Henry.
    Rand McNally, 1949.
Stormy, Misty's Foal, by Marguerite Henry. Rand McNally,
    1963.
The Superlative Horse, by Jean Merrill. Addison-Wesley,
    1961.
White Stallion of Lipizza, by Marguerite Henry. Rand Mc-
    Nally, 1964.

## Grades 8-12

The Call of the Wild, by Jack London. 1903.
Gay Neck: The Story of a Pigeon, by Dhan Gopal Mukerji.
    Dutton, 1927.
The Incredible Journey, by Sheila Burnford. Little, Brown,
    1961.
"National Velvet," by Enid Bagnold. Morrow, 1949.
Rascal: A Memoir of a Better Era, by Sterling North. Dut-
    ton, 1963.

Smoky, the Cow Horse, by Will James.   Scribner, 1926.
The Wolfling, by Sterling North.   Dutton, 1969.
Wonderful World of Horses, edited by Ned Hoopes.   Dell,
    1966.
The Yearling, by Marjorie Kinnan Rawlings.   Scribner,
    1938.


## Anthologies, Miscellaneous

### Preschool-grade 3

Better Homes and Gardens Story Book.   Meredith, 1950.
The Bumper Book, edited by Watty Piper.   Platt & Munk,
    1946.
The Gateway to Storyland, edited by Watty Piper.   Platt &
    Munk, 1954.
My Brimful Book, edited by Dana Bruce.   Platt & Munk,
    1960.
Stories That Never Grow Old, edited by Watty Piper.   Platt
    & Munk.

### Grades 4-7

Illustrated Treasury of Children's Literature, edited by
    Margaret E. Martignoni.   Grosset & Dunlap, 1955.
Nutshell Library, by Maurice Sendak.   Harper & Row, 1962.


## Anthropomorphic Animals

### Preschool-grade 3

Adventures of Peter Cottontail, by Thornton W. Burgess.
    Grosset & Dunlap.
Andy and the Lion, by James Daugherty.   Viking, 1938.
Angus and the Cat, by Marjorie Flack.   Doubleday, 1931.
Angus and the Ducks, by Marjorie Flack.   Doubleday, 1930.
Angus Lost, by Marjorie Flack.   Doubleday, 1932.
Animal Stories, by Edward W. and M. P. Dolch.   Garrard,
    1952.
Bear Party, by William Pene du Bois.   Viking, 1963.
Bessie, the Messy Penguin, by Joyce Holland.   Denison,
    1960.
The Biggest Bear, by Lynd Ward.   Houghton Mifflin, 1952.
Bobby Bear and the Bees, by Marilyn Olear Helmrath and
    Janet LaSpisa Bartlett.   Oddo, 1968.

Bobby Bear Finds Maple Sugar, by Marilyn Olear Helmrath
    and Janet LaSpisa Bartlett.   Oddo, 1968.
Bobby Bear Goes Fishing, by Marilyn Olear Helmrath and
    Janet LaSpisa Bartlett.   Oddo, 1968.
Bobby Bear in the Spring, by Marilyn Olear Helmrath and
    Janet LaSpisa Bartlett.   Oddo, 1968.
Bobby Bear's Rocket Ride, by Marilyn Olear Helmrath and
    Janet LaSpisa Bartlett.   Oddo, 1968.
Buttons, by Tom Robinson.   Viking, 1938.
Casey, the Utterly Impossible Horse, by Anita Feagles.
    Addison-Wesley, 1960.
Casper, the Caterpillar, by Celeste K. Foster.   Denison.
Cat and Dog, by Else H. Minarik.   Harper, 1960.
Come and Have Fun, by Edith Thacher Hurd.   Harper &
    Row, 1962.
The Curious Cow, by Esther Meeks.   Follett, 1960.
Curious George, by H.A. Rey.   Houghton Mifflin, 1941.
Curious George Flies a Kite, by Margret and H.A. Rey.
    Houghton Mifflin, 1958.
Curious George Gets a Medal, by H.A. Rey.   Houghton
    Mifflin, 1957.
Curious George Learns the Alphabet, by H.A. Rey.   Hough-
    ton Mifflin, 1963.
Curious George Rides a Bike, by H.A. Rey.   Houghton
    Mifflin, 1952.
Curious George Takes a Job, by H.A. Rey.   Houghton
    Mifflin, 1947.
Daffy, by Adda Mai Sharp.   Steck-Vaughn, 1950.
Dandelion, by Don Freeman.   Viking, 1964.
Danny and the Dinosaur, by Syd Hoff.   Harper, 1958.
The Extra Egg, by Edna A. Anderson.   Denison.
Father Bear Comes Home, by Else H. Minarik.   Harper,
    1959.
The Fire Cat, by Esther Averill.   Harper, 1960.
Flip, by Wesley Dennis.   Viking, 1941.
Flip and the Morning, by Wesley Dennis.   Viking, 1951.
George, the Discontented Giraffe, by Phillip Orso Steinberg.
    Denison.
Gertie the Duck, by Nicholas Georgiady and Louis Romano.
    Follett, 1959.
Gobble, Gobble, Gobble, by Mary Jackson Ellis.   Denison.
The Golden Egg Book, by Margaret Wise Brown.   Simon &
    Schuster, 1947.
Goodnight Moon, by Margaret Wise Brown.   Harper, 1947.
Harry and the Lady Next Door, by Gene Zion.   Harper,
    1960.
Harry the Dirty Dog, by Gene Zion.   Harper, 1956.

Harvey Hopper, by Bernice M. Chappel.  Denison.
The House at Pooh Corner, by A.A. Milne.  Dutton, 1928.
Jimmy, a Little Pup, by Clarence Jonk.  Denison.
Jonathan and the Octopus, by Celeste K. Foster.  Denison.
Julius, by Syd Hoff.  Harper, 1959.
Just Follow Me, by Phoebe Erickson.  Follett, 1960.
Katy No-Pocket, by Emmy Payne.  Houghton Mifflin, 1944.
The Kitten Who Was Different, by Lowell Saunders.  Denison.
Last One Home Is a Green Pig, by Edith Thacher Hurd.
    Harper, 1959.
Little Bear, by Else H. Minarik.  Harper, 1957.
Little Bear's Friend, by Else H. Minarik.  Harper, 1960.
Little Quack, by Ruth Woods.  Follett, 1961.
The Little Rabbit Who Wanted Red Wings, by Carolyn
    Sherwin Bailey.  Platt & Munk, 1945.
Mable the Whale, by Patricia King.  Follett, 1958.
Mouse House, by Rumer Godden.  Viking, 1957.
No Fighting, No Biting! by Else H. Minarik.  Harper, 1958.
Oliver, by Syd Hoff.  Harper, 1960.
Peter Churchmouse, by Margot Austin.  Dutton, 1941.
Rocky, the Rocket Mouse, by Alyce Bergey.  Denison.
The Runaway Bunny, by Margaret Wise Brown.  Harper,
    1942.
Sally Alligator, by Betty Molgard Ryan.  Denison.
Sammy the Seal, by Syd Hoff.  Harper, 1959.
The Story about Ping, by Marjorie Flack.  Viking, 1933.
The Story of Ferdinand, by Munro Leaf.  Viking, 1936.
Swimmer Is a Hopper, by Mary Jackson Ellis.  Denison.
Swimmy, by Leo Lionni.  Pantheon, 1963.
Sylvester and the Magic Pebble, by William Steig.  Simon
    & Schuster, 1969.
Tim Tadpole and the Great Bullfrog, by Marjorie Flack.
    Doubleday, 1934.
Timothy Turtle, by Al Graham.  Viking, 1949.
Too Many Dogs, by Ramona Dupre.  Follett, 1960.
Where Is Cubby Bear?  by Adda Mai Sharp.  Steck-Vaughn,
    1950.
Winnie-the-Pooh, by A.A. Milne.  Dutton, 1926.


Grades 4-7


A Bear Called Paddington, by Michael Bond.  Houghton
    Mifflin, 1960.
Charlotte's Web, by E.B. White.  Harper, 1952.
Elephi, the Cat with the High I.Q., by Jean Stafford.  Dell,
    1966.
The Hundred and One Dalmations, by Dodie Smith.  Viking,
    1957.

Junket, by Anne H. White.  Viking, 1955.
Rabbit Hill, by Robert Lawson.  Viking, 1944.
Stuart Little, by E. B. White.  Harper, 1945.
The Tough Winter, by Robert Lawson.  Viking, 1954.
The Trumpet of the Swan, by E. B. White.  Harper & Row,
   1970.
The Wind in the Willows, by Kenneth Grahame.  Scribner,
   1908.

## Anthropomorphic Inanimate Objects

### Preschool-grade 3

Becky Lou in Grandmother's Days, by Hazel Craig.  Denison.
Corduroy, by Don Freeman.  Viking, 1968.
Dandy, the Dime, by James S. Kerr.  Denison.
Katy and the Big Snow, by Virginia Lee Burton.  Houghton
   Mifflin, 1943.
The Little Engine That Could, by Watty Piper.  Platt &
   Munk, 1929.
The Little House, by Virginia Lee Burton.  Houghton Mifflin,
   1942.
Little Toot, by Hardie Gramatky.  Putnam, 1939.
The Lonely Doll, by Dare Wright.  Doubleday, 1957.
Mike Mulligan and His Steam Shovel, by Virginia Lee Burton.
   Houghton Mifflin, 1939.
Pony Engine, by F. M. Ford.  Grosset & Dunlap.

### Grades 4-7

Miss Hickory, by Carolyn Sherwin Bailey.  Viking, 1946.
Pinocchio: The Story of a Puppet, by Carlo Collodi.  1881.
The Velveteen Rabbit, by Margery Williams.  Doubleday,
   1926.

## Boys Growing Up

### Grades 4-7

The Bully of Barkham Street, by Mary Stolz.  Harper &
   Row, 1963.
Centerburg Tales, by Robert McCloskey.  Viking, 1951.
Dipper of Copper Creek, by John and Jean George.  Dutton,
   1956.
Don't Take Teddy, by Babbis Friis-Baastad.  Scribner, 1967.

Edgar Allan, by John Neufeld.  Phillips, 1968.
Hans Brinker:  Or the Silver Skates, by Mary Mapes Dodge.
    1865.
Henry and Beezus, by Beverly Cleary.  Morrow, 1952.
Henry and Ribsy, by Beverly Cleary.  Morrow, 1954.
Henry and the Clubhouse, by Beverly Cleary.  Morrow, 1962.
Henry and the Paper Route, by Beverly Cleary.  Morrow,
    1957.
Henry Huggins, by Beverly Cleary.  Morrow, 1950.
Henry Reed, Inc., by Keith Robertson.  Viking, 1958.
Henry Reed's Baby-Sitting Service, by Keith Robertson.
    Viking, 1966.
Henry Reed's Journey, by Keith Robertson.  Viking, 1963.
Homer Price, by Robert McCloskey.  Viking, 1943.
Huckleberry Finn, by Mark Twain.  1884.
It's Like This, Cat, by Emily Cheney Neville.  Harper &
    Row, 1963.
J.T., by Jane Wagner.  Van Nostrand Reinhold, 1969.
Little Lord Fauntleroy, by Frances Hodgson Burnett.  1886.
My Side of the Mountain, by Jean Craighead George.  Dutton,
    1959.
Onion John, by Joseph Krumgold.  T.Y. Crowell, 1959.
The Prince and the Pauper, by Mark Twain.  1882.
The Red Balloon, by Albert Lamourisse.  Doubleday, 1956.
Tom Sawyer, by Mark Twain.  1878.
The Wheel on the School, by Meindert DeJong.  Harper,
    1954.

Grades 8-12

And Now Miguel, by Joseph Krumgold.  T.Y. Crowell, 1953.
Drag Strip, by William Campbell Gault.  Dutton, 1959.
Durango Street, by Frank Bonham.  Dutton, 1965.
Good-Bye, Amigos, by Bob and Jan Young.  Messner, 1963.
Hot Rod, by Henry Gregor Felsen.  Dutton, 1950.
I'm Really Dragged But Nothing Gets Me Down, by Nat
    Hentoff.  Simon & Schuster, 1968.
Jazz Country, by Nat Hentoff.  Harper & Row, 1965.
The Nitty Gritty, by Frank Bonham.  Dutton, 1968.
The Outsiders, by S.E. Hinton.  Viking, 1967.
Penrod, by Booth Tarkington.  Doubleday, 1914.
The Pigman, by Paul Zindel.  Harper & Row, 1968.
Point of Departure, edited by Robert S. Gold.  Delacorte,
    1971.
Seventeen, by Booth Tarkington.  Harper, 1916.
Thunder Road, by William Campbell Gault.  Dutton, 1952.
Tom Brown's Schooldays, by Thomas Hughes.  1857.
Tuned Out, by Maia Wojciechowska.  Harper & Row, 1968.

## Early Childhood

Preschool-grade 3

Adventures in the Neighborhood, by Nila Voight.  Lawrence.
Angelo the Naughty One, by Helen Garrett.  Viking, 1944.
Anybody at Home? by H. A. Rey.  Houghton Mifflin, 1942.
Barney's Adventure, by Margot Austin.  Dutton, 1941.
Benny and the Bear, by Barbee Carleton.  Follett, 1960.
Big New School, by Evelyn Hastings.  Follett, 1959.
Blueberries for Sal, by Robert McCloskey.  Viking, 1948.
The Boy Who Would Not Say His Name, by Elizabeth Vreeken.
     Follett, 1959.
Caps for Sale, by Esphyr Slobodkina.  Addison-Wesley, 1947.
Circus Stories, by Edward W. and M. P. Dolch.  Garrard,
     1956.
Crow Boy, by Taro Yashima.  Viking, 1955.
Down, Down the Mountain, by Ellis Credle.  Nelson, 1934.
Exploring around the House, by Nila Voight.  Lawrence.
Flicka, Ricka, Dicka and the New Dotted Dresses, by Maj
     Lindman.  Albert Whitman, 1939.
The Four Friends, by Carol Hoff.  Follett, 1955.
Gilberto and the Wind, by Marie Hall Ets.  Viking, 1963.
Happiness Is Smiling, by Katherine Gehm.  Denison.
The Happy Birthday Present, by Joan Heilbroner.  Harper,
     1961.
Happy Hospital Surprises, by Winifred Talbot.  Denison.
Harold and the Purple Crayon, by Crockett Johnson.  Harper,
     1955.
Have You Seen My Brother? by Elizabeth Guilfoile.  Follett,
     1962.
Here Comes the Strikeout, by Leonard Kessler.  Harper &
     Row, 1965.
The Hole in the Hill, by Marion Seyton.  Follett, 1960.
I Like You, by Sandol Stoddard Warburg.  Houghton Mifflin,
     1965.
In John's Back Yard, by Esther Meeks.  Follett, 1957.
In My Mother's House, by Ann Nolan Clark.  Viking, 1941.
In the Forest, by Marie Hall Ets.  Viking, 1944.
Jeanne-Marie Counts Her Sheep, by Francoise.  Scribner,
     1951.
Journey Cake, Ho! by Ruth Sawyer.  Viking, 1953.
Just Me, by Marie Hall Ets.  Viking, 1965.
Lentil, by Robert McCloskey.  Viking, 1940.
Little Black Sambo, by Helen Bannerman.  Stokes, 1900.
Little Chief, by Syd Hoff.  Harper & Row, 1961.
Little Eddie, by Carolyn Haywood.  Morrow, 1947.

The Little Family, by Lois Lenski.   Doubleday, 1932.
The Little Old Woman Who Used Her Head, by Hope Newell.
     Nelson, 1935.
Madeline, by Ludwig Bemelmans.   Viking, 1939.
Madeline and the Bad Hat, by Ludwig Bemelmans.   Viking,
     1957.
Madeline and the Gypsies, by Ludwig Bemelmans.   Viking,
     1959.
Madeline in London, by Ludwig Bemelmans.   Viking, 1961.
Madeline's Rescue, by Ludwig Bemelmans.   Viking, 1953.
Mike's House, by Julia Sauer.   Viking, 1954.
Mop Top, by Don Freeman.   Viking, 1955.
My Own Little House, by Merriman Kaune.   Follett, 1957.
Nobody Listens to Andrew, by Elizabeth Guilfoile.   Follett,
     1957.
Norman the Doorman, by Don Freeman.   Viking, 1959.
One Morning in Maine, by Robert McCloskey.   Viking, 1952.
Play with Me, by Marie Hall Ets.   Viking, 1955.
The Poppy Seed Cakes, by Margery Clark.   Doubleday, 1924.
Sam, Bangs and Moonshine, by Evaline Ness.   Holt, Rine-
     hart & Winston, 1966.
The Secret Three, by Mildred Myrick.   Harper & Row, 1963.
Show and Tell, by Patricia Miles Martin.   Putnam, 1962.
The Smallest Boy in the Class, by Jerrold Beim.   Morrow,
     1949.
Snipp, Snapp, Snurr and the Big Surprise, by Maj Lindman.
     Albert Whitman, 1937.
Snipp, Snapp, Snurr and the Buttered Bread, by Maj Lindman.
     Albert Whitman, 1934.
Snipp, Snapp, Snurr and the Gingerbread, by Maj Lindman.
     Albert Whitman, 1936.
Snipp, Snapp, Snurr and the Magic Horse, by Maj Lindman.
     Albert Whitman, 1933.
Snipp, Snapp, Snurr and the Red Shoes, by Maj Lindman.
     Albert Whitman, 1932.
Snipp, Snapp, Snurr and the Yellow Sled, by Maj Lindman.
     Albert Whitman, 1936.
The Snowy Day, by Ezra Jack Keats.   Viking, 1962.
Spaghetti Eddie, by Mary Jackson Ellis.   Denison.
Springtime for Jeanne-Marie, by Francoise.   Scribner, 1955.
Tell Me Some More, by Crosby Newell Bonsall.   Harper,
     1961.
Time of Wonder, by Robert McCloskey.   Viking, 1957.
Umbrella, by Taro Yashima.   Viking, 1958.
Wee Gillis, by Munro Leaf.   Viking, 1938.
What Mary Jo Shared, by Janice May Udry.   Albert Whit-
     man, 1966.

What Mary Jo Wanted, by Janice May Udry.  Albert Whit-
    man, 1968.
Where Is Everybody? by Remy Charlip.  Addison-Wesley,
    1957.
Whistle for Willie, by Ezra Jack Keats.  Viking, 1964.
Who Will Be My Friends? by Syd Hoff.  Harper, 1960.
Who's a Pest? by Crosby Newell Bonsall.  Harper & Row,
    1962.
"Why" Stories, by Edward W. and M. P. Dolch.  Garrard,
    1958.


## Fairy Tales and Fables

### Preschool-grade 3

Fairy Tales and Fables, edited by Doris Duenewald.  Grosset
    & Dunlap, 1970.
The Five Chinese Brothers, by Claire H. Bishop.  Coward-
    McCann, 1938.
Goldilocks and the Three Bears.  About 1831.
Henny Penny, by Paul Galdone.  Seabury.
Little Red Riding Hood, by Jakob and Ludwig Grimm.  1812.
The Monkey and the Crocodile:  A Jataka Tale from India,
    by Paul Galdone.  Seabury.
Once a Mouse...  A Fable Cut in Wood, by Marcia Brown.
    Scribner.
Pelle's New Suit, by Elsa Beskow.  Harper, 1929.
The Steadfast Tin Soldier, by Hans Christian Andersen.
    1835.
The Tall Book of Fairy Tales, edited by William Sharp.
    Harper, 1947.
The Tall Book of Make-Believe, edited by Garth Williams.
    Harper, 1950.
The Tall Book of Nursery Tales, edited by Feodor Rojankov-
    sky.  Harper, 1944.
The Tasha Tudor Book of Fairy Tales, edited by Dana Bruce.
    Platt & Munk, 1961.
Three Fox Fables (adapted from Aesop), by Paul Galdone.
    Seabury.
The Three Little Pigs, by Jakob and Wilhelm Grimm.  1812.

### Grades 4-7

Aesop's Fables, edited by John Warrington.  Dutton.
Aesop's Stories, by Edward W. and M. P. Dolch.  Garrard.
At the Back of the North Wind, by George MacDonald. 1871.

Charlie and the Chocolate Factory, by Roald Dahl. Knopf, 1964.

Folk Stories, by Edward W. and M. P. Dolch. Garrard, 1952.

Grimm's Fairy Tales, by Jakob and Wilhelm Grimm. 1812, 1815.

Hans Andersen's Fairy Tales, by Hans Christian Andersen. 1835.

The Happy Prince and Other Stories, by Oscar Wilde. 1888, 1891.

James and the Giant Peach, by Roald Dahl. Knopf, 1961.

The Lost Princess: A Double Story, by George MacDonald.

The Magic Wishbone, by Sister Adele Marie, C. S. J. Lawrence.

New Illustrated Just So Stories, by Rudyard Kipling. Doubleday, 1912.

Pepper and Salt, by Howard Pyle. Harper, 1885.

Peter Pan, by James M. Barrie. Scribner, 1949.

The Three Toymakers, by Ursula Moray Williams. Nelson, 1971.

## Fantasy, Nonsense Stories, and Satire

### Preschool-grade 3

And To Think That I Saw It On Mulberry Street, by Dr. Seuss. Vanguard, 1937.

The Cat in the Hat, by Dr. Seuss. Random, 1957.

The Cat in the Hat Comes Back, by Dr. Seuss. Random, 1958.

The 500 Hats of Bartholomew Cubbins, by Dr. Seuss. Vanguard, 1938.

Green Eggs and Ham, by Dr. Seuss. Beginner, 1960.

Hop on Pop, by Dr. Seuss. Beginner, 1963.

One Fish, Two Fish, Red Fish, Blue Fish, by Dr. Seuss. Beginner, 1960.

Walt Disney's Mary Poppins, by Alice Chase. Golden, 1964.

Where the Wild Things Are, by Maurice Sendak. Harper & Row, 1963.

Yertle the Turtle, and Other Stories, by Dr. Seuss. Random, 1958.

### Grades 4-7

Alice's Adventures in Wonderland, by Lewis Carroll. 1865.

The Enormous Egg, by Oliver Butterworth. Little, Brown, 1956.

Gulliver's Travels, by Jonathan Swift.  1726.
Pippi Goes on Board, by Astrid Lindgren.  Viking, 1957.
Pippi in the South Seas, by Astrid Lindgren.  Viking, 1959.
Pippi Longstocking, by Astrid Lindgren.  Viking, 1950.
The Pushcart War, by Jean Merrill.  Addison-Wesley, 1964.
The Story of Doctor Dolittle, by Hugh Lofting.  Lippincott, 1920.
Through the Looking Glass, by Lewis Carroll.  1872.
The Twenty-One Balloons, by William Pene du Bois.  Viking, 1947.
The Voyages of Doctor Dolittle, by Hugh Lofting.  Lippincott, 1922.
The Wonderful Wizard of Oz, by L. Frank Baum.  George M. Hill, 1900.

## Folk Tales

Grades 4-7

English Folk and Fairy Tales, edited by Joseph Jacobs. Putnam, 1904.
Old Peter's Russian Tales, by Arthur Ransome.  1916.
Paul Bunyan Swings His Axe, by Dell J. McCormick.  Caxton, 1936.
Pecos Bill, by James Cloyd Bowman.  Albert Whitman, 1937.
Shan's Lucky Knife, by Jean Merrill.  Addison-Wesley, 1960.
Stone Soup: An Old Tale, by Marcia Brown.  Scribner, 1947.
Tales from a Finnish Tupa, by James Cloyd Bowman and Margery Bianco.  Albert Whitman, 1936.
Tall Tales from the High Hills, by Ellis Credle.  Nelson, 1957.
Walt Disney's Uncle Remus Stories, by Joel Chandler Harris. Golden, 1946.
The Wise Men of Helm and Their Merry Tales, by Solomon Simon.  Behrman, 1945.

## Girls Growing Up, and Family Stories

Grades 4-7

All-of-a-Kind Family, by Sydney Taylor.  Follett, 1951.
Bright April, by Marguerite De Angeli.  Doubleday, 1946.
Ellen Tebbits, by Beverly Cleary.  Morrow, 1951.
Eloise, by Kay Thompson.  Simon & Schuster, 1955.

The Empty Schoolhouse, by Natalie Savage Carlson.   Harper
    & Row, 1965.
The Four-Story Mistake, by Elizabeth Enright.   Rinehart,
    1942.
The Good Master, by Kate Seredy.   Viking, 1935.
The Happy Hollisters, by Jerry West.   Doubleday, 1953.
The Happy Hollisters at Sea Gull Beach, by Jerry West.
    Doubleday, 1953.
The Happy Hollisters on a River Trip, by Jerry West.   Dou-
    bleday, 1953.
Harriet the Spy, by Louise Fitzhugh.   Harper & Row, 1964.
Heidi, by Johanna Spyri.   1884.
Jo's Boys, by Louisa May Alcott.   1886.
Little Men, by Louisa May Alcott.   1871.
Little Women, by Louisa May Alcott.   1868.
Melindy's Medal, by Georgene Faulkner and John Becker.
    Messner, 1945.
Rebecca of Sunnybrook Farm, by Kate Douglas Wiggin.
    Houghton Mifflin, 1903.
Roller Skates, by Ruth Sawyer and Kate Seredy.   Viking,
    1936.
The Saturdays, by Elizabeth Enright.   Rinehart, 1941.
The Secret Garden, by Frances Hodgson Burnett.   Lippincott,
    1912.
Sensible Kate, by Doris Gates.   Viking, 1943.
Understood Betsy, by Dorothy Canfield Fisher.   1916.

Grades 8-12

Candy Stripers, by Lee Wyndham.   Messner, 1958.
Fifteen, by Beverly Cleary.   Morrow, 1956.
Hold Fast to Your Dreams, by Catherine Blanton.   Messner,
    1955.
Junior Miss, by Sally Benson.   1941.
Lisa, Bright and Dark, by John Neufeld.   Phillips, 1969.
The Peter Pan Bag, by Lee Kingman.   Houghton Mifflin,
    1970.
The Soul Brothers and Sister Lou, by Kristin Hunter.
    Scribner, 1968.
The Summer of the Swans, by Betsy Byars.   Viking, 1970.
Up a Road Slowly, by Irene Hunt.   Follett, 1966.


Historical Fiction


Grades 4-7

Blue Willow, by Doris Gates.   Viking, 1940.

By the Shores of Silver Lake, by Laura Ingalls Wilder.
    Harper, 1939.
Cotton in My Sack, by Lois Lenski.  Lippincott, 1949.
Diddie, Dumps and Tot, by Louise Clarke Pyrnelle.  Harper,
    1882.
Farmer Boy, by Laura Ingalls Wilder.  Harper, 1933.
King Arthur and the Round Table, by A. M. Hadfield.  Dutton,
    1953.
Little House in the Big Woods, by Laura Ingalls Wilder.
    Harper, 1932.
Little House on the Prairie, by Laura Ingalls Wilder.
    Harper, 1935.
Little Town on the Prairie, by Laura Ingalls Wilder.
    Harper, 1941.
On the Banks of Plum Creek, by Laura Ingalls Wilder.
    Harper, 1937.
Queenie Peavy, by Robert Burch.  Viking, 1966.
The Red Badge of Courage, by Stephen Crane.  1895.
The Silver Sword, by Ian Serraillier.  Phillips, 1959.
The Singing Tree, by Kate Seredy.  Viking, 1939.
Skip, the Pioneer Boy, by Gwendolen L. Hayden.  Denison.
Snow Treasure, by Marie McSwigan.  Dutton, 1942.
The Song of Hiawatha, by Henry Wadsworth Longfellow.
    1855.
Strawberry Girl, by Lois Lenski.  Lippincott, 1945.
Thee, Hannah! by Marguerite De Angeli.  Doubleday, 1940.

Grades 8-12

Across Five Aprils, by Irene Hunt.  Follett, 1964.
Adam of the Road, by Elizabeth Janet Gray.  Viking, 1942.
Johnny Tremain, by Esther Forbes.  Houghton Mifflin,
    1943.
Megan, by Iris Noble.  Messner, 1965.
Men of Iron, by Howard Pyle.  1891.
Tales of the Sea Foam, by Lisette G. Brown.  Naturegraph,
    1969.
The White Stag, by Kate Seredy.  Viking, 1937.
Winter on the Johnny Smoker, by Mildred H. Comfort.
    Denison.
The Witch of Blackbird Pond, by Elizabeth George Speare.
    Houghton Mifflin, 1958.

## Holiday Stories

Preschool-grade 3

Blink, the Patchwork Bunny, by Matthew V. Howard.
    Denison, 1959.
Bobby Bear's Halloween, by Marilyn Olear Helmrath and
    Janet LaSpisa Bartlett.   Oddo, 1968.
The Country Bunny and the Little Gold Shoes, by Dubose
    Heyward.   Houghton Mifflin, 1939.
The Littlest Angel, by Charles Tazewell.   Children's, 1966.
Mei Li, by Thomas Handforth.   Doubleday, 1938.
Nine Days to Christmas, by Marie Hall Ets and Aurora
    Labastida.   Viking, 1959.
The Tall Book of Christmas, edited by Dorothy Hall Smith.
    Harper, 1954.

Grades 4-7

The Birds' Christmas Carol, by Kate Douglas Wiggin.
    Houghton Mifflin, 1886.
Christmas:   A Book of Stories Old and New, compiled by
    Alice Dalgliesh.   Scribner, 1934.
A Christmas Carol, by Charles Dickens.   1843.
Christmas Nutshell Library, by Hilary Knight.   Harper &
    Row, 1963.
The Egg Tree, by Katherine Milhous.   Scribner, 1950.
Why the Chimes Rang, by Raymond MacDonald Alden.   Bobbs-
    Merrill.

## Mother Goose

Preschool-grade 3

Big Book of Mother Goose, illustrated by Alice Schlesinger.
    Grosset & Dunlap.
Book of Nursery & Mother Goose Rhymes, by Marguerite
    De Angeli.   Doubleday, 1954.
Mother Goose, illustrated by Gyo Fujikawa.   Grosset &
    Dunlap.
Mother Goose:   The Classic Volland Edition, edited by Eula-
    lie O. Grover.   Hubbard, 1915.
Mother Goose Rhymes.   Platt & Munk.
The Real Mother Goose, illustrated by Blanche Fisher Wright.
    Rand McNally, 1916.
The Tall Book of Mother Goose, illustrated by Feodor Rojan-
    kovsky.   Harper, 1942.

The Tenggren Mother Goose, illustrated by Gustav Tenggren.
    Little, Brown, 1940.
The Very Young Mother Goose, edited by Margot Austin.
    Platt & Munk, 1963.

## Mysteries

### Preschool-grade 3

The Case of the Cat's Meow, by Crosby N. Bonsall. Harper
    & Row, 1965.
The Case of the Hungry Stranger, by Crosby N. Bonsall.
    Harper & Row, 1963.
Rabbit and Skunk and The Scary Rock, by Carla Stevens.
    Addison-Wesley, 1962.

### Grades 4-7

The Boxcar Children, by Gertrude Chandler Warner.  Albert
    Whitman, 1950.
Encyclopedia Brown and the Case of the Secret Pitch, by
    Donald J. Sobol.  Nelson, 1965.
Encyclopedia Brown, Boy Detective, by Donald J. Sobol.
    Nelson, 1963.
Encyclopedia Brown Finds the Clues, by Donald J. Sobol.
    Nelson, 1966.
Encyclopedia Brown Gets His Man, by Donald J. Sobol.
    Nelson, 1967.
Encyclopedia Brown Keeps the Peace, by Donald J. Sobol.
    Nelson, 1969.
Encyclopedia Brown Saves the Day, by Donald J. Sobol.
    Nelson, 1970.
Encyclopedia Brown Solves Them All, by Donald J. Sobol.
    Nelson, 1971.
The Horse in the Camel Suit, by William Pene du Bois.
    Harper & Row, 1967.
Spooks and Spirits and Shadowy Shapes, by Emma L. Brock
    et al.  Dutton, 1949.
Surprise Island, by Gertrude Chandler Warner.  Albert Whit-
    man, 1949.

## Novelty Books

### Grades 8-12

Mad Libs, by Roger Price and Leonard Stern.  Price Stern

Sloan, 1958.
Mad Libs No. 5, by Roger Price and Leonard Stern.   Price
    Stern Sloan, 1968.
Mad Libs Six, by Roger Price and Leonard Stern.   Price
    Stern Sloan, 1970.
Monster Mad Libs, by Roger Price and Leonard Stern.
    Price Stern Sloan, 1965.
Son of Mad Libs, by Roger Price and Leonard Stern.   Price
    Stern Sloan, 1959.
Sooper Mad Libs, by Roger Price and Leonard Stern.   Price
    Stern Sloan, 1962.


## Plays

### Grades 8-12

Tales from Shakespeare, by Charles and Mary Lamb.   1807.
Ten Short Plays, edited by M. Jerry Weiss.   Dell.


## Remedial Reading--Adventure Stories

### Preschool-grade 3

Cowboy Sam, by Edna Walker Chandler.   Benefic, 1960.
Cowboy Sam and Big Bill, by Edna Walker Chandler.   Benefic,
    1970.
Cowboy Sam and Dandy, by Edna Walker Chandler.   Benefic,
    1962.
Cowboy Sam and Flop, by Edna Walker Chandler.   Benefic,
    1971.
Cowboy Sam and Freckles, by Edna Walker Chandler.
    Benefic, 1971.
Cowboy Sam and Freddy, by Edna Walker Chandler.   Benefic,
    1970.
Cowboy Sam and Miss Lily, by Edna Walker Chandler.
    Benefic, 1971.
Cowboy Sam and Porky, by Edna Walker Chandler.   Benefic,
    1971.
Cowboy Sam and Shorty, by Edna Walker Chandler.   Benefic,
    1962.
Dan Frontier, by William J. Hurley.   Benefic, 1959.
Dan Frontier and the Big Cat, by William J. Hurley.   Benefic,
    1961.
Dan Frontier and the New House, by William J. Hurley.
    Benefic, 1961.

Dan Frontier Goes Hunting, by William J. Hurley.  Benefic,
    1959.
Dan Frontier, Trapper, by William J. Hurley.  Benefic,
    1962.
Dan Frontier with the Indians, by William J. Hurley.  Bene-
    fic, 1959.
Sailor Jack, by Selma and Jack Wassermann.  Benefic, 1960.
Sailor Jack and Bluebell, by Selma and Jack Wassermann.
    Benefic, 1960.
Sailor Jack and Bluebell's Dive, by Selma and Jack Wasser-
    mann.  Benefic, 1961.
Sailor Jack and Eddy, by Selma and Jack Wassermann.
    Benefic, 1961.
Sailor Jack and Homer Pots, by Selma and Jack Wassermann.
    Benefic, 1961.
Sailor Jack and the Ball Game, by Selma and Jack Wasser-
    mann.  Bencfic, 1962.
Sailor Jack and the Jet Plane, by Selma and Jack Wasser-
    mann.  Benefic, 1962.
Sailor Jack's New Friend, by Selma and Jack Wassermann.
    Benefic, 1960.


Grades 4-7

City beneath the Sea, by Henry A. Bamman and Robert J.
    Whitehead.  Benefic, 1964.
Cowboy Sam and Sally, by Edna Walker Chandler.  Benefic,
    1959.
Cowboy Sam and the Airplane, by Edna Walker Chandler.
    Benefic, 1959.
Cowboy Sam and the Fair, by Edna Walker Chandler.  Benefic,
    1970.
Cowboy Sam and the Indians, by Edna Walker Chandler.
    Benefic, 1971.
Cowboy Sam and the Rodeo, by Edna Walker Chandler.
    Benefic, 1959.
Cowboy Sam and the Rustlers, by Edna Walker Chandler.
    Benefic, 1970.
Dan Frontier and the Wagon Train, by William J. Hurley.
    Benefic, 1959.
Dan Frontier Goes Exploring, by William J. Hurley.  Benefic,
    1963.
Dan Frontier Goes to Congress, by William J. and Jane
    Hurley.  Benefic, 1964.
Dan Frontier Scouts with the Army, by William J. Hurley.
    Benefic, 1962.
Dan Frontier, Sheriff, by William J. Hurley.  Benefic, 1960.

Fire on the Mountain, by Henry A. Bamman and Robert J.
    Whitehead. Benefic, 1963.
Flight to the South Pole, by Henry A. Bamman and Robert
    J. Whitehead. Benefic, 1965.
Hunting Grizzly Bears, by Henry A. Bamman and Robert J.
    Whitehead. Benefic, 1963.
Lost Uranium Mine, by Henry A. Bamman and Robert J.
    Whitehead. Benefic, 1964.
Sacred Well of Sacrifice, by Henry A. Bamman and Robert
    J. Whitehead. Benefic, 1964.
Sailor Jack and the Target Ship, by Selma and Jack Wasser-
    mann. Benefic, 1960.
Sailor Jack Goes North, by Selma and Jack Wassermann.
    Benefic, 1961.
The Search for Piranha, by Henry A. Bamman and Robert
    J. Whitehead. Benefic, 1964.
Viking Treasure, by Henry A. Bamman and Robert J. White-
    head. Benefic, 1965.
Yo-Ho and Kim, by Ruth Jaynes. Lawrence.
Yo-Ho and Kim at Sea, by Ruth Jaynes. Lawrence.


## Science Fiction

Grades 8-12

Around the Moon, by Jules Verne.
Around the World in Eighty Days, by Jules Verne. 1873.
Between Planets, by Robert A. Heinlein. Scribner, 1951.
Citizen of the Galaxy, by Robert A. Heinlein. Scribner,
    1957.
Farmer in the Sky, by Robert A. Heinlein. Scribner, 1950.
From the Earth to the Moon, by Jules Verne. Associated
    Booksellers, 1865.
Have Space Suit--Will Travel, by Robert A. Heinlein.
    Scribner, 1958.
Journey to the Centre of the Earth, by Jules Verne. 1864.
Red Planet: A Colonial Boy on Mars, by Robert A. Heinlein.
    Scribner, 1949.
Rocket Ship Galileo, by Robert A. Heinlein. Scribner, 1947.
The Rolling Stones, by Robert A. Heinlein. Scribner, 1952.
Space Cadet, by Robert A. Heinlein. Scribner, 1948.
The Star Beast, by Robert A. Heinlein. Scribner, 1954
Starman Jones, by Robert A. Heinlein. Scribner, 1953.
Starship Troopers, by Robert A. Heinlein. Putnam, 1959.
Time for the Stars, by Robert A. Heinlein. Scribner, 1956.
Tunnel in the Sky, by Robert A. Heinlein. Scribner, 1955.

Twenty Thousand Leagues under the Sea, by Jules Verne.
1869.
A Wrinkle in Time, by Madeleine L'Engle.    Farrar, Straus
& Giroux, 1962.

## Speech Improvement Stories

Grades 4-7

King Robert the Resting Ruler, by Donna Lugg Pape.    Oddo,
1968.
Liz Dearly's Silly Glasses, by Donna Lugg Pape.    Oddo,
1968.
Professor Fred and the Fid-Fuddlephone, by Donna Lugg
Pape.    Oddo, 1968.
Scientist Sam, by Donna Lugg Pape.    Oddo, 1968.
Shoemaker Fooze, by Donna Lugg Pape.    Oddo, 1968.
The Three Thinkers of Thay-Lee, by Donna Lugg Pape.
Oddo, 1968.

## Translation

Grades 8-12

Winnie Ille Pu:    A Latin Edition of Winnie-the Pooh, by
A.A. Milne and Alexander Lenard, translator.    Dutton,
1960.

## NONFICTION

### Activity Books

Preschool-grade 3

Colonial Williamsburg Coloring Book, by Marian Cannon.
Colonial Williamsburg Foundation, 1948.
Creative Thinking Activities:   A Highlights Handbook, by
Garry Cleveland Myers.    Highlights, 1965.
Creative Writing Activities:   A Highlights Handbook, com-
piled by Walter B. Barbe.    Highlights, 1965.
Dot to Dot, by Isobel R. Beard.    Follett, 1969.
Draw with Dots, by Isobel R. Beard.    Follett.
Fun with Dots, by Madeline May.    Follett, 1969.

Holiday (Craft) Handbook No. 1, compiled by Caroline Clark
    Myers.   Highlights, 1965.
Holiday (Craft) Handbook No. 4.   Highlights For Children,
    1965.
Join the Dots, by Isobel R. Beard.   Follett, 1969.
Learning Begins at Home--A Stimulus for a Child's I. Q.,
    by Doris V. Brown and Pauline McDonald.   Lawrence.
Link the Dots, by Isobel R. Beard.   Follett, 1969.
Puzzles and Riddles, by Isobel R. Beard.   Follett.
Puzzles for Pleasure, by Isobel R. Beard.   Follett.
Tricks and Teasers:  A Highlights Handbook.   Highlights
    For Children, 1965.

Grades 4-7

Junior Crossword Puzzle Book.   Platt & Munk.
My First Crossword Puzzle Book.   Platt & Munk.

## Anthologies of Essays, Etc.

Grades 8-12

Edge of Awareness, edited by Ned E. Hoopes and Richard
    Peck.   Dell, 1966.
The Outnumbered, edited by Charlotte Brooks.   Dell, 1967.

## Arts

Grades 4-7

Creative Art Activities for Home and School, by Doris V.
    Brown and Pauline McDonald.   Lawrence, 1966.
Famous Paintings:  An Introduction to Art, by Alice Eliza-
    beth Chase.   Platt & Munk, 1951.
Make It Yourself, by Bernice Wells Carlson.   Abingdon-
    Cokesbury, 1950.
The Pantheon Story of Art for Young People, by Ariane
    Ruskin.   Pantheon, 1964.

Grades 8-12

Art.   Boy Scouts of America, 1968.
Basketry.   Boy Scouts of America, 1968.
Clay, Wood and Wire, by Harvey Weiss.   Addison-Wesley,
    1956.

Droodles, by Roger Price.   Price Stern Sloan, 1965.
Leatherwork.   Boy Scouts of America, 1970.
Pencil, Pen and Brush, by Harvey Weiss.   Addison-Wesley,
    1961.
Photography.   Boy Scouts of America, 1960.
Wood Carving.   Boy Scouts of America, 1966.
Woodwork.   Boy Scouts of America, 1970.


## Biographies

Preschool-grade 3

Color Me Brown, by Lucille Giles.   Johnson (Chicago).

Grades 4-7

Abraham Lincoln, by Ingri and Edgar Parin D'Aulaire. Dou-
    bleday, 1940.
Abraham Lincoln, by Clara Ingram Judson.   Follett, 1961.
Abraham Lincoln:  For the People, by Anne Colver.   Gar-
    rard, 1960.
Afro-American Contributors to American Life, by John M.
    Franco.   Benefic, 1971.
Afro-Americans Then and Now, by Doris Haynes and Jane
    Hurley.   Benefic, 1969.
Amos Fortune, Free Man, by Elizabeth Yates.   Dutton,
    1950.
Ben and Me, by Robert Lawson.   Little, Brown, 1939.
Benjamin Franklin, by Ingri and Edgar Parin D'Aulaire.
    Doubleday, 1950.
Benjamin Franklin:  Man of Ideas, by Charles P. Graves.
    Garrard, 1960.
Christopher Columbus, by Clara Ingram Judson.   Follett,
    1964.
Columbus, by Ingri and Edgar Parin D'Aulaire.   Doubleday,
    1955.
The Courage of Sarah Noble, by Alice Dalgliesh.   Scribner,
    1954.
Daniel Boone Taming the Wilds, by Katharine E. Wilkie.
    Garrard, 1960.
Famous American Indians, by Edmond L. Leipold.   Denison.
Famous American Negroes, by Edmond L. Leipold.   Denison.
Florience Nightingale:  War Nurse, by Anne Colver.   Gar-
    rard, 1961.
Frederick Douglass, Freedom Fighter, by Lillie Patterson.
    Garrard, 1965.

George Washington, by Ingri and Edgar Parin D'Aulaire.
   Doubleday, 1936.
George Washington, by Clara Ingram Judson.   Follett, 1961.
George Washington:   Father of Freedom, by Stewart Graff.
   Garrard, 1964.
George Washington Carver, Negro Scientist, by Sam and
   Beryl Epstein.   Garrard, 1960.
Helen Keller:   Toward the Light, by Stewart and Polly Anne
   Graff.   Garrard, 1965.
John F. Kennedy:   New Frontiersman, by Charles P. Graves.
   Garrard, 1965.
Kon-Tiki for Young People, by Thor Heyerdahl.   Rand Mc-
   Nally, 1960.
Mr. Revere and I, by Robert Lawson.   Little, Brown, 1953.
Mustang, Wild Spirit of the West, by Marguerite Henry.
   Rand McNally, 1966.
The Real Diary of a Real Boy, by Henry A. Shute.   Bauhan,
   1902.
Sam Houston:  Hero of Texas, by Jean Lee Latham.   Gar-
   rard, 1965.
Stories of Champions:  Baseball Hall of Fame, by Sam and
   Beryl Epstein.   Garrard, 1965.
Story of the Trapp Family Singers, by Maria Augusta Trapp.
   Lippincott, 1949.
They Were Strong and Good, by Robert Lawson.   Viking,
   1940.
A World Explorer:   Marco Polo, by Charles P. Graves.
   Garrard, 1963.

Grades 8-12

Albert Einstein, by Elma Ehrlich Levinger.   Messner, 1949.
Atlas of the Presidents, by Donald E. Cooke.   Hammond,
   1964.
Carry On, Mr. Bowditch, by Jean Lee Latham.   Houghton
   Mifflin, 1955.
Daniel Boone, by James Daugherty.   Viking, 1939.
Dr. George Washington Carver, Scientist, by Shirley Graham
   and George D. Lipscomb.   Messner, 1944.
Electronics Pioneer, Lee De Forest, by I. E. Levine.
   Messner, 1964.
The First Woman Doctor:  The Story of Elizabeth Blackwell,
   M. D., by Rachel Baker.   Messner, 1944.
The Great Houdini, Magician Extraordinary, by Samuel Ep-
   stein and Beryl Williams.   Messner, 1950.
Invincible Louisa, by Cornelia Meigs.   Little, Brown, 1933.
Jackie Robinson of the Brooklyn Dodgers, by Milton J. Shapi-
   ro.   Messner, 1966.

The Jim Thorpe Story:   America's Greatest Athlete, by Gene
     Schoor.  Messner, 1951.
John F. Kennedy, by Norman Richards and John P. Reidy.
     Children's, 1967.
Joseph Pulitzer, Front Page Pioneer, by Iris Noble.  Messner,
     1957.
Marco Polo, by Manuel Komroff.  Messner, 1952.
Martin Luther King Jr., 1929-1968; An Ebony Picture Biog-
     raphy.  Johnson (Chicago), 1969.
The Presidents in American History, by Charles A. Beard.
     Messner, 1948.
Sigmund Freud, by Rachel Baker.  Messner, 1952.
Sitting Bull, Champion of His People, by Shannon Garst.
     Messner, 1946.
The Will to Be Free:  Great Escape Stories, edited by Eric
     Williams.  Nelson, 1971.


## Careers and Occupations

### Preschool-grade 3

I Want to Be a Nurse, by Carla Greene.  Children's, 1957.
Peter's Policeman, by Anne Lattin.  Follett, 1958.
The True Book of Our Post Office and Its Helpers, by Irene
     S. Miner.  Children's, 1955.
The True Book of Policemen and Firemen, by Irene S.
     Miner.  Children's, 1954.


### Grades 4-7

The Story of Linda Lookout, by Keith Lundy Hoofnagle.   Na-
     turegraph.


### Grades 8-12

Animal Industry.  Boy Scouts of America, 1944.
Aviation.  Boy Scouts of America, 1968.
Careers Outdoors, by James Joseph.  Nelson, 1962.
Conservation of Natural Resources.  Boy Scouts of America,
     1967.


## Conduct of Life, Etc.

### Grades 4-7

The Stork Didn't Bring You, by Lois Loyd Pemberton.  Nel-

son, 1948.
What Do You Say, Dear? by Sesyle Joslin.    Addison-Wesley,
   1958.

## Grades 8-12

Facts of Life and Love for Teenagers, by Evelyn Millis
   Duvall and Sylvanus Duvall.    Association, 1950.


## Dictionaries

### Preschool-grade 3

The Cat in the Hat Beginner Book Dictionary, by Phillip D.
   Eastman.    Random, 1964.
Courtis-Watters Illustrated Golden Dictionary for Young Read-
   ers, by Stuart A. Courtis and Garnette Watters.  Golden,
   1952.
Follett Beginning-to-Read Picture Dictionary, by Alta Mc-
   Intire.    Follett, 1959.
The Golden Dictionary, edited by Ellen Wales Walpole.
   Golden, 1944.
The Rainbow Dictionary, edited by Wendell W. Wright.
   World, 1947.

### Grades 4-7

Golden Picture Dictionary, by Lilian Moore.    Golden, 1954.
Webster's Elementary Dictionary.    Merriam, 1966.


## Health, Safety, and Self Improvement

### Grades 8-12

Automotive Safety.   Boy Scouts of America, 1962.
Firemanship.   Boy Scouts of America, 1968.
First Aid.   Boy Scouts of America, 1960.
Lifesaving.   Boy Scouts of America, 1965.
Personal Fitness.   Boy Scouts of America, 1968.
Public Health.   Boy Scouts of America, 1969.
Public Speaking.   Boy Scouts of America, 1969.
Reading.   Boy Scouts of America, 1965.
Safety.   Boy Scouts of America, 1971.
Scholarship.   Boy Scouts of America, 1970.

## History, Government and Politics

### Preschool-grade 3

The True Book of Indians, by Teri Martini.   Children's,
1954.

### Grades 4-7

The Civil War, by Fletcher Pratt.   Doubleday, 1955.
The First Thanksgiving, by Lou Rogers.   Follett, 1963.
The How and Why Wonder Book of Explorations and Discov-
eries, by Irving Robbin.   Wonder-Treasure.
The Indians of New Jersey:  Dickon among the Lenapes, by
Mark Raymond Harrington.   Rutgers University, 1963.
Minn of the Mississippi, by Holling Clancy Holling.   Houghton
Mifflin, 1951.
The Negro in America, by Earl Spangler.   Lerner.
Paddle-to-the-Sea, by Holling Clancy Holling.   Houghton Mif-
flin, 1941.
The Story of Mount Vernon, by Natalie M. Miller.   Chil-
dren's, 1965.
The Story of the Liberty Bell, by Natalie Miller.   Children's,
1965.
The Story of the Lincoln Memorial, by Natalie Miller.   Chil-
dren's, 1966.
The Story of the Star-Spangled Banner, by Natalie Miller.
Children's, 1965.
The Story of the Statue of Liberty, by Natalie Miller.   Chil-
dren's, 1965.
Tree in the Trail, by Holling Clancy Holling.   Houghton
Mifflin, 1942.
You and the Constitution of the United States, by Paul Witty
and J. Kohler.   Children's, 1948.
You and the United Nations, by Lois Fisher.   Children's,
1951.

### Grades 8-12

America and Its Presidents, by Earl S. Miers.   Grosset &
Dunlap, 1959.
The Book of the Ancient Greeks, by Dorothy Mills.   Putnam,
1925.
The Book of the Ancient Romans, by Dorothy Mills.   Putnam,
1927.
The Book of the Ancient World, by Dorothy Mills.   Putnam,
1923.

Citizenship. Boy Scouts of America, 1966.
The Day They Marched, edited by Doris E. Saunders. Johnson (Chicago), 1963.
Flags of American History, by David D. Crouthers. Hammond, 1964.
Indian Lore. Boy Scouts of America, 1959.
The Kennedy Years and the Negro, edited by Doris E. Saunders. Johnson (Chicago), 1964.
The Middle Ages, by Dorothy Mills. Putnam, 1935.
Renaissance and Reformation Times, by Dorothy Mills. Putnam, 1939.
Story of the Bible World, by Nelson Beecher Keyes. Hammond, 1962.
The Story of the Jew, by Harry Gersh and Elma E. and Lee J. Levinger. Behrman.


## Hobbies

Grades 4-7

Cub Scout Magic. Boy Scouts of America, 1960.

Grades 8-12

Coin Collecting. Boy Scouts of America, 1966.
Cooking. Boy Scouts of America, 1967.
Dog Care. Boy Scouts of America, 1969.
Fingerprinting. Boy Scouts of America, 1964.
First Aid to Animals. Boy Scouts of America, 1963.
Home Repairs. Boy Scouts of America, 1961.
Pets. Boy Scouts of America, 1969.
Radio. Boy Scouts of America, 1965.
Signaling. Boy Scouts of America, 1940.
Stamp Collecting. Boy Scouts of America, 1966.


## Jokes and Riddles

Grades 4-7

Jokes and Riddles, by George Carlson. Platt & Munk.
1001 Riddles. Platt & Munk.
Tell Me a Joke, edited by Dana Bruce. Platt & Munk, 1966.
Tell Me a Riddle, edited by Dana Bruce. Platt & Munk, 1966.

## Grades 8-12

The Elephant Book, by Roger Price, Leonard Stern, Larry
  Sloan, and Lennie Weinrib.  Price Stern Sloan, 1968.
Elephants, Grapes & Pickles, by Roger Price, Leonard
  Stern, and Larry Sloan.  Price Stern Sloan, 1964.
M Is for Monster, by Roger Price, Leonard Stern, and Larry
  Sloan.  Price Stern Sloan, 1965.
The World's Worst Jokes, by Price Stern editors.  Price
  Stern Sloan, 1969.


## Miscellaneous Information and Reference

## Preschool-grade 3

Airplanes & Trucks & Trains, Fire Engines, Boats & Ships,
  & Building & Wrecking Machines, by George J. Zaffo.
  Grosset & Dunlap, 1968.
Big Book of Airplanes, by Charles L. Black.  Grosset &
  Dunlap, 1951.
Big Book of Building and Wrecking Machines, by George J.
  Zaffo.  Grosset & Dunlap, 1951.
Big Book of Real Trucks, by Elizabeth Cameron.  Grosset
  & Dunlap, 1950.
Big Book of Submarines.  Grosset & Dunlap.
The Boats on the River, by Marjorie Flack.  Viking, 1946.
Chicken Little Count-to-Ten, by Margaret Friskey.  Chil-
  dren's, 1946.
Dr. Seuss's ABC, by Dr. Seuss.  Beginner, 1963.
A Friend Is Someone Who Likes You, by Joan Walsh Anglund.
  Harcourt, Brace, 1958.
Happiness Is a Warm Puppy, by Charles M. Schulz.  Deter-
  mined, 1962.
A Hole Is to Dig:  A First Book of First Definitions, by
  Ruth Krauss.  Harper, 1952.
How Big Is Big?  by Herman and Nina Schneider.  Addison-
  Wesley, 1946.
Lots More Tell Me Why, by Arkady Leokum.  Grosset &
  Dunlap, 1971.
Love Is a Special Way of Feeling, by Joan Walsh Anglund.
  Harcourt, Brace, 1960.
More Tell Me Why, by Arkady Leokum.  Grosset & Dunlap,
  1967.
Red Light Green Light, by Golden MacDonald.  Doubleday,
  1944.
The True Book of Holidays, by John W. Purcell.  Children's,
  1955.

Winnie-the-Pooh's Calendar Book, by A. A. Milne.    Dutton.

## Grades 4-7

The Answer Book, by Mary Elting.    Grosset & Dunlap, 1959.
Answers and More Answers, by Mary Elting.    Grosset &
    Dunlap, 1961.
Better Homes and Gardens Junior Cook Book.    Meredith,
    1955.
Big Book of Real Trains, edited by Doris Duenewald.    Grosset
    & Dunlap, 1970.
The Boy Scout Encyclopedia, by Bruce Grant.    Rand McNally,
    1952.
How Maps and Globes Help Us, by David Hackler.    Benefic,
    1962.
Still More Answers, by Mary Elting and Franklin Folsom.
    Grosset & Dunlap, 1970.
Still More Tell Me Why, by Arkady Leokum.    Grosset &
    Dunlap, 1968.
Tell Me Why, by Arkady Leokum.    Grosset & Dunlap, 1969.
UNICEF Festival Book, by Judith Spiegelman.    United States
    Committee for UNICEF, 1966.

## Grades 8-12

The Book of Marvels, by Richard Halliburton.    Bobbs-Mer-
    rill, 1938.
Illustrated Atlas for Young America.    Hammond Incorporated,
    1967.
Would You Believe? by Don Adams.    Price Stern Sloan,
    1966.

## Mythology

### Grades 4-7

The Adventures of Odysseus, by Andrew Lang.    1879.
D'Aulaires' Book of Greek Myths, by Ingri and Edgar Parin
    D'Aulaire.    Doubleday, 1962.
Tanglewood Tales, by Nathaniel Hawthorne.    1853.
A Wonder Book, by Nathaniel Hawthorne.    1851.

### Grades 8-12

Greek Gods and Heroes, by Robert Graves.    Doubleday, 1960.
Mythology, by Edith Hamilton.    Little, Brown, 1942.

## Poems and Verses

Preschool-grade 3

Around and About, by Marchette Chute. Dutton, 1957.
A Child's Garden of Verses, by Robert Louis Stevenson.
   1885.
Did You Ever See? by Walter Einsel. Addison-Wesley,
   1962.
The Gingham Dog and the Calico Cat, by Eugene Field. Fol-
   lett, 1956.
Hailstones and Halibut Bones, by Mary O'Neill. Doubleday,
   1961.
Now We Are Six, by A.A. Milne. Dutton, 1927.
When We Were Very Young, by A.A. Milne. Dutton, 1924.

Grades 4-7

A Child's Book of Poems, compiled by Gyo Fujikawa. Gros-
   set & Dunlap, 1969.
Favorite Poems Old and New, edited by Helen Josephine
   Ferris. Doubleday, 1957.
Illustrated Treasury of Poetry for Children, edited by David
   Ross. Grosset & Dunlap, 1970.
Miracles: Poems by Children of the English-Speaking World,
   edited by Richard Lewis. Simon & Schuster, 1966.
One Thousand Poems for Children, edited by Elizabeth
   Hough Sechrist. Macrae Smith, 1946.

Grades 8-12

Poems for Youth: An American Anthology, compiled by
   William Rose Benet. Dutton, 1923.
You Come Too, by Robert Frost. Holt, Rinehart & Winston,
   1959.

## Religion

Preschool-grade 3

Baby Born in a Stable, by A.H. Kramer. Concordia.
Bible Stories, by Mary Alice Jones. Rand McNally, 1952.
Boy Who Gave His Lunch Away, by Dave Hill. Concordia,
   1967.
Boy Who Ran Away, by Irene Elmer. Concordia, 1964.
Boy with a Sling, by Mary P. Warren. Concordia, 1965.

Braggy King of Babylon, by Yvonne McCall.   Concordia,
    1969.
A Child's Garden of Bible Stories, by A.W. Gross.   Con-
    cordia, 1948.
A Child's Garden of Prayer, by Herman W. Gockel and Ed-
    ward J. Saleska, compilers.   Concordia, 1948.
The Christ Child, by Maud and Miska Petersham.   Double-
    day, 1931.
Daniel in the Lion's Den, by Jane Latourette.   Concordia,
    1966.
Donkey Daniel in Bethlehem, by Janice Kramer.   Concordia,
    1970.
Egermeier's Bible Story Books, by Elsie E. Egermeier.
    Warner, 1923.
Eight Bags of Gold, by Janice Kramer.   Concordia, 1964.
Fishermen's Surprise, by Alyce Bergey.   Concordia, 1967.
Good Samaritan, by Janice Kramer.   Concordia, 1964.
Great Escape, by Mary P. Warren.   Concordia, 1966.
House on the Rock, by Jane Latourette.   Concordia, 1966.
Hurlbut's Story of the Bible, by Jesse Lyman Hurlbut.
    Revell, 1966.
If Jesus Came to My House, by Joan Gale Thomas.   Lothrop,
    Lee & Shepard, 1951.
Jesus, the Little New Baby, by Mary Edna Lloyd.   Abingdon,
    1951.
Jon and the Little Lost Lamb, by Jane Latourette.   Concord-
    ia, 1965.
Little Benjamin and the First Christmas, by Betty Forell.
    Concordia, 1964.
Little Boat That Almost Sank, by Mary P. Warren.   Con-
    cordia, 1965.
Little Book about God (Protestant), by Lauren Ford.   Dou-
    bleday, 1934.
Little Folded Hands, by Allan H. Jahsmann.   Concordia,
    1959.
Little Sleeping Beauty, by Brenda Prior.   Concordia, 1969.
Little Visits with God, by Allan H. Jahsmann.   Concordia,
    1957.
Marian's Big Book of Bible Stories, by Marian M. School-
    land.   Eerdmans, 1947.
Marian's Favorite Bible Stories, by Marian M. Schoolland.
    Eerdmans, 1948.
Mary's Story, by M.M. Brem.   Concordia, 1967.
Man Caught by a Fish, by M.M. Brem.   Concordia, 1967.
More Little Visits with God, by Allan H. Jahsmann.   Con-
    cordia, 1961.
My Bible Story Book, by Gerhard L. Wind.   Concordia, 1956.

My Picture Story Bible, by Dena Korfker. Zondervan.
Princess and the Baby, by Janice Kramer. Concordia, 1969.
The Rich Fool, by Janice Kramer. Concordia, 1964.
Secret of the Star, by Dave Hill. Concordia, 1966.
Simeon's Secret, by Janice Kramer. Concordia, 1969.
Small Rain: Verses from the Bible, edited by Jessie Orton
    Jones. Viking, 1943.
Story of Noah's Ark, by Jane Latourette. Concordia, 1965.
The Tall Book of Bible Stories, edited by Katherine Gibson.
    Harper, 1957.
Tell Me about Christmas, by Mary Alice Jones.   Rand Mc-
    Nally, 1958.
Tell Me about God, by Mary Alice Jones.   Rand McNally,
    1943.
Tell Me about Heaven, by Mary Alice Jones.   Rand McNally,
    1956.
Tell Me about Jesus, by Mary Alice Jones.   Rand McNally,
    1944.
Tell Me about the Bible, by Mary Alice Jones.   Rand Mc-
    Nally, 1945.
Three Men Who Walked in Fire, by Joann Scheck.   Con-
    cordia, 1967.
Unforgiving Servant, by Janice Kramer. Concordia, 1968.
Walls Came Tumbling Down, by Dave Hill. Concordia, 1967.
Water That Caught on Fire, by Joann Scheck. Concordia,
    1969.
World God Made, by Alyce Bergey. Concordia, 1965.

Grades 4-7

Beggar's Greatest Wish, by Alyce Bergey. Concordia, 1969.
Boy Who Saved His Family, by Alyce Bergey. Concordia,
    1966.
The Child's Story Bible, by Catherine F. Vos. Eerdmans,
    1949.
The Christmas Story, edited by Marguerite Northrup. Metro-
    politan Museum of Art, 1966.
Great Promise, by Alyce Bergey. Concordia, 1968.
Great Surprise, by Mary P. Warren. Concordia, 1964.
King's Invitation, by Virginia Mueller. Concordia, 1968.
Lame Man Who Walked Again, by Mary P. Warren. Con-
    cordia, 1966.
Most Wonderful King, by Dave Hill. Concordia, 1968.
One God: The Ways We Worship Him, by Florence Mary
    Fitch. Lothrop, Lee & Shepard, 1944.
One Hundred Bible Stories (Illustrated King James edition).
    Concordia, 1966.

A Picture Book of Palestine, by Ethel L. Smither.   Abing-
    don, 1947.
Secret Journey, by Virginia Mueller.   Concordia, 1968.
Tell Me about Prayer, by Mary Alice Jones.   Rand McNally,
    1948.
Two Men in the Temple, by Joann Scheck.   Concordia, 1968.
Young Readers' Bible, edited by Henry M. Bullock and Ed-
    ward C. Peterson.   Abingdon, 1968.


## Science

Preschool-grade 3

Animals Everywhere, by Ingri and Edgar Parin D'Aulaire.
    Doubleday, 1954.
Dash and Dart: Two Fawns, by Mary and Conrad Buff.
    Viking, 1942.
The Day We Saw the Sun Come Up, by Alice E. Goudey.
    Scribner, 1961.
The Hole in the Tree, by Jean Craighead George.   Dutton,
    1957.
Houses from the Sea, by Alice E. Goudey.   Scribner, 1959.
Let's Go Outdoors, by Harriet E. Huntington.   Doubleday,
    1939.
The Little Island, by Golden MacDonald.   Doubleday, 1946.
Mr. Mighty, by M. Worden Kidder and Barbara Kidder.
    Denison.
Mr. Wonderful, by Barbara Kidder.   Denison.
Rain Drop Splash, by Alvin Tresselt.   Lothrop, Lee &
    Shepard, 1946.
Seeds and More Seeds, by Millicent Ellis Selsam.   Harper,
    1959.
Songs of the Swallows, by Leo Politi.   Scribner, 1949.
A Tree Is Nice, by Janice May Udry.   Harper, 1956.
The True Book of Air around Us, by Margaret Friskey.
    Children's, 1953.
The True Book of Animal Babies, by Illa Podendorf.   Chil-
    dren's, 1955.
The True Book of Birds We Know, by Margaret Friskey.
    Children's, 1954.
The True Book of Dinosaurs, by Mary L. Clark.   Children's,
    1955.
The True Book of Farm Animals, by John Lewellen.   Chil-
    dren's, 1954.
The True Book of Insects, by Illa Podendorf.   Children's,
    1954.

The True Book of Moon, Sun and Stars, by Illa Podendorf. Children's, 1954.
The True Book of Pebbles and Shells, by Illa Podendorf. Children's, 1954.
The True Book of Plants We Know, by Irene S. Miner. Children's, 1953.
The True Book of Science Experiments, by Illa Podendorf. Children's, 1954.
The True Book of Seasons, by Illa Podendorf. Children's, 1955.
Where Does the Butterfly Go When It Rains? by May Garelick. Addison-Wesley, 1961.
White Snow, Bright Snow, by Alvin Tresselt. Lothrop, Lee & Shepard, 1947.

## Grades 4-7

Album of Horses, by Marguerite Henry. Rand McNally, 1951.
Atoms, Energy, and Machines, by Jack McCormick. Creative Educational Society, 1967.
Backyard Bandits--Including California Raccoons and Other Exciting Patio Visitors, by David D. Oliphant, Jr. Naturegraph, 1968.
Bird Life in Wington, by John Calvin Reid. Eerdmans.
Birds in Their Homes, by Addison Webb. Doubleday, 1947.
Bobby Discovers Bird Watching, by Marjorie Wackerbarth. Denison, 1962.
Bobby Discovers Garden Friends, by Marjorie Wackerbarth and Lillian S. Graham. Denison, 1960.
Bobby Learns about Butterflies, by Marjorie Wackerbarth. Denison, 1963.
Bobby Learns about Squirrels, by Marjorie Wackerbarth. Denison, 1966.
Bobby Learns about Woodland Babies, by Marjorie Wackerbarth. Denison.
The Desert, by Alexander and Elsie Klots. Creative Educational Society, 1967.
Dinosaurs, by Herbert S. Zim. Morrow, 1954.
Dinosaurs and Other Prehistoric Animals, by Darlene Geis. Grosset & Dunlap, 1959.
The Earth's Story, by Gerald Ames and Rose Wyler. Creative Educational Society, 1967.
Field and Meadow, by Etta Schneider Ress. Creative Educational Society, 1967.
Food and Life, by Gerald Ames and Rose Wyler. Creative Educational Society, 1966.

Forest and Woodland, by Stephen Collins.   Creative Educa-
tional Society, 1967.
Fresh and Salt Water, by B. Bartram Cadbury.   Creative
Educational Society, 1967.
Golden Book of Science, by Bertha Morris Parker.   Golden,
1952.
The How and Why Wonder Book of Ants and Bees, by Ronald
N. Rood.   Wonder-Treasure.
The How and Why Wonder Book of Birds, by Robert Mathew-
son.   Wonder-Treasure, 1960.
The How and Why Wonder Book of Deserts, by Felix Sutton.
Wonder-Treasure, 1965.
The How and Why Wonder Book of Ecology, by Shelly and
Mary Louise Grossman.   Wonder-Treasure, 1971.
The How and Why Wonder Book of Insects, by Ronald N.
Rood.   Wonder-Treasure, 1960.
The How and Why Wonder Book of Oceanography, by Robert
Scharff.   Wonder-Treasure, 1964.
The How and Why Wonder Book of Reptiles and Amphibians,
by Robert Mathewson.   Wonder-Treasure, 1960.
The How and Why Wonder Book of Sea Shells, by Donald F.
Low.   Wonder-Treasure.
The How and Why Wonder Book of the Human Body, by
Martin L. Keen.   Wonder-Treasure.
Junior Science Book of Icebergs and Glaciers, by Patricia
Lauber.   Garrard, 1961.
Junior Science Book of Penguins, by Patricia Lauber.   Gar-
rard, 1963.
Junior Science Book of Rain, Hail, Sleet, and Snow, by
Nancy Larrick.   Garrard, 1961.
Junior Science Book of Volcanoes, by Patricia Lauber.   Gar-
rard, 1965.
Keer-Loo, by Laura Louise Foster.   Naturegraph, 1965.
Let's Find Out about Heat, Water and Air, by Herman and
Nina Schneider.   Addison-Wesley, 1946.
Mr. Wizard's Experiments for Young Scientists, by Don
Herbert.   Doubleday, 1959.
The Ocean Laboratory, by Athelstan Spilhaus.   Creative Edu-
cational Society, 1967.
Parks and Gardens, by Robert S. Lemmon.   Creative Edu-
cational Society, 1967.
Planets, Stars and Space, by Joseph M. Chamberlain and
Thomas D. Nicholson.   Creative Educational Society,
1962.
Robin Deer, by Olga Cossi.   Naturegraph, 1968.
Snakes, by Herbert S. Zim.   Morrow, 1949.
Space, by Marian Tellander.   Follett, 1960.

Up Above and Down Below, by Irma E. Webber. Addison-Wesley, 1943.
The Way of the Weather, by Jerome Spar. Creative Educational Society, 1967.
What's Inside the Egg? by May Garelick. Addison-Wesley, 1955.
Wild Animals I Have Known, by Ernest Thompson Seton. Scribner, 1898.
Wonders of the Human Body, by Anthony Ravielli. Viking, 1954.

## Grades 8-12

Astronomy. Boy Scouts of America, 1971.
Bird Study. Boy Scouts of America, 1967.
Chemistry. Boy Scouts of America, 1962.
Electricity. Boy Scouts of America, 1964.
Forestry. Boy Scouts of America, 1971.
Gardening. Boy Scouts of America, 1971.
Geology. Boy Scouts of America, 1953.
Handbook of Nature Study, by Anna Botsford Comstock. Cornell University, 1939.
Insect Life. Boy Scouts of America, 1963.
Nature. Boy Scouts of America, 1952.
Nature Atlas of America, by Emil L. Jordan. Hammond, 1952.
Reptile Study. Boy Scouts of America, 1971.
Ring of Bright Water, by Gavin Maxwell. Dutton, 1961.
Soil and Water Conservation. Boy Scouts of America, 1968.
Weather. Boy Scouts of America, 1963.
Wildlife Management. Boy Scouts of America, 1952.

## Scout Handbooks

## Grades 4-7

Bear Cub Scout Book. Boy Scouts of America, 1967.
Cub Scout Fun Book. Boy Scouts of America, 1967.
Webelos Scout Book. Boy Scouts of America, 1967.
Wolf Cub Scout Book. Boy Scouts of America, 1967.

## Grades 8-12

Boy Scout Handbook. Boy Scouts of America, 1910.
Den Chief's Denbook. Boy Scouts of America, 1968.
Explorer Member's Guide. Boy Scouts of America, 1969.

Patrol Leader's Handbook.  Boy Scouts of America, 1967.
Scout How Book.  Boy Scouts of America, 1969.


## Songbooks and Music

Preschool-grade 3

Golden Song Book, by Katharine Tyler Wessels.  Golden,
    1945.
The Songs of Sesame Street (Sesame Street Book and Record
    Package), written by Jeffrey Moss, Joe Raposo, and
    Jon Stone.  Children's Television Workshop, 1970.

Grades 4-7

American Folk Songs for Children, by Ruth Crawford Seeger.
    Doubleday, 1948.
Chapbook 2.  Bethany, 1966.
Cub Scout Songbook.  Boy Scouts of America, 1969.

Grades 8-12

Boy Scout Songbook.  Boy Scouts of America, 1971.
Music.  Boy Scouts of America.  1968.


## Sports

Grades 4-7

Baseball, by Frank F. DeClemente.  Creative Educational
    Society, 1962.
Basketball, by Joe Hutton and Vern B. Hoffman.  Creative
    Educational Society, 1962.
Football, by J.R. "Bob" Otto.  Creative Educational Society,
    1962.
Golf, Swimming and Tennis, by Otis J. Dypwick and Helen
    Hull Jacobs.  Creative Educational Society, 1962.
Recreational Sports, by Clifford Brownell and Roy Moore.
    Creative Educational Society, 1962.
Track and Field, by Earl "Bud" Meyers and Rich Hacker.
    Creative Educational Society, 1962.

Grades 8-12

The Answer Book of Sports, by Bill Mazer.  Grosset &
    Dunlap, 1969.

Archery.    Boy Scouts of America, 1964.
Athletics.    Boy Scouts of America, 1964.
Camping.    Boy Scouts of America, 1966.
Canoeing.    Boy Scouts of America, 1968.
Cycling.    Boy Scouts of America, 1971.
Fieldbook.    Boy Scouts of America, 1967.
Fishing.    Boy Scouts of America, 1954.
Hiking.    Boy Scouts of America, 1962.
Horsemanship.    Boy Scouts of America, 1969.
Junior Illustrated Encyclopedia of Sports, by Herbert Kamm.
    Bobbs-Merrill, 1960.
Learning How Baseball, by Dick Siebert.    Creative Educa-
    tional Society, 1968.
Motorboating.    Boy Scouts of America, 1962.
Pioneering.    Boy Scouts of America, 1967.
Rifle and Shotgun Shooting.    Boy Scouts of America, 1967.
Rowing.    Boy Scouts of America, 1964.
Small-Boat Sailing.    Boy Scouts of America, 1965.
Swimming.    Boy Scouts of America, 1960.

WITHDRAWAL